Republican learning

Politics, culture and society in early modern Britain

General editors

PROFESSOR ANN HUGHES
DR ANTHONY MILTON
PROFESSOR PETER LAKE

This important series publishes monographs that take a fresh and challenging look at the interactions between politics, culture and society in Britain between 1500 and the mid-eighteenth century. It counteracts the fragmentation of current historiography through encouraging a variety of approaches which attempt to redefine the political, social and cultural worlds, and to explore their interconnection in a flexible and creative fashion. All the volumes in the series question and transcend traditional inter-disciplinary boundaries, such as those between political history and literary studies, social history and divinity, urban history and anthropology. They contribute to a broader understanding of crucial developments in early modern Britain.

Republican learning

John Toland and the crisis
of Christian culture, 1696–1722

JUSTIN CHAMPION

Manchester
University Press

Manchester and New York

distributed exclusively in the USA by Palgrave

Published by Manchester University Press
Oxford Road, Manchester M13 9NR, UK
and Room 400, 175 Fifth Avenue, New York, NY 10010, USA
www.manchesteruniversitypress.co.uk

Distributed exclusively in the USA by
Palgrave, 175 Fifth Avenue, New York NY 10010, USA

Distributed exclusively in Canada by
UBC Press, University of British Columbia, 2029 West Mall,
Vancouver, BC, Canada V6T 1Z2

British Library Cataloguing-in-Publication Data
A catalogue record for this book is available from the British Library

Library of Congress Cataloging-in-Publication Data
A catalog record for this book is available from the Library of Congress

ISBN 13: 978 0 7190 8049 4

First published in hardback 2003 by Manchester University Press
This paperback edition first published 2009

Printed by Lightning Source

Contents

Preface

This book has been ongoing for a number of years. I have many debts. The AHRB generously matched a period of leave awarded by the Department of History at Royal Holloway that allowed the bulk of the text to be written. I have tried many of the ideas out on tolerant audiences in Los Angeles, Victoria, Edmonton, Ferrara, South Bend, Belfast, Dublin, Paris, Wolfenbuttel, Oxford, York, Sheffield and London (strangely enough not yet in Cambridge): I am grateful to all these audiences. Some of the material has been rehearsed in print: due acknowledgement has been made in the appropriate place, but many thanks to Dan Carey, David Hayton, Antony McKenna, Ole Grell and the now sadly departed Roy Porter for offering editorial help in these instances. In the course of the research I have received help and advice from a huge range of scholars. Mark Goldie has been a constant inspiration. Michael Hunter has consistently laboured over the various versions, always offering invaluable suggestions and insights. Margaret Jacob offered robust encouragement and graciously forwarded research materials – many of the themes explored here were originally inspired by her path-breaking work. Blair Worden has been an important influence on the development of the work. He graciously read and commented on Part II. Antony McKenna has both delivered calm commentary and introduced me to a number of scholars – Pierre Lurbe, Laurent Jaffro, and Tristan Dagron. All the latter have shared their research and offered useful advice. Giancarlo Carabelli was for a long time known to me only by his extraordinary bibliography. Having met him in Ferrara, I can only salute his commitment and energy to excavating the infrastructure of Toland's life. Alan Harrison has been a sounding board over the past years; again, despite his own burdens he has shared his thoughts and researches. Miguel Benitez has generously offered robust advice and shared his profound learning. Other scholars, Jim Dibykowski and James Alsop, graciously shared their own researches with me prior to publication. The History of Parliament Trust in the learned trinity of David Hayton, Andrew Hanham and Stuart Handley have been exceptionally patient with me. They've all made me think harder about political realities, when I may have been tempted to spiral off into hyper-textuality. Similarly Clyve Jones of the Institute of Historical Research has patiently offered suggestions and important references. If this book has any claims to be more rooted in the real world of politics than most intellectual history usually is, blame these men.

Other historians and friends have offered an ear to rant in, and an arm to lean on. Mike Braddick has been a stable influence and encouraging commentator. Although it may not be immediately apparent his own work on authority and power has exercised a profound and deep influence on the way I think about the culture Toland lived in. Harvey Shoolman has offered more references than I could ever read, but also and importantly a fierce reassurance that subjects like Toland deserve our attention. Robert Iliffe continues to keep me on my toes. John Marshall has kept up a conversation on these matters for nearly twenty years. Closer to home Francis Robinson, Jack Pridham, Roy Miller, Paul Finch and Klaus Dodds have kept my spirits up with dedication and skill. A decade's worth of special subject students have helped me reread many of Toland's works: I can honestly say that on regular occasions I have learnt as much from them as they have from me. Thanks too are due to my persevering co-convenors at the Institute of Historical Research – John Miller and Ian Roy especially. The spirit of disinterested historical enquiry exists still in these gatherings. The University of London, and especially Royal Holloway College, has been a stimulating place to work. Despite the ever expanding burdens of administrative endeavour, the History Department has always prided itself on a commitment to scholarship. Colleagues such as Tony Stockwell, Pat Crimmin, and Alison Brown have always offered encouragement and support for which I am very grateful. Sam Barnish has been a tremendous font of knowledge (and fine wine): it is a privilege to be able to make idle enquiry of him. Such requests always prompt profound response. Michael Drolet has been a partner in crime for a number of years too. My research students, Eduardo Gasca, David Wilson, Lee McNulty, Nicholas Keene, Sheila Seymour, Debbie Kepple, Kris Josephs and Vanessa McMahon have all kept me firmly in touch with current research.

Committing one's thoughts to paper is an engaging but distracting activity. It requires an enormous infrastructure of institutional and economic support. It relies however on social and emotional dimensions which are very rarely costed in the various academic audits. I have upon occasions wondered whether writing books is a suitable pastime for a father and partner. The number of sunny summer days consumed in some dreary library, or stifling conference room, which should have been spent more profitably at the seaside or cooking supper are lost to me now. Dedicating the proceeds of such indulgence to the victims seems rather inappropriate in the circumstances, but it must do.

Royal Holloway, University of London

Abbreviations

Berti *et al. Heterodoxy*   S. Berti, F. Charles-Daubert, R. H. Popkin (eds) *Heterodoxy, Spinozism, and Free Thought in early eighteenth century Europe* (Klewer, 1996)

Collections 1, 2   John Toland *A collection of several pieces of Mr John Toland* 2 volumes (1726)

Correspondence   E. S. De Beer (ed.) *The correspondence of John Locke* 8 volumes (Oxford, 1978–)

Darbishire *Early lives*   H. Darbishire *The early lives of Milton* (1932)

Errata   G. Carabelli *Tolandiana. Errata, addenda e indici* (Ferrara, 1978)

Forster *Letters*   T. Forster (ed.) *Original letters of John Locke, Algernon Sidney and Lord Shaftesbury* (1847)

Jacob *Radical*   M. C. Jacob *The Radical Enlightenment* (1981)

Kemble   J. M. Kemble *State papers and correspondence* (1857)

Klopp 2   O. Klopp (ed.) *Correspondence de Leibniz avec L'électrice Sophie de Brunswick-Lunebourg* volume 2 (1874)

Nazarenus   John Toland *Nazarenus* ed. J. A. I. Champion (Oxford, 1999)

Pantheisticon   John Toland *Pantheisticon, sive Formula Celebrandæ Sodalitatis Socraticæ*, ed. M. Iofrida and O. Nicastro (Pisa, 1996)

Portland Mss IV and V   *Historical Manuscripts Commission. Report on the manuscripts of his Grace the Duke of Portland volumes IV and V* (1899)

Ricuperati 'Libertinismo'   G. Ricuperati 'Libertinismo e deismo a Vienne: Spinoza, Toland e il "Triregno"' *Rivista storica italiana* 79 (1967) pp. 628–695

Sullivan *Toland*   R. Sullivan *John Toland and the Deist controversy: a study in adaptions* (Harvard, 1982)

Tolandiana   G. Carabelli *Tolandiana. Materiali bibliografici per lo studio dell'opera e della fortuna di John Toland (1670–1722)* (Florence, 1975)

Various Mss VIII   *Historical Manuscripts Commission. Report on the manuscripts in various collections volume VIII* (1913)

Wootton *Republicanism*   D. Wootton (ed.) *Republicanism, liberty, and commercial society 1649–1776* (Stanford, 1994)

Worden *Ludlow*   A. B. Worden (ed.) *Edmund Ludlow: a voyce from the watchtower* (1978)

Introduction

◆

Locating John Toland

Toland was desperately ill. He had recurring 'pains in my thighs, reins and stomach' accompanied by 'a total loss of appetite, hourly retchings, and very high colour'd water'. His hopes that this suffering was the symptom of 'gravel' that would pass with the stones were dashed. Confined to his chamber for weeks, he could keep down nothing but weak broth, and was scarcely able to walk. Reduced to relying on the kindnesses of others by disastrous investments in the fashionable speculations of South Sea Company, Toland was on his uppers. Only a few years previously his pen had been at the command of government ministers and European princes: he had written for German queens, Savoyard princes, Irish peers and English earls.[1]

Despite his international celebrity, John Toland eventually died a slow, painful death in lowly circumstances, passing away in a rented back room of a carpenter's cottage in March 1722. This was less than gentle scholarly poverty. Given the radical character of his reputation, perhaps it was no coincidence that the churchyard was that of St Mary's Putney, which had entertained the political debates of the Levellers in the 1640s. Having suffered for months from a combination of the stone, severe rheumatism and 'black-jaundice', the final 'violent indisposition' that carried him away was a fever which 'proved mortal to him about three of the clock on Sunday morning, the 11th instant, in the 53rd Year of his Age'.[2] Typically for a man steeped in the writings of classical antiquity, Toland, called in one obituary 'the Lucian of our times', approached death with a 'philosophical patience', although papers left scattered in his room indicated he blamed the incompetence and greed of physicians for much of his misery.[3] He was bedridden for over a month but his friends and patrons did what they could to make him comfortable. Their concern was genuine.[4]

Even while confined to his bed he continued to write. He drafted a work against the incompetence of physicians and a political pamphlet for the coming election. Completion of the latter work, attacking the dangers of mercenary parliaments, was interrupted only by his demise. Even on his deathbed, Toland appeared more interested in books than his own health, after all it was books and ideas that had dominated his life. Crammed into his back room, books were his most precious belongings. Stacked on chairs, teetering in piles on chests, or packed into boxes, these works, and his intimacy with their contents, were the foundation of Toland's reputation. A mixture of recondite theology, classical learning and political tracts, the eclecticism of his library underscores the range of his interests and erudition. Even the last letters he wrote, which as well as describing in harrowing detail his sickness, also included remarks about books. He would lend Lady 'H' a copy of the fine romance *Zayde* so that she could be freed from the drudgery of the 'longwinded and unwieldy *Cleopatra*'. To Molesworth, he wrote of Cicero's *de republica* and a projected volume on the 'history of the late Wars from King William's death to Queen Anne's peace'.[5]

Surrounded by close intimates, even in the moment of his death, Toland was an enigma. The day before he died, one of his friends noted that 'upon his appearing somewhat more than ordinary cheerful [I said] ... I hoped he was better'. Toland responded promptly, 'Sir, I have no hopes but in God'. Even a few moments before he expired, 'looking earnestly at some friends that were in the room, and being asked *if he wanted anything*, he answered with the greatest resolution, *I want nothing but death*'. In another account, his last words uttered with tranquillity bidding farewell to those about him, were 'he was going to sleep'. Newspaper obituaries in the following days sanctimoniously reported the decease as a providential punishment for a man who had systematically attempted to 'shock the faith of Christians in the glorious person and divinity of their redeemer, and to sap and undermine the principle and foundations of the orthodox faith'. Noting that the 'anti-Christian' Toland refused the ministrations of the Church on his deathbed the general opinion was that Toland had received his just deserts. As Hearne put it, he was no more than an 'impious wretch'.[6]

Some contemporaries did, however, mourn his death. According to his friends, the clamours against his reputation had been undeservedly prompted by 'those Upstarts who envied his Learning' and by 'conceited priests' who had neither read his works nor 'could have understood them if they had'. In 'An elegy on the death of the famous Mr J. Toland', published later in his posthumous works, he was celebrated as a champion of British liberties. A man who stood firm against the torrent and 'impetuous flood, of bigotted Enthusiasts, and tricks of pedantry, and priestly politicks!' Toland's genius for 'reason' worked like the morning sun to 'dispel Dark clouds of Ignorance, and break the spell of Rome's Inchantments, and the lesser frauds of Churches protestant, and English Lauds'. This achievement of defending liberty and truth, breaking both political and intellectual chains, would inspire 'noble emulation' in the youth of the nation. Far from being an icon of impiety, Toland was a hero of liberty, who had 'freed our minds of superstitious pains'. Typically, for a man sensitive to his reputation, Toland wrote his own epitaph. He was no man's follower or dependent but maintained his status as 'an assertor of liberty, a lover of all sorts of Learning, a speaker of truth'.[7]

Toland today is little known outside the world of academia. Born in Ireland in 1670 he escaped his 'popish' background under the sponsorship of the dissenting minister Dr Williams, being educated successively in Scotland, Holland and Oxford.[8] Exploiting his intimacy with figures like John Locke in Oxford in the mid-1690s, Toland burst onto the intellectual firmament with his first major publication, *Christianity not mysterious* (1696), a work which antagonised the Anglican mainstream by its assertion that all fundamental doctrine was accessible to human reason unaided by the Church. Having secured public notoriety with this work (which was both prosecuted and burnt by official means) Toland spent the later 1690s producing an influential series of political works. This labour included an important collection of republished republican writings from the 1650s, as well as specific pamphlets contributed to controversial debates concerning issues like the standing army.

Throughout the 1690s, and the early 1700s, working closely with powerful political figures like the third Earl of Shaftesbury, Robert Harley and Sir Robert Molesworth, Toland became one of the most consistent and vocal publicists for Protestant liberties and the Hanoverian succession. During the 1700s he continued this public role writing (amongst many contributions) detailed defences of the Act of Settlement and the rights of the Electress and Elector of Hanover, of the Toleration Act, as well as fierce attacks upon the 'popery' of the High Church party in Convocation and Parliament. Alongside this explicitly political writing, Toland was involved in the production of works of profound erudition and scholarship. Much of this material was circulated in clandestine form amongst a circle of elite figures that included Sophia of Hanover (the successor apparent to the British Crown), Prince Eugene of Savoy (leading military strategist of the Protestant cause), and English gentlemen like Anthony Collins. Ultimately this erudition, which was also published in print form, earned Toland a significant and contentious reputation in the European 'republic of letters'.

From 1710, in the aftermath of the defeat of the Whig Party at the hands of an electorate smarting from the consequences of the Sacheverell Trial, Toland became explicitly associated with the cause of the Protestant succession against what he (and many contemporaries) saw as a resurgent Jacobite interest. To this end he published a series of increasingly virulent pamphlets exposing the High Church as crypto-popish and Tory politicians as pro-Stuart. Breaking completely with his former patron Robert Harley, whom he regarded as a traitor to the cause of liberty, Toland became a leading propagandist for Sophia and George, commending their virtues and Protestant legitimacy. After the accession of George I in 1714, Toland reaped the benefits of his life-long association with commonwealth politicians like Robert Molesworth. Between 1717 and 1720, at the height of his literary and scholarly powers, he produced a series of popular pamphlets and learned studies that acted as a platform for the reforms of the radical ministry of Stanhope and Sunderland.

Toland combined this public writing with a clandestine circulation of ideas amongst a more elite community. While his private commitments were highly heterodox, his public identity was devoted to the defence of what he called 'Protestant Liberties'. Dedicated to reforming the Established Church by removing its residual popery, and keen to institute a radical form of civil toleration, Toland hoped to achieve profound political change through the agency of his writings. Ultimately these ambitions were defeated by the political triumph of Walpole in 1720. Walpole's judgement that the Church of England was a powerful ally of the Whig establishment against the threat of Toryism, meant that the anticlerical project which was fundamental to Toland's (and the commonwealth party's) objectives was defeated. The political fallout from the disaster of the South Sea Bubble implicated many of those committed to the radical reforms of the earlier ministry. By 1722, Toland was a marginal figure, alienated from serious political circles, living in poverty in Putney, and suffering from a terminal illness.

This book has broader ambitions than a straightforward intellectual biography of Toland. By locating Toland's writings within a wider intellectual, social and political culture, the ambition is to contribute to an understanding of the nature of political debate in the period of his life. Toland moved in a, at times, bewildering set of different circles and milieux; as previous historians have noted with a touch of understandable exasperation, his 'identity' is elusive. This mercurial ubiquity, while frustrating to those who might wish to capture Toland's essence, makes him a fertile resource for exploring the dimensions of early eighteenth-century intellectual culture. Toland's ambiguity was a reflection of the compound structure of political and religious culture after the Glorious Revolution.

Historians have debated for many years whether 1689 was a watershed in the creation of the modern world, or merely another 'restoration' of *ancien regime* constitutions in Church and State. Whether insisting that British culture stood on the brink of modernity, or that the nation was not so much transformed as secured, it is clear that one of the major issues of public and private life was the status and role of religion in political culture.[9] Far from ending debates about the political power of the Church, or the role of Christianity in society, the consequences of ecclesiological reform in 1689 were a blend of innovation and tradition. In the same breath as allowing a diversity of Protestant worship, the statutory reforms underscored the singular juris-dictional authority of the Church of England. By default these debates about the nature of religion were intimately bound up with questions about the legitimate character of political authority. Despite the catastrophe of the fall of James II it was still a broad cultural assumption that monarchy was authorised from divine sources. Continuing debates about whether the divine origins of monarchical authority were shaped more by dynastic lineage or Protestant identity dominated the political landscape between 1689 and the 1720s.

The period between the Revolution of 1688–89 and the ascendancy of Walpole in the early 1720s was dominated by the 'rage of party'.[10] Whether examining the conceptual dimensions of Whig and Tory ideologies, the development of the mechanics of 'party' politics at Westminster and in the localities, or the rise of the dominance of a propertied and landed 'old corruption', the centrality of religious controversy to politics is indisputable. It is clear that the development of rival party ideologies, and the consequent fractured and divided society, was driven by the 'troubles' that had dominated the crises of authority in the seventeenth century. Recent writing has under-scored how the day-to-day battles of both national and local politics were fought out over a series of persisting issues.[11] The security of the Protestant succession, the claims of tender conscience, the rights of the Christian Church, the privileges of Parliament, the corruption of the political administration were amongst the core issues of debate. Whether defending 'revolution principles' or the sacred memory of the martyred Charles I, politicians and pamphleteers exploited a deep reservoir of ideas, prejudices and convictions. In an age of repeatedly contested elections, and an explosion of print culture, these issues were debated furiously and repeatedly in public. Pamphlets, addresses and petitions spewed from the presses and the localities. Although it is difficult to be precise about the impact of this printed discourse, it is clear that the successive swings in electoral fortunes from the 1690s and 1700s were shaped by ideological convictions. As the political crises surrounding the issue of occasional conformity in the early 1700s, and the aftermath of the Sacheverell trial in 1710, illustrate, both parliamentary politics and the conduct of the nation 'out of doors' was volatile and potentially insurrectionary. Men like Toland, feeding this public controversy, were playing with fire but for high stakes.

There is a parallel historiographical account of the same period. Eschewing the practical world of parliamentary and civic politics, a broader history of ideas has identified the period as initiating an 'age of reason'.[12] In this view the period is characterised by a general decay of religious sensibility. So for example the decline in magic and witchcraft, the fracturing of doctrinal orthodoxy and the critical attack upon the integrity of Revelation have been regarded as evidence of a general cultural crisis. The intellectual manifestations of this disenchantment of the world have been described with a variety of labels – deism, atheism, and a more diffuse heterodoxy.[13] This loose cultural combination of 'enlightenment' and 'secularisation' produced what John Locke called the 'reasonableness of Christianity'.[14] This forward-looking account has been comprehensively refuted by historians of the eighteenth-century Church of England. From a variety of perspectives it has been shown how clerical institutions (pastoral, political and intellectual) were robust and adaptable in the period.[15] Far from withering away into the foothills of the 'Enlightenment', theological culture and authority retained a persistent social power into the nineteenth century. While reinforcing the point of how deeply entrenched theological perspectives on the world were in the early eighteenth century, this work will also explore how it was possible to unpick some of the power of these discourses and institutions. To acknowledge the persistence of theological imperatives is not the same as claiming it was either unchangeable or uncontested. One of the central planks of Toland's cultural project was to censure the political status of clergyman and the 'Church' as an independent institution.[16] This was, by necessity, an assault on Christian ideas as much as on ecclesiastical men and tradition. For Toland corrupt ideas laid the foundations for a perverted civil polity.

Examining the life and works of John Toland will enable a reconsideration of the nature of English politics and society in the Augustan age. The early eighteenth century was an age when literary culture dominated the world of politics in the form of an explosion of printed materials ranging from the newsletter, the polemical pamphlet, the folio edition and the broadsheet. Public discourse in the period was made of a variety of competing, contested converging languages: popery and priestcraft, liberty and tyranny, virtue and corruption, politeness and barbarity, monarchy and commonwealth, interest and honour. Toland contributed to most, if not all of these forms. Toland's writings throw deep shafts of light not only into these discursive complexities but also into the under-explored dimensions of elite political culture. Toland acts then as a prism that refracts light into a number of diverse spaces: high politics, clandestine literature and the European republic of letters.

John Toland was first and foremost a politician. His ambition was to replace the rule of tyranny with liberty. In order to achieve this objective he intended to alter the culture he lived in by changing the way people thought and behaved: to this end he wrote, talked and published a number of different sorts of intellectual discourse. Ranging from translations of obscure Italian treatises on coins to innovative research upon questions of biblical canonicity, all his works contributed in different ways to this single-minded project of a war against what he, and many of his contemporaries, called 'priestcraft'.

Exploring what Toland thought he was doing, how contemporaries understood his objectives, and how effective he was in his conduct will be the simple objective of this book.

During the course of his life John Toland was beaten up in the street, prosecuted in civil and ecclesiastical courts, and snubbed by prime ministers. The same man, and at the same times, was entertained by dukes, earls and lords, collaborated with leading ministers and flirted with the potential successor to the British throne. Toland moved in a number of different social, political and intellectual spaces. He was certainly an *habitué* of the coffee-houses of London, Oxford and Edinburgh. Sometimes he was indiscreet in his conduct, trashing kings and scripture in an outrageous manner. At other times he was more circumspect, gathering opinions, listening, drawing out the convictions of his company. Toland was at home too in the spaces of learning; in the libraries and archives of the great European universities like Leiden, Oxford and Edinburgh, as well as the more intimate collections of private figures like Benjamin Furly, Eugene of Savoy and Anthony Collins. Just as his conduct in the coffee-houses brought him into contact with a variety of communities, so his intimacy with books enabled his participation in a different social world – if the coffee-house can be thought of as a public and political place, perhaps feeding the pulse of public opinion, then the libraries of the great and the good not only provided a series of powerful intellectual and cultural resources, but also an avenue of intimacy into the elite circles of political power.[17]

Public association with Toland after 1696 – as a consequence of both the dreadful reputation of his religious writings and his equally subversive editorial work upon the republican canon – became a dangerous thing. As will be discussed below, one man – John Locke – certainly thought better of his friendship and made it apparent he wanted no connection with him. Powerful political figures like Robert Harley, although keen to exploit Toland's polemical abilities, only made contact under cover of darkness or the back doors of anonymous meeting places. It is so much more significant then (and perhaps a surprise too) to find Toland associating with powerful people like Sophia, Electress of Hanover, her philosophically inclined daughter Sophia Charlotte, Queen of Prussia, and Prince Eugene of Savoy. Although diplomatic advisors and court politicians like Leibniz counselled discretion in all public dealings with Toland, nevertheless, both women encouraged communication and intimacy with him. As his literary dedications and private correspondence suggests, Toland was comfortable with, and well regarded by, leading members of the Whig aristocracy. He was, it seems, as at ease in close collaboration with men like Shaftesbury, as he was in the more public context of the aristocratic drawing room. While there is little doubt that Toland was master of the political brief or philosophical disputation, it is also important to indicate that he dabbled in the more frivolous activities of dancing, romancing and play-acting. The fragments of Toland's romantic poetry do not establish with any certainty the merits of his abilities; sadly the plays he wrote for the polite female company he associated with in the early 1720s do not survive. The point to reinforce is, however, simple. Toland was ubiquitous, he was everywhere important, at the elbow of the great and good, in the coffee-house, in the precincts of parliaments and courts. He communicated simultaneously with a variety of audiences, a bespoke powerful elite and a semi-anonymous public, tuning his ideas and writings to the demands of these communities.

If it is difficult to penetrate the membrane of Toland's personal identity, it is easier to establish his contributions to, and criticisms of, the broader culture from the evidence of his books and other writings. Drawing together the remnants of scribal and printed materials it is possible to reconstruct an archive of Toland's various transactions with a variety of political, economic, social and intellectual communities. These papers, whether letters to nobles, diplomats and princes, or more intimate communications with patrons, potential lovers and friends, tell us something about Toland the man and his associates as well as describing some of the structures of sociability in the period. Other fragments in this archive – the contracts with printers, the draft works, book-lists and working notes – allow us to enter cautiously (perhaps uninvited) deeper into the sanctum of Toland's working life.

In the absence of a diary or journal, reconstructing Toland's social life has to be done from the miscellany of material preserved in his correspondence and the reports of others in his company. We get glimpses of him, indiscreet in his attacks on monarchy and Church in coffee-houses in Edinburgh and London. Others reported him upsetting noble compatriots with his bad manners in Holland (for which he was given a good beating). Being hissed out of lecture rooms in Leiden University, or promising to write Sophia Charlotte, Queen of Prussia, a novel that never materialised. Hounded out of Dublin unable to pay either for food or fresh linen and wigs, or playing music and acting out parlour-room games with well-off women. A frequent house-guest of men like Anthony Collins and Molesworth, Toland was easeful in the gentlemanly environment of the country house. Indeed he idealised the benefits of such a rural retreat from the bustling commerce and conflict of the city in classical terms as places of reflection and philosophical contemplation. A very well-travelled man, one of the consistent themes of his itinerant life was the presence of books and libraries. Whether examining the heterodox holdings of Benjamin Furly's library in Rotterdam, or the no less irreligious collections of Prince Eugene or Baron d'Hohendorf in Vienna, or Collins's remarkable collection in Great Baddow, or more respectable locations such as the Bodleian in Oxford, or the University Library at Glasgow, Toland, it could be argued, measured his life in books and manuscripts. Toland was not only a politician, but a scholar too. His perceived learning was one of his distinctive qualities and certainly a factor in making his public status.

The Toland that haunts the following chapters is, I think, a very different figure from the man most historians (if they have heard of him at all) may have encountered. Although Edmund Burke, writing in the 1790s, insisted that no one read him any more (and indeed no one ought to), Toland's afterlife and reputation was still vigorous into the nineteenth century. The clearest testimony to the significance of Toland's intellectual and political contribution to eighteenth-century history is the monumental labour of Giancarlo Carabelli's bibliography *Tolandiana* which is the starting point not only for the contextual study of Toland's ideas, but also for the development of the historiographical reception of his work. Since the 1720s Toland has been the persistent subject of a widespread European historical account. German, French, but especially Italian scholars have devoted considerable efforts to investigating the significance of Toland's contribution.[18] In the twentieth century this story continued with the most serious examinations of his thought being undertaken by distinguished historians like the Frenchman Paul Hazard and the Italian Franco Venturi. In Anglophone writing, perhaps suffering from Burke's distaste, and the more hostile dismissal of Leslie Stephen, who regarded Toland as both an inconsequential thinker and a thoroughly reprehensible character, no major study of Toland was made until the 1970s and 1980s. The work, first of Margaret Jacob and then of Blair Worden, Robert Sullivan and Stephen Daniel, brought Toland to the attention of a more mainstream historiography.[19]

Yet Toland came to the mainstream as a maverick, a man on the radical margins, involved in clandestine counter-cultural sodalities, disseminating an esoteric materialism derived from the dark occultism of Renaissance texts composed by men like Giordano Bruno. Privileging the significance of Toland's natural philosophy, and his intimacy with the *libertin* circle of men like Rousset de Missy and Prosper Marchand, the writings of Margaret Jacob described a radical democratic tradition that drew its sap from the commonwealth traditions of the 1650s, and ultimately saw fruition in revolutions of the later eighteenth century. Toland was thus an important transmitter of a radical secular and materialist ideology to the revolutionary traditions embodied in the work of men like Baron de Holbach. Self-consciously distinct from the respectable liberal tradition of political ideology represented by the Lockean defence of the Glorious Revolution of 1689, Toland and his fellow-travellers of the 'Radical Enlightenment' become significant by their difference and uniqueness. In a mirror image of the celebratory interpretation advanced by Jacob, the historical understanding of the durability of traditional theological structures of institutional and ideological authority described by Jonathan Clark has also underscored the 'radical' (and by default unsuccessful) qualities of Toland's contribution. In contrast to Jacob's emphasis upon the importance of natural philosophy, and especially pantheistic materialism, to Toland's project, Clark is insistent that the characteristic quality of the polemic was a variety of religious heterodoxy. Far from ushering a new age of secular modernity, Toland and his ilk were a submerged and defeated interest, always outweighed (in the account of Brian Young) and out-thought by the overwhelming orthodoxy of traditional Christian theology.[20]

If Jacob's Toland turned God into matter, Clark's version advanced a picture of a rather unadventurous heretic. In contrast to these works of bold brush strokes, painting Toland either into the pantheon of Enlightenment or into the *chiaroscuro* of dissenting tradition, the work of Worden and Sullivan devoted more detail to locating the man and his thought into the context of his own times. In his fine edition of Toland's version of Edmund Ludlow's *Voyce from the watchtower*, Worden, concentrating upon Toland's relationship with the Commonwealthsmen of the 1690s, established the literary credentials of his subject. Meshing the heterodox account of Toland's religious convictions with his remodelling of the republican heritage of the 1650s, Worden argues that Toland performed an important role in adapting the languages of a political ideology drenched in biblical vocabulary to the exigencies of a more civil context. Toland's achievements were those of the pen rather than the intellect, employing high literary skill to manufacture ideological legitimation of the eighteenth-century constitution.[21] If Worden's focus dealt with political languages, then Sullivan applied considerable energy to locating Toland's religious identity within the broad carapace of reformed Protestantism. Accepting Toland's self-presentation as a sincere and convinced Christian, the picture that emerges in Sullivan's account is of a man concerned to reform religion to its primitive verities. Absorbing these arguments, Sullivan's Toland is conceived as blending civil and religious ambitions into a latitudinarian conception of organised religion that emphasised the moral dimensions of theology at the expense of the sacramental. Toland was then on the radical fringes of orthodoxy but still within the fold. There are then, it seems, almost as many Tolands as there are books about Toland.

It would be wrong and arrogant to suggest that this present work is any more than a development of the historiography discussed above. Although this author has a distinct view of each of the contributions so crudely epitomised here, each of them brings important and critical elements to this portrait of Toland. There are many versions of his life – Toland the radical, the religious thinker, the paid writer, the marginal and clandestine figure, the editor of texts. Toland was all of these. While one account pays attention to Toland's skills as an author, another underlines the philosophical or theological innovation of his ideas. For all these facets and accomplishments Toland still remains peripheral to the arterial routes of mainstream eighteenth-century history. This marginalisation of Toland's importance is a consequence not simply of his historical role, but of the broader attitude to the practice of the history of ideas in the period.

Toland's work is a useful starting point for engaging with the complex relationship between cultural diffusion and political agency, between the articulation of ideas and political action. So for example, one of the reasons for discussing with precision Toland's transactions with Harley and other politicians is to reinforce the argument that his writings played a significant role in the dynamics of early eighteenth-century political culture. Toland was part of the mainstream. This is not to suggest that he determined the nature of national politics, but that he was a participant in the community of the powerful elite that governed and managed that process. Although Toland was a man of relatively low social status, his education, learning and personal charisma advanced him to places of social power all over Europe. Whether in Berlin, Vienna, Amsterdam, Dublin or London, Toland managed to intrude himself into courts, salons, conversations and polite company. The interplay between his reputation for learning, the broader republic of letters that conferred status and credit on this learning, and the diverse political communities that employed and used this credit, meant that Toland acted as a mediator and intermediary between, and across, a number of social, geographical and political spaces. One moment he might be flirting with Sophia Charlotte in Berlin, while another he can be seen defending his reputation from frontal assault by Convocation. In another context he can be observed in clandestine communication with Eugene of Savoy, while writing diplomatic reports for Harley.

In all of these moments Toland was communicating with a number of audiences. When he debated the nature of the canon with continental clergymen in front of German princesses he was clearly engaged in a distinct form of intellectual activity than when he published works such as *Christianity not mysterious*. Toland was both a source and a conduit of ideas, opinions, beliefs and ideologies. As he put it, again, he could both 'draw' and 'diffuse' information. Simply because Toland moved in these diverse and powerful circles, he is an important subject to examine. Although it is not possible to recover the full dimension of his interaction with many of these elite people (in particular the recapture of his oral communication is, with some singular exceptions, elusive), we do have a large textual archive to examine as a starting point for exploring the purpose of his life. Toland's writings are the textual sediments of his attempts to communicate with a number of audiences. These texts are not only carriers of ideas but are also testimonies of his attempts to change established cultural convictions by intellectual persuasion. To understand the purpose of these texts we need to examine not simply their intellectual content, but also the material form and concomitant relationship with a readership or interpretative community. Whether a text was composed in French, Latin or English, distributed in scribal, printed or oral format, reprinted, published or simply proposed, shaped the function of the act of intellectual meaning. Toland's lifetime project was an engagement with the politics of cultural authority: his ambition was to challenge, overturn and reconstruct what he regarded as a corrupt rule of priestcraft. The major weapons in this engagement were ideas. As Toland was very well aware ideas became powerful when communicated effectively.

Toland, however, wrote in an age of censorship. Although the strict legal mechanisms for policing print material had lapsed in 1695, in a broader and more culturally diffuse sense, censorship was still an overwhelming and determining force in the realm of public communication. As the example of *Christianity not mysterious* indicates, there were still institutional means, civil and spiritual, for enacting legal prosecution of texts, authors and printers. Even beyond these acts of physical repression there was a form of powerful discursive restriction: the hegemonic authority of Christian culture meant that there was a defined structure for the production of orthodox discourse and knowledge. Conformity to that set of speech-codes was the process whereby legitimate (and therefore potentially successful) discourses became authorised. Strategies for the subversion of this cultural hegemony had to engage with the linguistic commonplaces in order to gain a foothold in the debate. Cultural criticism was necessarily dialogic: in order to compromise authority, the language that defined the legitimacy of that authority had to be appropriated to the act of censure. Transgressive projects were then both conceived and articulated within the idiom of orthodoxy: performing cultural criticism was to make a claim to power.

When Toland circulated his ideas (in scribal, printed or oral form) he was distributing information through social space: the point of this communication was political. The power of Toland's discourses was made, not purely by the intellectual coherence or elegance of their arguments, but in the negotiation between the reader's mind and the residual authority of contextual languages. In Toland's case it is important to think about how, and to whom, he was talking, rather than simply about what he was saying. It is almost certainly true that Toland very rarely meant what he actually said: this was not simply because he subscribed to a complex epistemological understanding of esoteric and exoteric truth (which he indeed did), but because the work of making meaning was done in the reception rather than the utterance of speech-acts. This relationship between textual utterance, reader reception and the generation of meaning and belief, was rendered even more complex by the bibliocentric nature of Christian theology in the period. In a political culture defined by Protestant orthodoxy, the institutions of Church and State were the most powerful forgers of authority when supported by the 'truth' of revelation. The pervasive authority of Scripture, and its availability to those with competent literacy, meant that there was a powerful textual resource for the legitimation of ideas and beliefs. The authority of different religious polemics was built upon an ability to capture the meaning of Scripture. Scriptural interpretation was a 'public' means for making true ideas, and a source by which many readers could authenticate or deconstruct the value of the works they examined. Little wonder then that Toland devoted considerable energies to developing an erudition in matters of biblical criticism and textual scholarship, because these would be powerful instruments for establishing the authority of his own writing.

The cultural system of early modern England was based upon the connection between Christian knowledge and institutions that made that knowledge. Ideas were then intimately related to the distribution of social authority and power.[22] This nexus between knowledge and institutional power was the one at which Toland worried. He hoped to reform corrupt Christian society by compromising the commonplace codes and vocabularies of orthodox language. The specifically Christian dimensions of early modern culture underscored the powerful relationship between ideas and institutions: the power of the monarchy and church was premised upon a true understanding of religion. Episcopacy as a political institution was right, because it conformed to the 'true' idea of the primitive Church. Obedience to the monarch was right because it was authorised by the divine injunctions of Christian belief, and the repeated vocal and print reiteration of the Church. The clergyman was right because he spoke in the divinely ordained language of Scripture. Toland's attack upon the cultural components of this system of power (the textual integrity of Scripture, the *de jure divino* status of clergymen, the doctrinal accounts of the soul) was ultimately a political act, although articulated in the language of theology, learning and history. This attack upon the ideological and institutional basis of clerical authority took a cultural form but had a political objective. Certainly, as the reception of his works indicates, contemporaries (whether hostile or supportive) acknowledged the power and danger of his labours. In undertaking this war of ideas against a prevailing cultural system that made monarchs and priests divine, Toland developed a series of cultural tools and practices that could replace the compromised system.

These acts of discrediting the conventional 'knowledges' of Christian culture allow a route into the debate about the relationship between ideas and historical change raised in the pertinent phrase of Roger Chartier, 'Do books make revolutions?'[23] Toland, as will be discussed below, engaged in a series of challenges to a number of authorities (Biblical, sacerdotal, political). The complex intellectual components of authority provided the cultural frameworks for the generation of public truth, or at least providing the grounds for making the institutions, texts and convictions of the status quo 'believable'. 'Truth' was made by men and institutions. It was forged by routine proce-

dures of credibility, textual hermeneutics and public communication. Ruptur-
ing, capturing and transforming the logic of such cultural procedures was a
discursive manoeuvre that had profound and explicit social and political
consequences. As will be examined at length, Toland conducted a sustained
and public assault upon the clerical cultural system for making authority. By
embroiling his priestly opponents in public debate he dislodged the mortar
that bound the stones of Christian order.

Toland's strategy for cultural subversion was a subtle and sophisticated
matter. Unlike contemporary 'heretics' like Arthur Bury or William Whiston
who articulated their objections as a full-frontal rebuttal of orthodox conceptions of religious truth, and were consequently met with the powerful forces of
persecution and destruction, Toland adopted a more dialogic method, adapting,
expanding and appropriating the commonplace routines of cultural authority
to his own purposes. Exploiting the growing cultural authority of the way of
print and especially the ambiguity of reader reception and response, Toland
consistently presented himself as a man of learning and theological erudition.
Rather than trash the claims of Scripture, the Church Fathers and ecclesiastical tradition, Toland became expert in the knowledge of these discourses.
By learning the trade he was able to engage more effectively in deconstructive
ambitions, teasing readers and audiences with a variety of ruses and ambiguities. Although, as the example of the execution of Thomas Aikenhead
establishes, the consequences of heterodoxy could be fatal, it is clear that the
orthodox state was only capable of exercising rudimentary control over the
circulation of ideas in the printed and spoken form.[24] Toland's adoption of the
authorial personae of 'sincere' Christian, or devout 'scholar', was a simple but
effective way of bypassing censorship, if not of avoiding public censure and
hostile rebuttal.

This book then will attempt to probe the relationship between discursive
performance and political action. Despite doubt about whether the world of
ideas can ever affect anything beyond the text itself, it will be a premise here
that ideas were powerful instruments in the transactions of cultural politics in
the period. Whether by manipulation of conventional languages, thereby
altering the perceptions, values, attitudes and understandings of audiences
and readers, Toland's writings and communications affected the durability of
some Christian configurations of power and authority. By effective capture of
the languages of orthodox discourses (in politics and theology) he developed a
repertoire of discursive ruses that deconstructed commonplaces, exposed
contradictions, and appropriated the affective power of key vocabularies to his
own purposes. As will be established in detail below, because Toland disseminated his ideas in a variety of forms to a variety of audiences, both elite and
popular, it is possible to relate the articulation of his ideas to precise social and
political communities. In the broadest possible sense then this work takes its

lead from the speech act arguments advanced by the Cambridge School. Central to this position is the assertion that there is a relationship between saying and doing: by recovering the historical context and performance of a text it is possible to retrieve the historical meaning of a set of discourses beyond the purely lexical content of the writing. In an age when issues of belief and conviction were fundamental to questions of religious identity, the simple existence of Toland's contributions made an impact.

The example of Toland and his social relationships provides ample material for making a model of cultural and intellectual change. Writing, reading and conversations were forms both of intellectual interaction and sociability. Toland's ideas did not float free-form in the ether of the public sphere, but were read and discussed in coffee-houses, aristocratic salons, scholars' libraries, political meetings and royal courts. These places and moments of communication did have an effect: perhaps the most obvious evidence of his influence on the public culture of his time can be seen in the thousands of pages written against his arguments. These hostile works were not simply counter-arguments, but material evidence of the way his books were read. Robert Darnton has repeatedly made enquiry into the question of how ideas penetrated into society in the eighteenth century. His account of the relationship between forbidden books and intellectual change has made a bridge between what has been identified as 'diffusion studies' and 'discourse studies'. Arguing for an understanding of the history of ideas that involves not simply the study of conceptual propositions but also the material and social dimensions of the production of books rather than texts, he has insisted that the matter of 'how the diffusion of books affects public opinion and how public opinion inflects political action' remains largely unresolved. The communicative network made by the serial transactions of writing, selling, buying and reading a book is the place to start thinking about the dynamics of change.[25]

Darnton's work has focused in detail upon the functional role of 'forbidden' books in eighteenth-century French society: in such subversive works the transformative intentions were explicit. The focus on the heterodox, the marginal and the polemic writings, while admirable and important, has tended to obscure the same processes in the reading and production of 'orthodox' discourses. Recovering the cultural procedure that authorised and made convincing the commonplace Christian and monarchical discourses is as critical as exploring the radical and controversial. The relationship between the two sorts of texts (and the two sorts of readers) is central to understanding the dialogic process of cultural change. How readers might accept, reject, misunderstand, and censor what they examined is key to thinking about how the power of ideas worked. In the case of Toland, his literary skill at exploiting the different authorities of printed and scribal formats of writing, as well as his successful mimicking of the literary styles of orthodox discourses, meant that the relationship between reading and conviction was dynamic rather than passive. Although the trend of recent historical approaches to the book has stressed the important role reader-reception played in making meaning from textual sources, it is also important to note that some writers were facile in exploiting the diversity of some of the predictable responses particular audiences might have to certain sorts of book. Toland's self-presentation as a man of erudition and biblical learning in works like *Amyntor* and *Nazarenus* was calculated to make a text suitable for, or conformable to, the expectations of an identifiable clerical readership. Readers of texts were neither passive sponges, nor were books indeterminate collections of meanings awaiting definition by readers. Making meaning was a social activity that involved a negotiation with the specific text, the full range of cultural and discursive conventions about both the content and the form of the work, as well as social and communal dimensions of where the book was bought, read and discussed. The book then, was both a material and cultural artefact, as well as a collection of literary codes: meaning was made in specific sites and by specific ways of reading. The same work might very well mean different things to different people at the same time: the function of the work was thus determined by a complex and changing mixture of the material, the cultural and the social.

Without doubt, books, manuscripts and writings of a more ephemeral quality were central in the making of belief in the period. These texts were closely related to the social authority of their authors and the community that produced them. The model of biblical interpretation is the most evident example of the relationship between the truth of a text and the authority of those that explained the text. How readers formed these beliefs was a complex psychological and epistemological process: knowledge was made credible by a cultural technology that combined the social and political power of institutions like the Church, with literary conventions that reinforced the social credit of the authors as well as the 'truth' of the texts. What Toland achieved was the intrusion of his dissident and disaffected discourses into this cultural procedure. We know he convinced some people (powerful ones like Sophia, Molesworth, Shaftesbury and Harley) at the same time as alienating others (in particular those clerical men who wrote repeatedly against his works and their reputation). While it is clear that Toland's writings did not prompt a revolution, a close examination of the relationships between his ideas and the political activities of the cadre of radical Whigs in the period indicates an intimacy between his anticlerical discourse and attacks upon the *de jure divino* constitution of the status quo.

This is a book about how books were used to fight a war of ideas against political and cultural corruption. It is also about the readers and audiences for those books. It sets out to examine how the ideas in the books Toland wrote became beliefs and convictions. Not only is it a study of the construction and meaning of a series of political and religious discourses, it is an examination of the cultural dimensions of power in the period. Ultimately it is a case study of the relationship between words and deeds. Its subject, a coiner of neologisms, articulator of impieties, and forger of scholarship, lived in a world of ideas. By invoking the different intellectual contexts, the range of institutional relationships, and Toland's membership of a number of communal networks, the intention is to attempt to examine not only the intimacies between the world of ideas and the world of power, but also to explore the nature of discursive power in the period: in other words, how and why ideas made convictions. This book is not a biography. Neither is it a narrow study of the philosophical or political dimensions of his writings and ideas. It is an examination of how Toland attempted to neutralise the authority of established Christian values and to challenge the hegemony of the Church. By necessity then it is also a story about the limits of that process of cultural transformation. The book then will approach the history of ideas not simply in a philosophical way: that is, it is not only concerned with the matter of intellectual coherence or conceptual sophistication, but with the 'use' made of such ideas. It will then be explicitly concerned with the nature of the 'circulation' of ideas, as much as their content.[26] Thinking about the textual productions of Toland and his contemporaries as acts of communication rather than purely as repositories of intellectual propositions allows a consideration of not only the ideas themselves, but also the different media of transmission, the various social spaces involved in the reception of such ideas, and the implicit purposes of their production. As will be suggested, Toland acted as a cultural broker making connections between different social networks, transforming the function of key cultural resources by skilful appropriation and 'publishing' them in a variety of public forms.

The book is built around three connected parts – the first part will place Toland in his social and intellectual milieu; the second will explore his engagement with what might be called public writing; while the third part will explore his involvement in a pan-European scribal community focused around the exchange and circulation of clandestine literature. The common theme of the chapters will be how Toland used his facility with the written word and a variety of literary forms to unpick the commonplace values of orthodoxy. This was as much a political as intellectual project. Toland's achievement was to exploit his erudition and literary skills as a means for establishing an intimacy with a number of very powerful elite figures. This meant he was communicating corrosive ideas to an influential audience who as the concluding chapters suggest had direction of national government in the years immediately after the accession of George I. A central theme of the book will be then that the war of ideas in which Toland campaigned was not an intellectual side-show, but intimately related to the practical tasks and problems of contemporary politics. The fact that the after-life of Toland's textual production projected him onto a canvas of 'Enlightenment' thought, a stepping-stone on the incremental progress of public reason to 'modernity', is another story that has often obscured his significance in the day-to-day turbulence of early eighteenth-century politics.

The first part of the book then will deal with what we might call the material and social infrastructure for Toland's 'life of the mind'. To many readers, Toland is encountered as a maverick figure on the margins of the mainstream, a hack writer constantly short of money, desperate for any income and social purchase to advance his cause. As the chapters will argue, Toland, on the contrary, was intimate with a powerful elite throughout his career – importantly this intimacy brought access to the most crucial resource (at least in Toland's view) for his project – libraries and books. Toland did most of his dangerous work in 'the library'. Establishing which libraries, and perhaps more significantly, whose libraries, Toland had access to will lay the foundations for exploring the 'content' of the works he composed and circulated. Importantly, these chapters will reinforce Toland's role as a connector between different social networks in England and on the continent – he was one of the links between men in the radical republic of letters such as Benjamin Furly, Anthony Collins, the third earl of Shaftesbury, Robert Harley and Viscount Molesworth. In this sense if the traffic in books made revolutions, their exchange also made communities of revolutionaries. In essence Toland engaged in a series of intellectual and social transactions that turned 'knowledge' into politics.

The second part of the book will explore the dimensions of Toland's political arguments. Toland was an effective and controversial author from the days of the mid-1690s when his first work *Christianity not mysterious* (1696) shattered the complacent 'reasonableness' of mainstream Anglican theology, to the period after 1714 when Toland wrote as a mouthpiece of the radical Whig ministry led by Stanhope and Sunderland. Whether composing pamphlets defending specific ministerial objectives, or compiling and editing more detached accounts of political philosophy, Toland pursued a common core of political and religious objectives identified in the defence of Protestant liberties and the Hanoverian succession. Central to Toland's public writings was the insistence that 'liberty' in matters of religion was an essential foundation for 'freedom' in politics. Fundamental to his thinking was a powerful redefinition of classical republican ideas as a means for establishing the government of reason, rather than as simply an anti-monarchical discourse. Elemental to these political writings was a practical agenda of legislating against the primary agencies of irrational corruption identified most readily in the 'popery' of the Church.

If the theme of the second part of the book is to explore how Toland used printed work to communicate with a public audience in an attempt to convince them of the best strategy for compromising the tyranny of clerical politics, the final part examines the arguments he advanced in more intimate circumstances. By scrutinising the ideas advanced in the diverse scribal works he circulated it is possible to see how he set about making conviction in the salon. Here, rather than communicating with a political public, Toland was intent upon persuading politicians, ministers and princes. As will be shown, there was a profound connection between the public writings, and these rather more privileged and exclusive forms of work.

NOTES

1 *Collections* 2 pp. 484–495 reproduces the correspondence that covers the final weeks of Toland's life: see p. 491 for his own description of his pain.

2 Anon *The life of Mr. John Toland* (1722) p. 90.

3 *Collections* 2 p. 487.

4 *Collections* 2 p. 484.

5 *Collections* 2 pp. 487–489.

6 *The life of Mr. John Toland* p. 91; *Collections* 1 p. lxxxviii; See *Tolandiana* pp. 243–245; T. Hearne *Remarks and collections* (Oxford, 1886) volume 7, p. 343.

7 *The life of Mr. John Toland* p. 92; *Collections* 1 pp. xciii–xciv. See *Collections* 1 pp. lxxxviii–lxxxix, for the Latin text, and BL Add Mss 4295 fos. 76–77 for a contemporary translation, cited here.

8 See A. Gordon *Freedom after ejection* (1917) pp. 182–183.

9 See the collection of essays addressing this issue, A. Houston and S. Pincus (eds) *A nation transformed: England after the Restoration* (Cambridge, 2001).

10 For the most recent statement, see D. Hayton *The House of Commons, 1690–1715: introductory survey* volume 1 (Cambridge, 2002).

11 See J. Hoppit *A land of liberty? England 1689–1727* (Oxford, 2000); G. Holmes *British politics in the age of Anne* (revised edition, 1987); W. A. Speck *Tory and Whig* (1970); W. A. Speck *The birth of Britain: a new nation 1700–1710* (1994); J. P. Kenyon *Revolution principles: the politics of party, 1689–1720* (Cambridge, 1977).

12 For a useful overview, see B. Worden 'The question of secularisation' in Houston and Pincus (eds) *A nation transformed* pp. 20–40.

13 See for a useful overview R. D. Lund (ed.) *The margins of orthodoxy: heterodox writing and cultural response 1660–1750* (Cambridge, 1995). See also J. A. I. Champion '"May the last king be strangled in the bowels of the last priest": irreligion and the English Enlightenment, 1649–1789' in T. Morton and N. Smith (eds) *Radicalism in British literary culture, 1650–1830* (Cambridge, 2002) pp. 26–44.

14 See J. G. A. Pocock 'Religious freedom and the desacralisation of politics: from the English civil wars to the Virginia Statute' in Merrill D. Petersen and Robert C. Vaughan

(eds) *The Virginia Statute for Religious Freedom* (Cambridge, 1988) pp. 43–73: see also J. G. A. Pocock 'Post-Puritan England and the problem of the Enlightenment' in P. Zagorin (ed.) *Culture and politics: from Puritanism to the Enlightenment* (Berkeley, 1980) and J. G. A. Pocock 'Clergy and Commerce: the conservative Enlightenment in England' in *L'Eta dei Lumi: Studi Storici sul Settecento Europe in onore di Franco Venturi* (Naples 1985); M. A. Goldie 'Priestcraft and the birth of Whiggism' in N. Phillipson and Q. Skinner (eds) *Political discourse in early modern Britain* (Cambridge, 1993).

15 See J. Walsh, C. Haydon and S. Taylor (eds) *The Church of England c. 1689–c. 1833* (Cambridge, 1993); W. M. Jacob *Lay people and religion in the early eighteenth century* (Cambridge, 1996); D. A. Spaeth *The Church in an age of danger: parsons and parishioners, 1660–1740* (Cambridge, 2000); J. Gregory *Restoration, reformation and reform, 1660–1828: Archbishops of Canterbury and their diocese* (Oxford, 2000); B. Young *Religion and Enlightenment in eighteenth century England: theological debate from Locke to Burke* (Oxford, 1998).

16 See J. A. I. Champion '"Religion's safe, with priestcraft is the war": Augustan anticlericalism and the legacy of the English Revolution, 1660–1720' *The European Legacy* 5 (2000) pp. 547–561; J. A. I. Champion '"To govern is to make subjects believe": anticlericalism, politics and power 1680–1720' in N. Aston and M. Cragoe (eds) *Anticlericalism in early modern England* (2001) pp. 42–66.

17 See J. Van Horn Melton *The rise of the public in Enlightenment Europe* (Cambridge, 2001).

18 See most recently G. Brykman (ed.) *John Toland (1670–1722) et la crises de conscience européenne* in *Revue de synthèse* 2–3 (1995) pp. 221–439; G. Palmer *Ein Freispruch für Paulus* (Berlin, 1996); G. Carabelli (ed.) *I castelli di Yale. Quaderni di filosofia* 4 (1999); A. Santucci *Filosofia e cultura nel settecento britannico: Fonti e connessioni continentali John Toland e il deismo* (Bologna, 2000). In France new editions of Toland's works are forthcoming from Pierre Lurbe, Laurent Jaffro and Tristan Dagron.

19 P. Hazard *The European mind 1680–1715* (1953); F. Venturi *Utopia and reform in the Enlightenment* (Cambridge, 1971); M. C. Jacob *The Newtonians and the English Revolution 1689–1720* (Cornell, 1976); Jacob *Radical Enlightenment*; Sullivan *Toland*; Worden *Ludlow*; S. Daniel *John Toland: his methods, manners, and mind* (Montreal, 1984).

20 J. C. D. Clark *English Society 1660–1832: Religion, ideology and politics during the ancien regime* (Cambridge, 2000); Young *Religion and Enlightenment in eighteenth century England.*

21 This argument has been developed further in B. Worden *Roundhead reputations: the English civil war and the passions of posterity* (2001) and 'Whig history and puritan politics: the *Memoirs* of Edmund Ludlow revisited' *Historical Research* 75 (2002) pp. 209–237.

22 See J. A. I. Champion '"To govern is to make subjects believe": anticlericalism, politics and power c. 1680–1717' and Champion '"Religion's safe, with priestcraft is the war"'.

23 R. Chartier *The cultural origins of the French Revolution* (1991) chapter 4 'Do books make revolutions' especially at pp. 81–91. For an useful discussion of Chartier's work see D. Goodman 'Public sphere and private life: towards a synthesis of current historiographical approaches to the Old Regime' *History and Theory* 31 (1992).

24 See M. Hunter '"Aikenhead the Atheist": the context and consequences of articulate irreligion in the late seventeenth century' in *Science and the shape of orthodoxy* (Woodbridge, 1995) pp. 308–332.

25 R. Darnton *The forbidden bestsellers of pre-revolutionary France* (1996) p. 179. For a discussion of these issues see H. T. Mason (ed.) *The Darnton debate: books and revolution in the eighteenth century* (Oxford, 1998).

26 See M. de Certeau *The capture of speech and other political writings* (Minnesota, 1997).

Part I

Republics of learning

———◆———

'The traffic of books':
libraries, friends and conversation

J OHN Toland read a great deal. The scholarly apparatus to his written work is
ample evidence of this. A more intimate view of his own library survives in
the manuscript fragments recording the piles of books left at his death in the
room he rented in Putney. Gathered on top of chairs, a chest of drawers and
on the floor was Toland's working library of some one hundred and fifty
volumes.[1] The collection was eclectic. It contained a number of foreign
language works in French, Spanish and Italian while the majority of the works
were in the commonplace scholarly languages of Greek and Latin. The range
of subject matter was broad, although a few suspect books were evident (a
book was noted without full title to be a 'Family of Love' work), the vast
majority were concerned with the staples of orthodox erudition. Biblical and
patristic studies were a constituent part: amongst many significant titles were
those, for example, by his own tutor at the University of Leiden, Frederic
Spanheim, a number of volumes by the controversial Arminian theologian
Jean Leclerc, the collected works of the Lutheran Biblical critic Johann Albertus
Fabricius, philological studies by the orientalist Von Hardt of Helmstadt, as
well as key grammatical volumes by the younger and older Buxtorfs. He
owned copies of the Bible in Greek, Latin, English and Irish. Alongside these
works of orthodox (in the main Protestant) piety were volumes of and about
rabbinical learning, as well as reasonably modern studies of Islam. So for
example, Toland owned the rather rare Italian work of Simon Luzzatto on the
politics of the Hebrew state: as we will see, he used the work as the basis for
his arguments in favour of naturalising the Jews, and indeed proposed an
English translation in 1714. Another work by the eminent Dutch orientalist
Adrian Reland was plundered by Toland to bring scholarly credit to his own
work on the *Gospel of Barnabas*. He also had a number of volumes of studies in
alchemical experiments and medicinal texts. The study of antiquities – Roman,
French or Celtic – was abundant. Again as will be discussed below, many of

these books by a variety of continental scholars (men like the Frenchman Pezron or the Irish scholars O'Flaherty and MacCurtin) formed the basis for intellectual projects undertaken by Toland.

Without doubt this was a working collection: the dictionaries, lexicons and grammar books show the grounding of Toland's scholarly routines. What is intriguing about the collection is its utterly unexceptionable character. It is clear that its owner had perhaps fashionably broad tastes (and certainly an erudition capable of digesting books in a number of difficult or unfamiliar languages). Supplementing the works of religious learning are a generous collection of classical sources by Cicero, Justin, Caesar, Seneca, Lucan, Virgil, Horace, and, perhaps significantly both a Latin and Italian edition of Lucretius *de rerum natura*. It would not however be sensible or appropriate to suggest that somehow these works were a determinant of the character of Toland's intellectual disposition. In contrast to the works on theology and classical antiquity, there were, scattered amongst the piles in the room, a few volumes (by Sarpi, Selden, Herbert of Cherbury and John Locke) which might be considered unorthodox in the wrong company, but which also were a staple of many clerical libraries. Owning copies of the *Gospel of Nicodemus*, the works of Hermes Trismegisticus, and Claude Berigard's *Circulus Pisanus* did not necessarily imply a bent towards heresy or heterodoxy, since they were works that cropped up in other scholarly libraries with unremarkable frequency.

What can be said then about any man from his books? It has been a common-place of historical studies to try to deduce the intellectual disposition of an individual from the bibliographical character of books they owned. Whether studying the remarkable cosmological world of Menocchio the miller of Fruili, or the mental worlds of more elite figures like John Webster, Samuel Jeake, John Locke and Isaac Newton, a close examination of their books has been a suggested means for casting a shaft of illumination into the real nature of their intellectual temperament. This historiography has tended to assert a rather reductive, and indeed passive, relationship between owner and reader, and between the content of a book and the experience of reading it. More recently much more attention has been paid to the various social contexts for the encounter between men (and women) and books. In this view the significance of reading a book may lie not in a purely intellectual transaction, but in a combination of this with other factors such as where the work was read (in a public library, in an intimate's parlour), or who recommended it, or indeed who condemned it. A specific invitation to read a particular book in a special location provided a different experience to that of stealing a view of a work in a clandestine moment. As we will see, for Toland, and the individuals he cultivated, books were as much instruments of sociability as carriers of intellectual meaning. The pursuit of certain books caused intimacies amongst booksellers, authors, buyers: the composition of works similarly required, and produced, patrons, printers, booksellers and reviewers. The books Toland wrote, and used, were given cultural value by a combination of the sociabilities necessary to produce them (both material and cultural); their reception (readers bought them, read them, answered them) and circulation (reviewers identified their worth, people lent and borrowed them). Books were important to Toland, not simply as bearers of arguments but as means for brokering political and social transactions.

Exploring the encounters Toland had with a series of individuals and their 'libraries' will lay the foundations for establishing the extent of the community of readers in which he lived.[2] An insight into the social dimensions that underpinned this world of books can be seen in the very first surviving letter in Toland's printed correspondence very possibly written in 1694 to John Locke, an early sponsor of his studies in Oxford. In this letter the young student, fresh from studying in Leiden, described his arrival in Oxford late on a Monday evening in the middle of a tempestuous storm, having narrowly escaped robbery by highwaymen. Having spent the journey in the company of a Fellow of New Hall, 'a violent partisan of the clergy', Toland insisted that he was well informed about the 'abilities, genius and disposition of the Doctors of the University'. His first impression of the 'air' of university was that of learning. Having settled into lodgings at Mr Bodington's by All Soul's College, a location convenient for the Bodleian Library, Toland immediately found himself at the centre of attention. Through the agency of the 'extraordinarily civil' Mr Creech he was introduced to 'three or four of the most ingenious men in the university', as well as being visited by powerful scholars like Dr John Mill and White Kennet. Toland described in some detail the trials of his encounter with these men of learning, as he put it 'a la mode de France'. 'At great agonies ... to answer the expectations of those grand virtuosos', Toland noted that he was subjected to a barrage of testing enquiries 'especially [by] some of their Antiquaries and Linguists, who saluted me with peals of bar-barous sounds and obsolete words'. He responded in kind. 'I spent upon them all my Anglo-Saxon and old British etymologies; which I hope gave them abundant satisfaction'. Preparing for future encounters Toland commented 'Hebrew and Irish, I hope, will bear me out for some weeks' but by then he realised that he would have to recharge his intellectual capital 'furnish'd from the library'.

Access to the collections in the Bodleian would provide Toland with material upon which he could maintain his intellectual credibility: this repute also opened doors to further avenues of learning. Upon establishing himself in Oxford, Toland was immediately integrated within a network of lending, borrowing and recommending books. Toland passed on news of Mr Creech's new edition of Lucretius and Manilus, indicating his intimacy with prepublication projects. He noted too that the famous Biblical scholar, John Mill, 'has already communicated his Testament to me'. This is clear evidence of Toland being made part of the informal collaboration of scholars working on the critical edition of the New Testament finally published in 1707. In fact, Toland was inundated with books; as he modestly wrote 'others sent me several books, I only inquired after, without any design of making bold so soon to borrow; all which I attribute to the respect they own their friends'.[3]

There are some significant themes to tease out of these descriptions of the callow fledgling scholar immersed in a complex web of scholarly personality and learning. The first point to underline is the connections between status and erudition: Toland's initiation into the world of Oxford learning was conducted through a robust inquisition of his skills. Reading books and displaying knowledge derived from them had positive benefits. Convincing performance created cultural status and authority, which in turn laid the foundations for further absorption into the circle of Oxford Fellows. Admission to this milieu was helped by the duties and protocols of friendship. Toland was introduced to men like Creech and Mill because of the 'respect' they owed to a mutual friend. One of the ways in which the tendrils of such friendship manifested themselves was in the lending of books. As we will see below this was one of the powerful mediums by which books dispersed amongst a community of the learned. As Anne Goldgar has underscored, in commentary on the sociability underpinning the republic of letters, such bibliographical transactions and exchanges of reciprocal service were central to establishing what can be called intellectual communities.[4]

Toland's intimacy with a number of individuals and their libraries illustrates the function of books and learning in his life. The theme to foreground here is not that these liaisons just brought him into contact with dangerous books, but that the pursuit of 'bad' books initiated him into a circle of powerful and radical figures. In the early 1690s Toland first came to the notice of the republic of letters through his association with Benjamin Furly, the radical Quaker friend of John Locke. Typically, Toland acted as a carrier of books between Locke and his friends (organised through the recommendation of Furly). His intimacy with Furly, reinforced by his connections to figures like Anthony Ashley (third Earl of Shaftesbury), Prince Eugene of Savoy, and Anthony Collins who were also closely associated with the Quaker, brought him acquaintance with a series of libraries of international repute. The jewel in the crown of such libraries was that belonging to Benjamin Furly.

Furly, merchant of Rotterdam, was extraordinarily proud of his library. The notoriety of his intellectual hospitality prompted his close friend Anthony Ashley to decline his offer of accommodation on the grounds that the house was too 'public' for his requirements of 'easy and private' philosophical tranquillity.[5] From the early 1680s the reputation of Furly's library attracted many learned and philosophically *avant garde* visitors. Toland followed in the path of many others. The library's attraction was not simply the intellectual resources found on the shelves but also the people that met there. Furly's library was a space of sociability in which Toland made many acquaintances. Evidence of the content of the library, and the large quantity of correspondence with a range of late seventeenth-century figures that Furly had, can provide a significant pathway into the sociability of the world of ideas in which Toland moved. As a collector and reader Furly came to know many of the learned authors and publishers associated with the radical side of the republic of letters. Men like Charles Levier, Thomas Johnson and Jean Aymon also came to work closely with Toland on a number of projects through intimacy with Furly.

The dubious reputation of Furly's library was widespread. Having described the approximately 4,000 volumes shelved along the walls of the *comptoir*, the visiting bibliophile Von Uffenbach noted that the books were 'mostly on theological subjects, of the *suspectae fidei* order, and appear to be well suited to Mr. Benjamin Furly's taste, who is a paradoxical and peculiar man, who soon gave us to understand that he adhered to no special religion'.[6] Historians, like the German visitor, have readily made the connection between the possession of suspect books, and Furly's heresy and irreligion. Furly admitted that the 'infection of heresie' was cultured within this environment of suspect books.[7] At least one regular meeting known as the 'Lantern' met in Furly's house. On these occasions a sociability based on the consumption of drink, the communal reading of books and consequent conversation, according to Furly, commonly encouraged heresy to 'rise up a pace in the Lanterne when so watered'.[8] Even the cautious Locke feared he might be 'heretickated' by such company.[9] The radical potential of Furly's intimate meetings can best be seen in the fact that it was in this library that the compilation and scribal distribution of the manuscript text *Le traité des trois imposteurs* was composed. This work (which dismissed all organised religion as imposture and tyranny) was a *bricolage* of works readily available in Furly's collection.[10] It was no coincidence that this work, one of the most celebrated and feared clandestine works of the eighteenth century, was the product of Furly's sociability. As the evidence of a number of archives shows, the first copy of the work was made in 1711 in Furly's library. Many of his friends were responsible for expanding various scribal and printed 'versions' between 1711 and 1719. Other evidence indicates that one of the other libraries with which Toland was familiar (that of Eugene and Hohendorf in Vienna) was also a source for the distribution of the same work. As will be discussed below (chapter 7), through his relationship with Furly and Eugene of Savoy, Toland was certainly intimate with its content and most probably was involved in making additions to the text. Libraries were places not only for reading but for writing too.[11]

Visitors to Furly's library were not without their own collections. Libraries were not simply spaces where books sat dumbly on shelves, but were where like-minded men gathered to discuss books, create ideas and compose texts. Although it is not possible to be precise in detail, it was through Furly that Toland met many of the powerful men who provided the intellectual and political platforms for his public mission. These connections might originally have been made through the medium of a mutual interest in books, but they were to develop into relationships that produced a compelling series of public discourses. In reading these men's books, Toland made himself a broker of cultural authority. Men like Anthony Collins (a gentlemen freethinker and intimate of Locke in his last years who was known to Toland from the early 1700s) threw open their substantial libraries for Toland's use. As evidence of the manuscript catalogue of Collins's collection establishes, his library offered Toland many heterodox resources.[12] Collins was in his own words, 'a severe judge of books' who had the reputation of being a relentless hunter of books. One contemporary described Collins as a man 'whom I thought no book could escape'.[13] Although there has been no systematic study of Collins's collection the case could certainly be put for describing it as erudite, and perhaps *libertin erudit*.[14]

Just like Furly's volumes, Collins's collection was not simply made up of works of dubious piety, but included a range of orthodox theology, patristics and biblical commentary, as well as an impressive holding of classical Roman and Greek literature (very often in multiple editions and translations). Reflecting a continental rather than insular learning, the majority of these works were in Latin, and in French. The theology ranged from hyper-Catholic and High Church Anglican (Bellarmine and Bossuet, Hickes and Dodwell), to broadly reformed apologetics (Allix, Limborch and Hoadly). Again, a little like Furly's collection, the radical sectarians of the English revolution were well represented in the works of Muggleton, Penn and Naylor. Notably, the commonwealth political tradition, to which Toland was to make a seminal contribution, was also well represented in the form of *monarchomach* and republican works by Hotman, Buchanan, Milton, Harrington, Gordon and Molesworth. To supplement this variety of orthodox and radical material were 'dangerous books' by Bruno, Spinoza, Vanini, Blount and Tindal. Toland's intimacy with the library can be seen in Collins's possession of a number of his manuscripts. Like others in Toland's circle, Collins accumulated these books by the intellectual recommendation found in the full range of literary journals such as the *Acta Eruditorum* (1682–1719), the *Journal des Sçavans*, the *Journal Littéraire*, and various *Bibliotheques* of French and German literature, which he owned. For comparison (and perhaps purchase) he also owned twenty-one catalogues of private and institutional libraries, including those of his friends Furly and Hohendorf as well as those for the universities of Oxford and Leiden and the Vatican. This library (like the others that Toland haunted) was a material manifestation of the intellectual culture of the republic of letters.

Making such libraries involved both economic and intellectual trans-actions. The purchase, selection and circulation of books brought men together creating networks of communication and cultural power. The example of Collins indicates that his pursuit of titles led him into a series of relationships with a variety of people and places. He had met Locke in Churchill's book-shop. He had also used the same London bookshop (Christopher Bateman's in Paternoster Row) as Eugene of Savoy and Baron d'Hohendorf. The intimacy of contact is further evidenced in Collins's visit to Furly in 1711. Here he met Eugene of Savoy, noting that '[I] was several times in conversation with Prince Eugene there'. One can only speculate about what books they discussed, but it seems a very remote possibility that the three men who owned the most dangerous collections in Europe did not share bibliographical secrets and desires. It also seems unlikely that Toland, who was conducting a secret correspondence with Eugene at the time, as well as visiting Collins regularly, did not share these secrets. Certainly, Collins owned a copy of the *La vie et l'espirit de Spinoza*, as well as a trinity of very anti-Christian manuscripts written by Spanish Jews like Troki, Mortiera and Orobio which, according to Desmaiseauz, he had acquired in Holland before 1714.[15]

Toland used the access he had to these libraries in a variety of ways. One significant role was to act as a broker of 'lost' ideas. This can be best be seen in his role in the circulation of Giordano Bruno's works, which is typical of how he spent a lifetime springing dangerous works from library shelves. Toland first came into contact with Bruno's work in 1698. From this point he was conducting a lengthy correspondence with Leibniz and others over the mean-ing of the *Spaccio*, one of Bruno's most subversive texts. By 1713 he was implicated in the publication of a translation of the same work.[16] The list of 'lent' manuscripts (which will be explored in more detail in the following chapter) indicates that as late as 1719–20 Toland was still undertaking the distribution of Bruno's works. He sent a 'Life' of Bruno to Nicholas Hartsoeker in Holland, and two other minor works to Englishmen.[17] Further evidence of Toland's labours in translating and commenting on Bruno's work are found both in his archive and in the (1726) printed collection.[18] In distributing such texts he was acting both as an intermediary between geographically dispersed archives, and between private collections and the public sphere. The Viennese library of Baron d'Hohendorf and Prince Eugene, as Toland acknowledged to Leibniz, was another resource he exploited in this role.[19] Anthony Collins's library was the source of the translation that ultimately resulted in the printed edition of the *Spaccio* (1713). The translation had originally been made 'for the private use of Mr Collins, nor ever intended to be printed'. Toland borrowed it, promptly sending it to the press.[20] It was no surprise then that after his death

Collins anxiously wrote inquiring about a number of volumes Toland had failed (repeatedly) to return.

Another powerful visitor to Furly's library with whom Toland became intimate was Anthony Ashley, the Third Earl of Shaftesbury. Although Shaftesbury's writings have been subjected to close study by literary scholars, the full dimensions of his political commitments in the 1690s and 1700s have not been fully explored. Having entered Parliament in 1695, Shaftesbury was a focus for the 'true Whig' war for 'common liberty' until his retirement from national politics in 1704. As evidence of his correspondence with Goldophin shows, even after this date he was a powerful figure in elite politics, potentially brokering support for various ministries in the late 1700s. The earl was not simply a mediator of commonwealth commitments in England, but importantly had a network of connections with key figures in European politics, like Furly, Eugene of Savoy and Sophia of Hanover herself. Again these relationships were cast in opposition to the 'foreign and universal tyranny' of Louis XIV. As Shaftesbury's lengthy correspondence with Furly establishes, his relationships were based upon a defence of liberty and free government. This devotion stayed with Shaftesbury throughout his life: as he commented after the trial of the 'seditious priest' Sacheverell in 1710, never 'was the principle of liberty and hatred of slavery and priestcraft ever higher in its ascendant'. For the earl, liberty would be preserved by the security of the Protestant succession. The tenure of free government was secured then by parliamentary measures like the Act of Settlement.[21] From the late 1690s Toland and Shaftesbury collaborated upon a number of 'commonwealth' political projects. In turn this relationship brought, not only patronage, but also access to further library collections and circles of intimates. The evidence of Shaftesbury's own substantial library catalogue suggests he was a keen and discerning owner. The manuscript catalogues in Latin, Greek and English compiled *c.* 1708 for his Chelsea residence indicate a sophisticated collection dominated by a comprehensive range of classical texts. The quality and size of editions as well as place of publication were prestigious (folios from Amsterdam, Rome, Paris, and Venice) reflecting Shaftesbury's wealth. The library contained an impressive collection of republican political theory from Buchanan to Harrington, and the *Vindicae contra tyrannos* (Edinburgh, 1579) to Machiavelli. Supplementary were works of erudition (Spanheim, Kircher, Fabricius, Vossius, Selden) and biblical criticism (including the works of Richard Simon 'suivant la copie de Paris'). But there was also a batch of more popular pamphlet literature. Especially prominent were the political writings from the 1680s and 1700s in particular those produced by the Commonwealth publishers Richard Baldwin and John Darby. Overall the collection is eclectic although more secular than theological, although there were significant holdings of Calvinist, Catholic and Anglican works (including writings by Whiston, Stillingfleet, and Tillotson) as well as High Church works by Atterbury and Hickes.[22] It is important to acknowledge that the intellectual culture in which Toland and his ilk operated was learned as well as subversive. Their ideas were formed in dialogue with libraries that contained the canons of orthodox culture rather than simply generating new views unanchored from commonplace tradition.

From the fragments of correspondence we know, then, that Toland had access to a series of significant libraries. These introduced him into learned circles in Oxford, heterodox communities in Rotterdam, and gentle society in London. His acquaintance with Eugene of Savoy, which started as early as 1708, brought him into contact with not only a patron of European-wide reputation and status, but with a book collector on an immense scale. Whereas Shaftesbury's library was dominated by classical works, and Furly's was replete with theology, Prince Eugene's library, reflecting his wealth, was, perhaps simply because of its size, a much more determinedly 'erudite' collection. Whereas Furly owned perhaps as much as a few shelves of impious works and a handful of clandestine manuscripts, Eugene owned rooms of such books, and dozens of such manuscripts.[23] Eugene's contemporary reputation as 'a soul inaccessible to superstition' and a 'man of reason' was prompted by his collections.[24] His librarian, the minor poet Jean-Baptiste Rousseau noted 'the astounding fact is that there is hardly a book which the Prince has not read, or at least looked through, before sending it to be bound'.[25] One contemporary warned him of the danger of his books, 'Take care, monsieur, for your vast knowledge will damn you, but my ignorance will be my salvation'.[26] To complement Eugene's collection his friend Baron d'Hohendorf, gatekeeper to Eugene's more dangerous works, had accumulated his own impressive collection, which again is distinguished by its resolutely secular contents. The character of the library is perhaps best indicated by the absence of theological works (in any significant numbers).[27] This was the intellectual culture that underpinned Prince Eugene's reputation and role as leading military defender of the international Protestant interest. As will be argued in a later chapter, we know that Toland's relationship with these two figures prompted him to compose a number of works which were initially only conceived of as private scribal works intended for inclusion in their libraries. In these connections and encounters with men and books lie the origins of Toland's lifetime work. This cultural encounter prompted first dialogue, and then transformation of the commonplace certainties of that orthodox culture. How he set about establishing this dialogue will form the backbone of this current study.

The 'library' (the sort of space Toland studied in, in the houses and palaces of men like Furly, Shaftesbury, Collins and Eugene), was then both a place where a network of individuals met for conversation and collaboration, and also a material resource in the form of a collection of books and manuscripts.

Bearing in mind Borges' remark 'that books in themselves have no meaning', we need to think harder about how the intellectual community focused on the late seventeenth-century library worked. Rather than simply regarding it as a place where books were stored, the intention will be to make an inquiry into how the library's human subjects interacted with books, to explore how books (and their writers and readers) not only produced intellectual statements, but also forged political relationships and brokered cultural power.

A starting point is to ask what Toland's contemporaries thought a library was for. By examining the surviving catalogues of various collections it is possible to be quite precise about the contents of any particular library, but it is not quite so easy to grasp its broader cultural function. Reconstructing the dynamics of the material process of making a library is to underscore the complex relationships formed between authors, booksellers, purchasers and readers.[28] A convenient contemporary perception of the cultural function of a library is Gabriel Naudé's *Instructions concerning the erection of a library* (translated by John Evelyn, London 1661). The work sets out to discuss how a gentleman might 'regulate himself concerning the choice of books, the means of procuring them, and how they should be disposed of'.[29] A good library was the premise for being cosmopolitan. Books were not only the instruments of cultural ornament but crucial for study too.

How did one exercise refinement and discretion in the purchase of works? In making a library, what books ought to be bought and what excluded? The best means of identifying a 'canon' of good books was to peruse the sales-catalogues of book auctions: 'by this means', commented Naudé, 'one may sometimes do a friend service and pleasure; and when we cannot furnish him with the book he is in quest of, shew and direct him to the place where he may find some copie'.[30] Men like Collins, Shaftesbury and Locke used such catalogues to identify desired books. Again, as the evidence of Toland's letter suggested above, the importance of the intimacy between books and sociability is underscored. Circulating knowledge about books and using ownership of books as part of the protocols of friendship and service was essential. Naudé was pragmatic in his description of the motives for purchase and pursuit of titles. It was well known 'that every man who seeks for a book, judges it to be good'.[31] Importantly for our consideration of the sources of Toland's impiety, Naudé recommended that books on all subjects ought to be included in a collection, even those that might be considered dangerous or heretical.[32] Although more interested in the provision of public libraries, Naudé was insistent that libraries were to be used for the benefit of as many as possible: access to libraries thus ought to be regulated by rules of civility and sociability.[33]

The principal points to be made here are inter-related. The contents of a library were to be calculated for instrumental purposes rather than mere display. As a consequence the perceived intellectual value of books was shaped by individual desires and appreciation. Books were meant to mean things. The merits and cultural status of any particular book was the product of shifting conventional standards. Collections of books (libraries) represent, then, the results of a series of such changing aspirations, the material accretion of human inter-action, choice and cooperation. One consequence of this slow accretive process of making a collection suggests that historians ought to exercise considerable caution about too readily defining a library as radical or orthodox. Such a description would presume some single-minded objective behind its making, when in fact a collection was the result of a series of exchanges and conversations. It also raises a number of points in relation to the arguments of historians who have suggested with confidence that the circulation and ownership of radical books laid the foundations for radical political action in the period. As this book will endeavour to argue, the radicalism of Toland's project was determined not simply by his access to radical resources in the form of dangerous ideas contained in a corpus of clandestine and heterodox literature, but in how he attempted to subvert the commonplaces of orthodox discourses by appropriating their status and values. The presence of clandestine literature in these various libraries may have been a symptom rather than a cause of a subversive intellectual disposition. The primary function of these texts may not have been intellectual as much as social: subversive works may have acted as badges of identity, rather than carriers of precise philosophical meaning. The intellectual work of attacking the hegemonic discourses of orthodoxy carried out by Toland was undertaken by immersion in works of theology, scripture and patristics rather than by mere imitation and reproduction of the radical arguments of a subversive tradition.

The pursuit of books was driven by both the ambitions of sociability and the intellectual priorities of the period. In buying books intellectual aspiration, economic logistics and social protocols converged. A library was after all a physical collection of books: a material residue of an intellectual culture. Not only do the books themselves indicate the contours of debate and controversies, but they are also a sediment of 'intellectual' problems. These same books were the products of a series of economic transactions and social negotiations: books were bought by individuals from booksellers for themselves or others. The decisions determining purchase were made by assessment of intellectual and economic worth. Ownership was determined both by availability and a network of knowledge about where such a book could be got. Making libraries was a collective act.

For men like Furly, Shaftesbury, Eugene and Collins, books were the very stuff of life. Intellectual 'conversation' about books amongst this group of men had its own form of social etiquette. Exploring these protocols of conduct will lay some foundations for thinking about how the circulation of ideas in the period functioned. Harold Love has persuasively asserted that there was a connection between sociability and the circulation of scribal texts. Patterns of cultural exchange made not only readers, but also communities of readers.[34] Toland, as will be established below, certainly acted as a broker and maker of such a radical milieu by his transmission of books and 'clandestine' texts. Just as the circulation and exchange of manuscripts made communities, so did libraries. The exchange of news about books, gleaned from literary journals, or on the recommendation of a helpful bookseller, meant that any one individual had potential access to a network of information across Europe. As we will see, Toland not only contributed many works that became the subject of this literary exchange, but also was responsible for circulating other texts for communal discussion.

One insight into the sort of 'conversation' about books can be gleaned from the long and intimate correspondence between Furly and Locke, cementing a friendship that developed when Locke was in exile in the 1680s. Much of the conversation concerned the pursuit of books and discussion of their merits. It is in this cut and thrust of bibliographical erudition that such men formed, changed, developed and altered their beliefs and opinions. Men in pursuit of important books were tenacious. Evidence of a collaborative concern to track down titles in England and abroad is prevalent in the correspondence.[35] Each man would borrow catalogues, arrange for intermediaries and warn the other of sharp practice in the second-hand trade.[36] Throughout the letters there are repeated instructions from both men about the transport of books between Holland and England, sometimes carried by themselves, sometimes by friends and sometimes by carriers (in which case strict details were given on how the package should be wrapped).[37] It is possible to trace the shared interest in a particular author through the correspondence: Locke repeatedly wrote to Furly in quest of the critical works of Richard Simon, complaining of the delay and loss of volumes in transit.[38] We should recall that Toland's first introduction to this circle was as a book carrier between Furly, Locke and Leclerc.

One of the key benefits of this sort of community was the mutual lending of books. As Collins recalled he, repeatedly, lent books to Toland which were difficult to retrieve.[39] The swift exchange of volumes, accompanied by some sort of commentary or reflection is a repeated theme of many letters passed between Furly and Locke. At some moments it seems that the two men were reading the same book simultaneously, separated only by the North Sea. So for example in December 1690 having discussed a number of polemical writings Furly noted similarities with 'that book we read together'.[40] At other points both men asked for the written opinions of the other on books they were about to read. In August 1692 Furly sent Locke a parcel of books (some of which came from Jean Leclerc) including a volume of Van Helmont's which he noted, I 'now expect your account of it I never having read it'.[41] Again in 1694, Furly requested Locke to give his commentary on a difficult book, 'I doubt not, but you have read the book through, and desire you would freely, as a friend give me your thoughts of it'.[42] Writing in 1697 about a book examining obscure terms in the New Testament, Furly concluded his remarks, 'But I will not trouble you any longer with my observations on this treatise, desiring rather to see yours, when you have read them'.[43]

These letters are peppered with such exchanges about books read, books sought out, books lost, books recommended. The discussion of an issue might lead to recommendations of further reading or as Furly commented 'this has made me search my library'.[44] Toland's skill was to absorb the dynamic of inquiry, and to set up his own lines of controversy. Although the subject matter debated between Locke and Furly covered a range material – politics, natural philosophy, and theology – a recurrent and persistent interest was a concern about the textuality of Scripture.[45] This was to be a theme that Toland developed as a central issue in many of his public writings. Having identified the 'weak' points in orthodox learning through forensic discussion with others, in works like *Amyntor* and especially *Nazarenus*, Toland would contrive material for similar discussion. Responding to new polemics, contemporary scholarship, and often very controversial writings, was the declared ambition of such conversations. This process of answering and absorbing the arguments of a variety of works enabled individuals to construct their respective intellectual critiques. Books were the staple of this process of making conviction. It was this intellectual substance, pondered by a community of readers, which produced beliefs and principles. In this way, as Furly put it, I may 'weigh my reasonings'.[46]

That the 'traffick in Books' (in their material form as well as their intellectual meaning) provided the stuff of intellectual community is also readily exemplified in the relations between John Locke and the fledgling 'freethinker' Anthony Collins.[47] Their friendship was cemented 'past ceremony' when Collins successfully and swiftly completed Locke's instructions for binding books on his behalf.[48] An interesting insight into this relationship can be seen in the very exact instructions Locke gave Collins about the physical preparation of his Bibles. Their material condition was important for his intended use. The size of margins was critical to how he would use the books, as he explained in one letter, he required a Bible with 'ordinary binding but strong and that will open well' and in another a binding 'so well sown and ordered in the back that it will lye open anywhere'.[49] If the task was not well undertaken he was critical and complained to Collins of the faults of the binder by 'the running of his pareing knife too deep into the margent'.[50] Like Locke and Collins, we must imagine Toland carefully reading, annotating and collating his own copies of the Bible.

Books were for Locke, as for many of his friends, 'instruments of truth and knowledge'. They were (in his pithy phrase) the 'fodder of our understanding'. Men informed themselves by a 'tiresome rummaging in the mistakes and jargon of pretenders to knowledge'.[51] A presumably tired Locke sometimes resented the labours he had devoted to reading bad books.[52] Regardless of these critical remarks, as with Furly, Locke's correspondence with Collins was structured by the pursuit of sought after books. 'There is nothing publish'd of late in England worth acquainting you with', 'at present wee have but few worth taking notice of' are repeated phrases from Collins's letters. Encouraged by Locke to keep him informed of new works in Holland and France, Collins sometimes supplied him directly with his own copies of books.[53] Locke was particularly keen to get hold of a copy of Jean Leclerc's edition of the New Testament: 'I shall be glad to see it since Mr Bold has told you how desirous I was to see it. I have expected one of them from Holland ever since they have been out, and so I hope to restore it you again in a few days'. Collins had unexpectedly received a copy and could 'therefore very well spare it for your use'.[54] Eventually, Locke received two copies of the work and suggested Collins take one 'unless you have some particular reason to desire your own again'.[55] Throughout these series of transactions Locke repeatedly asked Collins to supply him with any details of how Leclerc's volume had been received: did it 'make any noise amongst the men of letters or divinity in your Town?'[56] Again the urgency of acquiring a copy of a particular work was only matched by the desire to know what other readers thought of the book. Toland's publications repeatedly set up such ripples of expectation and criticism across the republic of letters.

As well as being concerned to identify and provide details of books that a 'rational man' could take pleasure in and instruction from, Locke and Collins also exchanged a number of recommendations and reviews. Sometimes this involved them in the posting of volumes, other times a recommendation led to the individual reading a book he already possessed. As Collins noted to Locke's suggestion that he lend him a copy of Limborch's *Vita Episcopii*, 'I have the book and will read it upon your recommendation'.[57] As well as examining the worth of recent publications, Locke and Collins also gave each other very explicit accounts of why they read books. When Collins offered Locke a copy of Bossuet's work against Richard Simon (direct from the publishers in Paris) he indicated he was only interested in reading the book if it discussed matters beyond that of the status of the Vulgate: 'if it gives any light into the true sense of the S. Scripture by establishing the Greek text or explaining the sense of any obscure or difficult passages I shall be glad to see it'.[58] Locke, in his turn, attempted to give Collins careful advice about the necessary 'application' required when reading Scripture, only to be rebutted by Collins who insisted that his method of reading was adequate, 'for I have no design to find any particular opinion there but only to endeavour to get the same idea that the author had when he wrote'.[59] Again these different strategies for reading texts, and making meaning from them, were born in epistolary conversation with friends. This unrelenting dialogue with print culture was a self-conscious and collective enterprise: being part of the conversation meant potentially having the ability to shape and determine the beliefs and convictions of a community of people.

One important thing to note about the tone of these epistolary exchanges is the equality of discussion. Despite clear distinctions in wealth and social prestige, men like Locke, Collins, Furly and Toland treated each other as equals in debate. Clearly men like Locke and Collins had financial advantages that allowed them to participate in the relatively expensive business of book buying. Although an element of deference was evident (especially to Locke whose public intellectual status was profound) there was considerable disagreement and free expression. As part of this community it is possible to imagine how, despite his lowly birth and lack of wealth, Toland's intellectual facilities qualified him for participation in the conversation. His intimacy with men like Furly and Collins gave him access to large and diverse collections of books, but also to a different set of personal networks to the world of print culture. Furly was best connected in the Low Countries, being intimate with *libraires* like Leers, Wettstein and Johnson. Locke conducted most of his business through the services of Awnsham Churchill, while Collins, through the agency of Pierre Desmaizeaux, had efficient relations with French book-sellers in London like Vaillant and Du Noyer. These routes for acquiring the latest volumes, or the most valuable edition, were also available to Toland to distribute his own work. In tracing the cut and thrust of changing interests, the responses to new works and the debates about the merits of particular arguments and ideas it is possible to see the process by which individual conviction was made. In these routine, mundane, repeated and habitual transactions the grit of cultural change was gradually deposited amongst this community of friends and associates. Toland was a master at making ripples of controversy in these constantly ebbing waters.

In the letters passed between two of Toland's other close friends – Anthony Collins and Pierre Desmaizeaux – it is evident that the 'traffick in books' was not insular, but involved participation in a European-wide republic of letters. As we will see later in this book, one of Toland's supreme skills was to be able to broker intellectual resources from a variety of cultural capitals – London, Hanover, Leiden, Dublin and Vienna being the most obvious. Pierre Desmaizeaux's massive correspondence is an ideal archive for reconstructing the cultural mechanics of book buying in some detail.[60] The letters between him and Collins give a sense of these transactions, close to the experience of Toland. Unlike the exchange of letters with Locke, although it is clear that

Collins has respect for Desmaizeaux's learning and bibliographical taste, he was treated as an intermediary rather than an equal: very few of the letters have extended discussion of the contents of the works sought out or received. Collins's relationship with the Frenchman was based upon his efficiency as a mediator and networker with a variety of booksellers in London, Paris and Holland. Like many of his friends, Collins relied on a combination of news by word of mouth, letter or literary review to make his choice of books to buy. A recurrent request was to be told the 'literary news of the town'.[61] Collins subscribed to a variety of literary journals and was particular that he received them punctually. He took seriously the reviews he read. When purchasing duplicate copies of works like Adrian Reland's *de religione mahommedica* (a work that Toland exploited in *Nazarenus*) he noted 'that there are very considerable additions in it'. When enquiring after a new edition of Naudé's *Apologie* he instructed purchase only 'if the notes are in your opinion curious; for I have an old edition of it, printed at The Hague without notes'.[62] On his regular visits to London, Collins took the opportunity, as he put it 'to try some of the books in the catalogues you sent me'.[63] Sometimes Collins appealed to Desmaizeaux for help with books he could not find like Richard Simon's *Discourse upon Ecclesiastical Revenues*, 'it is a book I want very much; and you would do me a favour if by any means you could procure it for me'. His regular booksellers Vaillant and Du Noyer could not get hold of a copy, but Desmaizeaux could.[64]

Collins was not profligate in his purchases: through the agency of Desmaizeaux he exercised a refined discrimination. His books were not for mere ornament. Keen to have them used, Collins encouraged access to his collection at Great Baddow, repeatedly inviting and entertaining men like Toland, Sallengre and another of Toland's friends Hugh Wrottesley. He promised one visitor 'good fires, good books, good wine, philosophers meals, and country appetites'.[65] Inviting Desmaizeaux to stay in 1710, he noted that 'you may be so private as not to be subject to any manner of animadversion on for keeping bad company'.[66] Again the provision of books laid the foundation for a form of intellectual sociability. Like Furly's meetings at the Lantern, the evidence of Collins's correspondence indicates that at the same time as ordering his books he made sure a plentiful supply of good wine was bought too. Collins, although reluctant to borrow books himself, freely lent copies to others. Some borrowers like Hewett and Toland failed to return volumes causing Collins to buy duplicates.[67] Although a generous lender Collins was anxious about 'losing' volumes as he explained to Desmaizeaux: 'as to the other books I am willing you should keep them till you have don with them; but then I would have them returned; for tho they are of no great value, I would not be without them, as wanting sometimes to consult them, and knowing not where to get them again'.[68]

When thinking about the milieu in which Toland lived we need to be cautious about over-emphasising the intellectual 'radicalism' of his contacts. There is little doubt that one of the results of his involvement with these people (and many others) was constant conversation. The 'traffic' of ideas was carried out in both the material form of books and the social process of communication. A model of reading based upon passive consumption or absorption of the content of books is untenable given the evidence of the interactions of these men. Toland, like Furly, Collins, Locke *et al.* were not just interested in reading 'radical' books, but primarily wanted to engage with the arguments of the mainstream. It is also important to emphasise the diversity of the 'community' that Toland engaged with. Men like Furly, Jean Leclerc, Phillip Limborch, John Locke, Anthony Collins, Shaftesbury, Charles Levier, Jean Aymon, Eugene of Savoy, and d'Hohendorf did have common interests, but they also offered different intellectual and political opportunities. Toland's skill was to be able to exploit a range of different (and sometimes conflicting) political interests. As we will see, Toland compromised some of these relationships: it is quite clear that John Locke was keen to disassociate himself from Toland, while his close friends Anthony Collins and Furly kept up their intimacy throughout their lives.

John Toland established his cultural credentials by a variety of relationships with the written word. In his life books were lent, borrowed, lost, misplaced, annotated, condemned, hidden, and even (as we will see in the next chapter) imagined. Access to libraries, deals with booksellers, controversies with authors, contracts with printers, and failed editorial projects structured the shape of Toland's intellectual and social environment. In the material form of books we have the residue of this complex current of communication between, and amongst, individuals. The books that Toland wrote, read and circulated were not simply passive texts, but also a forum where ideas and convictions were made. A considerable amount of thought has been devoted to thinking about how individuals formed their Christian beliefs in dialogue with Scriptural discourses; less labour has engaged with the cultural processes of disengagement from such traditional forms of reading. The books owned collectively by men like Furly, Toland and Eugene were possessed to be read as part of a collaborative enterprise. These men were 'reading for action'.[69] The 'fodder' contained within books cultivated beliefs and convictions. Whether imagining Furly and Locke in conversation about the difficulties of establishing the precise textual integrity of Scripture, mirrored in Locke and Newton exchanging dissertations about specific textual corruptions in the *Gospel of John*, or John Toland and Robert Molesworth using the margins of a particular book to discuss their project on the history of Celtic learning, it will be central to this book that the cultivation of ideas worked in this dynamic of oral or literary conversation.[70] Books had meaning read into them. Within this world of books we can see different trajectories and characters: the theological eclecticism of Furly's library both reflected, and determined, the character of his tolerant attitude to all sincere theological opinion; the more actively hostile and irreligious contents of Eugene and Hohendorf's collections both made, and were made, by their anticlerical and anti-theological commitments. The variety of books found in the libraries of Furly, Shaftesbury, Locke, Collins, Eugene and Hohendorf provided a cultural infrastructure for the making of authority. The provision, reception and circulation of books, manuscripts and ideas amongst this community also brought Toland enormous cultural credibility and status. In these conversations (literary and oral) Toland formed the relationships that meant his ideas had a theatre of influence that unfolded across Europe.

NOTES

1 For a full list see *Nazarenus* pp. 302–314.

2 See A. Ophir and S. Shapin 'The place of knowledge: a methodological survey' in *Science in Context* 4 (1991) pp. 3–21.

3 *Collections* 2 pp. 292–294.

4 A. Goldgar *Impolite learning* (New Haven, 1995).

5 Foster *Letters* pp. 198, 201.

6 W. I. Hull *Benjamin Furly and Quakerism in Rotterdam* (Swarthmore College Monographs, 1941) p. 152.

7 *Correspondence* No. 947 p. 230.

8 *Correspondence* No. 986 p. 316.

9 *Correspondence* No. 993 pp. 332–333.

10 See S. Berti *Trattato dei tre impostori* (Turin, 1994) 'Introduction'.

11 P. Marchand 'Impostoribus' in Berti *et al. Heterodoxy* p. 510.

12 See *Bibliotheca Antonii Collins* (1731). BL 270 I 23 (1–2) has prices marked. A manuscript version is at Keynes Mss 217, King's College, Cambridge.

13 *Correspondence* No. 3391 p. 129; No. 3326 p. 53.

14 See J. O'Higgins *Anthony Collins: the man and his works* (The Hague, 1970) pp. 23–39.

15 BL Add Mss 4282 fo. 242. See Keynes Mss 217: fos. 235. 305, 325 [the Spanish mss], 431 [*Le vie et L'espirit*]. On the acquisition of the Spanish works see BL Add Mss 4254 fo. 11; O'Higgins *Anthony Collins* p. 38.

16 See S. Ricci *La Fortuna del Pensiero di Giordano Bruno 1600–1750* (Florence, 1986); G. Carabelli 'John Toland e G.W. Leibniz: otto lettere' *Rivista critica di storia della filosofia* 29 (1974) pp. 412–431: Champion *Pillars* pp. 150–154.

17 See Carabelli 'John Toland e G.W. Leibniz' p. 425.

18 See BL Add Mss 4295 fo. 64r 'A Psalm before Sermon in Praise of Asinity' and fo. 65r

'A very pious Psalm after Sermon about the meaning of the Asse & her Foal'. The 1726 collection included *De genere, loco, et tempore mortis Jordani Bruni Nolani* (dedicated to Hohendorf dated 1709) and an account of Bruno's 'Of the infinite Universe'.

19 Carabelli 'John Toland e G.W. Leibniz' p. 425, 'I found my self oblig'd to send as farr as Vienna a kind of dissertation on this subject'.

20 See Ricci, *Giordano Bruno*, p. 250.

21 See Foster *Letters* p. 200 and *passim*. On Shaftesbury's political career see L. Klein *Shaftesbury and the culture of politeness* (Cambridge, 1994). The best account is M. L. de Miranda 'The moral, social and political thought of the third earl of Shaftesbury, 1671–1713: unbelief and Whig republicanism in the early Enlightenment' (Cambridge University PhD, 1994).

22 See the catalogues in PRO 30/24/23/10–11.

23 See Ricuperati 'Libertinismo'. A manuscript copy of the library is to be found at Östereichische Nationalbibliothek (ONB) 13,966.

24 J. Banks *The life of Prince Eugen of Savoy* (1702) pp. 291, 350.

25 D. McKay *Prince Eugene of Savoy* (1977) p. 197.

26 McKay *Eugene* p. 199.

27 Archer Taylor *Book Catalogues: their variety and uses* (1986) p. 246.

28 See R. Chartier *The order of books* (1994).

29 G. Naudé *Instructions concerning the erection of a library* (translated by John Evelyn, London 1661) p. 2.

30 Naudé *Instructions* p. 14.

31 *Ibid.* p. 24.

32 *Ibid.* pp. 30–31.

33 *Ibid.* pp. 89, 90, 91.

34 See H. Love *The culture and commerce of texts: scribal publication in seventeenth century England* (Amhurst, 1998).

35 *Correspondence* No. 993 p. 333.

36 *Correspondence* No. 995 p. 335.

37 *Correspondence* No. 1506 p. 461.

38 *Correspondence* Nos. 1356, 1364, 1371, 1379, 1392, 1400, 1407.

39 *Correspondence* No. 1325 p. 147.

40 *Correspondence* No. 1344 p. 172.

41 *Correspondence* No. 1533 p. 512.

42 *Correspondence* No. 1702 p. 2.

43 *Correspondence* No. 2287 p. 161.

44 *Correspondence* No. 2200 p. 2.

45 *Correspondence* No. 995 p. 337; No. 1480 pp. 416–418; No. 1533 p. 512.

46 *Correspondence* No. 1480 p. 418.

47 *Correspondence* No. 3530 p. 287.

48 *Correspondence* No. 3293, 3435 pp. 177–178, 3438.

49 *Correspondence* No. 3474 p. 217; No. 3483 p. 232; No. 3530 p. 287.

50 *Correspondence* No. 3556 p. 314.

51 *Correspondence* No. 3449 p. 189; No 3556 p. 314.

52 *Correspondence* No. 3311 p. 24. The book was Broughton's *Psychologia*; Samuel Bold dismissed it as worthless No. 3326 pp. 50–53.

53 *Correspondence* No. 3385 p. 123; No. 3422 p. 169; No. 3361 p. 98; No. 3372 p. 111.

54 *Correspondence* No. 3311 p. 26; No. 3318 p. 33.

55 *Correspondence* No. 3332 p. 62.

56 *Correspondence* No. 3342 p. 73.

57 *Correspondence* No. 3488 p. 238; No. 3493 p. 247.

58 *Correspondence* No. 3387 pp. 125–126, replying to Collin's letter No. 3385 p. 123.

59 *Correspondence* No. 3567 p. 332.

60 See J. Almagor *Pierre Desmaizeaux (1673–1745), Journalist and English correspondent for Franco-Dutch periodicals, 1700–1720* (Amsterdam, 1989).

61 BL Add Mss 4282 fos. 206, 208.

62 BL Add Mss 4282 fos. 144, 180.

63 BL Add Mss 4282 fo. 208.

64 BL Add Mss 4282 fos. 186, 192.

65 BL Add Mss 4282 fo. 224.

66 BL Add Mss 4282 fo. 232.

67 BL Add Mss 4282 fos. 228, 190.

68 BL Add Mss 4282 fo. 180.

69 See A. Grafton and L. Jardine '"Studied for action": How Gabriel Harvey read his Livy' *Past and Present* 129 (1990) pp. 30–78.

70 See below, chapter 9.

2

Publishing reason:
John Toland and print and
scribal communities

TOLAND did more than simply read and write books: he was a key agent in disseminating ideas around the elite salons of early eighteenth-century Europe. In the last chapter Toland's involvement in a world of learning and the library was explored. One of the intentions was to underscore the social dimensions of this world of learning: gaining entrance to the inner sanctum of a man's library was a means of getting inside his head. In locating Toland in this milieu we only get glimpses of his conduct and status from the surviving records. A more straightforward means of establishing his presence and the purpose of his literary activities can be achieved by disinterring his involvement in the business of scribal circulation and print production. Toland's skill at manipulating both print and scribal works laid the foundation for his political ambitions: his literary transactions produced both cultural and political effects.

Toland's archive provides a wealth of material for reconstructing, in some detail, what Robert Darnton has called a communication circuit. A fluent and talented public author, facile in the rhetoric of print culture, Toland also played a critical role in the production and dissemination of manuscript material in England and on the continent in the early eighteenth century. Traditionally, Toland has been regarded as one of the pivotal polemicists of the 'Radical Enlightenment', because of his involvement in the production and circulation of scribal works such as the *Traité des trois imposteurs*, a story which will be rehearsed in detail in a later chapter.[1] Toland, as we will see, was a figure adept at exploiting both scribal and printed 'forms' of communication to persuade elite and public audiences. He was involved in much more than the distribution of one clandestine work. By exploring his facility with different forms of writing, his abilities to manipulate and construct diverse audiences for similar works, and his intimacies with the mechanics of the business of printing and publishing, it will be possible to reconstruct his attempts to communicate his ideas to powerful and politically effective communities. Questions of audience and readership, of access and inclusion, can be explored with precision in the case of Toland where it is possible to see him inventing a community of readers by the circulation of his works. This community was a platform for his political ambitions.

The starting point for this investigation is Toland's private archive which, as well as preserving many original manuscript works, includes a great deal of fragmentary material relating to Toland's transactions (both financial and literary) with booksellers and printers, as well as correspondence with sympathetic readers and notes towards works in progress.[2] Amongst the various papers and palimpsests there is one particular fragment which casts a shaft of light onto the identity of the community established by Toland's scribal efforts. On a small scrap piece of paper, dating from after 1718, Toland noted a record of 'Manuscripts of Mine Abroad'. The manuscript list was compiled over a period of time: the recording of names and titles are made in the same hand but in different qualities of ink. Indicating periodic amendment of the record, six of the items are crossed through, suggesting that the text had been read and returned.[3] 'Manuscripts of mine abroad', although a modest document (it is fewer than 100 words), tells us a good deal about the range of Toland's scribal activities and contacts. Twelve people are named: nine men and three women. Seven of these individuals can be identified. Sixteen manuscripts were in circulation, although only fourteen titles are named. Of these works ten can be identified: two were published during Toland's life and three in the posthumous collection of 1726. Only four of the texts remain obscure.

Who were these men and women bound together in intellectual intimacy by Toland? A prosopographical study of the people identified on the 'lent list' establishes that at the same time as moving amongst European figures, Toland belonged to a circle at the heart of elite Whiggism. It was one of Toland's skills to be able to fabricate, participate and move between these divergent intellectual, social and political communities. Of the list of twelve people, with some exceptions, the majority are unknown to mainstream historiography. Five of the individuals (Robert Molesworth, Thomas Hewett, Lord Castleton, Matthew Aylmer and Lady Carriere) were intimately connected with the Hanoverian Whig political establishment, most of them favouring the neo-republican wing of the party.[4] As will be discussed in detail below, Robert Molesworth was a significant political figure, author of influential 'commonwealth' works, and political principal of the 'Old Whigs' in and out of Parliament. Like Molesworth, four of these men had been Whig members of Parliament, who consistently supported the tolerant and sometimes anti-clerical platforms of the true Whigs. Castleton, Aylmer and Parker had all received promotion and peerages as rewards for political loyalty to the Hanoverian regime after 1714. Matthew Aylmer, a former client of the irreligious second Duke of Buckingham (and regarded by Swift as a violent partisan) was a senior naval officer, ultimately becoming Rear-Admiral of Great Britain after 1718. James Sanderson, who trained as a lawyer, represented Lincolnshire as a Member of Parliament, and was rewarded for political loyalty between 1714 and 1720 by being made successively Baron, Viscount and Earl of Castleton. The other minor Whig figures – the architect Thomas Hewett and the antiquary Hugh Wrottesley, as well as the bookseller Robinson – also displayed a commitment to anticlerical and tolerationist principles.

Thomas Parker, husband of Lady Carriere, was perhaps one of the most powerful people receiving material from Toland. A key legal figure in the early eighteenth century, as a staunch Whig he made his name defending Whig printers such as John Tutchin. He explicitly used his legal skills to defend toleration and the Hanoverian succession. A fierce prosecutor of Sacheverell, Parker became Lord Chief Justice and ultimately Lord Chancellor of England (April, 1718).[5] As a legal officer Parker was a key administrative figure in the succession of George I, meeting him on his arrival in Greenwich in 1714. A popular courtier, Parker also gained favour with George I because of his judgement affirming the King's rights over his grandchildren. Parker became first Lord of the Regency between 1718 and 1725. As a legal officer, Parker was hostile to the Test and Corporation Acts and defended the interests of Quakers in 1722. An examination of his correspondence between *c.* 1704 and 1730 indicates that he was also a man of letters.[6] He corresponded with Pierre Desmaizeaux over the receipt of the standard foreign literary journals.[7] Parker, with his legal power and popularity with George I, was clearly a significant figure: it is of profound interest that Toland (admittedly through the agency of Parker's wife) was able to include him in his circle. Toland's messages were then getting through to elevated circles.

These men and women were not simply connected by their literary relationship with Toland. Most of them, for example, also had relationships with either Anthony Collins or Pierre Desmaizeaux, whose exchanges of letters between 1712 and 1727 frequently mention intellectual or political transactions.[8] For example, Desmaizeaux visited Parker at Shirburn Castle in the winter of 1716, and conferred with Wrottesley about translating various legal documents for a case Parker was pursuing. Wrottesley also inquired of Desmaizeaux whether he could recommend a French-speaking tutorial companion for a child of his acquaintance in Bristol. Collins periodically wrote to Desmaizeaux asking for accounts of Wrottesley's welfare and asking him to pass on invitations to stay at his Essex house. Collins married Wrottesley's sister Elizabeth in 1724. Robert Molesworth, a leading Whig politician from the 1690s, had links with almost all of the other figures in the circle: he was friendly with Thomas Hewett, who also worked on projects on his estate. Molesworth's son, John, corresponded with Parker about the allocation of a clerical living. He also knew Lord Castleton and corresponded with both Collins and Desmaizeaux. Although there were intimacies between these men independently of their connection with Toland, by his distribution of manuscripts he brought them into a different sort of dialogue.[9]

Beyond the listing of recipients this fragment also illuminates a number of other themes. It confirms Toland's involvement in the dissemination of a number of clandestine works both in England and on the continent. For example, amongst the material that Lord Castleton received was 'The Cloud & Pillar', a work which was later published in 1720 as part of *Tetradymus* under the title of *Hodegus: or the Pillar of Cloud and Fire*. The text was, however, first circulated in scribal form in French *c*. 1710 in the collection of the *Dissertations Diverses* sent to Prince Eugene and Baron d'Hohendorf.[10] As will be discussed in a later chapter, this work originally derived from the researches Toland had pursued in the Low Countries. Some of the material was published in Latin in the Hague, the other extracts (which are similar to passages in the *Traité des trois imposteurs*) Toland disseminated in scribal form to an audience of two. The fact that Toland was able to recycle the material that made the 'Cloud & Pillar' across a decade of time, and in Holland, Vienna and England, illustrates a measure of his flexibility and skill at adapting his ideas to different circumstances and readers. Toland was capable of adjusting his ideas to different contexts and attempting to persuade quite distinct groups of people to a common agenda. That Toland could have worked upon a text for over a decade, and thought it viable for a different audience, is testimony both to the continuity, and the flexibility, of his intentions in communicating his opinions. As will be seen (in chapter 8 below) in the discussion of his life-long labour on the manuscript work on the history of the Christian canon, Toland revised and remodelled his work continually.

Toland undoubtedly kept many of his intellectual activities hidden from public knowledge, but he also quite commonly, and deliberately, drew attention to projected works. It is possible in a number of cases to identify the scribal outcome of such advertisement. Many of Toland's announcements denoted intellectual hubris, rather than any serious intention. In *Christianity not mysterious* (1696) he announced a work called 'Systems of divinity exploded'; in *The Militia reform'd* (1698) his proposal was for an account of 'Brutus, or the history of liberty and tyranny'; in the 1700 edition of Harrington's works, he claimed that he was going to draw a 'parallel' between Socrates and Christ.[11] Such rumours of intended works were calculated to cultivate public expectation (and clerical anxiety).[12] Commenting on the project for a comparative history of Socrates and Christ, Toland admitted 'that I have been some time about it, I freely avow; yet not in the manner those officious informers report, but as becomes a disinterested Historian, and a friend to all mankind, as will more fully appear to the world whenever the Book itself is published'.[13] In 1706 Elisha Smith commented to Thomas Hearne that 'Mr Toland is making collections for his Brutus yt he promis'd and for ye life of Socrates'.[14] Unfortunately, no fragments of these works exist to allow an assessment of their intellectual intentions.

There is little doubt that Toland liked to exploit processes of literary rumour in order to set off the anxieties of the orthodox: for example, the hearsay that he was about to reveal evidence of a 'new Gospel' convulsed the Church in 1713–1714, and prompted attack prior to publication.[15] Not all of these announcements were unsubstantiated provocation. In *Amyntor* (1699) Toland published a short consideration of apocryphal scripture: using this as a starting point he announced his intention of composing a fuller 'History of the Canon of the New Testament' in 1710. In another printed preface (1718) he mentioned that his history of the canon 'whereof I have written ... in two parts, to be publish'd in convenient time'.[16] The 'lent list' recorded that Mr Hewett had borrowed and returned a text called 'History of ye canon'. The 1726 collection reproduced *A Catalogue of Books ... as truly or falsely ascrib'd to Jesus Christ, his Apostles, and other eminent persons*, which is an expanded version of the original printed fragment in *Amyntor*. Toland, thus, had produced a text that was originally printed, which he expanded in scribal form for circulation between *c.* 1710–1720. The evidence of this practice of making public his intentions, and then consequently circulating such material, suggests a sophisticated process of self-publicity based in a complex relationship between print and scribal publication.

These were not isolated instances. Toland persistently employed the prefaces of his printed works to 'hint' at ongoing works. One of the most significant of the 'missing' works of Toland is his 'Respublica Mosaica'. He first drew attention to such a work in the manuscript dissertations he sent to Prince Eugene, *c.* 1708–1710.[17] By 1718, he reported in print 'I can now gladly tell you, my materials are in such a readiness; that one half year, free from all other business, wou'd be sufficient for me to form and finish the whole work'.[18] Two years later the work had still not appeared, but Toland again drew attention to the 'promis'd' work which would be controversial. As he noted, warning his readership to brace itself, 'I find it highly necessary to publish before-hand some short specimen of my undertaking'. This was to 'prevent surprise' in his readers at the novelty of his arguments. The probable result of advertising the work in this way was (again) to prompt anxiety rather than comfort amongst his potential audience.[19] Beyond the evidence of his library, which contained a number of important works on the history of Judaism, there is nothing to suggest that the work was circulated in specimen or indeed even completed.

Toland, by straddling the bridge between scribal and print culture in this way, was able to 'circulate' the idea of a text without material form.

As the evidence of yet another non-extant, possibly fictive, text, *A treatise upon tradition*, suggests, Toland devoted some efforts to ensuring that his projected works would provoke a hostile reception amongst the orthodox. In responding to clerical critics of *Nazarenus* (1718), Toland insisted that he would 'publish a tract on this subject very soon'.[20] Indeed the evidence of Anthony Collins's correspondence with Desmaizeaux (in March 1722) does confirm that Toland had devoted some effort to researching such a work.[21] Toland's 'promise that I both will write, and dare publish a treatise concerning TRADITION before Midsummer next, my life and health continuing', was broken perhaps only by his ultimately fatal ill-health.[22] Certainly, Toland indicated that although he had intended to publish the work in 1720, upon 'second thoughts' he had delayed publication, perhaps anxious that its reception would not be good.[23] Toland contrived, then, by using the medium of his printed work, to generate a potentially hostile audience for a project, before embarking upon the production of such a work. Presumably this enabled him to scrutinise the reactions of his audience through oral or printed responses, and so adapt his work to take account of this. The evidence of the rewriting of works like *Nazarenus* for different audiences indicates that Toland was adept at reconfiguring his work according to its potential reception.[24]

Some of the most enduring relationships Toland had were with a series of booksellers, printers and *libraires* (even though these were largely unprofitable in financial terms). Figures like Samuel Buckley, John Darby, Abigail and Richard Baldwin, James Roberts, Thomas Johnson and Bernard Lintott were all periodically involved in the publication and circulation of Toland's printed work. These engagements did not always result in 'published' works however. For example, in 1712 Toland made an agreement with John Humfreys of Bartholomew Lane, London to print *Cicero illustratus*.[25] The terms dictated the amount and quality of the paper, the costs of printing and extra payment for 'working the title in red'.[26] The work cost Toland in total £6.17s, of which he made three payments leaving an outstanding bill of £3.12s 6d. Toland undoubtedly put money and effort into the production of this Latin work, which was dedicated to Prince Eugene and Baron d'Hohendorf. Desmaizeaux reproduced the work in Toland's posthumous collection pointing out that 'it is very scarce; and the reason is, that it was never made publick'. In fact, Toland had only 'printed a few copies at his own charge, to distribute among his friends and subscribers'.[27]

Toland exploited what Harold Love calls 'author publication' to establish his credentials amongst the powerful.[28] Although Toland used print technology his text was not distributed as a printed work, but he attempted to retain a precise control over the distribution of copies, and consequently over the audience for the work. Further evidence for this bespoke dispersal is found in the manuscript annotation Toland added to the copy of the work in the Bodleian: 'in token of respect, and for his old acquaintance-sake this book is presented to Doctor John Carr, by his most humble servant, Septr. 30: 1712. J. Toland'.[29] Toland wished to produce an edition of the entire works of Cicero furnished with critical notes. To attract subscription for such an enterprise (especially given his reputation) he set out to create a community of readers through the distribution of his proposal. Since no Toland edition resulted we might presume either that the project was unpalatable, or the costs too great. As we will see in a later chapter he acted in the same way with one of his more controversial works, the *Pantheisticon* (1720).

Toland often tested the waters of public reception in a more conventional manner by preparing a series of mock title-pages for publishers.[30] The example of one of the surviving copies ('The Critical History of the Celtic Religion & Learning: Containing An Ample Account of the Druids') suggests that these proposals were serious.[31] The 'lent list' shows that a manuscript with this title was circulated. It was to be posthumously printed in the 1726 collection. The mock title-page differs from the circulated manuscript in that it indicates four parts rather than three. That the work was destined for print publication is suggested by the remark that the book would be 'illustrated with copper cuts'. As will be discussed at length below, this work was a product of Toland's political intimacy with Robert Molesworth. The circulation of scribal work to other contemporaries implicated them in the political agenda associated with Molesworth's commonwealth projects. Another title-page, *Priesthood without priestcraft*, dated 1705, not only included a title-page, but also a list of sixteen chapter headings divided between two books. That a text under this title was circulated is confirmed by the evidence of Anthony Collins's library catalogue (*c*. 1720) which recorded a volume under that name.[32] The other works designed in this way do not seem to have reached maturity in circulated versions.

It was a key part of Toland's skill as a public writer to operate in both scribal and print culture. He also was adept at recognising the opportunities of translation between the two media. The power of his skills as a communicator lay, not necessarily in the articulation of new ideas, but in the redeployment of ideas, sources and texts into different social and cultural contexts. Toland developed an arsenal of different authorial strategies when writing for a print audience, including the presentation of scholarly apparatus, the appropriation of orthodox rhetoric, and the careful presentation of typographical style. The function of this variety of authorial *personae* was to attempt to engage with as many types of reader as possible, simultaneously. Insinuation, appropriation and ambiguity were strategies adopted by Toland to capture the reader's mind and initiate the process of persuasion or corrosion of accepted patterns of authority and belief. The imperatives and constitution of scribal publication determined a different set of conventions and relationships between author and reader. In particular, scribal publication offered the author a potentially untrammelled dominion over audience: the author could choose to whom he would send a text, and might *encumber* that transfer of material with precise stipulations about when and where other access might be allowed to the manuscript, and by whom. The effect of this was a conversation with a specific group of people. The evidence of the list 'manuscripts abroad' illustrates with precision one community of readers created by Toland: the circulation of manuscript works thus not only spread ideas but made a platform for political action.

Lawyers, booksellers, aristocrats, politicians, admirals and architects formed the circle made by Toland's manuscripts. This intellectual intimacy established the social groundwork for access to power. One of the significant minorities of people to whom Toland distributed texts was that of women. The gentle status of Lady Janet Carriere may in some sense explain her presence on the list: clearly Toland used her, in part, as a conduit to pass scribal material to her husband. The fact that she was a useful instrument in establishing such a relationship is significant in itself. Her later involvement in the sale of legal offices suggests she had a measure of intellectual and even political independence.[33] In the face of a paucity of information about the lives of the other women to whom Toland lent works, it is necessary to broaden the context to consider the nature of Toland's associations with other women. He encountered women most frequently in the print-bookselling trade. Abigail Baldwin, Ann Dodd and Mrs Smith were three women *libraires* who published a number of Toland's works between 1700 and 1718. Baldwin published material overwhelmingly in defence of the Hanoverian succession, while Dodd was involved in producing the second edition of *Nazarenus* (1718), and Mrs Smith the virulently anticlerical *An appeal to honest people against wicked priests* (1712).[34]

Toland had a predilection for talking with powerful women too. In the early years of the 1700s, Toland (as a result of various diplomatic missions) had established a close conversational association with both Sophia, Electress of Hanover, and consequently Sophia Charlotte (her daughter) in Berlin. One important literary result of this relationship was Toland's *Letters to Serena* (1704). Addressed to Sophie Charlotte, Toland took the opportunity to defend the female sex against male 'prejudice'. He claimed to have demonstrated 'the Parity of the intellectual Organs in both sexes, and that what puts 'em both on the same foot in discourse of ordinary business (which is deny'd by no body) makes em equally capable of all improvements, had they but equally the same advantages of education, travel, company, and the management of affairs'.[35] Later he was to publish Sophie's work on patristic scholarship as a means of reinforcing the Protestant piety of the Hanoverian succession. In the face of

considerable conservative opinion, Toland insisted that women were potentially capable of apprehending the highest philosophy, virtue and religion.[36]

In a preface to a much earlier work *A lady's religion in a letter to the
Honourable My Lady Howard* (1697) Toland had horrified his readers with the
suggestion that women had an equal facility for reasonable 'plain, short and
intelligible' religion (and thus for priesthood) as men. He had underscored
this point about the potentially clerical role of women, in the 'Primitive
constitution of the Christian Church' (c. 1705), when he had provided patristic
evidence for the status of deaconesses in Christian antiquity.[37] Later in
Hypatia (1720), Toland took the fate of the ancient philosophess of Alexandria
who was assassinated in 415 AD, as indicative of the cruelty and perfidy of
priestcraft. The work was intended to celebrate the 'vast number of Ladies,
who have in every age distinguished themselves by their professions and
performances in learning'. Women had been eminent in all kinds of literature
but 'especially in Philosophy; which as it is the highest perfection, so it
demands the utmost effort of human nature'.[38] One of the manuscripts Toland
circulated (to Mr Robinson) the 'Piece of ye Roman education', celebrated the
role women like Theano and Muia, wife and daughter of Pythagoras, undertook in the raising and education of children.[39] In print and scribal publications Toland self-consciously laid emphasis upon the intellectual abilities of
women: while much of this may be the manifestation of his desire to
ingratiate himself with an elite social and political milieu, the evidence of his
correspondence also reveals a similar attitude.

There is no doubt that Toland used his pen for personal advancement, even
for more intimate advantage. At some point after 1720, Toland fell in love with
a young women he identified only by the letters 'A.B.C.D.'. Rumour had
misidentified the object of his amour. Writing to 'Mrs D***', Toland intended
to clarify the misunderstanding that had been made worse by the insinuations
of various balladeers. While he acknowledged that he had used some 'roguish
expressions, which I know to be one of her favourite diversions' he was ready
to swear on his 'corporal oath, she was never the object of my thoughts'.
Toland had engaged his heart to be 'constant to merit in the person of one
excellent creature', even though this meant 'that I may ruin my self all at once
with some other Darlings of mine (meaning the venerable society of vain and
wanton Widows, the honourable company of Virgin, that have large fortunes
and small understandings; with the faded skins, and cherry-cheeks of both
sorts)'. The robust language suggests an intimacy and assured playfulness
with the *moeurs* of gentle female company. Toland continued to give 'the
character of my real or imaginary mistress': she 'ever thinks before she
speaks, tho she never speaks half she thinks'. While not the 'monster they call
a learned lady' she joined moderate reading with prudent observation,
combining the wit and beauty of youth with the 'sense and virtue' of age. Her

religion 'lyes not in her tongue, but in her heart'. Her command of the social graces meant she was 'genteel without affectation, gay without levity, civil to strangers without being free, and free with her acquaintance without being familiar'. Toland sadly acknowledged that there was no 'return of mutual love' partially because he had not 'made her a positive declaration'.[40] In a subsequent letter to the same woman Toland, describing his own love as combining the 'ardour of the youngest man, ... with all the constancy of the oldest philosopher', continued to laud the physical beauty of his mistress which verged on the sensual.[41]

That Toland's infatuation was real rather than fictional is substantiated by some fragmentary drafts of letters to a mother and daughter written *c.* 1720 found in his archive. The prompt for his correspondence was his gift of a copy of *Hypatia* to the daughter. Assuring the mother that the small present was 'purely honorable' he 'hope[d] you have a better opinion of my charming Sory (I am sure I have) then that she would exchange her heart for a sixpenny pamphlet'.[42] In the course of his letter Toland gave directions about how he expected the volume of essays should be read. The account of Hypatia 'will most affect you, considering that a young lady of your distinguished merit must needs be sensibly touch'd to find such an unparallel'd example of her sex, but the envy and reproach of ours'. The second discourse (*Clidophorus*) would convince her 'that men do commonly use as little sincerity to each other as to all women; in w[ch] charge no way you are nothing concern'd, since your beauty and virtue, joined to so many good qualities, have privileged you against all dissimulation'. The first and last parts of the work (*Hodegus* and *Mangoneutes*) are described as 'idle comments' designed to 'amuse where they cannot instruct you'.[43] Here, although perhaps driven by desire for the particular woman, Toland provides confirmation of the motivation for circulation of (printed or scribal) texts to other women in his circle. Women were a legitimate and responsive audience for his critique of prejudice, dissimulation and priestcraft. Toland was at intellectual and social ease in the company of women whether queens, printers, ladies or lovers. His dispersion of texts was a means of engaging with female sociability, in itself a convenient means for accessing power and for countering orthodox clerical discourses about the intellectual competence of women.[44]

The people Toland sent manuscripts to, both men and women, were a group with common characteristics. They shared a platform of similar political and religious beliefs that (as we will see in chapters 4 to 6) can be described as republican. This 'commonwealth' ideology made a firm connection between political and religious liberties. It was commonly articulated as an attack upon the legal foundations of the confessional state or what we could call 'political anticlericalism'. The significance of the affinity is its identity as a politically active group closely allied with the Hanoverian court. Toland's community of readers was not marginal and radical but included figures (like Molesworth and Parker) that laboured at the very centre of national politics. Toland's scribal writings were contrived to integrate him into a circle of patronage, and were in that sense instruments in creating a social connection that would enable him to advance ideas and opinions in an oral or conversational context. At the same time the texts themselves contrived to act as stimulants of political activity. We need then to be sensitive to both the social and intellectual purposes of these textual exchanges.

Toland's relationship with the men of power he came to know can be best explored in the associations he had with Robert Harley, Anthony Ashley Cooper and Robert Molesworth. His liaison with women of power like Electress Sophia of Hanover will be considered at length below, but should be thought of as underpinning the legitimacy of his relations with all these other figures. Defending the legitimacy of a tolerant Protestant succession was a central plank of his political agenda. In the immediate aftermath of the fiercely contested General Election of 1705, Toland wrote to an anonymous correspondent (probably William Penn) in late June in answer to the queries 'why I was not employ'd before, and how I wou'd be employed at present?'. Combining a touching reflection upon his own youthful political *naïveté*, with an account of the vagaries of ideological controversy in the late 1690s and early 1700s, he admitted 'I thought everybody meant what they said as well as my self'. The consequence of this inexperience was that 'in the most public manner I promoted the party I had espous'd, without once considering that their adversaries wou'd all very naturally become my enemies'. This public espousal involved the defence of liberty and free government 'against what is arbitrary and despotic'. The government of 'standing and indifferent laws' was to be preferred to the 'uncertain and byast will of any Prince'. As Toland clarified, the best form of a free government was 'our own mixt constitution'. It was a shock then, to this young and 'ardent' lover of liberty who had embarked on the public service of republishing the works of Milton, Harrington and 'some others' (Ludlow, Holles and Sidney at the very least), to find himself mischaracterised and traduced as a 'most violent republican'. The immediate political point of the letter was to distance himself from intimacy with the Whig Junto (and in particular Somers and Halifax: protesting perhaps too much Toland insisted that, 'I have no personal obligations to either of them, nor have every enter'd into any manner of transactions with themselves or on their behalf, either here at home, or any where abroad').[45]

This experience taught Toland a lesson: most politicians 'of whom I had hitherto entertain'd a high opinion, meant nothing by the public but themselves'. Those who might have been able to offer serious counsel to such figures instead became 'the mean tools of their avarice or ambition, being their exchange or coffee-house heralds, and the trumpeters of their praises in all public meetings'. The point was to distinguish between 'men and things, between professions and performances'. The conduct of the apostate Whigs (who by principle ought to be 'the patrons of the liberty of mankind') in the matters of parliamentary legislation (especially the Judge's Bill, the Triennial Bill and for the regulation of trials) was shockingly partial. The 'business of the standing army finished all', driving a rift between honest and corrupt men, between friends and flatterers. Toland's point was to establish a clear ideological distance between the Junto Whigs and 'the persevering Whigs' like himself and the Duke of Newcastle, who were never 'tainted with notions of arbitrary power ... and who are most unlikely to be seduc'd or corrupted hereafter by reason of their great quality, plentiful fortunes, and honest principles'. Importantly, Newcastle was the cornerstone of Harley's policy of attracting Whig support to his ministry.[46]

The letter was then an application for political employment. Toland acknowledged that his own reputation was controversial: some Whigs, most Tories and all Jacobites hated him. For Toland however 'words are but wind (as they say) and therefore names go for nothing with me': as long as men were good countrymen and defended the constitution and the 'Protestant Religion and Succession' they were 'true Englishmen' regardless of party affiliation and 'narrow bottom'd faction'. In the early years of Queen Anne's reign Toland was protected by 'high born persons' from the accusations of both parties; 'for at one and the same time I had a Tory Secretary of State writing letters against me to foreign Courts as Agent to the Whigs, if not obnoxious to the laws'. At the same time leading Whigs were describing him as 'Mr Harley's creature, which was a higher crime by far than being a Tory'. Sadly, Toland noted that he had not 'spoke one word to Mr Harley, nor receiv'd one letter or message from him, since King William died'. Since then Toland had been treated in the manner of those 'coquet ladies, who tast all the bitter of the scandal without enjoying any of the sweets of the sin': he was accused of being a creature of Harley, while being distrusted by the man himself. Noting that he had offended Marlborough, Nottingham and Rochester, Toland underscored the importance of his political relationship with the leading noble figures: Shaftesbury, Somers, Halifax and Newcastle.[47]

Although he had been ill-used in the past, perhaps deservedly, Toland offered his services on trial: 'I wou'd not desire any public establishment for some time, 'till my patron had got experience of my fitness and ability'. The grounds for this arrangement were to be 'on such a foot as is agreeable to my principles and for the particular benefit of the Succession'. Allowing him the opportunity to offer counsel would soon cure the prejudices against his character, even those advanced by the Church 'which is so much exasperated against me'. Toland's immediate proposition was that he should go to

Germany 'and keep a constant weekly correspondence with his Lordship, not only according to his instructions, but likewise as to all observations of my own, I shou'd think deserving of his curiosity or notice'. Although he would travel throughout Germany the purpose of his mission would be to exploit his own standing at the Hanoverian court 'that when absent I shou'd know all that past there and could communicate what I thought fit to them from other places'. Such an 'appointment' would be paid quarterly and 'continued no longer than I shall be judg'd to deserve the same or better'. Toland's role was to be neither 'Minister nor Spy', but would prove to be 'of extraordinary use' to the Lord Treasurer Godolphin. Toland's credit in this matter was derived, notwithstanding the savagely critical memorials of Nottingham, from the strength of his reputation with the Electress of Hanover, who was only restrained from acknowledging her respect for him 'in a public manner' by the fear of upsetting Anne.[48]

Two months later, writing to Robert Harley, Toland was still in pursuit of place. Through the agency of William Penn, he had re-established his connections with Harley. 'The complication of parties, principles and designs' and the potentially hostile construction of 'both the violent Whigs and Tories', meant that 'prudence' about the extent of their relationship, would be Harley's best policy while it was 'both my interest and duty to be secret'. Toland had declined to be a 'mercenary tool' and had consequently suffered persecution: 'they loosed all their little curs of Booksellers and others upon me at once, knowing I could not be able to satisfy my creditors (though my debts were very small) if they came upon me all together'. These financial difficulties were moderate and ought not to be blown out of proportion as a tool to compromise Toland's reputation. Toland proposed a 'method' which would 'make me useful to yourself and the public without incurring the censure of any faction or letting it be known to your best friends, till I have time and opportunity to wear off those prejudices which my own want of experience and the treachery of others have raised against me'. Toland would abandon his 'tattling and mean acquaintance' and indiscreet frequenting of coffee-houses: Harley, with the connivance of Godolphin, could 'make me a new man without changing my old principles'.[49]

At the same time as he was negotiating with Harley, Toland felt compelled (in order to maintain his political relationship with the third Earl of Shaftesbury) to offer some explanation of his conduct and associations. He noted that his earlier applications for political service had been unsuccessful: 'for what my Lord Somers' Ministry wou'd not give me, and what I wou'd not ask of my Lord Nottingham's Ministry, the present Ministry unsought has offer'd, and I am willing to accept'. Unwilling to proceed without clearing the air, Toland requested a private and confidential meeting to discuss the 'terms' and 'purposes' of his employment. It was 'absolutely necessary that I begin on clear ground'. A further letter in October 1705, regretting that no meeting had taken place, attempted to make transparent his objectives by including the first fruits of his labours for the Ministry (accompanying the letter was a copy of Toland's *Memorial of the State of England* a work composed in response to James Drake's furiously High Church polemic, and encouraged by Harley). Toland was concerned to clear his name of the charge of being a turncoat: the 'confidence' between the two men had not been tarnished by his conduct. As he commented, 'by this memorial you may perceive what sort of Tory I am grown, and at the same time what sort of politicians they are at the Grecian, who (as I am inform'd by no mean person) report that I am become a Tory'. This was a 'spightfully' contrived by 'certain unforgiveing managers' to 'oppress' him. Far from regarding the *Memorial* as a work of purely Harleian purposes, Toland encouraged Shaftesbury to see the book as part of his own political project: 'I shall only tell your Lordship, that it is really your fault, if this book be not so good as you wou'd have it, since my Design of Seeing you some weeks ago was to advise about it'.[50]

In these letters we can see Toland the politician at work, offering services, producing polemics, engineering wider intellectual support for particular policies. Even the minor episode of the *Memorial* establishes the breadth of his connections, and the intimacy between his writings and the highest elites of the political world. As Toland proudly noted in a letter to Harley in December 1705, 'It is no small satisfaction to me, that the judgement of the Queen, the Parliament, and the Ministry, do unanimously concur with the Book'. Although Toland acknowledged Harley's encouragement in the production of the book, he also noted that there might be some things in the book 'not according to your sentiments'. As Harley well knew this was because 'I wanted opportunity to consult you personally'. The work was rushed, 'I having finish'd it in a very few days, without any to advise me but Mr P[enn], being in the country, and not master of time enough to polish the very language'.[51] Although the *Memorial* might not have reflected the opinions of Harley in every iota it clearly contributed to the political agenda of refuting Tory claims that the Church was in 'danger'. By 20 December 1705, both the Houses of Lords and Commons had resolved to condemn such opinions and insist 'that whosoever goes about to suggest and insinuate that the church is in danger under her Majesty's administration is an enemy to the queen, the church and the Kingdom'. Instructions were sent to magistrates to prosecute any who contradicted the resolution.[52] While, no doubt, Toland over-exaggerated the influence of his own contribution, here there is unmistakable evidence of his writings having some sort of causal relationship with the development of public policy against the High Church Tories. Whether Toland was merely the agent of Harley's machinations, or (as the correspondence with Shaftesbury might suggest) had his own agenda in the composition, will be a matter for debate. What is manifest is his intimacy with the agents of political power. Writing could make a difference.

Toland was proud of his abilities to influence public debate: indeed he forwarded to Harley evidence of the reception of the *Memorial* by the dissent-ing minister John Shower who regarded it as 'the most judicious and seasonable of anything lately printed'. So much was Shower impressed that he intended to buy twenty-five copies for distribution 'as to occasion the buying and reading of a much greater number'.[53] Given such a reception, it was unsurprising that Toland attempted to broach further designs to Harley, 'and therefore as well as for that, as for some other reason, I humbly and earnestly beg the favour of one half hour's Discourse with you, wherever or in what manner you please to appoint'. The next piece of writing would be 'without a fault; which I shall judge it be, if it has but your concurrence or approbation'. For this and other such writings and counsel it was rumoured that Toland was to be made Keeper of the Paper Office worth about £400 per annum.[54] However, as Toland miserably complained to Harley two years later, 'I own myself disappointed'. He had not even received 'as much as copy-money' for his writings.[55]

While Toland evidently considered himself suitably qualified for senior duties in the Ministry (and the appropriate recompense), he was not success-ful. In a long letter of woe to Harley ('the best friend I have on earth') he unburdened his feelings of despair. He was (as he put it rather immodestly) 'a great deal more capable in all respects, than several in the long list of such as have been employed in that space of time'. As an 'absolute stranger to all bargaining', Toland objected bitterly to the nepotism and self-interest that had governed political appointments: 'I have neither bought with some, nor sold with others ... I have neither betrayed, nor been betrayed; I am neither akin to this family, an enemy to that, nor a retainer to any: I have never a favourite brother or sister, nor am myself for such gentle services in the good graces of any Lord or Lady whatsoever; I have neither flattered nor lampooned with my prostitute rhymes'. Toland had 'silently endured the greatest hardship imagin-able' and was modest in his demands: yet still the 'centre of preferment' eluded him. The slanders of 'some hotbrained pert fellows from Christchurch' had compromised his reputation. Harley had, according to Toland, 'supplied me now for two whole years out of your own pocket, in diet, clothes, lodging and all other expenses'. Toland had been led to imagine, possibly by the promptings of William Penn, that these provisions had been made on the instructions of the Lord Treasurer 'till something became vacant proper for me to accept or execute'. Only lately had he realised his dependence on Harley, 'and truly all the world are persuaded you are my patron, and look on me as your creature'. Since Toland had often approved of Harley's 'impartial measures' in politics he resolved to 'have no other interest but yours' as the most 'certain method of being always for the good of my country'. He would abandon his approaches 'to some great person to whom I was lately recommended'.

Reassuring Harley that his imminent trip out of the kingdom would not lead him to visit either Berlin or Hanover (and thus possibly compromise diplomatic relations between Anne and Sophia by the shadow of his reputation) he also took the opportunity to submit another claim for expenses. It was, he commented, high time 'for me to have new clothes'; the cost of new linen, the settlement of some small debts, and the charge for 'subsistence till November next' would come to a sum of £50. Although Toland was indebted to Harley ('I had no other resource in the world but your protection and friendship') he was careful to indicate he retained his independence by keeping an 'account of all I have received from you hitherto, and I make no question but if I live I shall be able to repay you, as you have enabled me to pay others'.[56] The relationship between Harley and Toland, for all the claims of honour and obligation, was not one based upon trust. Certainly in this instance in 1707, Toland did not keep his promise to avoid Hanover, and in fact Harley (rightly) doubted him enough to have his various diplomatic representatives report his movements. D'Alais reported in October, 1707 that Toland had not only visited the Elector at Dusseldorf (who presented him with 'considerable presents'), but also paid his respects to the Electress at Hanover. Toland had claimed 'that he was accredited by the government to the Elector for affairs of importance'. Howe passed on an account of Toland's arrival in Hanover describing the three or four hour private meetings he held with the Electress: he noted that 'this scandalous fellow pretends to come from several people of quality in England'.[57] Toland's ability to present himself as an intimate of the powerful was a consistent part of his conduct in Germany. Proffering all sorts of testimonials and references as he moved from court to court he fashioned himself as a conduit of influence between England and Hanover. As Lord Raby explained to Leibniz in January 1708, Toland's claim to be employed by the English government was deceitful, 'Mr Harley himself has written to me that so far from having any commission from him, he made difficulties in giving him a passport to leave England, not knowing what business he could possibly have abroad'. Harley's own capacity for duplicity is perhaps evident in the supplementary comment that Raby passed on: 'it is true that for some time he suffered him in his company, as a man reputed to have a good deal of reading, but that he was very far from ever having any friendship for or confidence in him'.[58]

When Harley returned to political power in 1710 Toland offered him hearty congratulations and reopened his offer of political counsel as did other commonwealthsmen like Robert Molesworth.[59] Addressing a number of 'memorials' to the first minister, Toland delivered a series of practical political 'advices' for brokering a scheme of coalition from 'a person of undoubted credit among the Whigs'.[60] The tone of these exchanges was one of increasing alarm about the danger to the Hanoverian succession implicit in Harley's diplomatic entanglements with France: Toland finished one letter with the injunction 'delays are dangerous'. Repeatedly underlining the 'difficulty of access' and his inability to speak with Harley directly, Toland offered his 'liberal education and experience in foreign Courts' and his 'credit abroad' to the service of the ministry. He would use both his tongue and his pen to reinforce the security of the Succession: because of his connections he could 'draw' information from the Hague, Hanover, Berlin, Dusseldorf and Vienna, as well as 'diffuse' policy in the same places. In return for these services he expected payment: perhaps ultimately a salary of £200 per annum (paid quarterly) but in the interim £20 would do. Acknowledging that the attentions of the 'Jesuits of Christchurch' meant that significant office would not be his, he commented that 'I know there are places very little subject to notice or envy'. Such an appointment would 'make me not a little useful to your Lordship, as well as easy to myself'.[61]

It is worth pondering for a moment the nature of these services Toland offered to the minister. Toland denied he was a spy although many hostile contemporaries made the accusation. Toland described himself as 'very busy'. As he expanded 'I have been at times in all places and with all people'. He had been long absent from London which had given him 'a good pretext for an unaffected reserve' and encouraged others 'desirous to inform me on the foot of their own schemes and principles'. Toland characterised himself as a monitor and conduit of political opinion: 'I therefore hear and see everything'. Haunting the coffee-houses Toland had developed the 'art of disburthening' opinions from men by 'bantering and fooling, indifference and doubtfulness'. By 'pumping' he drew out of some people their political designs.[62] The purpose of this was to find the pulse of public political opinion so that he might acquaint Harley 'with the general notions, right or wrong, that obtain at any time in the town; with perhaps a true account of their original and tendency, what might be hoped or feared, done or undone, by such means'.[63] Toland proffered practical political prudence driven by a series of confirmed objectives which converged upon securing the Hanoverian succession against the combined threats of popery and the French. At this juncture Toland's advice was that in order 'to settle the minds of the subjects' an open and hearty support for the House of Hanover must be established: 'Dry and general expressions will not do: friends must be confirm'd, and enemies put out of hope'. The lengthy letter continued to give specific and detailed advice about the treatment of diplomatic matters, financial affairs and particular individuals. The rhetoric of this advice was one of humanist counsel: Toland warned that a method must be found of stalling the malicious designs of enemies at home and abroad because 'I have known a boat overset, because the skipper wou'd not slacken his sail at the desire of a passenger'.[64] In effect and intent, this memorial was a coded warning to Harley that his policies and negotiations with France were perceived as dangerous to the true national interest by both Whigs and Tories.

Unmistakably, Toland was not the only man offering such counsel to Harley, but the tone and expediency of the communication is significant. Toland was not bashful in his guidance. Reflecting on the nature of this relationship one might be tempted to regard Toland as the creature and instrument of the clever politician, a man who wrote (unsuccessfully in this case) for reward and place, a hack, a hired-hand. As the evidence of the various contracts Toland entered into with a number of booksellers, publishers and printers indicates, he wrote for a living having no other visible means of support. The implication that what Toland wrote was commissioned to order and therefore, if not insincere, then certainly not the product of pure intellectual conviction, is not sustainable from the evidence of his relationship with patrons like Harley, Shaftesbury and Molesworth. Ultimately perhaps the question comes down to a matter of private motivation, an issue ever elusive from the purview of the historian. Toland made, repeatedly during the course of his life, attempts to associate himself and his writings with a series of elite political figures. At one level such relationships provided him with material benefits and ease, but importantly they also provided him with a forum, a platform and the opportunity for the broadcast and articulation of his ideas and beliefs. Toland's skills at public writing, his reputation for learning and scholarship, his personal intimacies with a European community of letters, were all elements that made him attractive to courtiers and politicians. Indubitably Toland thought of himself as a figure at the centre of a complex web of intellectual and political relationships: he could both 'draw' and 'diffuse' information, ideas, learning, opinions and beliefs from this network. His performance in this circuit of communication was both covert and public, clandestine and communal. The texts Toland composed had meanings implicit in their languages, but also derived sense from these wider cultural contexts.

Toland's relationship with Harley was not simply one of hierarchy, of patron and client. At one level Harley needed Toland as much as he was needed by him. Although, as we have seen, Toland described himself as a 'creature' devoted to Harley's sole interest, it is important to stress that this relationship was determined by Toland's perception of Harley's commitment to a shared political agenda. When this communal platform was compromised Toland rapidly and determinedly withdrew his involvement with the politician. The evidence for the principled foundation of his working relationship with Harley is best displayed in the lengthy 'memorial' he sent in December 1711, a time when serious doubts about Harley's motives were developing. Premising his remarks with a description of his awareness of the protocols of true counsel ('principibus placuisse viris, non ultima laus est') and an assertion of his own proved intimacy with political 'company', he bemoaned the increasing difficulty of access he experienced, compared with the success of men 'the most opposite to you in principles' whom he met 'going up your stairs or coming down'.[15] In order to smooth his way, Toland took the opportunity to remind Harley of the sources of their 'familiarity ... founded upon the same love of Letters and Liberty, which to generous spirits are stronger ties, than even those of blood or alliance'. From this foundation Toland invoked 'the rights of friendship'. Unlike those men whom Harley used as 'tools ... to say and do, to unsay and undo as they are bid', Toland was 'just the reverse' in his principled consistency; he explained, 'My management abroad, my behaviour at home, what I whisper'd in private, and what I printed to the world, all speak the same language, all tend to the same end'. This end had been served by Toland's personal loyalty to Harley, a thing he had never exploited to personal benefit when men had 'sollicited my interest for access to your person, or intercession in their behalf; constantly refusing the most tempting offers, and often when I had not many guineas left for superfluous expence'. The premise of Toland's service was 'to communicate to your Lordship my observations on the temper of the ministry, the dispositions of the people, the condition of our enemies or allies abroad, and what I might think most expedient in every conjuncture'. Qualified by experience, languages and contacts, in combination with his devotion to the 'publick' interest, Toland acted as a 'private monitor', most emphatically not a spy. Of recent times Toland had begun to suspect his counsel was not used and fearful of betraying his friends he had become 'very cautious and reserv'd'. Toland had only the 'good of my country' at heart. As the evidence of his conduct in the 'impenetrable negotiation at Vienna' with Prince Eugene of Savoy indicated, 'they who confided to my management affairs of a higher nature have found me exact as well as secret'.

Toland pondered whether difficulties were prompted by 'the conditions demanded by me, or in the principles on which we are both to proceed?'. The matters of providing for his 'competent maintenance' were insubstantial; the principles of communion 'which with me are unalterable and indispensable, are civil liberty, religious toleration, and the Protestant Succession' were 'conditions *sine qua non*'. As Toland underscored 'he that will not agree with me on this foot, must never employ me nor ever trust me'. Recalling that Harley had encouraged Toland's edition of Harrington and commissioned the *Memorial of the State of England,* he reiterated their joint subscription to Whig and Commonwealth principles. Reviewing the defence of government by rule of law rather than will, the 'human and heavenly principle of Toleration' and the defence of the succession, Toland intended to reinforce the consistency of his service to Harley. If Harley had compromised his convictions, especially his allegiance to Hanover, then, lamented Toland, 'what a wretched politician am I? How greatly misled my self? And how great a misleader of others?' Although Toland feared the worst (especially given his own shoddy treatment), he refused to be convinced by any 'but your self ... that we are not embarked upon the same bottom'. Anxious that he might be considered self-important or hectoring in his address, Toland insisted that he simply acted the just duty of the 'free subject'. In the same breath as he confirmed his respect, love and duty towards Harley, he commanded something be done to head off an infamous and dangerous peace with France.[66] To cover his own back and vindicate his own reputation, Toland made sure that he distributed copies of the memorial to others.[67]

That Toland's relationships with powerful men were built upon principle rather than private interest is best exemplified in his reaction to Harley's apostacy from 'revolution principles'. This prompted furious and powerful criticism from Toland. In private correspondence Toland explained that because Harley had uttered 'ambiguous words' against the House of Hanover, he had 'utterly renounc'd his friendship' and had broken off all contact (spoken or written). This of course left him bereft of support while still reaping the unjust opprobrium attached to his former relationship. Retired from the bustle of business in Epsom, Toland devoted his energies to destroying Harley's reputation: the product was *The art of restoring* which skilfully compared Harley's conduct to that of General Monck, bracketing the restoration of the Stuarts in 1660, with that of the Pretender in 1714. The evidence of this long and tortuous relationship tends to suggest that Toland was a principled man with an eye to self-advancement but not to hypocrisy: he had clearly formed some personal attachment to Harley, perhaps drawn by the natural charisma of the latter's power and learning. The last letter he wrote used the metaphor of lovers to describe his relationship; there were however strict limits to the extent of this devotion: these parameters were defined by political conviction.

There are some important themes that can be extracted from this account of Toland's relationship with Harley. First, and most obvious, is the point that Toland defined himself as a commonwealth Whig: his allegiance to this identity was powerful and consistent from the 1700s to his death. Importantly this subscription to a party label for Toland meant that he was neither 'king-ridden nor priest-ridden': it implied a set of arguments about the nature of civil politics, the constitution of the Church, and the nature of the monarchy, all of which were encompassed by the vocabulary of liberty. Committed to a set of core republican values, Toland engaged in a powerful polemic against 'tyranny' whether it was located in a corrupt monarchy, a persecuting priest-hood, or a self-interested parliament. In the broadest possible terms, then, Toland was engaged in a political endeavour that had objectives of reforming

the corrupt and corrupting elements of society. The evidence of his relationship with Harley, which can be compared to parallel associations he had with
other powerful figures like Shaftesbury, Molesworth, Eugene of Savoy and
Sophia of Hanover, suggests that Toland was a man intimate with the mechanics and personnel of elite politics. Like contemporaries of his, the historian
needs to be wary of Toland's claims to influence and connection, but there was
clear substance to his assertion of intimacy with princes, nobles and men of
political power. The significance of these connections needs to be carefully
considered: the relationship between 'access' and 'influence' invokes some
particularly thorny issues in the history of ideas.

The connections Toland established through the circulation of manuscripts
c. 1720 shifts the place of his relationship with elite political culture from the
margins closer to the centre. It is clear from the trajectory of his career and the
concatenation of his political patrons that from the late 1690s to the end of his
life Toland was intimate with the mechanics of power. Whether acting as
purveyor of arguments in defence of the Hanoverian succession, editing the
canon of republican texts for the Whig commonwealthmen, or composing
livres de circonstance against Tory enemies, it can be argued that Toland was a
subtle and effective political pamphleteer. Even as a political writer Toland
exploited the scribal form in writing private memorials for Harley, Shaftesbury
and later Molesworth. Some of these materials survive both in manuscript and
in printed versions in the 1726 collection: works like *A project of a journal* and
A scheme for a National Bank were original essays composed presumably to
persuade his patrons (Shaftesbury and Molesworth) to pursue his advice in
the arena of national politics.[68] If these texts were meant to persuade within a
political context, we can only speculate about what role the less straightforwardly political works on the 'lent list' performed. When Molesworth
announced to Toland his plans to run for election at Westminster, he reassured
him: 'believe me when I tell you, you shall fare as I do'. Toland replied (a week
before his death) 'Since you will embark once more on that troublesom sea, I
heartily wish you all good luck, and wish I had been able to run for you night
and day, which with great ardour I wou'd'.[69] It would be wrong to separate this
political relationship from the intellectual intimacy established between the
two men represented in the exchange of scribal material. How far the content
of the manuscript material set the context for the development and articulation of the 'political' tenets is difficult to establish with precision. However, it
is possible to indicate that far from consigning him to the radical margins, at
least in England, Toland's scribal labours projected him into the swell of
national politics.

NOTES

1 See Jacob *Radical Enlightenment*; M. Benitez 'La coterie hollandaise et la réponse à m. de la Monnoye sur *le Traité de Tribus impostoribus*' *Lias* 21 (1994) pp. 71–94.

2 For earlier versions of this argument see, J. A. I. Champion '"Manuscripts of mine abroad": John Toland and the circulation of Ideas, c. 1700–1722' *Eighteenth-Century Ireland* 14 (1999) pp. 9–36 and '"Publiés mais non imprimés": John Toland et la circulation des manuscrits, 1700–1722' *La Lettre clandestine*, 7 (1998) pp. 301–341.

3 BL Add Mss 4295 fo. 43 'Manuscripts of mine abroad'.

4 See C. Robbins *The eighteenth century commonwealthmen* (Cambridge MA, 1959); J. P. Kenyon *Revolution principles* (Cambridge, 1977); W. Laprade *Public opinion and politics in the eighteenth century* (New York, 1936).

5 See G. Holmes *The trial of Dr Sacheverell* (1973) pp. 149–155. On Parker, see J. Campbell *The lives of the Lord Chancellors* (1846) volume 4.

6 See BL Stowe 750, *passim*.

7 See BL Add Mss 4287 fos. 210–216.

8 See the calendar in J. Almagor *Pierre Desmaizeaux (1673–1745), journalist and English correspondent for Franco-Dutch periodicals 1700–1720* (Amsterdam, 1989).

9 See Champion 'Manuscripts' p. 30. On Hewett see E. McParland *Public architecture in Ireland 1680–1760* (New Haven. 2001) pp. 9–11.

10 See 'Projet d'une dissertation sur la colomne de feu et de nuée des Israelites: dans une lettre à Megalonymus'. OBN 10,390.

11 See *Christianity not mysterious* Preface, p. xxvi; *Militia Reform'd* [*Tolandiana* p. 3]; J. Toland (ed.) *Harrington's works* p. xli.

12 See *Tolandiana* p. 64.

13 E. Curll *An historical account of the life and writings of the late eminently famous Mr John Toland* (1722) p. 22.

14 *Errata* p. 3.

15 *Tolandiana* pp. 169–170.

16 *Nazarenus* p. ix.

17 ONB 10,325 'Projet' fos. 4–5.

18 *Nazarenus* Appendix I p. 2.

19 *Tetradymus*: Hodegus p. 6.

20 *Tetradymus*: Mangoneutes p. 209.

21 See BL Add Mss 4282 fo. 190 (March 15. 1722).

22 *Tetradymus*: Mangoneutes p. 209.

23 *Tetradymus* 'Preface' p. xxii.

24 See *Nazarenus* 'Introduction' *passim*.

25 See *Tolandiana* pp. 157–158. 162.

26 See BL Add Mss 4295 fo. 24.

27 P. Desmaizeaux 'Introduction' *Collections* 1 p. lxvii.

28 H. Love *Scribal publication in seventeenth-century England* (Oxford, 1993) p. 47.

29 See *Tolandiana* p. 158.

30 See Add Mss 4295 fos. 25 and 4, for examples of other 'contracts'.

31 BL Add Mss 4295 fo. 61. For a transcription see *Tolandiana* pp. 6–7.

32 See King's College, Cambridge, *Bibliotheca Collinsiana* Keynes 217 fo. 469. Collins also owned another manuscript title 'Christianity Restored'. A contract is in BL Add Mss 4295 fo. 4.

33 See *Lives of the Lord Chancellors* p. 544.

34 For full details of all their publications, see *Tolandiana*.

35 *Letters to Serena* (1704) Preface, §3, 5.

36 *Ibid.* §7, 8.

37 *Collections* 2 pp. 191–192.

38 *Tetradymus* pp. 105–106.

39 See *Collections* 1, 'A letter concerning the Roman Education', pp. 1–27.

40 *Collections* 2 pp. 357–363

41 *Collections* 2 pp. 364, 367, 368.

42 See BL Add Mss 4465 fo. 44.

43 BL Add Mss 4465 fo. 45

44 See H. Smith 'English "Feminist" writings and Judith Drake's *An essay in defence of the female sex*' (1696) *Historical Journal* 44 (2001) pp. 727–747.

45 *Collections* 2 pp. 337–353. I am very grateful to James Alsop for allowing me to read an account of these letters. This is a corrective to the account found in F. H. Ellis (ed.) *Jonathan Swift: a discourse of the contest and dissentions between the nobles and the commons in Athens and Rome* (Oxford, 1967) pp. 39–42.

46 W. Speck *The birth of Britain: a new nation 1700–1710* (1994) p. 83.

47 *Collections* 2 pp. 345–346.

48 *Collections* 2 pp. 351–353, 340–343.

49 *Portland Mss* IV p. 235.

50 F. H. Heinemann 'John Toland and the age of enlightenment' *Review of English Studies* 20 (1944) pp. 134–135, citing Toland to Shaftesbury, 22 October 1705.

51 *Collections* 2 pp. 354–355.

52 Kenyon *Revolution* p. 100.

53 *Collections* 2 pp. 356–357.

54 Heinemann 'John Toland' p. 137.

55 *Portland Mss* IV p. 408.

56 *Ibid.* p. 410

57 *Ibid.* p. 456.

58 Kemble *State Papers* p. 465.

59 *Portland Mss* IV p. 572.

60 See *Collections* 2 pp. 215–219 which is a slightly different version of that reproduced in *Portland Mss* V pp. 126–127.

61 *Portland Mss* V pp. 259–260.

62 *Collections* 2 p. 404.

63 *Portland Mss* V p. 258.

64 *Collections* 2 pp. 406–409.

65 *Collections* 2 p. 221.

66 *Collections* 2 pp. 221–238 *passim*.

67 *Collections* 2 p. 429.

68 See *Collections* 1 pp. 448–474; volume 2 pp. 201–215. See BL Add Mss 4295 fo. 68, and Add Mss 4465 fos. 39–42, for manuscript copies.

69 See BL Add Mss 4465 fos. 27, 29.

3

Reading Scripture: the reception of *Christianity not mysterious,* 1696–1702

'A s for religion ... it is more easy to guess what he was not, than to tell what he was. 'Tis certain, he was neither Jew nor Mahometan: But whether he was a Christian, a Deist, a Pantheist, an Hobbist, or a Spinozist, is the Question'.' Toland's writings had 'alarm'd all sober well-meaning Christians, and set the whole clergy against him'. Having explored how Toland lived and worked in a world of libraries and books, it is time to examine how his books worked in the public sphere. One of the persistent problems Toland faced throughout his life was the question that hung over his reputation: an anxiety that was driven by the disastrous reception of his first venture into print, a work that engaged directly with the status of the most important text in early modern culture – the Bible. If doubts voiced about the orthodoxy of Toland's private beliefs were hardly unsurprising at the end of his career, clerical worries about the integrity of his Christian faith were also manifest before he made his mark in the intellectual firmament. As a young man, it was reported, Toland had declared that 'Religion is a plain & easy thing, & that there is not so much in it, as Priestcraft would persuade: taking it for granted to be part of this Doctrine, that what is to be done in order to Salvation, is as easy, as what is to be known, is plain'.' If libraries were good places to meet powerful people, and manuscripts were effective ways of making influential friends, Toland's first work argued that the Bible was a non-mysterious book accessible to all rational readers. By default this was a political claim which compromised the social power claimed by the Church over their exclusive rights of interpreting revelation. Reading books, under the advice of Toland, became a political act.

The conflict between Toland's public reputation and private faith came early in his career. Some time in early 1694 a concerned cleric had left Toland a long letter expressing anxieties that he had 'great learning but little religion'. Toland's outraged reply insisted that he was orthodox, confirmed by a short *credo* of his Christian faith. First, he claimed to believe in an 'infinite, good, wise and powerful Being, which in our language we call God, substantially different from the universe he created'. Second, he upheld belief in Christ, foremost as a 'perfect example' for humanity sanctified by the Holy Spirit. Thirdly, he insisted that it was the duty of all Christians to 'live temperately, justly and piously: to love God above all things; and my neighbour as myself'.[3] Although Toland maintained these statements as his rule of faith he was also very keen to uphold the necessity of toleration. Toland's anonymous clerical correspondent claimed he had not intended to provoke the young scholar. The accusation of having 'little religion' was not meant to imply irreligion, but that 'you were one who dealt somewhat too freely with it, a man of aspiring and uncontrouled reason, a great contemner of credulity'.[4] Although Toland was anxious to protect his public reputation he did not hesitate to challenge these criticisms.

The anxious clergyman of Oxford had been driven to caution Toland because of the rumour of a work he was supposed to have written. That work was *Christianity not mysterious,* published without Toland's name or details of either publisher or bookseller between December 1695 and June 1696. Draft 'papers' had possibly been sent to John Locke in late March 1695, via his friend John Freke.[5] Reports about Toland's work were widespread in Oxford through the year.[6] Advertisements for the work appeared in the *Post-Man* in late December 1695. By early June the book was being attacked from London pulpits for its 'most arrogant and impudent treatment of God and the Holy Scriptures'.[7] By late June 1696 Toland placed adverts in the *Post Man* acknowledging his authorship. By August the book had been announced on the Continent.[8] To accompany this revelation a 'second edition enlarg'd' was published with Toland's name on the title-page. He revelled in the celebrity. Writing in 1702, defending his original publication, Toland insisted that he would never allow another edition of the work to see the light of day, he had 'refus'd my Consent to make any edition of it since the second of the same year with the first 1696'. This was deceitful nonsense.[9] In the very same year (probably after May) a third edition was published with the addition of the *Apology* (1697) Toland had written to defend himself against charges of blasphemy and irreligion.[10]

Despite the work masquerading as the penmanship of a sincere Christian (a passage from Archbishop Tillotson had been included prominently on the title-page), the outcry of rage was immediate and intense. Within the first two years there were over twenty responses to the book, almost all by clergymen, ranging from massive single volumes to cheap ephemeral pamphlets. The response prompted more powerful legal and political institutions to react too. In mid-May 1697 the Grand Jury of Middlesex 'presented several books as scandalous', condemning *Christianity not mysterious* in the company of two other anonymous works *The Reasonableness of Christianity* and *A Lady's Religion*.[11] Toland's book had fallen foul of one of the initiatives aroused by the drive for moral reformation that periodically convulsed the Williamite regime. In defending the sanctity of scripture and the truth of the Trinity, the presentment suggested that 'all care possible ought to be taken for the speedy discovery of all such books'. Authors, printers and publishers should be dealt with 'according to the utmost severity of the Laws'. All editions should be suppressed, and all future printing be prevented for the 'time to come'.[12]

The evidence of the presentment by the Middlesex Grand Jury is a keen illustration of how the publication of *Christianity not mysterious* perturbed the authority of public religion. Both Mary and William had issued successive proclamations reinforcing magisterial injunctions against profanity and debauchery.[13] This drive for discipline was also advanced in the House of Commons. Reacting in particular to the explosion of irreligious works that were published as a consequence of the expiry of the Licensing Act in 1695, MPs devoted their energies to promoting legislation against blasphemy and profaneness.[14] The proclamation issued in William's name 'for preventing and punishing immorality and profaneness' attacked the 'several wicked and profane persons [who] have presumed to print and publish several pernicious books and pamphlets' and charged all 'persons that they do not presume to write, print or publish any such pernicious books or pamphlets, under the pain of our huge displeasure and of being punished according to the utmost severity of the law'. Ultimately a Blasphemy Act gained the statute book in 1698.[15]

Christianity not mysterious was published then into a context riven by orthodox disquiet about the connection between private immorality and public depravity. The presentation of the book, as a common nuisance, was intended to act as a 'precedent for others to do the like'.[16] Jean Gailhard, gentleman, a man intimate with Sir Thomas Rokeby (who had issued the directions to enforce morality that the Grand Jury had responded to) had later in November of the same year published his *The blasphemous SOCINIAN HERESIE disproved and confuted* (1697). The main body of this work painstakingly rebutted Socinian attacks upon the Trinity, although he also included a last lengthy chapter that put forward 'some animadversions upon a book called Christianity not mysterious.' Gailhard complained bitterly, 'to what purpose is Popery or Idolatry expell'd, if Socinianism or Blasphemy be let in?' While 'Atheism, Deism, Prophaneness, Immorality, yea, and Idolatry, &c. doth bare and brazen-faced walk in our streets' it was necessary in Gailhard's view, to invoke 'extream Remedies' to reform the nation. The 'Devil hath his instruments of several sorts' and had caused 'Achans' to trouble 'our Israel'. Some out of pride, others 'out of a Vain Glory or affectation of Singularity and Self conceit of Learning' had struck at the 'most holy Godhead it self'. The remedy was clear: imposition of the 'heaviest punishment to make the Pain hold a proportion with the offence' should be enacted against blasphemers. Citing *Leviticus* 24.24, he insisted, that 'The Blasphemer was by God's immediate Command, *stoned to death*, by the whole congregation, because the sin and scandal were Publick, so was the punishment to be'. English law allowed the same treatment. Reciting the cases of Bartholomew Legate and Edward Wightman, who were both burnt for heresy, Gailhard insisted that such 'Ishmaels' might be 'delivered into the Civil Magistrate's hand'.[7]

Gailhard's language was drenched in providential discourses which justified magisterial authority in restraint of the public exercise of reason in all conversation and books. He happily cited the magisterial example of the Scottish Parliament which had recently reinforced the 1661 statute against blasphemy, but also enacted further penalties against those 'whosoever in Discourse or Writing shall deny, quarrel, argue or reason against the Being of a God, or any of the Persons of the blessed Trinity, or against the Authority of the Holy Scripture, or Providence of God in Governing the World'. A third offence would be capital. The proceeding that the Emperor Theodosius undertook against heretical Manichees or Donatists should be re-invigorated 'at least strictly to be practised against live Socinians as dead Manichees'.[8] It is unlikely that Gailhard was unaware that these Scottish statutes had been employed against the Edinburgh University student Thomas Aikenhead resulting in his execution in January 1697: the language of capital punishment was not mere magisterial rhetoric.[9] For men like Gailhard then, such books were fundamentally dangerous.

At least one set of Parliamentarians rebutted Gailhard's suggestions and defended the 'natural right' to the exercise of reason in the matter of belief.[20] This free 'natural right' to the exercise of individual reason in the realm of public religion was precisely what Gailhard reviled.[21] Severe and brutal execution of penalties was not ungodly, as Gailhard explained, because 'The truth is, that Society of men are against all manner of restraint in matters of religion, they would have everyone believe and profess what seems good in his Eye; and so of the Church, which is the House of God, to make a meer Babel and confusion without order and rule, which frame will at last rend in pieces and ruin it'. What started in the Church would end in politics: 'you thereby introduce confusion into the Church, which may soon become Anarchy in Government'.[22] Men of Gailhard's ilk were convinced that elevating human reason against the grace of God would cause 'Bedlam' to reign where true religion ought to exist. The full power of the law could, and should, be turned against such miscreants. In the face of such hostility and the tragic example of Aikenhead in Scotland, Toland chose to follow one of his political patrons, John Methuen, to Ireland where he had been made Lord Chancellor in 1697.[23] Toland arrived in Dublin some time towards the end of March and early April

1697: his reception was hostile. In London he had fallen foul of a minor figure Sir John Bucknall, presented only as a common nuisance. In Dublin he was pursued though the Irish Commons and his book was burnt in September 1697. He fled the country in poverty and disgrace.

Examining the public and private reception of Toland and his work will allow an evaluation of the subversive implications of the work both as an intellectual and social statement. The first place to explore this is in the reaction of Toland's first powerful patron. Much has been written about the relationship between John Locke and Toland. It is commonly suggested that Locke had very little intellectual intimacy with the corrosive and indiscreet Toland. A close examination of the correspondence between Molyneux and Locke suggests to the contrary that Locke only chose to cut off his contact with Toland after the latter's public behaviour had compromised any private understanding they may have had. Locke and Toland first met in early August 1693 when Toland had acted as a book carrier on his behalf. Limborch had introduced Toland as 'an excellent and not unlearned young man ... if perchance you meet him you will find him frank, gentlemanly, and not at all a servile character'.[24] Furly commended the book-bearer as 'a free spirited ingenious man' who 'having once cast off the yoak of Spirituall Authority, that great bugbear, and bane of ingenuity, he could never be perswaded to bow his neck to that yoak again, by whom soever claymed'. This 'free spirit' had put Toland in difficulties regarding employment and Furly wrote on his behalf to encourage Locke 'to be assistant to him, wherein you can; not for my sake, but for his own worth'.[25] Nearly four years later William Molyneux again brought up the subject of Toland, this time suggesting that much of the hostility Locke's *Essay* had attracted from clerical opponents like Bishop Stillingfleet was due to the misuse of his arguments by books like *Christianity not mysterious*.[26]

At this time Locke expressed no hostility to Molyneux, indeed there is the suggestion, from the tone of a letter written by John Freke and Edward Clarke at the same time, that he felt some sympathy for Toland's condition. Freke, who had subsidised Toland's living expenses, thought that Locke would be interested enough to know that Toland having gone to Ireland, had left behind debts of some £80.[27] On the same day Locke was sent a further letter from Molyneux giving much more detail of Toland's conduct in Ireland. Molyneux spoke highly of Toland and especially of his relationship with Locke: 'But that for which I can never Honour him too much is his Acquaintance and friendship to you, and the Respects which on all occasions he expresses for you'. Molyneux found Toland congenial company and took a 'great deal of satisfaction in his Conversation' which had not been discreet since he further commented that 'I take him to be a Candid Free Thinker, and a good Scholar'.

Toland had, according to Molyneux, a rough reception in Dublin, 'there is a violent sort of spirit that Reignes here, and begins already to shew itself against him; and I believe will Increase Dayly, for I find the Clergy alarm'd to a mighty degree against him'. Toland had been welcomed 'to this Citty by hearing himself Harangued against out of the Pulpit'.[28]

Locke answered this letter about a month later commenting that he was 'glad' that 'the gentleman ... does me the favour to speak well of me on that side of the water, I never deserved other of him, but that he should always have done so on this'. Although Toland was diminished by 'his exceeding great value of himself', he might make a useful contribution. Indeed Locke spent some space in the letter talking about Toland 'freely' with Molyneux, 'because you are my friend for whom I have no reserves', although he introduced a caveat that 'I say it to you alone, and desire it may go no further'. Importantly, although Locke had read *Christianity not mysterious* and was undoubtedly aware of the controversy that raged in public about its significance, he was still positive (if cautious) about his support for Toland. As he clarified to Molyneux, 'For the man I wish very well, and could give you, if it is needed, proofs that I do so. And therefore I desire you to be kind to him; but I must leave it to your prudence, in what way and how far. If his carriage with you gives you the promise of a steady useful man, I know you will be forward enough of your self, and I shall be very glad of it'. If Toland through his actions spurned such friendship 'it will be his fault alone'.[29]

By the time he replied to Locke, Molyneux was beginning to articulate doubts and 'apprehensions' about Toland. It was not only Toland's vanity that perturbed him, but his lack of prudent management in his public carriage, for 'he has raised against him the clamours of all parties; and this not so much by his Difference in opinion, as by his Unseasonable Way of Discoursing, propagating, and Maintaining it'. Contrary to the current historiography about the location of the public space of the coffee-house as one of the places for the articulation of reason, Molyneux insisted that 'Coffee-houses and Publick Tables are not proper places for serious discourses relating to the most important truths'. Molyneux called on Locke to administer a friendly admonishment, 'for his conduct hereafter'. Furthermore, Locke was made aware that Toland brought ignominy to him because he takes 'a great Liberty on all occasions to vouch your patronage and Friendship, which makes many that rail at him, rail also at you'. Still, with all this disreputable behaviour, Molyneux looked upon Toland 'as a very ingenious man, and I should be very glad of any opportunity of doing him service, to which I think myself bound by your recommendation'. Molyneux completed his comments on Toland by pondering 'what might be the occasion of Mr T. coming at this time into Ireland'. Toland had 'no fortune or Imploy, and yet is observed to have a subsistence; but from whence it comes no one can tell certainly. These things joyn'd with his great forwardness in appearing publick makes people surmise a thousand Fancys'.[30] Locke's reply to Molyneux in mid-June 1697 was blunt and to the point: 'as to the gentleman, to whom you think my friendly admonishments may be of advantage for his conduct hereafter, I must tell you that he is a man to whom I never writ in my life, and, I think, I shall not now begin'. Toland was no intimate of Locke's and could not expect such concern: Molyneux should consider himself discharged of any 'over-great tenderness to oblige me'. It was left to Molyneux's discretion 'and therefore, whatsoever you shall, or shall not do for him, I shall no way interest myself in'. Locke terminated his discussion of Toland with the remark that he was unhappy at having spent so much 'of my conversation, with you, on this subject'.[31] Although Molyneux passed on information about Toland's travails in two further letters between 20 July and 11 September giving an account of his presentment by the Dublin Grand Jury and condemnation by the Irish Commons, he provoked no further response from Locke on the subject of Toland.[32]

In the course of his stay in Dublin, Toland had thus managed to alienate not only the local churchmen, but also Locke and Molyneux. Locke, perhaps predisposed to value Toland, was forced by the nature of his public carriage to end his support of him. Molyneux's description of Toland's imprudent actions suggests a man deliberately courting controversy and running himself 'against rocks to no purpose'. Not that Molyneux suggested that 'any man can be dispensed with to dissemble the truth, and full perswasion of his mind in religious truths, when duly called to it, and upon fitting occasions. but I think prudence may guide us in the choice of proper Opportunities'.[33] Toland, by the gait in which he appeared 'Publick', compromised such prudence. Molyneux did not abandon Toland to his fate but spoke up in his defence when clerics like Peter Browne assaulted him with 'foul language and Opprobrious Names'. In particular Molyneux rebutted what he called the 'killing argument'. 'Calling in the aid of the civil Magistrate and delivering Mr Toland up to secular punishment' was a 'matter of dangerous consequence, to make our Civil Courts judges of Religious Doctrines'. The Dublin Grand Jury, following the example of their brother jurors of Middlesex had also presented *Christianity not mysterious* even though not one of them had 'ever read One Leaf in Christianity Not Mysterious'.[34] Although no surviving copy exists, the Dublin presentment was said to be a reprint of the one reproduced by Gailhard, with a new 'emphatical title and cry'd about in the streets'.[35] Toland's 'imprudent management' had prompted a universal outcry against him which meant that 'twas even dangerous for a man to have been known once to converse with him'. Such was Toland's reputation that 'all wary men of reputation decline[d] seeing him, insomuch that at last he wanted a Meals meat (as I am told) and none would admit him to their Tables'. Toland, poor when he arrived in Ireland, was reduced to 'borrowing from anyone that would lend him 1/2 a

Crown; and run in debt for his Wigs, cloaths and Lodging'. Faced with the burning of his work and prospective prosecution by the Attorney-General Toland 'fled out of this kingdom'.[36]

Toland's narrative of his time in Dublin gives a different account. He published two defences – *An Apology for Mr Toland, in a Letter from himself to a member of the House of Commons in Ireland* (1697) and *A Defence of Mr Toland in a* LETTER *to Himself* (1697).[37] Citing Jude 9, 'We read, an archangel was not permitted to rail against the very devil', Toland declared that he would be restrained by the message of the Gospel, in his response, even if the pulpits of Dublin handled him roughly.[38] The indictment of his book by the jurors of Dublin, who had neither read nor (if they had) understood it similarly could not provoke Toland to unchristian reaction. He was irritated though by the fact that those who held any conversation or intellectual intimacy ('of either sex') with Toland found themselves under suspicion as 'proselytes'. Toland insisted his conversations with such 'worthy persons (for he always chose the best company)' was irreproachable. He never talked of religion, or made 'his opinions the subject of his common talk' indeed 'he declin'd speaking of 'em at all'.[39] Toland represented himself, contrary to the account found in the correspondence between Locke and Molyneux, as a discreet and careful man who kept his opinions to himself. Controversy was fanned by the industrious hostility of the orthodox rather than by his ideas.

Toland's arraignment by agencies of pulpit, jury, court and press was merely the preamble to Parliamentary censure. By 14 August the combined forces of moral reform, embodied in the polemics of men like Handcocke and Browne, 'concluded at last to bring his Book before the Parliament'. *Christianity not mysterious* was presented to the Committee of Religion in the Irish Parliament.[40] The matter of Toland's book was considered by 'a very full Committee, wherein this business was a great while debated'. It is clear from Toland's published account that he had access to someone who participated in the Committee's deliberations. There were 'several persons eminent for their birth, good qualities or fortunes' who objected to and opposed the whole proceedings 'being of opinion it was neither proper nor convenient for them to meddle with a thing of that nature'.[41] Such scruples were ignored and the offending passages of *Christianity not mysterious* were read out and examined. Some MPs encouraged Toland in his purpose of appearing before the Committee in person to answer their charges and 'to declare the sense of his book and his design in writing it'. To that end Toland composed a letter to the Committee defending his work and pleading for an oral examination. Again this personal appeal was rejected. The last thing the orthodox wanted was Toland to plead his cause in the forum of Parliament.[42]

Although it seems likely that there was significant and vocal support in defence of Toland coming from the Whiggish anticlerical interest in the Irish

Commons, which may have included Robert Molesworth and William Molyneux, *Christianity not mysterious* was declared heretical. It was to be burnt twice (once before Parliament and once before the civic buildings). Toland was to be brought into custody by the Sergeant at Arms in order to be prosecuted by the Attorney General. All copies of *Christianity not mysterious* were to be impounded and further imports banned.[43] Toland reported that 'in the committee it was mov'd by one that Mr Toland himself should be burnt, as by another that he should be made to burn his book with his own hand; and a third desir'd it should be done before the door of the house, that he might have the pleasure of treading the Ashes under his feet'.[44] The sentence was executed on 11 September. The public campaign against Toland did not stop there. As he commented 'there came abroad a printed sheet' with the specific purpose of terrifying 'any body from appearing publicly for Mr Toland'. Any who spoke out against the 'just prosecution or censure of it or him' did the same as denying 'our Saviour before men' and should, like Toland, suffer the consequences of their wilful heresy.[45]

Toland was to suffer yet further persecution at the hands of English priests in the early 1700s. By the later 1690s the anxieties about the consequences of the Toleration Act and the moral laxity of the nation had prompted High Churchmen like Francis Atterbury to cry out loudly and mobilise a powerful interest around the dictum of the 'Church in Danger'. Focused upon key figures in Oxford University like Henry Aldrich and William Jane, the High Church interest organised its polemic through the reinvigorated Lower House of Convocation.[46] Asserting the rights of Convocation to defend true religion, a full-scale counterblast was launched against irreligion. One element of this assault involved using Convocation to root out heresy and irreligion. Convened under the chairmanship of Dr William Jane, Dean of Christchurch, Oxford in February 1701, Convocation established a Committee of Religion 'appointed for the examination of books lately published against the Truth of the Christian Religion'.[47] The Committee pursued a vendetta against not only obvious heretics like Toland, but also the enemy within like Bishop Gilbert Burnet whose exposition of the 39 Articles was condemned along with *Christianity not mysterious*.[48] The Committee produced a precise account of five positions against *Christianity not mysterious*, reciting exact passages and phrases from the book. Having condemned the books the Lower House of Convocation passed them on to the Upper House for judicial censure. Here the anti-heretical ambitions of the Lower House fell victim to the ecclesiological powers of the more liberal Bishops in the Upper House, who pointed out that Convocation had no legal abilities to proceed against 'heretical, impious and immoral books' without specific licence from the civil sovereign.[49]

Although no further legal proceeding followed, Toland did not shirk his perceived duty of self-defence. Ordering his bookseller to supply him with all the hostile works written against his own volume, he was dismayed 'to see what a task I had on my hands'.[50] Initially as he sat down to read his way through the pile of antagonistic criticism, Toland was insistent that he would not trouble 'the Publick ... about my sentiments or private concerns'. Hearing, however, that Convocation intended to investigate him as 'the author of an Atheistical and Detestable book' Toland saw the necessity of a 'Publick Defence'. While it had been mere individuals who had responded to *Christianity not mysterious* Toland was content to rest his pen, but confronted with institutional criticism he felt compelled to retort.[51] He defended his right of 'writing in a free country' and called for the right to defend himself before the clergy.[52] Convocation refused to call Toland, presumably not wishing to give him a public platform for trumpeting further dissent from orthodoxy. It was clear that unlike many confronted with censure, Toland actively embraced the cause of controversy. As he wrote, 'It is not scribere est agere with me, for I have not only publisht but also own'd my books'.[53]

Between its first and third editions (1696–1702) *Christianity not mysterious* was condemned and reviled by a number of different institutions and in a number of different public spaces. The Middlesex and Dublin Grand Juries had used the laws of public nuisance and the climate of moral reform to attack the book. The world of print culture had been inundated with counter blasts (and would continue to be so throughout the first half of the eighteenth century in both Great Britain and the continent). Toland had been subject to personal vilification in newspapers and broadsides. Two national institutions, one civil and one spiritual, had also turned their authority and power against the text. Toland in each case presented himself as a reasonable and adaptable controversialist, willing to defend but also to compromise. Importantly, he consistently defended his right to publish such opinion, and more importantly his duty to defend himself against both political and religious authority. It was this *performance* of public dissent which was almost more significant than the intellectual or theological propositions advanced by Toland in *Christianity not mysterious*.

Christianity not mysterious has traditionally been understood as part of the ongoing debate about the nature of the Trinity that convulsed theological discourse in the 1690s.[54] In particular the relationship between *Christianity not mysterious* and John Locke's *The Reasonableness of Christianity* (1695) and the critical reception of the latter work within an anti-Trinitarian context, has meant that historiography has commonly seen Toland's work as a subversive and insidious attack upon the Trinity.[55] It is clear that Toland exploited non-Trinitarian sources on 'mystery' in his book, although he refuted the label socinian.[56] Many contemporaries also assumed that in removing mystery from religious belief Toland intended to strike a blow at the doctrine of the

Trinity. Anglican theology defended the doctrine as a matter of faith – if not contrary to reason, then certainly above rational understanding. Explaining precisely how the doctrine of the Trinity was to be understood and how it fitted into the broader texture of Protestant soteriology had bedevilled the Church in the 1690s, with many hyper-orthodox Churchmen arguing themselves into heresy in the very act of trying to defend the Athanasian Creed. Although the arguments of *Christianity not mysterious* had clear implications for the Trinity, Toland allowed his readers to pursue those implications for themselves: his purpose was to engage, not with the details of any specific theological doctrine, but with a more fundamental discussion of the politics of knowledge.

The epistemological context of Toland's discussion has often led historians to indicate the intellectual intimacies between *Christianity not mysterious* and John Locke's *Essay concerning human understanding* (1690).[57] Certainly Edward Stillingfleet, Bishop of Worcester, attempted to tar Locke's work with Toland's intellectual consequences, much to Locke's disgust and horror.[58] Toland acknowledged that he had borrowed key concepts (in particular the distinction between nominal and real essences), but denied that Locke's *Essay* was a fundamental influence.[59] Reiterating this point some twenty years later Toland commented against the accusations of a clerical antagonist 'now this is to inform all those who have not read Xtianity not mysterious, that I have never nam'd Mr Locke in any edition of that book: & that far from quoting him, I have not as much as brought one Quotation out of him to support notions he never dreamed of'. Locke merely commented that Toland 'says something which has a conformity with some notions in my book, but it is to be observed, he speaks them as his own thoughts, & not upon my Authority, nor with taking any notice of me'. Reviewing the Stillingfleet–Locke debate, Toland proudly noted that 'The Bishop himself was forc'd at last to own, that Mr Locke & I went upon different grounds; nay he averr'd that mine were the better'.[60]

Toland's appreciation of his own intellectual worth undoubtedly led him to draw a sharper distinction between his own thought and that of Locke. The two men had very different purposes in their writings. Locke had devoted careful thought and attention to preserving the epistemic distinction between matters of 'Faith' and 'Knowledge' in the *Essay* (Book IV Chapter xviii). Toland, on the other hand, was to collapse Locke's distinction by the assertion that 'Faith is knowledge'.[61] Both men pursued a resolution to the perennial debate about the legitimate 'rule of faith' in questions of religious belief. Locke set out to resolve a specific theological enquiry with philosophical tools: his objective was to provide a level of functional theological certainty for the true believer. Toland, as we will see, was concerned with epistemological certainty too, but the context for the performance of that certainty was not theological truth but a broader social community. Whereas Locke intended to enfranchise the human intellect with the potential competence to understand theological propositions, Toland attempted to lay epistemological foundations for the conduct of authentic civil and social relations.

Whereas Locke's epistemic system still looked to heaven, Toland's was rooted in social understandings of the production of knowledge. Negotiating the different epistemological relationships between faith and knowledge held implications for both the relationship between individual conscience and public authority, but also for the important institutional nexus between believer and church. These debates were more than merely intellectual debates but constitutive of the cultural structures of social power in the period. This theme of the challenge to the epistemological competence of the Church was pronounced and highlighted in the many clerical responses to *Christianity not mysterious*. The central link was made between Toland's account of the capacity of human reason and the consequent negation of clerical authority in the exposition of religious truth. As Richard Willis wrote 'when they would convince us of the uselessness of the Clergy, they tell us that the Scripture has deliver'd our Duty in such a plain and excellent manner, that the meanest capacity may understand it without the assistance of a Teacher, or the Trouble of Thought and Study'.[62] For Willis the priesthood was part of the providential means of preserving and elucidating the true word of God. Reason had to be tied to learning in order to render scripture 'perspicacious'. Divine providence had preserved the texts of scripture and the 'monuments and antiquities of history', and more importantly an 'order of men ... whose particular duty and business it is ... to understand and deliver the meaning of the Scriptures'. Such a 'right understanding' was to be disseminated 'whether by Publick Preaching, or by private application to the consciences of particular persons'.[63] Human reason was, in general, too fallible to understand all the mysteries of God without the aid of authority, either in the form of God's revelation or clerical declaration.

Toland claimed that men could read and think for themselves. His opponents challenged this optimistic description of a universally proficient human reason. Matters of divine truth were often elusive to human reason. The proposition that evidence was more important in matters of belief than the injunctions of authority was also refuted. God's authority, mediated though the Church, was and should be persuasive. John Norris, rector of Bemerton near Sarum, pursued these dual themes in his lengthy rejoinder. Toland's work was 'one of the most bold, daring and irreverent pieces of defiance to the mysteries of the Christian Religion that ever this Licentious Age has produced'.[64] Norris appealed to his readers to deconstruct Toland's general arguments by applying his criticisms.[65] The battle of the books was on. Human reason was 'not the measure of truth'. To suggest, as Toland and the Socinians did, that 'nothing is to be believ'd as revealed by God, that is above the comprehension of Human Reason; or, that a man is to believe nothing but what he can comprehend', was either to 'Humanize God' or 'Deify themselves and their own Rational abilities'.[66] Faith, unlike reason, was certain. True faith differed from all other forms of intellectual assent because it had 'no evidence at all, but only Authority for its ground'.[67] Faith was an act of belief prompted by divine authority without 'regard to Evidence'.[68] The strength of conviction brought by such faith was superior to the testimony of the finite capacities of human reason which was merely contingent and derivative from the 'necessary and eternal' truth of divine reason. Since truth was 'incomprehensible' to human reason 'we should not vainly go about to comprehend it, but be contented to be ignorant in many things'.[69]

The pronouncement that authority rather than evidence was the foundation of certain belief was at the heart of Peter Browne's censure of *Christianity not mysterious*. Toland had made two mistakes: the first (in logic) by insisting that 'evidence is the only ground of persuasion', and the second (in divinity) 'that now under the Gospel the veil is perfectly lifted'.[70] Revelation would ever dominate corrupt reason: 'and therefore I say it again, in opposition to this insolent man, that I thus *adore what I cannot comprehend*'.[71] Browne found fault with the anticlerical implications of Toland's discussion of human rationality.[72] The cognate thrust of Thomas Beverley's reply to *Christianity not mysterious* can be deduced from the sub-title of his pamphlet which asserted that 'Christianity is above Created reason, in its pure estate. And contrary to humane reason, as false and corrupted; and therefore in a proper sense, Mystery'. Toland had attempted to promote the 'Dead Child of reason and free-will' against the 'living Spirituous Christianity of the Scriptures'.[73] William Payne's sermons against *Christianity not mysterious* echoed these essays by insisting on the 'Infallibility and Authority of Divine revelation' against the feeble claims of reason.[74] Similarly, Oliver Hill affirmed that without the inspiration of faith and revelation natural reason was 'nothing'.[75] Churchmen were in broad agreement: Toland's defence of reason against the claims of faith compromised not only godliness but their authority too.

Jean Gailhard joined in too. Human reason was 'subject to error, a meer Chimera and fancy of man's shallow brain' fit only for natural knowledge 'for supernatural it must be supernaturally endowed'.[76] Divine knowledge was 'the Gift of God'.[77] Revelation transformed the disabled faculties of human understanding: 'God gives a new Heart, a new Spirit, new Thoughts, new Affections'. Without such inspiration human reason 'can no more know the nature of God and his attributes, than a little Bottle hold in all the water of the sea'.[78] Making religion depend on the senses rather than faith was Toland's sin. Faith for Gailhard was 'a strong perswasion, grounded and built not upon reason, but upon God's gracious and special Promises, infus'd into us by the Holy Ghost'.[79] For Gailhard the emphasis Toland laid upon the capacity of reason led to social bedlam and anarchy.[80] He insisted that although every private man might read scripture they could make no 'human private interpretation'. He acknowledged that all Protestants had the liberty to read Scriptures, but denied that this necessarily led to a right of interpretation: the conscience must be bound by a correct interpretation of Scripture established by the Church.[81] Richard Willis reinforced these suggestions by insisting that the clergy and church were the 'stewards of the mysteries of God'.[82]

For the Churchmen, Toland's arguments corroded ecclesiastical power by challenging their spiritual authority. Attempting to encourage or sanction the use of reason by private individuals was theological anathema. Indeed many of Toland's antagonists were not only unhappy with the nature of his arguments but also with the printed form of *Christianity not mysterious* itself. The book allowed and invited its readers to come to their own conclusions, rather than telling them what to believe. As Oliver Hill complained, Toland left 'his reader, like the clergymen of Rome (who arraign, Try and Condemn, then deliver to others to pronounce and execute their sentence on the patient), the conclusion to gather, which he makes ready for him'. By continually asserting that the Christian religion was mysterious Toland 'left to the reader' the conclusion that the Trinity was false.[83] Peter Browne, referring to the pretensions of the work as suitable only to be a 'sticht pamphlet ... cry'd about with Almanacks', also protested that 'all his Discourse is a meer rope of sand; many bold and false assertions, sly insinuations, and several things, nothing at all to the question, huddled up together on purpose to patch up a book; and amuse such persons who have just Logick enough to be imposed upon by a Fallacy, but not enough to see through it'.[84] Toland had written a book that both in its content and form un-picked the seams of clerical authority.

Toland was portrayed as manipulating his readers, most spectacularly in his abuse of scripture citation. Browne made the charge in robust terms: 'do but look over every text he hath quoted by way of proof, and try to make his inferences from it, and you will be satisfied that Quaker, or any other enthusiast never apply'd Scripture so impertinently'.[85] The consequence of Toland's insinuation would be that one must 'lay aside your Bibles, those lively oracles, (after you have read the Historical part of them) and let Reason be your only guide'.[86] Toland's antagonists were profoundly aware of the process of reading and readership that underlay the power of his book. They speculated about how the reader would digest and reflect upon *Christianity not mysterious*: one clear implication being that Toland's book would be read side by side with the Bible out of the purview of the clerical eye. This process of reading was perceived as potentially tremendously corrosive of cultural order. At least for the clergyman, such books did provoke revolution.

Turning to *Christianity not mysterious* itself it is possible to applaud the acuity of Toland's critics. In his preface, Toland defended the right of all men to speak 'their Minds in publick'. His own intellectual disposition was 'accustom'd to Examination and Enquiry': from an early age he had been taught 'not to captivate my understanding, no more than my senses to any man or society whatsoever'. His purpose was to encourage his readers to a similar liberty of enquiry especially in matters of religion which was 'calculated for reasonable creatures [so] 'tis conviction and not authority that should bear the weight with them'. Toland wrote against claims to infallibility whether 'popish' or Protestant.[87] The purpose of the book was to impeach 'all corrupt clergymen ... who make a meer trade of religion, and build an unjust Authority upon the abus'd consciences of the Laity'. Importantly (and dangerously) Toland declared his text was designed for the 'vulgar' and 'poor' rather than the 'philosopher'. He had worked hard to write with a clarity of style. He commented, 'I have in many places made explanatory repetitions of difficult words, by synonymous terms of a more general and known use'. The 'vulgar' could 'likewise be judges of the true sense of things, tho they understand nothing of the Tongues from whence they are translated for their use'.[88] In parts a technical treatise about the relationship between reason and faith, *Christianity not mysterious* was persistently given a practical slant, relating such philosophical discussions to the circumstances and practices of reading and thinking. As some of Toland's critics had perceived *Christianity not mysterious* was designed to be read side by side with the Bible: it was as much an advice book on how to read Scripture as a meditative dissertation.

The key themes were simple. The work unpicked deference and tutelage to the clerical 'Doctor'.[89] The combination of epistemological confidence (every man may believe according to his own sense) and political liberty (establishing toleration) would establish a system of intellectual liberty. This was central to Toland's lifetime project. Importantly, for Toland the liberty enshrined in this process of enlightenment was prompted by the act of reading. The act of (free) reading would have an effect on the social relationship between parishioner and cleric as well as an intellectual outcome. Despite the epistemological sophistication of *Christianity not mysterious*, Toland's objective was to advance a way of reading Scripture. His account of reason and faith suggested that true conviction was achieved by an individual understanding the Bible, unhampered by clerical doctrine and metaphysical mystery. Reason was the foundation of all certitude. Knowledge was defined as 'the perception of the agreement or disagreement of our ideas in a greater of lesser number, whereinsoever this Agreement or Disagreement may consist'.[90]

Crucially, Toland made the distinction between what he called the 'means of information' and the 'ground of perswasion' in the construction of beliefs. A rational assessment of the evidence, established through the 'means of information', caused assent to a proposition. God had predisposed humanity to accept and assent to proper evidence rather than capitulate before the injunctions of authority. He had 'put us under a Law of bowing before the light and majesty of evidence. And truly if we might doubt of anything that is clear, or be deceiv'd by distinct conceptions, there could be nothing certain: neither conscience nor God himself, should be regarded: no society or government could subsist'.[91] Revelation was, for Toland, 'not a necessitating motive of assent, but a means of information'.[92] This was contrary to commonplace Protestant notions which insisted that Revelation provoked assent by authority because it was the Word of God. For Toland, belief was prompted by correct understanding created by a rational assessment of the means of information. Men should believe nothing without evidence. It was thus 'not the bare Authority of him that speaks, but the clear conception I form of what he says, [which] is the ground of my perswasion'. Scripture must be read carefully and understood: 'the question is not about the Words, but their sense'.

There was for Toland no difference in the rules of interpretation to be followed in Scripture than 'what is common to all other books'.[93] He answered theological objections. Reason was not debilitated by sin, because corruption was cultural and individual rather than implicit in the human condition: 'there is no defect in our Understanding but those of our own creation, that is to say, vicious habits easily contracted, but with difficulty reformed'. Indulgence of our inclinations and debauched imaginations could lead us to ignorance and deceit but also could be transcended.[94] Toland blithely redefined 'faith' in a similarly robust manner. The word 'faith' simply 'imports Belief or Perswasion, as when we give credit to anything which is told us by God or Man'. Divine faith was of two varieties 'either when God speaks to us immediately himself, or when we acquiesce in the words or writings of those to whom we believe he has spoken'. As he continued, again explicitly and intentionally undercutting clerical understandings of faith as a gift of divine grace, 'all *faith* now in the world is of this last sort and by consequence entirely built upon *Ratiocination*'.[95] All faith was thus based on understanding: citing Romans 10.17 he explained '*Faith* is likewise said to *come by hearing;* but without understanding 'tis plain this hearing would signify nothing, Words and their ideas being reciprocal in all languages'.[96] Toland further illustrated this claim that faith was simply a state of believing, rather than a theological condition, by interpreting the Biblical actions of Abraham's willingness to sacrifice Isaac as an example of 'faith' as a process of 'very strict reasoning'. Hebrews 11.17–19 was thus interpreted as testimony to the power of Abraham's ability to reason about God's intentions towards him and Isaac: this directly contradicted the commonplace citation of the incident as an example of the blind faith demanded by God's authority.[97]

Faith was shorthand for indicating that an individual understood what they believed. Faith was knowledge. This was not to take away from the importance of revelation: it provided the means to inform humanity of God 'whilst the evidence of the subject persuades us'. Reason did not exceed revelation but was the means to understand it 'just as much as a Greek Grammar is superior to the New Testament; for we make use of Grammar to understand the language, and of reason to comprehend the sense of that Book'. Both reason and revelation came from God.[98] It was precisely because of the universality of reason and the accessibility of revelation that Toland compounded his heterodoxy by continuing to insist that even the poor could achieve such 'faith'.[99]

The bulk of *Christianity not mysterious* was devoted to an exegesis of scriptural passages to prove Toland's arguments about the reasonableness of Christian doctrine. Toland scrutinised the use of the word 'mystery'. Producing a concordance for the word showed that it was commonly used to mean something hidden and obscured, rather than incomprehensible. The New Testament always used the word in the sense of something hidden.[100] Christ had taken the veil away and rendered the 'mystery' of religion manifest. To aid the reader, Toland then proceeded to transcribe 'all the passages of the New Testament where the word mystery occurs, [so] that a man running may read with conviction what I defend'.[101] The point was that Toland wanted his readers to examine the scriptural evidence for themselves without recourse to the assistance of the Church. He cleverly grafted his anticlerical assault upon the Church onto his lexical account of the meaning of the word 'mystery'. Although he refused to comment in detail on the use of the word mystery in the Revelation of John, in the second edition of *Christianity not mysterious* Toland expanded his extracts insisting that, as he put it, 'that mystery is here made the distinguishing mark of the false or Antichristian Church'. As least one contemporary complained that Toland in this way made undue and insinuating reflections upon the Church of England.[102]

Toland established how manipulation of the concepts of mystery had been institutionalised by the Christian clergy after the second century. As he commented 'here's enough to show how Christianity became mysterious, and how so divine an institution did, through the craft and ambition of priests and philosophers, degenerate into mere paganism'. Priestly fraud monopolised 'the sole right of interpreting scripture and with it [a] claim'd infallibility, to their body', unfortunately, as Toland noted, 'and so it continues, in a great measure, to this day'.[103] Toland wanted his readers to think and believe for themselves. As he argued, 'how can any be sure that the scripture contains all things necessary to salvation, till he first reads it over? Nay, how can he conclude it to be Scripture, or the word of God, till he exactly studies it, to speak now of no other means he must use?'[104] Throughout the text there were injunctions to the reader to consult Scripture for themselves; at points Toland appealed to this extra-textual reading to confirm his own arguments.[105] It was his declared intention simply to provoke the reader to pursue their own beliefs rather than impose a particular view.[106] As he noted 'no particular Hypothesis whatsoever has a right to set up for a standard of reason to all mankind ... and so far am I from aiming at any such thing, that it is the very practice I oppose in this book'.[107]

Toland wanted to shatter the clerical ambition of establishing a conformity of beliefs to doctrinal orthodoxy. Truth was the product of individual rationality rather than a pattern determined by eternal verities. He hoped *Christianity not mysterious* had been successful in 'convincing people that all the parts of their RELIGION must not only be in themselves, but to themselves also must appear, sound and intelligible'. That achieved, he continued, 'I might justly leave everyone to discover to himself the reasonableness or unreasonableness of his religion (which is no difficult business, when once Men are perswaded that they have a right to do it)'.[108] These arguments provoked opposition because they corroded contemporary assumptions about the relationship between private belief and public authority. Toland's account of belief and conviction devolved authority away from public institutions into the private epistemological world of the individual conscience, scholarship and erudition. Libraries rather than churches became the spaces for making conviction. Books rather than priests became instruments of cultural value.

Unlike his clerical antagonists, Toland was confident about the possibility of building political stability upon this ground-bed of diverse and (perhaps) conflicting beliefs. For him, the origins of political authority lay in the civic pursuit of reason, rather than in merely establishing protection. One of Toland's earliest critics had suggested that his religious doctrines, rooted so firmly in conceptions of reason, held implications for the political order, in other words that just as religion was founded in reason so would dominion be. Toland embraced and reinforced this notion in his reply.[109] Civic rationality was the cultural infrastructure that Toland argued would be the consequence of freeing private conscience from tutelage to priests. Recovering from the bitter and dangerous reception conjured up by *Christianity not mysterious* Toland, in the later 1690s, turned to developing a more fully articulated political theory in defence of these liberties.

NOTES

1 A. Boyer *The political state of Great Britain* XXIII (1722) p. 342.

2 BL Add Ms 5853 fo. 385.

3 *Collections* 2 pp. 301–304.

4 *Ibid.* pp. 309–313.

5 See *Correspondence* V No 29.

6 See J. A. I. Champion 'John Toland: the politics of Pantheism' *Revue de Synthèse* 116

(1995) pp. 259–280. A more detailed account of the prosecution of *Christianity not mysterious* can be found in J. A. I. Champion 'Making authority: belief, conviction and reason in the public sphere in late seventeenth century England.' In *Libertinage et philosophie au XVIIe siècle. Le Public et le Privé* (1999) pp. 143–190.

7   *Tolandiana* p. 39.

8   See *Tolandiana* p. 28.

9   Toland *Vindicus Liberus* (1702) pp. 80, 104.

10 *Tolandiana* pp. 92, 320.

11 N. Lutterell *A brief historical narration of state affairs* 6 volumes (Oxford, 1857) IV pp. 226–227.

12 J. Gailhard *The epistle and preface to the book against the blasphemous Socinian heresie vindicated and the charge against Socinianism made good* (1698) pp. 81–82.

13 See J. Spurr 'The Church, the societies and the moral revolution of 1688' in J. Walsh, C. Heydon and S. Taylor (eds) *The Church of England c. 1689–c. 1833* (ed.) (Cambridge, 1993) pp. 127–142.

14 See D. Hayton 'Moral reform and country politics in the late seventeenth century House of Commons' *Past and Present* 128 (1990) pp. 48–91.

15 See *Calender of State Papers Domestic* 1698 p. 107; Hayton 'Moral reform' pp. 58–59.

16 Gailhard *Epistle* p. 81.

17 J. Gailhard *The blasphemous Socinian heresy* (1697) Epistle Dedicatory [unpaginated] pp. A3, A3r, A5r–A6, A6r, a3–a3r.

18 *Ibid.* Preface [unpaginated] pp. i–ii.

19 See M. Hunter 'Aikenhead the Atheist' in M. Hunter and D. Wootton (eds) *Atheism from the Reformation to the Enlightenment* (Oxford, 1992).

20 Anon *An apology for the Parliament, humbly representing to Mr John Gailhard some REASON why they did not at his request enact Sanguinary Laws against Protestants in their last session* (1697) pp. 3, 5, 6–7, 9–10.

21 Gailhard *Blasphemous* pp. 337, 320.

22 Gailhard *Epistle* pp. 5–6, 7, 13.

23 See A. D. Francis *The Methuens and Portugal 1691–1708* (Cambridge, 1966) pp. 356–358.

24 *Correspondence* IV 1646 p. 705.

25 *Correspondence* IV 1650 pp. 710–711.

26 *Correspondence* VI 2221 pp. 40–41.

27 *Correspondence* VI 2239 p. 80.

28 *Correspondence* VI 2240 pp. 82–83.

29 *Correspondence* VI 2254 p. 105–106.

30 *Correspondence* VI 2269 pp. 132–133.

31 *Correspondence* VI 2277 pp. 143–144.

32 See letters 2288 and 2311 *Correspondence* VI pp. 163–164, 192.

33 *Correspondence* VI 2269 at p. 133.

34 *Correspondence* VI 2288 p. 164.

35 Toland *An apology* pp. 5–6.

36 *Correspondence* VI 2311 at p. 192.

37 *Tolandiana* pp. 30–32.

38 Toland *An apology* pp. 4–5.

39 *Ibid.* pp. 6–7.

40 See *Journal of the House of Commons of Ireland* (Dublin, 1753–91) ii p. 903.

41 Toland *An apology* pp. 22–23.

42 *Ibid.*

43 See *Journal Ireland* ii 1697 pp. 903–904.

44 Toland *An apology* p. 25.

45 The text Toland condemned was *A letter to J.C. Esq upon Mr Toland's book* (Dublin, 1697).

46 See G. V. Bennett *The Tory crisis in Church and State 1688–1730* (Oxford, 1975).

47 See E. Cardwell *Synodolia* 2 volumes (Oxford, 1842) 2, pp. 701–705.

48 See M. Greig 'Heresy Hunt: Gilbert Burnet and the Convocation Controversy of 1701' *Historical Journal* 37 (1994) pp. 569–592.

49 See *Synodolia* 2 p. 706.

50 Toland *Vindicius Liberius* p. 1

51 *Ibid.* pp. 4, 6, 12–13.

52 *Ibid.* p. 16.

53 *Ibid.* p. 37.

54 G. Cragg *From Puritanism to the Age of Reason* (Cambridge, 1966).

55 See J. C. Biddle 'Locke's critique of innate principles and Toland's Deism' *Journal of the History of Ideas* (*JHI*) 37 (1976) pp. 411–422; D. D. Wallace 'Socinians, Justification by Faith and the sources of John Locke's Reasonableness of Christianity' *JHI* 45 (1986) pp. 49–67.

56 See G. Reedy 'Socinian, John Toland and the Anglican Rationalists' *Harvard Theological Review* 70 (1977) pp. 295–304.

57 See J. Yolton *John Locke and the Way of Ideas* (Oxford, 1956) pp. 110–126, 175–180.

58 *Correspondence* VI 2221 p. 40 and 2269 p. 132.

59 See *Christianity not mysterious* pp. 83, 87.

60 A contemporary transcription, possibly by Toland, also exists on a copy of Hare's sermon in Cambridge University Library call mark 8.2.51⁴.

61 *Christianity not mysterious* p. 139.

62 R. Willis *The Occasional Paper* (1697) p. 13.

63 *Ibid.* pp. 16, 25.

64 J. Norris *An Account of Reason and Faith* (1697) p. 4.

65 *Ibid.* p. 5.

66 *Ibid.* pp. 10, 14.

67 *Ibid.* pp. 53, 59.

68 *Ibid.* p. 89.

69 *Ibid.* p. 227.

70 P. Browne *A Letter in Answer to a Book intituled Christianity not mysterious* (Dublin, 1697) p. 4.

71 *Ibid.* p. 60.

72 *Ibid.* pp. 168–169.

73 T. Beverley *Christianity the great mystery* (1696) p. 4.

74 W. Payne *The mystery of the Christian Faith and of the Blessed Trinity vindicated* (1696) pp. 61–62.

75 O. Hill *A rod for the back of fools: in answer to a book of Mr John Toland called Christianity not mysterious* (1702) pp. 112–113.

76 Gailhard *Blasphemous* pp. 315–316.

77 *Ibid.* p. 320.

78 *Ibid.* p. 324.

79 *Ibid.* pp. 328, 332.

80 *Ibid.* p. 329.

81 Gailhard *Epistle* pp. 14–16.

82 Willis *Occasional paper* p. 22.

83 Hill *A rod* p. 18.

84 Browne *Letter* p. 81.

85 *Ibid.* p. 118.

86 *A Letter to JC Esq* (Dublin, 1697) p. 2.

87 *Christianity not mysterious* pp. iii, ix, xiv–xv.

88 *Ibid.* pp. xxx, xvii, xviii, xix.

89 *Ibid.* pp. 109–110.

90 *Ibid.* pp. 6, 12.

91 *Ibid.* pp. 22–23.

92 *Ibid.* pp. 38–39.

93 *Ibid.* pp. 34, 49.

94 *Ibid.* pp. 56–63 at 58.

95 *Ibid.* pp. 126, 127.

96 *Ibid.* p. 129.

97 *Ibid.* pp. 129–132.

98 *Ibid.* p. 140.

99   *Ibid.* p. 141.

100   *Ibid.* pp. 66–72.

101   *Ibid.* pp. 94–105.

102   Beverley *Christianity* pp. 53–54.

103   *Christianity not mysterious* pp. 162–163, 167, 169.

104   *Ibid.* p. xxv.

105   *Ibid.* p. 108.

106   See for example *Christianity not mysterious* p. 126.

107   *Ibid.* p. 122.

108   *Ibid.* p. 171.

109   See Browne *Letter* p. 173; Toland *An apology* pp. 13–14.

Part II

The war against
tyranny and prejudice

4

Editing the republic:
Milton, Harrington and the
Williamite monarchy, 1698–1714

A T some point in 1694, John Toland frequented Jack's Coffee House in King's Street, London. Recently arrived from Oxford, he struck up conversation with two persons 'wholly unknown to him'. Boldly he opened the discussion with a powerful statement of political identity: 'I am a common-wealth's Man, tho' I live at Whitehall, and that is a Mistery'. Continuing in this vein he challenged his auditors, 'if any man will give me Ten guineas, I will go to the King and Queen, and prove to their faces, that a Commonwealth is more fit for this Nation than Monarchy'.[1] Writing a little later in 1695, the philologist Edward Lhwyd commented upon the same young man who had impressed scholars in Oxford with his learning and abilities as 'being of excellent parts, but [with] as litle a share as may be of modesty or conscience'. With the reputation as being 'one of the best scolds I ever met with' Lhwyd noted too that Toland 'is eminent for railing in coffee houses against all communities in religion, and monarchy'.[2] By October of 1695, Dr Arthur Charlett wrote to Archbishop Tenison condemning Toland's notorious public behaviour that had prompted the Vice-Chancellor to banish him from the university. He was described as 'trampling on ye Common Prayer Book, talking against the scriptures, commending commonwealths, justifying the murder of K.C. Ist, railing against priests in general'. His insolent carriage made him contemp-tible to all: his parting shot, proclaiming all sorts of intimacies with 'some very great men', was that 'he should be a member of Parliament, and then should have an opportunity of being revenged on Priests and Universities'.[3]

It is quite clear then that amongst a variety of contemporaries in the 1690s (in Scotland, London and Oxford), Toland's reputation was as a violent and controversial firebrand, incautious in his enmity to the institution of monarchy, and disreputable in his religious conduct and beliefs. Although intelligent and pretending to learning, the violent nature of his temper had betrayed him in 'all places and countrys he has been in'.[4] It was no surprise then that contemporaries (especially clergymen) reviled the 'revived impertinences' of Toland's 'commonwealth fictions'. Toland was a 'spiteful young fellow' who had disturbed the 'sacred ashes' of Charles I's memory. In his assault on the Stuart monarchy and in particular on his attempted erasure of the commemorative sermons of 30 January, 'Milton Junior' executed 'as fatal a stroke to the Royal Martyr's reputation, as the Ax did his life'.[5]

Toland's radical disposition against the orthodoxies of Church and State had been rapidly established by his first ventures into print. While *Christianity not mysterious* advanced the claims of reason in religion, he also set about defending the sovereignty of reason in politics by undertaking the adventurous project of republishing the canonical works of the commonwealth tradition between 1697 and 1700. In both public projects Toland was cautious to stress his decorous approach to established Christian orthodoxy and political authority. Despite the furious disapproval of these works of the 1690s he publicly denied his intentions were incendiary. The reported coffee-house conduct of a man who railed against revelation and flung Scripture to the floor in the same breath as scolding the monarchy gives us an insight into Toland's less discreet aspirations. The starting point for this unorthodox political theory was a condemnation of divine right monarchy.

Printed in the '10th year of our redemption from Popery and Slavery' the short pamphlet *King Charles I. No such Saint, martyr, or Good Protestant as commonly reputed* (1698) made extraordinarily clear the author's commitment to an anticlerical republicanism. Vilifying Charles I as a 'cruel and oppressive Tyrant', Toland cast off the 'gaudy name of Majesty' as not only a religious but 'a civil kind of idolatry'. The Anglican obsession with the reputation of the (so-called) martyred king, Charles I, enshrined in the commemorative services on 30 January, was *au fond* the cause of contemporary political corruption. The pernicious tyranny of the Stuart monarchy was forged by a corrupt conspiracy of King, courtiers and clergy. This confederation was on-going. Charles I had encouraged the 'worst and corruptest sort of courtiers' and 'the most ignorant, profane and vicious clergy, learned in nothing but their pride, their covetousness and superstition'. Using the powerful resources of press and pulpit, the clergy reduced the people to the 'bondage of Tyranny and superstition' by inculcating a series of 'abominable enslaving doctrines' like passive obedience, non-resistance, and 'Obeying without reserve'. Such 'horrid notions' were enough to corrupt 'the best prince, and enslave the freest people'. Invoking the rights of the 'freeborn English man' and the injunctions of 'salus populi est suprema lex', Toland succinctly deployed the central aphorisms of popular sovereignty and resistance theory against divine right monarchy and passive obedience. His point was to hammer home that 'rebellion consists in resisting of just Governors in their just Government, and not in defending legal rights against a Tyrant'. The causes of this tyrannous corruption were obvious: 'why do the generality of the clergy and laity so much adore and idolise all Monarchy (whether good or bad) above the people?' The answer was manifest: wicked priests. Far from being the 'Christian advocates for the rights and privileges of millions of people', the clergy made 'miserable and lasting slaves'.[6]

One of the persistent claims made by contemporaries about republicans like John Toland forged the connection with the 'Calves-Head' club. Republicans were conspiring, seditious regicides plotting the destruction of monarchy. Occasions like the 30 January anniversary became powerful platforms for fixing the image of regicide in public discourse. The memory of 1649 was a starting point from which to condemn any political ideology that deviated from the shibboleths of *de jure divino* accounts of monarchy. That such occasions clearly caused not only conceptual difficulties, but also problems of 'image management' to the mainstream Whig publicists can be seen as testimony to the success of the projection of the 'Calves-Head' conspiracy by figures like Edward Ward. The tradition was an 'invention' of conservative propaganda, akin to the processes of popular print culture that projected anxieties about religious heterodoxy onto a national canvas under the name of the 'Ranters' in the early 1650s. The origins of the literary tradition can be located in Edward Ward's *The secret history of the Calves Head Clubb, or the republican unmasqu'd* published in 1703. Ward, sometime publican, was one of the marginal figures of London literary life who published a huge range of coarse anti-Whig material. Pilloried twice in 1705 for his attacks upon the ministry, Ward was an imaginative and satirical writer immersed in the popular political culture of London.

According to Ward, John Milton was the founder of the club. The republication of his works was a sign of resurgent regicidal aspirations. Ward cited the evidence of an 'active Whigg' who noted that although the meeting had taken place with a 'great deal of precaution' after the Restoration, by the 1690s it met 'almost in a publick manner, and apprehend nothing'.[7] Describing in detail the ceremonies of the club (meeting in Moorfields) Ward explained the republican meanings of the foods and anthems celebrated. The high point was the 'Anniversary Anthem' which was sung in combination with a 'Calves-Skull fill'd with wine or other Liquor' toasting 'the pious memory of those worthy Patriots that had killed the Tyrant, and deliver'd their country from his arbitrary sway'. Added to this historical introduction were transcriptions of these republican 'anniversary thanksgiving songs'. Between 1703 and 1714 the *Secret history* was published in at least nine editions in London, and two further in Dublin. More importantly the volume of the edition kept expanding from the slight pamphlet of 22 pages in 1703 to a more weighty book of over 220 pages. These subsequent editions 'with large

improvements' included more 'anthems', as well as supplementary vindications of the Royal martyr and polemics against 'Presbyterians' and 'modern
Whigs'. By 1707 a description of the Calves Head club 'curiously engrav'd on a
copper plate' gave a more visual dimension to the tradition. This was the
backcloth against which Toland had to paint his political theory.

The point of the *Secret history* was to rivet the connection between 'the
hellish mysteries of old republican rebellion' and 'the Whiggish faction'.[8]
Although there was little contemporary evidence for the existence of such a
club the power of Ward's writing was such that it created a powerful tradition
for stigmatising any who advanced republican ideas.[9] John Toland was right
at the heart of this political project both in terms of the production of books
and political patronage. Unpacking how Toland was able to balance his
defence of commonwealth principles against these hostile assertions that all
such argument was by necessity regicidal will be critical to establishing his
intentions. Like Ward and his contemporaries, the general assumption that
republicanism was by definition regicidal has penetrated deep into the seams
of modern historiography. As Worden has established in the case of the
works of the regicide Edmund Ludlow, the act of making republicanism
respectable was achieved by editorial methods rather than by conceptual
innovation. Toland packaged an older violent republicanism for a more
respectable audience by wielding a keen editorial knife.[10] Hostility towards
the regicidal reputation of interregnum republicanism, cultivated by the
rhetoric of the martyrdom of Charles I and the projection of the Calves-Head
myth, meant that in order to promote an effective political ideology in the
1690s republicans were forced to distance themselves from the antimonarchical and regicidal elements of their legacy.[11] After 1689, republicanism
became a 'language' rather than a 'programme'. As the politics of corruption
replaced that of revolutions, the central issues became the campaigns against
ministerial bribery, patronage, and the standing army, rather than opposition
to kingship.[12]

Republicanism then became more Tacitean, adapted to the political
problems of life under a king, rather than those of the Republic.[13] 'Commonwealth' language came to share many political objectives with the 'country
interest' of the early eighteenth century.[14] As the trajectory of political employment from the early 1690s to the 1700s turned oppositional voices into
established ones, so the radicalism of republicanism became moderated.[15]
Tactical accommodation rather than covert incendiary principle became the by-
word of political ambition. The point to stress here is that in Toland's hands
'republican' tradition became one of the most powerful ways of defending the
Protestant succession. As we will see, Toland understood this republican discourse to be entirely compatible with virtuous monarchy (in the form of
William III, or Sophia of Hanover), but fundamentally opposed to clericalist

accounts of the divinity of political authority. The sharp edge of republican thinking was to be turned against priests rather than kings. For Toland, the pursuit of respectability was not the result of conceding on true political principle, but a means to obtain a powerful instrument of civic reform.

Unsurprisingly, contemporary clergymen were profoundly apprehensive that a vibrant republicanism did persist into the 1700s. Toland did little to assuage their fears. Far from avoiding regicidal tradition, he deliberately set out to make the works of the 1650s available to a new audience. Despite the association with the regicidal memory of 1649 he devoted considerable time and effort to republishing works, which by their very nature, would reinforce rather than fracture such a link. Admittedly, especially in the case of Ludlow, many of the 'puritan' elements of his subject's prose were purged. As Worden has explained, the result of this editorial work was that 'far from converting country Whigs to republicanism, Toland helped to adapt republicanism to country Whig ends'.[16] This process of editorial appropriation requires some further scrutiny. During the course of the 1690s Toland published editions of works by Harrington, Sidney, Milton, Holles and Monck. Very little attention has been paid to the production, editorial intervention, and (perhaps most importantly) reception of these works. Many scholars agree that Toland's labours were critical in the transmission of republican ideas to the eighteenth century. As John Pocock has put it, Toland was the myth maker of English republican theory.[17]

As archivist of republican tradition, Toland made the eighteenth-century canon of writings that were later repeatedly republished through Europe and America. It was his editions that lined the shelves of many country house libraries.[18] The act of making these editions involved the editor (and presumably printer-publishers) in a considerable amount of labour. Copies of the original texts (either printed or scribal) had to be located, identified and then prepared for publication. Coupled with this administrative work were intellectual and political decisions about which texts would be produced, when, and in what form. Appropriation of texts from the 1650s involved an element of political imagination. Publishing them into a context that embraced traditions of monarchical authority was an act of courage. So Toland confronted, as editor, intellectual, textual and political problems. He was not simply recovering and refurbishing a tradition, but trying to do something practical in political terms.[19] Toland set out to compose republican arguments in the times of kings. In order to be effective he needed to accommodate his politics to circumstance. To do this without sacrificing his commitment to principle was a skilful achievement.[20] Like those who wrote under the Protectorate, Toland and his friends had to engage with the figure of the legislator or prince within the constitution. The irony that the safety of Protestantism was only secured by the British monarchy had not escaped Toland. Indeed the integrity of the regime became an increasingly delicate political question. Toland's response was to design 'republican' defences of the monarchy against the divine right claims of the tyrannous Stuarts.

John Toland was critical to the survival and persistence of republicanism after 1689. From the early 1690s to the early 1720s Toland was intimately involved with the public circulation of republican writings, ranging from the so-called 'Ludlow' pamphlets, through the canonical editions and anti-corruption works of 1698–1700, to the later writings defending the legitimacy of the 'limitations' upon monarchy and the programmatic manifestos of works like the tremendously popular *State anatomy of Great Britain* (1717). At different moments in his life Toland engaged with the tasks of politics and political communication in different ways. Sometimes he wrote detached works of political theory (or at least edited them); at other times, he engaged in polemics over particular political issues or debates. He also contributed a variety of practical 'memorials' reflecting upon the state of politics for men like Harley, Molesworth and Shaftesbury. Whether in print, in conversation, or in works of scribal advice, Toland projected himself as committed to the principles of liberty and toleration in both civil and religious matters. As he was to admit in private correspondence he would collaborate with any political figure to achieve the ends of liberty and freedom.[21]

Collaborating with men of political stature like John Trenchard, Walter Moyle, Robert Molesworth and Lord Ashley on the production of pamphlets attacking mercenary parliaments, standing armies, and the dangers of courtly patronage, Toland was intimate with the elite of republican politicians. At the very time when he was preparing his printed defence against the prosecution of *Christianity not mysterious* by Convocation, Toland was also working upon the editions of Milton, Ludlow, Sidney and Harrington. In terms of the sheer number of words and pages produced this was a Herculean task. The Sidney and Harrington volumes (1698, 1700) totalled together a sum of over a thousand pages of folio print. The Ludlow papers ran to over four hundred octavo pages, while the Holles memoirs were over two hundred quarto pages. One printer-publisher, John Darby (d.1704) convicted in 1684 for printing the libel *Lord Russell's speech* and regarded as a 'true assertor of English liberties', was responsible for the majority of this publication (the works by Ludlow, Milton, Sidney and Harrington). The remaining item, the *Memoirs* of Denzil Holles, were published by Tim Goodwin, an associate of Darby and also publisher of Robert Molesworth's controversial *An account of Denmark* (1694).[22] The Holles memoirs were regarded as useful contextual material for comparison with Ludlow's account.[23] Certainly, advertising material in (for example) later editions of Sidney's *Discourses* (1704) suggested that all these works were available through Darby's shop, even though initial imprints suggested other locations for their origins. The works did good business although they did not make Toland's fortune.

It was clear Toland needed collaborators to make these editions. As he acknowledged in both the editions of Harrington and Milton he had received rare or unpublished materials from families or contemporaries.[24] There is evidence to suggest that scribal copies of such republican material were in circulation in the 1690s. Sir Robert Southwell, Hans Sloane and Robert Harley owned copies of versions and extracts from *Oceana*.[25] Toland knew Southwell's son, and Robert Harley was supposed to have been one of the sponsors of the Harrington edition.[26] How the 'original' manuscript for the reproduction of Algernon Sidney's *Discourses*, came into Toland's hands is unknown. The papers had been preserved by the printing community surrounding John Darby and Richard and Abigail Baldwin. Whether they had been kept by Sidney's intimate Benjamin Furly and passed on to Toland by Shaftesbury is impossible to know. There is clear evidence to suggest that, at least in the case of the works of Harrington, both Shaftesbury and Furly collaborated in distributing the works amongst like-minded men in Holland.[27]

The dedications of these editions establish a circle of influence in which Toland operated. The Milton edition was dedicated to Thomas Raulins of Herefordshire, an intimate with whom Toland corresponded until 1714. He was directly involved in the printing contract between Toland and John Darby.[28] Possibly a member of Shaftesbury's 'independent club', Raulins was a trustee with John Trenchard of the Irish Forfeitures.[29] He was also named as one of Toland's London circle in the later 1690s by William Simpson, and associated with the radical Whig alderman Sir Robert Clayton.[30] The Holles *Memoirs* were dedicated to John, Duke of Newcastle, staunch Whig and Williamite, one of the wealthiest men in the kingdom who had encouraged Toland to publish the work. In 1705 Toland was to describe Newcastle as 'my true friend' who had 'been constantly infusing into me sentiments of peace and moderation, the profoundest respect for the Queen's Majesty and Government, and a largeness of soul towards all denominations of Englishmen'.[31] Newcastle, a friend of men like Somers, Shaftesbury, and the young James Stanhope, was also the dedicatee of Toland's important work *Anglia Libera* (1701). Throughout the 1690s and 1700s he was a key political figure in the elite sociability of the Whig party.[32] Publishing the memoirs of the 'famous Lord Holles, Your Great Uncle', a man who 'took up arms, not to destroy the King, or alter the constitution, but to restore the last, and oblige the former to rule according to Law', was intended as an incentive to Newcastle.[33] The Harrington volume was dedicated to the 'Lord Mayor, Aldermen, Sheriffs and Common council of London': the key figure here was Sir Robert Clayton (d. 1707) former Exclusionist MP, Lord Mayor of London and successful banker.[34] Clayton's Whig credentials were unimpeachable, he also attempted to encourage support for Toland and possibly finance for the publication.[35] In December 1698 Toland exchanged letters with Clayton consoling him on the death of his nephew with whom Toland had studied at Oxford.[36] It is possible that Clayton contemplated using his parliamentary interest in Surrey to get Toland elected to the House of Commons.[37]

It is important to stress then that Toland's project was not solitary but collaborative. In publishing these works he was not alone. The point of publication was as much to expose and identify the common political interest, as the ideas of the texts themselves. The production of the works involved a community of individuals of a variety of social and political status: dukes, earls, lords and MPs, as well as printers and publishers were involved. Whether providing the textual material for publication, financing the printing costs, typesetting the words, advertising the books, or lending cultural status by being identified as willing recipients of dedications, the publications are not simple evidence of Toland's singular role, but of his involvement in a much broader political community. Some of these men were also part of a more private circle of influence and conversation. Although the works were produced with significant public support from leading political figures like Shaftesbury, Newcastle, Molesworth and Harley they courted immediate controversy. In particular, Toland's edition of Milton 'the great Anti-monarchist', and more specifically his biography of the apologist of the Republic, sparked off a fierce response from Churchmen concerned to defend divine principles in Church and State.[38]

It is important to be clear here about Toland's editorial role. Unlike the case of Ludlow's memoirs in the major editions of Milton and Harrington's works it seems that Toland exercised very little systematic textual intervention. In the case of Harrington, as we will see he achieved his adjustment by the intrusion of supplementary texts not necessarily by the original author. In the case of Milton's work the bulk of his subject's prose works were prepared by other 'Calves-Head' editors – it was Toland's role (probably at the request to the printer John Darby) to provide a prefatory biography that shaped the way the prose was read.[39]

Toland's approach to biography was both narrative and thematic. The *Life* made Milton's writings relevant to the political concerns of the 1690s. Milton the apologist for regicide, the critic of the *Eikon Basilike*, and the putative founder of the Calves-Head club was an unambiguous and radical figure. Translations and editions of separate items from Milton's work were one means by which radical Whig polemicists attempted to rebut *de jure divino* Jacobite challenges. Toland's method was to observe 'the rules of a faithful historian' in reconstructing Milton's life and thought in precise detail: 'I shall produce his own words, as I find 'em in his Works'. Authentic citation allowed Milton to speak for himself, but also freed Toland from blame 'of such as may dislike what he says'. As he noted sometimes historians were accused of making 'their Hero what they would have him to be, than such as he really was'. To this end Toland used historical method to justify the reproduction of Milton's arguments. Some historians might 'put those words in his mouth which they might not speak themselves without incurring some danger': Toland (in general agreeing with Milton's ideas) justified the re-articulation of Milton's republican sentiments by the injunctions of the *ars historica*.[40]

Milton was presented as a man of learning and eloquence with a 'laudable passion for letters'.[41] Combining learning with travel, Milton was struck by the decline of Rome from the height of 'liberty and learning' to the 'most exquisit Tyranny': importantly, Toland suggested that the root of such civil corruption (according to Milton) was to be found in the power of 'effeminat priests' for 'deluding men with unaccountable Fables, and disarming 'em by imaginary Fears'.[42] These themes, of the defence of liberty and the critique of priestcraft, were the motors of Toland's biography, subtly focusing the republican tradition away from a straightforwardly regicidal quality to a hostility to a tyranny composed of both civil and spiritual deviance. Returning to England in the early 1640s Milton engaged in a learned and fundamental attack upon the agents of tyranny. His objective was (in his own words from the second defence) 'to rescue his fellow citizens from slavery'. Justifying his interpretation with long extracts from Milton's works, Toland commented that he was 'very severe upon the clergy'. All the corruptions of civil government came from 'the craft of prelates'; episcopacy by definition was 'always opposite to Liberty'. The idea of primitive and apostolic church government, as well as the veneration for patristic tradition was assaulted.[43] Milton's views on divorce became for Toland an opportunity to reinforce his commitment to 'domestick liberty' freeing men from 'a kind of servitude at home': importantly the distinction was made between this form of liberty and the licentiousness of libertinism.[44]

Throughout the *Life* all forms of attempted clerical domination are regarded as agencies of servitude and bondage whether Protestant or popish, Presbyterian or Anglican. Religious persecution was the starting point for civil tyranny. So *Areopagitica* (in Toland's reading) became a republican critique of tyranny: censorship was 'unjust in itself, and dishonourable to a free government'. Here the account of Milton's attack upon licensing had an obviously contemporary context for Toland and his audience. The suspension of the Licensing Act in 1695 and the attempted re-imposition of restraints upon liberty of religious expression, was as Toland put it 'more dangerous even than a standing army to civil liberty'.[45] The lengthy extracts from *Areopagitica* were not only part of the historical reconstruction of Milton's thought but were a direct commentary upon contemporary political problems: here the republican language of the interregnum had quite precise and direct application to the culture of the 1690s.[46]

The question of the regicide (and Milton's powerful justification) was dealt with in a short and simple account. Having been judged an enemy by Parliament and made a prisoner by 'their victorious Army', the King was 'judicially try'd and condemn'd, and the form of government was chang'd into a Democracy or Free State'.[47] Importantly, Toland made no reference to the execution of Charles, but took the opportunity to expose the hypocrisy of the Presbyterians who 'did tragically declaim in their Pulpits, that the King's usage was very hard, that his person was sacred and inviolable'. Rehearsing Milton's *Tenure of Kings and Magistrates,* Toland pointed out 'that such as had the power might call a Tyrant to account for his maladministration, and after due Conviction to depose him or put him to death, according to the nature of his crimes'. If the 'ordinary Magistrates' refused to execute this justice, 'then the duty of self-preservation, and the good of the whole (which is the supreme law) impowers the People to deliver themselves from Slavery by the safest and most effectual methods they can'.[48] The resonance between these unambiguous assertions of the legitimacy of regicide and the defence of a radical account of 1689 is clear. This assertion of republican political theory was reinforced in the eulogy of the *Defensio pro Populo Anglicano* a work that, according to Toland, equalled 'the old Romans in the purity of their own Language, and their highest notions of liberty'. Rather than reproduce extracts of the work, Toland insisted that since 'it deserves so much to be consider'd at length in the Original, or in the English version ... that I will not deprive any body of that pleasure'. The English translation of the work had been made by Joseph Washington in 1692, republished in 1695 and included in the collected edition of 1698. The invitation to read the text was further encouraged when Toland could not resist extracting two passages from the work that reinforced (in Milton's words) 'the common Rights of the People against the unjust domination of Kings, not out of any hatred to Kings, but Tyrants'.[49] Toland did not compromise Milton's ideas, but endorsed them for contemporary readers.

While Toland did not shrink from applauding and commending Milton's explicitly republican texts, he also paid very close attention to the ecclesiastical writings. One of the recurrent themes of the *Life* was the conspiracy of tyranny and superstition as the most pernicious threat to the liberty and virtue of a nation. Milton expressed hope that Cromwell would settle a 'perfect form of a free state' where no single person 'should injoy any power above or beside the Laws' but also where an 'impartial Liberty of Conscience' would be established.[50] 'Tyranny' was defined not only by deviant Stuart kingship, but also by the domineering ambition of clerical hirelings. Starting from Milton's rhetorical question 'what Government coms nearer to this precept of Christ, than a free Commonwealth?', Toland surveyed Milton's critique of all forms of priestly corruption: tithes, benefices, liturgies, and intolerance.[51] This survey resulted in the assertion that 'no true Protestant can persecute any persons for speculative Points of Conscience, much less not tolerat his fellow Protestant, although in som things dissenting from his own judgement'.[52] Ultimately, Toland argued, Milton embodied a 'disinterestedness and impartiality' about religious confession. This liberty of expression was linked directly to his defence of 'true and absolute freedom' which was the greatest 'happiness of this life, whether to societies or single persons'. Constraint was misery, thus he used his 'strength and faculties in the defence of liberty, and in direct opposition to slavery'.[53] Although Milton had a reverence for 'the Deity as well in deeds as words', Toland pointed out that 'he was not a profest member of any particular sect among Christians, he frequented none of their assemblies, nor made use of their rites in his family'. Toland hesitated to 'determine' whether this 'proceeded from a dislike of their uncharitable and endless disputes, and that love of dominion, or inclination to Persecution, which, he said, was a piece of popery inseparable from all Churches'.[54] For Toland, then, Milton's 'republican' project included both civil and mental liberty: the war against tyranny was to be fought in the debates about ecclesiastical power as much as monarchical authority. Religious superstition, persecution, censorship and intolerance were a form of 'tyrannical faction' that oppressed a free state.

This delicate shift of emphasis in Toland's biography can be seen most explicitly in his treatment of Milton's *Eikonoklastes*. Here Toland's reworking of the 'meaning' of Milton's republicanism was carefully and deliberately tailored for the political needs of the 1690s. One of the staple strategies of monarchist public discourse was the exploitation of Charles I's martyrdom in the powerfully emotive contexts of 30 January sermons (delivered in commemoration of his execution). An important constituent of the construction of Charles as a martyr was the print success of the *Eikon Basilike* (1649). Milton had made a commanding response to the work that attempted to counter its affective quality, and importantly cast doubt upon the authorship of the text. As Toland explained, Milton had 'discovered a piece of Royal plagiarism, or (to be more Charitable) of his Chaplains priestcraft'.[55] Exposing the use of passages from Sidney's *Arcadia*, and the 'stile' of the composition, Toland suggested that Milton perceived the work as the 'production of som idle clergyman, than the work of a distrest Prince'. It had the rank smell 'of a System of the Pulpit'. Toland intruded a supplementary account of the 'imposture' drawn from sources discovered after Milton's death. Using the so-called 'Anglesey memorandum' which suggested that Gauden had composed the *Eikon*, Toland implicated not only the Restoration Church but both Charles II and James II in a conspiracy to sustain the pretence. That the cheat of such a 'supposititious piece' could be foisted upon the public so effectively made Toland ponder how many forged pieces might have been attributed to Christ and the Apostles. As will be discussed in chapter 8, this was to form a platform for a radical deconstruction of scriptural canonicity, which Toland distributed in a clandestine work.

Even in its initial form this reflection sparked off a savage response in defence of the authenticity of Christian revelation. Toland's exposure of this fraud not only compromised the *Eikon Basilike* and the pious reputation of the martyred Charles, but also implicated the established clergy in the perpetration of a deception. Milton's *Eikonoklastes* became a text for the 1690s exposing the ideal of a divinely appointed monarch and the corruption of aspiring priestcraft. The subtlety of this narrative was to be seen in the emphasis placed upon the machinations of the clergy and the passivity of the monarch: kings could be tyrants but they were habitually prompted to such oppression by the ambition of priestly hirelings. Readers in the 1690s were aware of the debates over the authorship of the *Eikon*, and would also have experienced the sermonising on 30 January. Importantly, in one of the few editorial additions to Milton's prose, material concerning the Royal plagiarism and the 'Anglesey memorandum' (which exposed the forgery), was intruded into the collection between *Eikonoklastes* and the *Tenure of Kings and Magistrates*.[56] In Toland's edition of Milton late seventeenth-century readers could find an effective way of understanding the political significance of such matters and map them on to the contemporary struggle between liberty and slavery.

Many of Toland's contemporaries were more than disgruntled with his *Life of Milton*. In his 30 January sermon (1699) John Gilbert, Canon of Exeter, assailed the work for its defence of 'execrable traytors and proscribed regicides'.[57] Although clerical hostility was directed at the remarks Toland cast against the canonicity of Scripture, the republication of Milton's works was reviled as 'tending to promote the design of lessening and reproaching monarchy'.[58] Another reply condemned Toland for trying 'to turn the Gospel against Kingly government'. Toland was (as he predicted) accused of twisting Milton's reputation to his own ends. Just as Italian artists were notorious for painting pictures of the Virgin Mary according to the features of their mistresses, 'in truth I am of the opinion that the author design'd the like compliment to himself in forming Mr Milton's Character'. Toland had in particular modelled his account of Milton's religious identity ('an hypocrite in his youth, a libertine in his middle age, a deist a little after, and an atheist at last') 'so exactly [to] the authors own temper'.[59] The main criticism was that Toland had twisted Milton's words to attack the contemporary Church: 'to run down Fathers, Councils, Universities and publick maintenance for the ministry'. This attack upon the church was compounded with the assault upon monarchy: the 'main design' of the work was 'to promote the cause of a commonwealth' and to place the crown 'under the people's feet'.[60]

Never shy of controversial exchange, Toland published a robust defence of his biography, *Amyntor* (1699). Milton was a model of virtue. Far from misrepresenting his life or 'discovering truth not fit to be known', as he had stressed in the original *Life* he had simply reproduced Milton's own words 'to prove I had neither injur'd him nor abus'd my readers'.[61] Toland reacted badly to being told that 'I ought not to meddle with Milton's books, nor revive his sentiments'. He had no intention of stirring up controversy, but simply gave a truthful account of Milton's opinions; if this prompted doubts about the legitimacy of kingship or the virtue of the Church so be it. He actively encouraged the critics to 'defend your castles and territories against him with all the vigour you can'. Defending his historical duty, and reiterating the concluding points of the *Life*, Toland insisted whether writing a study of Tarquin or Brutus, the 'historian ought to conceal or disguise nothing; and the Reader is to be left to judge of the virtues he should imitat, or the vices he ought to detest and avoid'.[62] Again the injunction to the reader to 'judge' of the merit of Milton, and his works, is clear evidence that Toland was expecting the edition to have an edifying effect upon contemporary readers. The bulk of Toland's defence turned against mercenary churchmen who 'remember me oftener in their sermons than their prayers'. Importantly the defence of Milton's conduct was made by a much more active restatement of the case against the royal authorship of the *Eikon Basilike* and the debate about the canon of scripture.[63] The martyrdom of Charles was a fiction, the 'reliques' of this tradition, whether material or ideological were 'popish legends'.[64] There was a fundamental objection to hearing Charles I described as the 'best of kings, and the best of men', when there were many more suitable figures for admiration from antiquity or even the present.[65]

If Toland's edition of Milton was a means for reinvigorating the attack upon *de jure divino* accounts of Church and State, his handsome folio collection of James Harrington's works was an even more pronounced attempt to make republican texts suitable for contemporary consumption. Unlike the edition of Ludlow (where he adjusted the language of the text), or the collection of Milton's prose (where he showed the reader how to understand the meaning of the text by including a biographical guide), with Harrington's canon, Toland used a more subtle approach involving iconographical presentations, as well as inclusion of non-original work. Prominently on the title page Toland cited Cicero's *de republica*, 'That a commonwealth only exists where there is a sound and just government, whether power rests with a monarch or with a few nobles, or with the people as a whole', with the intention of underscoring the point that republican government was the rule of justice and reason, not necessarily a specific form of rule. This emphasis upon just government without reference to specific institutional form was also indicated in the sophisticated iconography of the frontispiece. Inscribed with the tag 'I. Tolandus libertati sacravit' the iconography illustrates how Toland remodelled Harrington's thought for the 1700s. The structure of the emblem is built in architectural form, reflecting classical republican ideas that the art of government is architectonic.[66] The centrepiece has the female form of Liberty clothed in Roman robes holding a hat on a stave of manumission, symbolising a state of freedom from slavery restored. Surrounding Liberty is an architectural monument, four Corinthian columns supporting a plinth and resting on a wall. At the top of the monument are representations of military prowess, glory and victory: drums, spears, arrows, axes, cannon, standard-flags, body armour and a plumed helmet. Behind the monument, a vista of a seascape is described complete with an armed fleet and evidence of military fortification. Liberty has been victorious on land and sea, but also has defensive qualities. Beneath the seat upon which liberty is seated are (left and right) representations of civic buildings and an agrarian scene named 'Commercio' and 'opificio'. Indicating the foundational components of civic freedom, commerce and land are seen as the 'balanced' premise of the free state.

The remainder of the engraving has three related levels of illustration. Most obvious is the joined symbols of 'Great Britain', Scotland, England and Ireland: the thistle, the rose and the harp. Linked to these images of national identity are portraits of Junius Brutus and William III (significantly wearing the laurels of victory). The relationship between these two facing portraits suggests that just as Brutus acted to restore liberty, so too did William III, the expulsion of the Tarquins and the Stuarts being commensurate acts of national liberation. This marriage of republican hero and regal authority was shorthand for the editorial ambitions of the entire volume. Reinforcing this ideal of the 'monarchy' of William III as a form of republican government, the last level of representation has five portraits of Moses, Solon, Confucius, Lycurgus and Numa. This canon of ancient figures invokes the celebration of classical political legislators encountered in key texts such as Machiavelli's commentaries on Livy's *Discourses*. Solon, the founder of Athens, Lycurgus founder of Sparta, and Numa, second king of Rome, were the staples of republican historical admiration. The addition of the Chinese philosopher legislator and the Hebrew prophet made the recommendation of the tradition of political legislators more complex, specifically highlighting the introduction of a religious relativism. While Machiavelli, and some of his contemporaries, had been content to represent Moses as a suitable pattern for republican government, little had been said about Confucius.[67]

To many late seventeenth-century readers the tradition of Solon, Lycurgus and Numa was fundamentally problematic because their politics were non-Christian. Certainly the accounts of their use of 'politic religion' found in Machiavelli's *Discourses* tended to underscore the impiety of the republican tradition against the *de jure divino* models of government. By the 1690s and 1700s the transformation of 'political legislators' into 'political impostors' had been made by the various clandestine works of European *libertins erudits*: describing Moses as a legislator was not therefore only a politically deviant act, but fundamentally an irreligious one too. One iconographical meaning of this engraving, then, suggests a lineage between the tradition of the ancient political legislators and William III. Just as Brutus restored liberty, so did William; just as Lycurgus laid the foundations for republican Sparta, so did William III for Britain; if Numa and Moses employed 'religion' to make laws more effective, so would William III. The frontispiece was then an invitation to readers to explore Harrington's works with a 'present-centred-ness' which was constructed as a legacy of the ancient prudence of Athens, Rome and Sparta.

Toland reinforced these themes in his dedication and introduction to the edition. London was described as 'a new Rome in the West'. The liberty of the city was built upon 'Trade and Commerce' which had elevated the citizens of London 'to so high a degree of Riches and Politeness'. The establishment of liberty, and especially the 'impartial liberty' of religious toleration, meant the city combined 'union, wealth and numbers of people'. Drawing attention to the city's reputation as a refuge from 'the glittering pomp and slavery, as well as [from] ... the arbitrary lust and rapine of their several tyrants', London had become 'everyman's country'. A source of liberty for the entire nation, it pumped liberty 'into all quarters of the land'.[68] The 'power' and 'freedom' of the national government was reflected in city institutions like the Bank of England, which was 'like the Temple of Saturn among the Romans'. Indeed, according to Toland, the constitution of the Bank 'comes nearest of any Government to Harrington's model'. Buttressing this republicanising of contemporary institutions, Toland imagined the government of the City of London as a republican foundation. The Lord Mayor was more than an 'Athenian Archon', the equivalent of a 'Roman Consul'. The solemnity of his election, the magnificence and extent of his authority was such that 'during a vacancy of the throne he is the chief person of the nation'. Extending the constitutional analysis of city government, as the common council was 'the popular representative, so the court of alderman is the aristocratical senate of the city'. The eldest alderman, Toland's erstwhile patron Sir Robert Clayton, was equivalent to the 'prince of the senate' at Rome. Indeed Toland's eulogy of Clayton was undertaken in republican terms: 'he universally passes for the perfect pattern of a good citizen' and just as Cicero was called the father of his country so was Clayton 'the father of the City'.[69]

Turning to Harrington's works, Toland reiterated the position he had adopted in the edition of Milton. He transmitted 'to posterity the worthy memory' of Harrington's ideas, which were in his view the best account of government, justice and liberty. Many 'roaring and hoarse Trumpeters of

Detraction' would 'proclaim that this is a seditious attempt against the very being of Monarchy, and that there's a pernicious design on foot of speedily introducing a Republican form of Government into the Britannic islands'. Toland countered by accusing them of the 'raging madness of superstition'. All those 'who talk by rote' attempted to make the name of 'commonwealths-man' invidious by foisting a false account of monarchy onto public discourse. Republicans had 'valiantly rescued our antient government from the devouring jaws of arbitrary power' and placed the crown under 'such wise regulations as are most likely to continue it for ever, consisting of such excellent laws as indeed set bounds to the will of the king, but that render him thereby the more safe, equally binding up his and the subjects hands from unjustly seizing one anothers prescrib'd Rights or privileges'. If a king was 'the man of his people' (like William III), he would be capable of 'uniting two seemingly incompatible things, Principality and liberty'.[70] English government was 'the most free and best constituted in the world' because it was a government of laws 'enacted for the common good of all the people, not without their own consent or approbation'. Just as Aristotle wrote under the government of Alexander, Livy under Augustus and Thomas More under Henry VIII, Toland felt that he was empowered to write 'freely, fully and impartially' with 'honour and safety' under a 'king that is both the restored and supporter of the Liberty of Europe'.[71] Republicans could work with good kings.

Just as Cremutius Cordus had spoken honourably of 'the immortal tyrannicides of Brutus and Cassius' regardless of the condemnation of Tiberius, so Toland reprinted Harrington's works for the 'public good'. *Oceana*, a work of 'so much learning and perspicacity', was a perfect model of a commonwealth. He encouraged Harrington's works to be read alongside a 'study of other good books, but especially a careful perusal of the Greec and Roman Historians' as a ground-work of liberty.[72] Explaining the key principle of the work, that 'foundation of all politics', that empire followed property, Toland drew attention to the fact that this principle was not 'form' specific. As he clarified, 'all that is said of this doctrine may as well be accommodated to a monarchy regulated by laws, as to a democracy or more popular form of government'.[73] It was perfectly possible then to be a republican and operate within a monarchical form without compromising fundamental principles. Toland was adamant that the role of 'legislator' was a more effective way of establishing and remodelling a commonwealth than the instruments of a popular assembly. The 'legislator' had to have 'a refin'd and excellent genius, a noble soul ambitious of solid praise, a sincere lover of virtue and the good of all mankind' if he was to be 'capable of executing so glorious a undertaking as making a people free'. This was a preamble to describing the aspirations for William III, although the consensual origins of his government were underscored with the succinct phrase 'we made him King'.[74]

Rethinking the nature of monarchy was central then to the intentions of the publication of Harrington's works. This element can also be seen in Toland's editorial advice. He specifically recommended the preliminary discourses to *Oceana* and its epitome, *The art of lawgiving*, as encapsulating Harrington's ideas. Neither 'private speculations' nor 'impracticable chimeras', Harrington had 'authoriz'd' his understanding by 'a world of good learning and observation'.[75] To digest these fundamental principles was the point of reading the edition. To this end Toland had deliberately not attempted to produce a complete collection, including some scribal works (like the 'System of politics' and 'The mechanics of nature'), but omitting the more trivial pamphlets which were 'solely calculated for that time'. Editors who included everything wanted judgement. Not making a distinction between 'the elaborate works which an author intended for universal benefit, and his more slight and temporary compositions, which were written to serve present terms' was a mistake. Many of the more marginal works were not only unintelligible, but 'useless'. The corollary of this editorial advice was that the published work still retained pertinence for contemporary politics.

That Toland exploited a number of literary strategies in his editions has become commonplace. Toland prepared his text for his readers. Attention has been drawn to the fact that Toland included in Harrington's works by another writer. It seems unlikely that Toland was attempting to pass off John Hall's *The grounds and reasons of monarchy*, originally published in 1650, as Harrington's work since he pointed out the real author in his preface.[76] Hall was a defender of the regicide.[77] Toland adjusted Hall's work to contemporary purposes. By the insertion of new words, changes of punctuation (in particular the substitution of full stops, for a maze of subordinate clauses) and the replacement of archaic expression Toland adapted the text to the 1700s.[78] This skill was employed to make the text a defence of the legitimacy of William III's kingship. The rewritten Hall text was still hostile to corrupt monarchy and the bewitching qualities of courts and priests. Divine right accounts were specifically condemned as superstitious prejudices clung to by the 'generality of mankind'. Corrupt monarchical rule was 'diametrically opposite' to civil happiness. The welfare of the people was 'the sovereign law and end of all government' because all men were naturally born equal. The contextual thrust of the reprint was to critique Stuart monarchy rather than the Williamite commonwealth. Passages that attacked the role of the clergy who 'borrow the face of Divinity', could be very well applied to those churchmen who used 30 January sermons to dazzle the community. Just as 'slavery enfeebles their minds' many people preferred temporary ease to 'real happiness'. A belief in 'succession' placed matters of government 'into the hands of fortune' rather than prudence. Such a monarchy was a 'disease of government' which ought to be replaced by 'pristine liberty and its daughter happiness'.[79] Having carefully integrated Harrington's works within Williamite discourses, it seems unlikely that Toland would have so deliberately compromised his own editorial aspirations by the inclusion of a rabidly anti-monarchical text, unless he intended to make a profound distinction between kingship and tyranny. The inclusion of Hall's work, suitably edited, showed readers that it was possible in 1700 to be both a republican and loyal to a virtuous monarchy.

This distinction was also at the heart of Toland's edition of Sidney's *Discourses* in 1698. He published the work so 'that nations should be well informed of their rights'. Denying that this was a seditious enterprise, Toland countered 'that as man expects good laws only from good government, so the reign of a Prince, whose title is founded upon the principle of liberty which is here defended, cannot be but the most proper'.[80] The use of a vocabulary of 'princes' rather than kings was a significant attempt to avoid the implications of a regal language. Later Toland defended himself from the charges of heresy and sedition. He 'freely' owned that 'I am a great common-wealths-man ... and value myself upon being so'.[81] Far from distancing his editorial project from republican charges, Toland embraced them: 'I have bin wholly devoted to the self-evident principle of Liberty, and a profest enemy to slavery and arbitrary power'. The abusive use of 'commonwealthsman' was the result of the vindictiveness of 'court flattererers and pensioners' whose objective was to insinuate that such men were 'irreconcileable enemies' to regal government. Acknowledging that it was lawful 'to resist and punish tyrants of all kinds', Toland insisted that although *in extremis* he preferred a democracy over tyranny, his support was for a commonwealth. This was defined as having no 'particular form' but as 'an independent community, where the commonweal or good of all indifferently is design'd and pursu'd'. Since all magistrates were made 'for and by the people' so with the settlement of the crown on William III, England became a commonwealth 'the most free and best constituted in all the world'. Invoking the authority of Cicero, Toland simply argued that 'all free governments' were commonwealths regardless of institutional form. The images of 'anarchy, confusion, levelling, sedition and a thousand other terrible things' were wrongly associated with a republic, which 'really signifies Liberty and Order, equal laws, strict and impartial justice'. Explicitly denying a continuity with the 'tyrannical usurpation of Oliver Cromwell' Toland defended 'the antient and present constitution of England under Kings, Lords, and Commons' reiterating his 'untainted loyalty to King William'. This loyalty he insisted 'will argue me to be a staunch commonwealthsman' and as such 'I shall continue all my life a friend to religion, an enemy to superstition, a supporter of Good Kings, and (when there's occasion) a Deposer of Tyrants'. For Toland, it was clear that republican principles of good government were entirely compatible with the rule of William.[82]

This theme was also found in Toland's poetic work *Clito: a poem on the force of eloquence* (1700) which as Nigel Smith has commented 'out Miltons, Milton'.[83] Premising his arguments upon a amalgam of Lucretian and Spinozist materialism, anticlericalism and the promotion of 'the good old cause', Toland presented himself as an active republican, as a 'fatal scourge of slavery. / Ambitious Tyrants, proud and useless drones, / I'll first expose, then tumble from their thrones'.[84] Eulogising 'Godlike Brutus' for his defence of liberty, Toland intruded a celebration of William III, in very similar terms as the dedication to Harrington's works, as 'a matchless Hero ... / that freedom he restor'd he will maintain, / incourage merit, and leud vice restrain. / Our Laws, Religion, Arms, our coin and trade, / All flourish under him, before decay'd'.[85] William would bring both the 'branch of peace, and thunderbolt of War': the free state of Britain would become an anti-tyrannical force 'to free those who slavish fetters wear'.[86] For Toland the more urgent war was to be fought against the instruments of spiritual slavery, the 'swarming herds of crafty priests and monks, / the female orders of religious punks, / Cardinals, Patriarchs, Metropolitans, / Franciscans, Jesuits, Dominicans'. Although anti-popish in idiom this war against priestcraft was against all deviant church-men: 'all holy cheats / of all Religions shall partake my threats'.[87] While con-temporaries reviled the work as both irreligious and treacherous, it is impor-tant to note that Toland, content with the regulated government of William III, turned the full force of his polemic against false religion as the urgent enemy of republican virtue. The war against priestcraft was more necessary than that against kings.

Although many contemporaries deliberately fashioned William III as a 'Godly' and providentially legitimated ruler, Toland was not alone in imagin-ing William III within the tradition of republican legislators.[88] For example, 'An essay on publick virtue', one of the scribal works of Shaftesbury written in the mid-1690s, before he became Toland's intimate, indicates how even the most principled republican could envisage virtuous government being the product of monarchical rule. Composed as a plea to reform public service from the degeneracy of private interest, William III was defended as 'a virtuous prince' who laboured hard for the 'publick good'.[89] William III, like Dion who restored 'the Sicilians to their freedome', had renovated religion and civil rights.[90] William's rule was a 'kingship limited and circumscribed by laws, or a king at the head of ye commonwealth'.[91] The important theme to note in this discourse, as in much of the 'true Whig' polemic of the late 1690s, was that the focal points of anxiety were civil institutions other than the monarchy. In the person of William, republicans like Toland and Shaftesbury seemed confident in the security of commonwealth virtues and justice. While they 'would not spare the monarchy', men like Toland when dealing with 'his present Majesty's person ... would deal gently with the monarch'.[92]

Toland's editorial efforts were subtle attempts to redefine legitimate monarchical government. The legality of the regicide, and of the right of resistance, was not abandoned. As Toland clarified, he was 'a supporter of Good Kings, and (when there's occasion) a Deposer of Tyrants'. Legitimate monarchy was one circumscribed by institutional limitations. From the republican perspective the most pressing political problem was the legitimacy of succession. The consequences of 1689 had established a legitimate form of government that coincided with a dynastic succession. While William III was a powerful example of the political legislator with whom republicans could work, the future in the late 1690s looked bleaker with the alternatives being the rule of the dangerously clerical Anne, or a return to the dangers of Jacobite restoration. Turning arguments that were calculated to defend rights of resistance and regicide into an intellectual defence of a dynastic succession involved considerable intellectual contortion. As we will see in the next chapter, Toland actively defended this limited form of monarchy by fusing it with a defence of Protestantism. Fresh from his editorial efforts in the late 1690s Toland became one of the staunchest defenders of the Hanoverian succession. This liberty was a language built as much out of Protestant languages of conscience as anti-monarchical sources. As Toland insisted in *Vindicus Liberius*, 'the greatest glory of a free government' was liberty of the understanding which was 'yet a nobler principle than that of the body, if this be not a distinction (as they say) without a difference; and where there is no liberty of conscience there can be no civil liberty'.[93]

NOTES

1 *A Letter to the Author of Milton's* LIFE (1699) postscript p. 6.

2 R. T. Gunther (ed.) *Early science in Oxford: life and letters of Edward Lhwyd* (Oxford, 1945) p. 278.

3 *Notes and Queries* vol 1 1862 p. 7.

4 *Ibid.*

5 See William Barron *A just defence of the Royal Martyr* (1699) p. 13; *ibid. Regicides no saints or martyrs* (1700) pp. 5–6, 114, 133. See, G. Watson 'The Augustan Civil War' *Review of English Studies* 36 (1985) pp. 321–337.

6 J. Toland *King Charles I No such Saint, Martyr or Good Protestant* (1698) pp. 2, 4–5.

7 See G. Sensabaugh *That Grand Whig, Milton* (Oxford, 1952) pp. 199–200.

8 Bibliographical details and title pages/contents are drawn from the English Short Title Catalogue (ESTC).

9 J. P. Kenyon *Revolution principles: the politics of party 1689–1720* (Cambridge, 1977) p. 76.

10 Worden 'Republicanism' in Wootton *Republicanism* p. 175.

11 Worden 'The Revolution and the English republican tradition' in J. I. Israel (ed.) *The Anglo-Dutch Moment* (Cambridge, 1991) pp. 241–277, at 241.

12 See J. G. A. Pocock (ed.) *The political writings of James Harrington* (Cambridge, 1977) pp. 15, 42.

13 See Worden 'Republicanism' pp. 156–157.

14 See D. Hayton 'The "country interest" and the party system, 1689–c. 1720' in C. Jones (ed.) *Party and management in Parliament 1660–1784* (London, 1984) pp. 37–85.

15 Worden 'Republicanism' p. 178. See also M. A. Goldie 'The roots of "true whiggism" 1688–1694' *History of Political Thought* 1 (1980) pp. 195–236.

16 Worden *Ludlow* p. 51.

17 J. G. A. Pocock 'Varieties of Whiggism from Exclusion to Reform' in *Virtue, Commerce and History* (Cambridge, 1985) pp. 232–233.

18 Worden 'Republicanism' pp. 177–178.

19 de Certeau *Capture of speech* pp. 92–93, 97, 105, 120–121.

20 D. Norbrook *Writing the English Republic* (Cambridge, 1999).

21 Letters to Harley, c. 1711.

22 Worden *Ludlow* p. 30.

23 *Memoirs of Denzil Lord Holles* (1699) p. x.

24 Darbishire *Early lives* p. 171, on the inclusion of Milton's model of a commonwealth and letters to Monck, which were 'communicated to me by a worthy friend'. For background to this community see J. B. Duke-Evans 'The political theory and practice of the English commonwealthsmen, 1675–1725' (DPhil Oxford University, 1980) especially pp. 111–139.

25 See A. Sharp 'The manuscript versions of Harrington's *Oceana*' *Historical Journal* 16 (1973) pp. 227–239.

26 For Harley's involvement see *Collections* 2, pp. 217–218, 345, 349–50.

27 See Forster *Letters* pp. 71, 120.

28 See BL Add Mss 4295 fo. 6 and BL Add Mss 4295 fo. 10.

29 See J. A. Downie 'William Stephens and the *Letter to the author of the memorial of the state of England*' *Bulletin of the Institute of Historical Research* 50 (1977) pp. 253–259; Toland's correspondence with Raulins is in *Collections* 2, pp. 433–436, 441–445.

30 See Jacob *Newtonians* p. 221.

31 *Collections* 2 p. 348.

32 See W. Sasche *Lord Somers: a political portrait* (Manchester, 1975).

33 *Memoirs of Holles* pp. v, xii.

34 See G. de Krey *A fractured society: the politics of London in the first age of party 1688–1715* (Oxford, 1985).

35 See Jacob *Newtonians* p. 221; Worden *Ludlow* p. 42.

36 *Collections* 2 pp. 318–331.

37 *Modesty mistaken: or a letter to Mr Toland upon his declaring to appear in the ensuing Parliament* (1702) p. 6. Toland placed a disclaimer in *The Postman* November 1701. See *Tolandiana* p. 78.

38 See N. Von Maltzahn 'The Whig Milton, 1667–1700' in D. Armitage, A. Himy and Q. Skinner (eds) *Milton and republicanism* (Cambridge, 1995) pp. 229–253, at p. 241.

39 For a detailed discussion see P. Lindenbaum 'Rematerialising Milton' *Publishing History* 41 (1997) pp. 5–22; Von Maltzahn 'The Whig Milton' pp. 248–252.

40 Darbishire *Early lives* reproduces Toland's *Life* between pp. 83 and 197; see pp. 83–84.

41 Darbishire *Early Lives* pp. 84, 86.

42 *Ibid.* p. 93.

43 *Ibid.* pp. 99–100, 102.

44 *Ibid.* pp. 120–23.

45 *Ibid.* pp. 127–29; see also p. 139.

46 *Ibid.* p. 133; the extracts are at pp. 129–133.

47 *Ibid.* p. 135.

48 *Ibid.* p. 136.

49 *Ibid.*; the extracts are pp. 156–158 from the conclusion of the *Defensio*.

50 *Ibid.* p. 166.

51 *Ibid.* p. 173.

52 *Ibid.* p. 189.

53 *Ibid.* p. 194.

54 *Ibid.* p. 195.

55 *Ibid.* p. 144; pp. 142–151 cover the entire episode.

56 See *A complete collection of the historical, political and miscellaneous works of John Milton* (1698) volume 2, between pp. 525 and 529.

57 See *Tolandiana* p. 64.

58 See *Tolandiana* p. 67.

59 *Remarks on the life of Mr Milton as publish'd by J. T.* (1699) pp. 2–3.

60 *Ibid.* pp. 24, 27.

61 *Amyntor* pp. 3, 4–5, 6.

62 *Ibid.* p. 9.

63 *Ibid.* pp. 20–41.

64 *Ibid.* p. 170.

65 *Ibid.* p. 166.

66 See J. A. I. Champion *The pillars of priestcraft shaken* (Cambridge, 1992) p. 205.

67 See A. Brown 'Savanarola, Machiavelli and Moses' in *The Medici in Florence: the exercise and language of power* (Florence, 1992) pp. 263–279.

68 Toland *The Oceana of James Harrington and his other works* (1700) dedication, pp. iv, ii–iii.

69 *Ibid.* p. v.

70 *Ibid.* pp. vii–viii.

71 *Ibid.* p. viii.

72 *Ibid.* p. ix.

73 *Ibid.* p. xix.

74 *Ibid.* p. xxi.

75 *Ibid.* pp. xxi–xxviii.

76 *The Oceana of James Harrington and his other works* p. xxviii; see Wootton *Republicanism* pp. 26, 30–31.

77 Norbrook *Writing* p. 218.

78 So for example compare page 3 (Toland edition), with page 3 Hall (BL 601.a.4: Edinburgh 1650) [knows/knoweth; retain/hold up; they are/it is] or page 3 (Toland) with page 4 (JH) opiniativeness/opiniatritirie; or page 4(Toland) with page 5 (JH) Kingcraft/kingship; page 6 (Toland) with page 13 (JH) types of divinity/the eclypse of divinity.

79 J. Hall *The grounds and reasons of monarchy* in *Oceana* (1700) pp. 3, 4, 6–8, 9, 10–11, 13.

80 A. Sidney *Discourses concerning government* (1698).

81 *Christianity not mysterious* p. 186.

82 *Ibid.* pp. 188, 190–191.

83 See N. Smith 'The English Revolution and the end of rhetoric: John Toland's *Clito* (1700) and the republican daemon' in *Essays and Studies* (1996) pp. 1–18, at 12.

84 Toland *Clito* (1700) pp. 10–11.

85 *Ibid.* pp. 11–12.

86 *Ibid.* p. 14.

87 *Ibid.* pp. 14–15.

88 See T. Claydon *William III and the Godly Revolution* (Cambridge, 1996) and C. Rose *England in the 1690s: revolution, religion and war* (1999).

89 'An essay on public virtue. Part Ist' BL Harleian 1223 fos. 6, 7, 20, 23, 28–29.

90 *Ibid.* fos. 31–32.

91 *Ibid.* fos. 34–35

92 *Modesty mistaken* pp. 2–3.

93 Toland *Vindicus Liberius* p. 182.

5

Anglia libera:
Protestant liberties and the
Hanoverian succession, 1700–14

WITH the publication of the splendid edition of Harrington's works, Toland secured his position at the heart of a 'true commonwealth' interest. This intimate collaboration with elite Whig politicians led to Toland becoming the leading defender of Protestant liberty. This took immediate form in a vindication of the legitimacy of the Hanoverian succession under the terms of the *Act of Settlement* 1701. For many 'commonwealthsmen' around Europe the act that confirmed the succession of Sophia of Hanover was a republican device to exclude both popery and tyranny. The third Earl of Shaftesbury even wrote to Benjamin Furly in Holland, claiming that his 'friends' had been involved in the committee for the legislation.[1] The subtitle of the act, 'for the further limitation of the crown and better securing the rights and liberties of the subject', established for many contemporaries its radical ambitions. A later commentator, echoing these points, described the act as 'the last great statute which restrains the power of the crown'.[2] As a direct response to William III's speech to Parliament encouraging swift settlement of the succession after the death of the Duke of Gloucester, Parliament set in train the political process that resulted in the act in early March 1701. Despite the aftermath of a bitterly contested General Election, the act was passed without controversy. A contemporary, the Whig William Blathwayt, suggested that Whigs and Tories were collaborating 'in weakening the Crown'.[3]

That an explicitly republican agenda was still tenable during the debates surrounding the act can be seen in works like *The limitations for the next foreign successor* (1701) that was sometimes (falsely) attributed to Toland. Reasserting the commonplaces of the 'true Whig' agenda against corrupt monarchy it argued for a radical reintroduction of the limitations of the 'original' bill of rights. Annual parliaments, limitations upon the exercise of prerogative, the abolition of 'dependence' upon the court, parliamentary counsel in the appointment of ministers like the Lord Chancellor and Lord Treasurer, as well as the parliamentary creation of nobility, were amongst the fifteen points of regulation proposed as limitations upon the crown.[4] These conditions 'would dissolve the monarchy, and reduce it to a commonwealth'. Citing Fortesque alongside a range of other medieval and more contemporary sources, the insistence was that such regulations were part of ancient usage that restrained kings from lapsing into tyranny. Even Moses had ruled with the counsel of limited government. Plato, Aristotle and Tacitus, in distinguishing between the rule of kingship and the degeneracy of tyranny, had determined that legitimate government established the common good over the private interest of the few.[5] As one respondent put it bluntly 'the drift of it tends to a commonwealth' and 'democracy and confusion'.[6] The author claimed to be in favour of monarchy when really 'he was preaching up the doctrine of Harrington's Oceana'.[7] Gilbert Burnet commented that the conditions were 'such extravagant limitations, as should quite change the form of our government, and render the crown titular and precarious'.[8]

Some contemporaries suggested that Toland had penned this piece, either at the request of Robert Harley or Shaftesbury, grasping the opportunity to press for a radical completion of the unfinished work of the 1689 revolution.[9] Nevertheless it is unlikely that Toland wrote the work. A central theme of the *Limitations* was an implacable hostility to the Hanoverian succession; by mid-1701, however, Toland emerged as the leading defender of the claims of Sophia, Electress of Hanover. Fresh from his editorial labours upon the supposedly regicidal texts of the republicans, Toland turned his literary talents towards not only defending the legitimacy of the Hanoverian succession, but actively propagandising the personal merits of the Electress and her German courts. This was personal as well as political. Toland described the 'extraordinary veneration and affection I have for the whole family, and which their conspicuous Virtues will put beyond all suspicions of flattery'.[10] By August of 1701, Toland was taking part in the ceremonial presentation of the *Act of Settlement* to Sophia in Hanover. He became 'the literary champion of the Protestant Succession'.[11] Accompanying Lord Macclesfield (another friend of Shaftesbury's), Toland managed to intrude himself into the centre of diplomatic formalities: as he boasted 'I was the first who had the Honour of kneeling and kissing her hand on account of the Act of Succession'.[12] In return for gifts of medals and portraits of Sophia and the Electoral Prince, Toland gave her a copy of his *Anglia libera* (1701) a work that was to be translated into Dutch, French and Latin.

This work is compelling evidence of how Toland reinvented republican traditions by becoming the advocate of a limited monarchy. *Anglia libera: or the limitation and succession of the Crown of England explained and asserted* (1701) which set about justifying the act clause by clause, was explicitly written for both British and European readers. Toland sent the work page by page to be translated into French for simultaneous publication.[13] German and Dutch editions followed, published in Hamburg and Rotterdam, reproducing only the first ten sections of the English work that dealt with the specific details of the legal succession. The more discursive commentary on English political tradition was omitted.[14] Through Leibniz there was direct collaboration with Sophia's court. The Germans had not been unaware of Toland, and his work, since many correspondents sent responses to his political writings. Clearing Toland from association with the radical *Limitations*, it was established that he had been encouraged to write *Anglia libera* by several leading figures in the government. Dedicated to the Duke of Newcastle, and presented to William III by Toland himself, the work was represented as an 'official' defence of the succession, 'pour servir d'information tant aux gens du pays qu'aux etrangers'.[15] This was, then, no seditious and marginal composition of a compromising and covert republican.

The doubts entertained by Sophia about her prospects in Britain, had been prompted by the publication of Toland's earlier editorial labours. George Stepney, envoy to Berlin and Vienna, had reassured her that although the nation had an excessive love for liberty this did not imply a deep disgust for monarchy. The republications of Harrington, Milton and Sidney amongst others, did not herald a return to 1649, as he commented 'pour le peu que je connois le genie des Anglois, qu'il est nullement porté aux principes Republicains'.[16] Leibniz, one of Sophia's philosophical and political advisors, reduced republican principles to an opposition to arbitrary power and the establishment of 'L'empire de la raison'. A variety of correspondents had alerted Leibniz to Toland's reputation. His judgement on the *Life of Milton* led him to describe Toland as a man of spirit and learning, if little moderation. It was only ignorant prejudice that led to accusations of atheism. As Leibniz clarified, simply because Toland loved 'true liberty' did not make him a dangerous republican: 'reasonable liberty', where 'good law' constrained both monarch and people, was preferable to a situation where 'arbitrary power' was exercised by either.[17] Political circumstance meant that there was little danger of a republic being established in England, because the threat of a transcendent French power meant that it was the best England could do to preserve itself from despotism.[18] Although Leibniz was mildly critical of some of Toland's views he admired the Flemish translation of *Anglia libera*.[19] Toland, writing to Shaftesbury in July 1701, described his reception abroad as delightful; 'I am informed that on my return from Germany I am to have some distinguishing mark of their acknowledgement. They have already put me in all their Gazettes for writing it, and look on me so farr to be some sort of ambassador from the people'.[20] Toland acknowledged his 'duty and gratitude' to both Shaftesbury and Newcastle for helping with the work and its reception. This was a long way from the Middlesex Grand Jury and book burning in Dublin.

Anglia libera had both intellectual and social functions. The work not only projected Toland's reputation onto a European canvas, but also opened the doors of the Hanoverian court. Both Sophia and her daughter Sophie Charlotte (Queen of Prussia) entertained Toland repeatedly throughout the 1700s. Although Sophia, because of Toland's poor reputation in England, was discreet about her intimacy with him, nevertheless her correspondence is littered with accounts of their meetings and conversations. At one point Toland suggested he might be tutor to the Electoral Prince, such was his standing.[21] Reports of his perambulations with Sophia in the gardens of Herrenhausen led observers to imagine 'that they were talking of important matters concerning affairs of state and that Her highness took him into great confidences'.

As Leibniz speculated, the conversations were mainly about philosophical and literary curiosities rather than politics, but nevertheless the presentations of medals and other gifts were rewards for his book on the succession.[22] Sophia received repeated warnings about Toland's character and the dangers of intriguing with him. His attempt to ingratiate himself with her by advancing proposals in print for inviting the Electoral Prince to England, backfired when the text was condemned by Parliament, and Sophia had to distance herself by rebuking Toland.[23] The Irishman persisted in his attentions, deliberately lodging near the court and passing on gifts and writings from England, at times exploiting unsuspecting collaborators like Spanheim and Archbishop Sharp into his intrigues.[24]

It is clear, that whether Toland was discoursing with Sophia about the metaphysics of matter and motion, or the nature of the Christian canon, he used his connections to attempt to embroil the Electress in anti-Tory politics. Sophia, although evidently encouraging Toland to discourse on a number of deep metaphysical and theological issues, managed carefully to avoid public political scandal. Although she repeatedly wrote to others confirming her distance from Toland, the evidence suggests she was in contact with him, especially through attendance at the court of her daughter, Sophie Charlotte, Queen of Prussia. Certainly, in many of her letters there is a barely hidden sympathy for Toland who was suffering the calumny of prejudiced clergymen. When Toland was reported to have defended the culture of the cannibals from the charges of the Spanish who had in his view invented such monstrous behaviour to justify their own cruelties, Sophia commented that she was not surprised that 'poor Toland took the part of the Cannibals, because one day they might possibly be his protectors, given that all Christianity was against him'.[25] The Electress' daughter, Sophie Charlotte, perhaps less concerned with diplomatic niceties, was more tolerant of Toland's public company, expressing disappointment when Toland had failed to visit her court.[26] Evidence suggests that Toland was indiscreet and challenging about matters of politics and religion, sometimes he spoke incautiously like a 'républicain'.[27] Sophie Charlotte commented that, 'it's true that his language is a little free, but I find that he is becoming more and more wise'.[28]

Toland did not moderate his views when walking with queens, yet he was undoubtedly committed to defending the Hanoverian succession. As one diplomatic observer put it Toland presented himself as 'the greatest and first promoter of the succession, and the man who drew out the deduction of the rights of your E[lectoral] H[ighness]'.[29] Throughout the 1700s and 1710s, Toland claimed he had 'favour' with various politicians like Harley who vigorously denied such a mission.[30] Establishing the exact nature of Toland's political credentials in 1701 is not easy given the shadowy quality of his connections. One thing is certain, *Anglia libera* was dedicated to the 'most noble and mighty prince, John, Duke of Newcastle', although it seems likely that this was omitted from the Dutch and German editions. Newcastle deserved the honour of the dedication because of his 'inviolable love' for the 'liberty of your country' and the particular zeal for 'the late settlement of our Crown in the House of Hanover'. Like the Valerii of ancient Rome, nobles such as Newcastle 'were extremely popular and rever'd, for the mildness of their nature, the easiness of their manners, and the affectionate esteem they paid their Fellow Citizens'. This celebration of aristocratic virtue was a reflection of the elite dimensions of republican political life in the period. Newcastle's virtue derived from his kinsman Holles, 'the ablest champion of *English* liberty, and the sincerest Lover of the true constitution of our Government'. The combination of property and virtue, meant that men like Newcastle had a 'natural right to share in the government of any place, where they have an interest to secure, and the people such a pledge of their Fidelity'. Newcastle's virtue was incorruptible. A stern defender of the Revolution and loyal to William III, he would approve of 'these new limitations to the Crown' which would preserve and enlarge the liberty that 1689 had restored. As Toland explained, his purpose was show 'all persons both at Home and Abroad' that the Parliamentary limitations were 'agreeable to the principles of justice and the ends of all good government, as well as according to the constant practice of this Kingdom'.[31] It was also designed, importantly, 'to acquaint the House of HANOVER with the true nature of their title'. *Anglia libera* was then a treatise upon republican kingship.

In *Anglia libera* Toland plundered many intellectual resources: Locke, Harrington, Cicero, Tacitus, Sallust plus many others were cited to establish 'the true principles of civil society'. The Lockean premise of his political thought was that 'men are born in the same condition, and that, when they come to years of maturity, they are equally free to dispose of themselves as Reason shall direct them'. These rational individuals incorporated themselves into 'civil society' for 'mutual delights and assistance' and 'greater security to their persons and possessions'. For the 'good of the whole community' certain rules and laws, 'the measure and standard of everyman's actions' were agreed and exacted by 'indifferent umpires'.[32] Although legislative power was supreme, it was not arbitrary, but fiduciary. The 'whole people may call them to account' if the trust of establishing the 'security, welfare and felicity' of the common good was compromised.[33] Arbitrary power was the rule of passion. Such rule, especially in the form of an absolute monarchy, was not really 'any kind of civil government' being 'infinitely worse than the very state of nature'.[34] On the contrary the genius of 'free governments' lay in the ability to 'perfect the Felicity of mankind'. The people were 'numerous, industrious, sober, wealthy, and martial', the architecture, agriculture and roads and rivers were 'equally stately and commodious'. Free states made a balanced, vigorous and thriving society where 'all orders of men maintain their proper Characters, but the stoutness, neat apparel, and good air of the common people particularly demonstrate their freedom and plenty'.[35] As well as economic and social success, 'arts, inventions, and learning are universally incourag'd, and in the most flourishing condition', there was no intolerance directed against the free exercise of religious or philosophical expression.[36]

The principles of 'civil liberty' were not the singular focus of Toland's recommendations in *Anglia libera*. Fundamental to the definition of liberty in a free state was the preservation of 'liberty of the understanding'. Eliding republican discourses with a Protestant vernacular (citing Harrington) Toland argued that 'religion it self is not more natural to man, than it is for every Government to have a national religion, or some public and orderly way of worshipping God, under the Allowance, Indowment, and Inspection of the civil magistrate'. The free constitution of the national church was arrayed against the tyranny of popish idolatry and superstition. 'Liberty of Conscience' was the premise of civil liberty. Dissidence from the national religion ought not to mean deprivation either in 'persons or possessions' for anyone 'from any privileges in the state to which they have a Right by birth, naturalisation, or otherwise'.[37] As Toland emphasised, the limitations in the *Act* specified that the monarch must be of the Protestant communion, so by default the common-wealth had a religious framework.[38]

This 'liberty' had a history. 'Great and various' had been the attempts to 'ruin it'. Invoking Harringtonian analysis, Toland insisted that the conflict between Kings, clergy, nobility and commons was driven by the material cause of the 'overballance of property (and consequently of power)'. Now the commons conjured power and authority. The 'new model'd' government, however, following Tacitus' dictum ('arcanum novi status, Imago Antiqui'), retained 'the image of the old': it still looked like a monarchy.[39] Toland condemned the tyranny of the Stuarts who had persistently 'redoubl'd their efforts to grasp at an arbitrary power'. Churchmen played a key role in this tyrannous attempt by infecting 'the understandings of the people, and ... mak[ing] them eternal slaves by their own concurrence as well as consent'. James II, by breaching the 'natural relation or original compact between all kings and their subjects', forfeited his right to 'regal government'. The 'free people' by inviting William to rule, had thereby 'successfully recover'd the just rights of themselves and their posterity'. Appropriating the language of radical contractarian traditions, Toland insisted that William was chosen by the judgement of the Convention Parliament because of his virtue, which gave him a secure title, for 'no king can ever be so good as one of their own making; as there is no title equal to their approbation, which is the only divine right of all magistracy, for *the voice of the people is the voice of God.*'[40]

The *Act of Settlement* was a framework for preserving 'liberty' from the threatened encroachments of 'a second Restoration' of popish Stuart Kings. Toland argued that Britain was already a free state.[41] As he explained, 'For tho we were a free nation before, and that at one time or other we enjoy'd the greatest part of the privileges contain'd in this *Act*, yet there never was the Time wherin they all at once had the Force of Laws'. The resonance with the idea of a remodelled monarchy found in the editions of Harrington, Milton *et al.*, and *Anglia libera* is profound. The *Act of Settlement* was a 'republican' measure intended to reinforce 'liberty' in the tradition of *Magna Charta* and the *Petition of Right*. This reworking of the relationship between kingship and liberty was initiated (according to Toland) by William III's dedication to the preservation of liberty. As indicated in his speech to Parliament in February 1701, William placed restraints upon prerogative just like Theopompus, King of Sparta, ordained 'the Ephori, or overseers, shou'd be created at Lacedemon, to be such a restraint upon the Kings there, as the Tribuns are on the Consul at Rome'. Monarchy, as bound by law, was a key part of 'our present form of government' thus 'shou'd never be abolisht'.[42] Although the history of the Stuart monarchy had made men 'like the Romans to abhor the very Name, or at least despair of having any king that should have no separat interest from the Nation', even the 'republicans' supported the 'naming' of Sophia as successor. 'There was', proudly exclaimed Toland, 'not one single person of the real or reputed Republicans in the whole Kingdom who did not heartily concur with his Majesty's Judgement'. This naming was also received with 'unanimity and cheerfulness' in Parliament; the 'most illustrious order of the *English nobility*' were especially zealous.

Just as the regal element was a fundamental part of the constitution, so was the aristocracy. Like the patricians of Rome, and those of Athens, Sparta and Venice, the 'nobility' were the leaders of the people in war and 'their protectors

and guides in peace'. Citing James Harrington, 'one of the greatest republicans that ever liv'd in the World', Toland applauded the 'nobility' as leaders
like officers in an army. 'Gentlemen' were critical to good government as the
examples of Moses, Lycurgus, Numa, Brutus and the Gracchi 'who lost their
lives for the people of Rome', and Cornelia daughter of Scipio, established.
The names to be added to the list were William of Nassau, founder of the
Dutch commonwealth and Sophia.[43] The ideological link was forged between
classical republican traditions and the legitimate status of the contemporary
regime.

By carefully detailing the 'limitations' in the settlement Toland claimed that
the measures would halt the pernicious contentions between 'prerogative and
privilege' forever.[44] The articles appealed to the political ambitions of Royalists
and Republicans, 'for the Royalists have still a king, under which magistrate
they thought liberty the most secure: and the Republicans injoy a Liberty
under a King, tho they once thought them things dissociable and scarce to be
reconcil'd'.[45] The distinction between 'Royalists' who supported 'our antient
form of government, consisting of King, Lords and Common', and those
'obstinat sticklers for the Divine Right of Monarchy' was critical for Toland to
be able to detach his understanding of monarchy from Jacobite discourses and
make common ground with more mainstream loyalists.[46] Extending the arguments he had refined in the editions of Harrington and Milton, Toland
reinforced republican commitment to the reformed monarchy: the 'Republicans are unanimously pleas'd with the new Limitation and succession of the
Crown'. Such men were lovers of 'liberty under any form or denomination': it
was 'not the name of any magistrate, but his power that ought to be chiefly
consider'd. The word KING, for example, has no other Force or Right than
what particular Nations are pleas'd to annex to it'. Exploring the variety of
linguistic usage (Caesar, Grand Segnior, Cham, Czar) Toland attempted to
dissociate the word from the thing: 'kings' in the commonwealth of Rome
were not only frequently deposed but were 'usually clients to the nobility'.
Indeed the Roman kings 'before Tarquin the proud, were but the chief
Magistrates of a free Government' like the kings of Athens and Sparta.

Applying a form of political nominalism, he observed 'that in government
the Names are often chang'd when the power is still the same, as at other
times the Power is actually chang'd tho the name remains unalter'd'. The
same titles thus 'have different significations in different places'. Kings of
Poland were formerly dukes, Venetian magistrates might be called kings or
dukes. Toland was insistent that the word 'commonwealth' did not mean a
form of democracy, nor indeed, any particular form of government 'but an
independent community, where the Common Weal or Good of all indifferently is design'd and pursu'd, let the Form be what it will'. Admittedly,
republicans had sometimes been hostile to corrupt kingship, but the reforms

of 1689 meant they were 'ready to pay all good *Kings* not only obedience but double Honor'.[47] The argument here prudently detached the 'form' from the 'nature' of government and in doing so (in a strict sense) implied there was no necessary connection between liberty and specific sorts of political institutions. It was perfectly possible for government by monarchy to produce the conditions for a 'free state' when regulated and limited.[48] This programme for republican reform was precisely what Toland advanced in *Anglia libera* to an audience that included the present and future monarchs.

Toland defended the English tradition: 'our manner of constituting the chief magistrate is the laudable mean between two most vitious extremes'. Electing a new person on the king's death would, as the example of Poland suggested, be to expose the nation to uncertainty, confusion and war. Making the succession 'absolutely hereditary' would potentially subject the nation to the successive government of 'tyrants, madmen, fools or idiots'. The English practice limited the succession to 'a certain line' thus avoiding the opportunity for contention, but still reserved the ability to 'transfer the Right of Succession from one line to another' according to necessity.[49] Citing a number of historical examples, drawn from John Somer's Exclusionist tract *The brief history of the succession*, documenting the 'free choice of the people of England' from the Saxons to the Tudors, Toland documented the 'power of Parliaments with relation to the Succession'. The limitations were no innovation, but an application of 'the fundamental rules of our Constitution to particular persons'.[50] Proposing a veneration for the 'sacred names' of heroes like Timolean, Junius Brutus and 'William the Old Prince of Orange', Toland wished for a 'stentoriean voice which might reach to all the regions of the world, and call mankind aloud to LIBERTY!'[51] A free England, in liaison with the Dutch republic could lead Europe out of slavery.

Anglia libera was a set piece of propaganda critical to the 'survival' of republican traditions of political thinking in the period. Sponsorship by leading noble politicians like Shaftesbury and Newcastle is significant, underscoring the theme of the text itself, that the 'patricians' of the nation had an important role in the preservation of virtue and liberty. Even though the work was by the hand of a man responsible for the 'republican editions' of the late 1690s, its reception in Germany by the nominated successor, Sophia and her advisors like Leibniz, suggests that the work was both successful and effective. Contrary to commonplace suggestions, republicanism was a serious, and still vigorous, way of conceptualising the task of politics and government in the early eighteenth century. Toland's propagation of this republicanism was not confined to the publication of such powerful set-pieces but took at least two other forms after 1700. First he advanced his republican arguments in a series of polemical political pamphlets, composed between 1701 and 1705 when his connections with Shaftesbury and possibly Harley, entangled him in the day-to-day exigencies of party politics. Second, and perhaps more importantly, he also promoted his vision of a republican monarchy by acting, almost single-handedly, as a publicist for Sophia of Hanover.

Dedicated to William III, 'supreme magistrate of the two most potent and flourishing commonwealths in the universe', *The art of governing by parties* (1701) published by Bernard Lintott who also produced *Anglia libera*, was premised upon Harringtonian conceptions of political counsel. He commended William III, for his 'unparalleled zeal for Liberty (a thing so unusual with crown'd heads)'.[52] Invoking the duty of counsel, implicit in citizenship of a 'free government', Toland explained, 'I write with in the reach of no Tyrant; but under the wings of a valiant, wise, and just Prince'.[53] The cast of the pamphlet was historical, establishing a narrative of Stuart tyranny, focusing especially on Charles II. Combining the dual ambitions of 'popery and despotick power' Charles II had established his tyranny by fomenting division amongst his people, creating an 'implacable animosity of contending parties'. Both in politics and religion, with the assistance of the 'peevish and ill-natured ecclesiastics', the brothers Charles and James attempted to execute their illegal designs. The most powerful solvent of liberty had been the creation of 'parties' in religion. Underpinning other differences it was the 'most success-ful machine of the conspirators against our government'.[54]

Charles II had divided his people and possessed 'the Royalists with apprehensions of a commonwealth' when 'all the world know that England is under a free Government'. Legislative power was directed by a mutual 'check and balance' of King, Lords and Commons, which 'indifferently designed and pursu'd' the common 'good of all'. Although England was a free common-wealth it was 'ordinarily stil'd a Monarchy because the chief magistrate is call'd a King'.[55] These party fears had been inflamed by the Church, 'men who then appropriated to themselves the name of the Church of England, but were really the scandal and betrayers of it, mercenary drudges of the court ... and tools of popery'. The tyranny of Charles II was systemic, successively corrupting the monarch, the church, the ministry, the judiciary, and the army.[56] By the use of 'parties, places and pensions' Charles II had compromised the indepen-dence of Parliament and local corporations, raising a 'sort of civil war, creating quarrels and perpetual animosities in all countys and corporations'. Such corruption of 'honor, preferments, dependences, or expectations' appealed to the private interests of all under the cover of the 'interest of their party': the 'good of the public was minded by none or a very few'. To dampen these potentially corrupting factors, Toland recommended the staple reforms of self-denying bills to remove temptation. The only sure remedy was the election of annual parliaments which would make bribery too expensive. An equalisa-tion of representation would also bring vigour back to the independence of

Parliament. Such measures would establish a 'sort of rotation among the Gentlemen into this great school of wisdom'.[57] Toland's commentary upon the corruption of late Stuart politics was intended as a reflection upon implicit dangers in the 1700s. William III was invoked as a reformer of these abuses.

Government by 'party' was government, ultimately, by the passions of self-interest. Ministers of state and counsellors who applied their passionate 'reason of state' in their service to Princes in the form of 'nauseous and repeated flatteries' compromised the common good.[58] Quoting the 'picture of corrupt ministers', described by Sidney in the *Discourses on government*, Toland condemned the venality of courts.[59] The consequence of government by 'party' was a tragic compromise of liberty; kings became 'rather the ring-leaders of Petty clubs, than the fathers of great nations'.[60] The only remedy against the 'mischief of parties' was a 'Parliament equally constituted'. The introduction of constitutional reforms like annual elections, a qualifying bill and an extension of the electorate to all those who paid church and poor rates would make a platform for civic virtue. An independent Parliament made of MPs of integrity and moderation would refurbish a declining liberty.[61] This theme of the need for fundamental institutional reform was taken even further in *Paradoxes of State* (1702), a work Toland composed in collaboration with Shaftesbury. The pamphlet was structured around the last speech of William III to Parliament in December 1701, affirming that when the court was not popish, prerogative and liberty might have a common interest. The political premise was that there was 'an ill balance still left in the state by the insufficiency of our hasty Bill of Rights'.[62] In this work, the remodelling of monarchical discourse to republican purpose, literally by appropriation of the King's words, was an effective and powerful political strategy. Lord Somers was reported to have composed the speech; certainly it became an icon of liberty, being translated into Dutch and French to be hung up in frames.[63] Echoing the last phrases of William's words, the text of *Paradoxes* insisted that distinctions between parties (Whig and Tory, Williamite and Jacobite) could be collapsed to one division between those of Liberty and Tyranny or England and France. After William had restored, confirmed and enlarged 'liberty', 'all republican pretences were out of doors' because England was 'the best, the most equal, and freest commonwealth in the world'.[64] If principles of tolera-tion, frugality and military valour could be preserved then Britain would be protected from both 'internal corruption' and 'external threat'.[65]

One of the recurrent themes of these political writings of 1698–1702 was confidence in William III's kingship, premised as it was on a commitment to 'liberty' in civil and religious matters. One of the consequences of this trust was that criticism of the conduct of politics was deflected from structure to conduct. 'Kingship' was not the pressing political problem, whereas corrupt courtiers and crafty priests were. Republican criticisms were not directed against the monarchy, because Toland and Shaftesbury were convinced that the legal and constitutional limitations after 1689, placed effective bridles on illegitimate conduct. They did not then hesitate to criticise limited regal government, but saw no need of so doing: the butt of their assault lay elsewhere. One of the presuppositions of much of Toland's political writing in this period (and later) was that much civic mischief was made by the misunderstanding of the vocabulary of political discourse. Such misunderstanding was the result not of ignorance but deliberate fraud 'as they are severally influenc'd by ignorance, prejudice, passion or design'.[66] The perpetrators of this deceit (whether courtiers or churchmen) were the targets of attack: anti-courtly and anticlerical polemic then became a fundamental element in the republican programme.

After the death of William III, the accession of Anne changed the emphasis of relations between crown and republican. Toland clearly avoided any direct commentary on the nature of her religious and political commitments: he preferred to look forwards to the Hanoverian option, or backwards to the example of William. While Anne was praised as an Elizabeth restored, the ambiguity of her religious and dynastic commitments were further complicated by her relationship with the dynamics of party politics in the period. The fury of the 'rage of party' and the intricate nature of parliamentary influence and political management focused on central issues such as religious toleration and the power of the Church. The continuity of political language with the 1690s, in the case of Toland, can be seen in the publication of his controversial *The Memorial of the State of England* (1705) an answer to the High Church anxieties that the 'Church was in danger'. Toland drew a powerful link between the divisions amongst Churchmen and dissenters and disputes about the nature of civil government: low churchmen limited the 'civil government with law' while high churchmen stressed 'the uncontroulable Power of the prince in Temporal affairs'. The dispute then was between liberty and prerogative.[67] Fomenters of discord like James Drake had attempted to tar dissenters with 'being Commonwealthsmen, or for popular government', when in fact they defended 'the liberty of the antient English Government', secured by laws 'and by divers other excellent regulations'. Such 'republicans' were indeed 'zealous for the House of Hanover' and Protestant liberties, only those who pursued 'designs of arbitrary and despotick power' were fearful.[68]

Elemental to Toland's arguments was religious toleration. William III had removed the 'civil sting' against liberty of conscience. Contrary to the clerical claims that compulsion in matters of conscience was legitimate, as acts both of religious duty and civil magistracy, Toland insisted that civil authority should take 'no cognisance of those inward dispositions which are wholly seated in the mind'. It was a mistake to confound 'persecution for opinions with punishment for crimes'. The nature of human epistemological competence

meant 'that as men have different capacities, apprehensions, and opportunities, so they cannot possibly but have different notions of things'. Whether
men lived in free or despotic dominions they would have different opinions,
consequently 'a great variety of opinions is a certain sign of a free government,
and no wonder, since men are there permitted to live as men, making use of
their reasoning faculties, and speaking what they think, as they think what
they please'.[69] Answering Augustinian assertions that the civil magistrate had
a Christian duty to induce men to a consideration of the truth by the
application of penalties, Toland countered that 'the Question is not if mens
opinions be true, or their ceremonies best, but if they be hurtful or not'. All
persecution and compulsion was illegitimate whether Protestant or Popish:
Calvin, Beza and Rutherford had all defended compulsion. Contrary to the
ambitions of those that wanted to make 'men in all things of one mind' Toland
asserted that a diversity of religions was beneficial to the state. Extending this
argument he suggested that the sacramental test be abolished. The debate was
au fond a question of civic participation and 'civil trusts': all men should be
'treated, as well as reputed, like good subjects, and admitted without any
partial distinction to all offices in the state'.[70] The suggestion that the Test be
abrogated was unacceptable to contemporary churchmen. It was however a
practical political objective, and as such, indicates the programmatic dimensions of republican politics.

Toland's *Memorial* was a plea for 'moderation' but one articulated in a
republican idiom. All 'good government' was '(under God) originally from the
choice of the people, for whom, and by whom' it was established. The end of
society was the pursuit of the common good regulated by the rule of law. The
mixed form of government was one means of achieving this end, and
although there was a regal line it was limited by the precept that princes were
made 'for the people, and not people for the use, will or lust of the Prince'.
Tyrants and usurpers could be legitimately resisted in the name of 'free
government'. Contrary to those Tory discourses that demanded a 'servil and
blind obedience to the prerogative', Toland argued that 'understanding and
vertue be the best foundation of the love of liberty'.[71] In private correspondence (probably with Harley), Toland reiterated that he was, 'for a free government against what is arbitrary and despotic, which is to say, that I prefer
standing and indifferent laws to the uncertain and byast will of any Prince'.
Acknowledging that there were many different forms of free government, he
still preferred 'our own mixt constitution'. He acknowledged that his editorial
efforts of the 1690s combined with his evident 'ardent love of liberty' had led
some to mischaracterise him as 'a most violent republican'.[72] Toland's
ambitions were to serve the cause of liberty and his country: he had drawn up
various memorials to advise 'true whigs' of the incipient dangers to liberty.
His terms of employment were simple, he would work for Harley (for

example) 'on such a foot as is agreeable to my principles, and for the particular benefit of the succession'.[73] These were no idle words, for Toland did indeed work hard for 'the benefit of the succession'.

For his 'early and great love to the House of Hanover', wrote the satirist John Dunton in 1716, Toland merited the reward of 'place or pension' from the new regime.[74] Launched into intimacy with the courts at Berlin and Hanover between 1701 and, at least, 1707, Toland was a regular (if sometimes unwelcome) visitor. A variety of correspondence indicates that Toland remained committed to the interest of Sophia's succession right up until her death. In 1711 when offering his services again to Harley, one of the skills he said he could contribute was good relations with Hanover.[75] An indication of his own hopes was expressed in a letter he wrote (to an anonymous correspondent) upon hearing of Sophia's death, 'Lord! How near was my Old woman being a Queen! And your humble servant being at his ease! All is not over yet, and some symptoms are promising enough'.[76] Relations between Hanover and England in the 1700s were delicate and made complex not only by diplomatic matters but by the difficult relationship between Anne and Sophia.[77] The fraught context of party politics in England made over-zealous public commitment to Hanover a dangerous business. Many gentlemen and politicians clearly kept their options open by paying their respects in Hanover. So for example, Sir Justinian Isham who, while studying at the Ducal Academy at Wolfenbuttel, was encouraged by his father to visit: 'I wou'd have you go to Hanover for some time to make your court there, which I believe may be kindly taken'.[78] Enthusiastic men like Sir Rowland Gwynne attempted to force the issue of Sophia's status by various political attempts (in collusion with Leibniz and others) to have her invited to England: the attempt in 1706 resulted in Parliamentary condemnation.[79] The issues of Sophia's naturalisation, the provisions for a Regency, the inclusion of prayers for her in religious services, invitations to England and funding for her court, were all the focus of convoluted political machinations between the Whig and Tory interests during the course of the 1700s.

Toland had nailed his colours to the mast while William III was still alive, with the publication of *Reasons for addressing his Majesty to invite into England their highnesses, the Electoral Dowager and the Electoral Prince of Hanover* (1702), which was 'Censur'd by ye Lords 16 May 1702, as a malicious villainous libel'.[80] Prompted by Louis XIV's recognition of 'the pretended Prince of Wales', Toland's work was an urgent response to (and defence of) the Attainder and Abjuration Acts of January 1702. Although statute had settled the succession, Toland had doubts that 'the ink and parchment of this law may prove but a small defence' against Jacobite military threats. 'For the safety and the benefit of the nation' both Sophia and Prince George should be accommodated in England. Sophia considered herself 'as an English woman, speaks our language as well as any of the natives' and looked forward to coming to her mother country. Bringing over the Prince would allow him to be 'educated in the language, laws, and the establisht religion of the nation he's to govern, not by his own will and discretion, but according to certain rules and limitations, whereof he shou'd not remain ignorant till the time they are put into practise'.[81]

Even as Toland propagandised on behalf of Hanover he was also inscribing its 'limited' nature, highlighting the irony and urgency of republican ambitions being attached to the insecurity of a dynastic succession. Indeed in the second part of the work, Toland launched a virulent attack upon the popish tyranny of the Stuart monarchy, which earned Parliamentary censure in Anne's reign. Abjuration and attainder of the Prince of Wales was necessary to defend 'liberty and Religion' and 'free government'. Since the 'whole right of succession in this Kingdom is founded on the good will of the people' it was only just that an oath should be tendered to all to establish their allegiance. Junius Brutus, a 'watchful guardian of Liberty', had encouraged the people of Rome to make an 'act of banishment against all those of the Tarquinian name'. Solon had made it a capital offence 'for any man to remain an unconcern'd spectator when any sedition shou'd happened in the city'. In Toland's view the abjuration should be administered to 'all manner of persons' including 'the King's majesty' and 'her Royal Highness the Princess of Denmark'. Hardly calculated to enamour himself to Queen Anne, he commented that 'Caesar's wife ought to be unsuspected as well as innocent'.[82] The examples of Brutus and Solon underscored the republican dimensions of inviting the people in public acclamation of the legitimate succession.

Having his fingers burnt by Parliamentary condemnation, and cautious of alienating Sophia's favour by compromising her own political strategies, Toland turned his pen to a more subtle form of pro-Hanoverian discourse. Despite the earlier representation of William III as a virtuous legislator, much republican polemic had been directed against the corruption inherent in royal courts. In reworking these themes, Toland laboured to characterise Sophia, and her court, as a source of virtue and reason. The vehicle for this representation was his *Account of the courts of Prussia and Hannover* first published in 1705 by John Darby, and also in subsequent editions with supplementary material in 1706 and 1714. A French edition (1706) was published by Thomas Johnson at The Hague with beautiful illustrations. It is worth noting that these publishers (Darby, Baldwin and Johnson) were part of a printing community that produced much of the radical political and heterodox literature of the period. Some insight into this is indicated in the small catalogue appended to Johnson's elegant edition of the *Account* advertising his other literary wares which included works by Sidney, Molesworth, Locke, Buchanan and Tyrrell, as well as dangerous works like the *Vie de Spinoza* and the *Turkish spy*.[83]

Dedicating the work to Charles Seymour, Duke of Somerset, a 'worthy Patriot', and defender of 'the most divine cause of Liberty', and co-Regent, Toland took the opportunity again to reiterate and applaud the role such 'nobles' took in the defence of 'free government'.[84] That the work had political intentions was established in the preface where Toland justified his inclusion of the oath of abjuration against James III that proscribed any 'to write or speak, or to commit any other overt act against the Protestant succession in the House of Hanover'.[85] Similarly Toland, denying charges of flattery, deliberately used the title of 'Royal Highness' that was not strictly necessary to describe Sophia's legitimacy against the claims of the Pretender.

Deliberately constructing a positive account of both the Prussian and Hanoverian governments, Toland presented them as wise and regulated, calculated to preserve both religious and civil liberty. Entire, rather than partial, liberty of conscience, was established and no one suffered civil penalties for religious difference. The Hanoverian court was polite 'both for civility and decorum': the clergy neither attended court nor played any role in government. Since there was a 'complete liberty of conscience' the clergy tended to be eirenic rather than persecuting. Sophia, 'long admir'd by all the learned world, as a woman of incomparable knowledge in Divinity, Philosophy, History and the subjects of all sorts of books, of which she has read a prodigious quantity', was a model of a virtuous ruler. She was without doubt above party distinctions.[86] In the account of the ordinances of the Royal Academy at Berlin, Toland presented a 'plan of education' that escaped the dominance of 'the servile fetters of systems, commonplaces, childish ceremonys, and ridiculous habits' in favour of the advancement of virtuous knowledge which would produce a 'learned nobility'. Citing Cicero, Toland applauded this schedule of learning, because the education of youth in the correct principles of virtue was key to the health of the commonwealth.[87] The Electress' daughter also established a rule of virtue in Prussia. Sophie Charlotte had such a just idea of government that she was known as 'the republican queen'. Not only was she beautiful but learned too: 'her reading is infinite, and she is conversant in all manner of subjects; nor is she more admir'd for her inimitable wit, than for her exact knowledge of the most abstruse parts of philosophy'.[88] Combined with such reasonable philosophy, the Prussian militia received favourable compliment, establishing a model close to that recommended in Toland's *Militia reform'd* (1698).[89] It is important to emphasise that Toland intended to make a presentation that contrasted Hanoverian virtue with popish decadence.[90]

In the anxious days of 1714, when the imminence of the succession became urgent, Toland published not only a new edition of the *Account*, but also a shorter abridgement of the work, *Characters of the Court of Hannover* (1714), which made explicit the alternatives between the regulated, virtuous monarchy of Hanover and the pretended, despotic and popish tyranny of the Stuarts. Prudentially, 'crying fire before the House was burnt down', Toland defended the Hanoverian succession against charges that the new regime would introduce 'foreign' traditions. The 'limitations' of the act of settlement would regulate the new government to render the influence of foreign ministers minimal compared with the rule of the French-influenced Pretender. The 'personal virtues' of Sophia and George (extracted from the 1705 work) were compared directly with the personal characteristics of the Pretender.[91] In an earlier short pamphlet Toland had justified the creation of the Electoral Prince as a peer of the realm reproducing Queen Anne's letters patent to establish that the succession had English credentials. In this work Toland pointed out that Sophia was not only a legitimate descendant of James I, but also of Matilda, Henry II's daughter. Reinforcing this, Sophia had medals struck with images of Matilda for presentation to the British Embassy in 1701. The point, of course, was to establish dynastic continuity. As Toland explained, although 'I shall ever adhere to sound Revolution principles, yet I am no means fond of frequent revolutions'. The constitution of Britain was a 'medium between an absolute hereditary, and an absolutely elective, monarchy'. In defining it as an 'hereditary right, under parliamentary limitations' Toland was able both to invoke obedience to the succession, while simultaneously reinforcing the regulated and consensual origins of its authority.[92] By April 1714 Toland stepped up his efforts with the publication of *The reasons and necessity of the Duke of Cambridge's coming* (1714) which argued that it was both 'reasonable and necessary' that the young prince be brought to England. This would be a security for the future and a sign that the ministry was supportive of the Hanoverian succession. The prince (and his children) would become a 'country-man', tutored in the constitutional traditions of the nation. He was 'our Scipio, from whom we expect the rescuing of our liberties'. As a good soldier and virtuous prince 'his wisdom and prudence make him admired, whilst his affability makes him belov'd'.[93]

The cynosure of this veneration of the Hanoverian monarchy can be found in Toland's publication of *The funeral elogy and character, of Her Royal Highness, the late Princess Sophia* in September 1714. A translation of the Latin 'Eloge' of Johann Cramer, the text was based upon a reading of the commemorative medal cast upon the Electress' death, representing 'Sophia, coelo, recepta'. The starting point for the work was a reiteration of the *Act of Settlement* and the emphasis of Sophia's descent from the Plantagenet line of Henry II. Sophia was 'the most finish'd pattern' for people of 'all degrees' to imitate. Learned, yet cultivated in the 'female arts', Sophia established a 'regulated' court which was the 'repository of good sense, virtue and wisdom, as well as the temple of the Loves and Graces'.[94] Whether walking, talking or in correspondence, Sophia combined elegance, wit, 'politeness and temper'.

Her attitude to approaching death was stoical: 'she ever expected death with a countenance as intrepid as her mind; and being thus serenely prepar'd to receive him, her understanding was too much irradiated by Philosophy, to repine at anything that to human nature is incident or unavoidable'. Like Astrea, goddess of Justice, driven from earth by the iniquity of men, the Electress 'was Sophia no less in effect than in name'.[95] The images of her funeral medal underscored these philosophical accomplishments. Dressed as the goddess of Wisdom, she ascended in apotheosis in the manner of the 'deification of the old Roman heroines and empresses'. Her soul was in flight to the stars. Surrounding Sophia, three angels carried different branches representing glory, love and honour. In his translation of the explication from Cramer's Latin, Toland carefully stressed the Protestant quality of Sophia's heritage while omitting reference to her immediate hereditary titles. She was 'call'd to the succession of the British throne by the unanimous voice of the people, and the sanction of laws'.[96] Sophia was the embodiment of republican self-mastery, 'governed by the dictates of reason'. Her restraint of passion and ambition was such 'that what in duty she was bound to do by the law of nature, she likewise willingly perform'd by the complete victory she had obtained over her own passions'. The crown of stars symbolised an ensign of immortality as reward for her 'heroic virtue'.[97] This pattern of regal virtue was transmitted to George I whose overwhelming zeal was directed against 'the long intended project of a universal monarchy'. For George, the pursuit of glory 'consists in justice'. Committed to liberty of conscience while being a thorough Protestant, George was destined to be the leader of Protestant liberty in Europe. Transforming the Hanoverian monarchy into a critique of illegal kingship, as Toland warned, 'Hear ye tyrants, and tremble ye persecuters'. George would continue the 'most happy legacy of the never to be forgotten William'.[98]

Toland composed many other polemical works defending the succession between 1711 and 1714 that reinforced the theme of the Hanoverian monarchy as the most effective means of preserving English liberties and the Protestant interest across Europe. Privately he also campaigned urgently on behalf of Sophia. As he explained to Harley, 'dry and general expressions will not do, friends must be confirm'd, and enemies put out of hope'.[99] Toland held suspicions that some Tories, like the October club and the dons of Christchurch, were plotting against Hanover: 'the allegorical health [at Christchurch] in Confusion to philosophy' was directed at 'Sophia and her friends'.[100] To this end Toland composed a number of practical 'memorials' of advice to Harley, searching for a political means to preserve the succession. The most adventurous suggestion, restating some of the principles of *The art of governing by parties,* was his scheme for a coalition of 'moderate Whigs and moderate Tories' who were 'true friends to their country'. Offering his insights into the state of domestic electoral politics and his standing in Hanover and Holland, Toland hoped to broker a platform for security: as he concluded his letter, 'delays are dangerous'.[101] Republican politics then had a very practical focus. For Toland the objective was clear, as he explained, 'my management abroad, my behaviour at home, what I whispered in private, and what I printed to the world, all speak the same language, all tend to the same end': the preservation of liberty, the succession and public welfare.[102] 'Civil liberty, religious toleration and the Protestant succession' were the unalterable and indispensable ambitions of his political service. His support for Hanover was based on his 'commonwealth' defence of liberty as 'a government of laws and not of will'.[103] Importantly these principles were to be pursued against both party politics and the 'spiritual tyranny' of 'Protestant popery' and the 'pride and power of priests'.[104] Practical devices such as oaths of allegiance and abjuration would winnow out the corrupt and conspiratorial.

It is a measure of Toland's commitment to these political values that when Harley's fidelity to Hanover was compromised by 'ambiguous words', Toland 'utterly renounc'd his friendship' and launched a powerful print campaign against him. It was, he said, 'impossible for a soul that's really fir'd with the love of his country, not to express in the most pathetic terms a detestation for tyranny, a contempt for slaves, an aversion to traytors, and resentment of injur'd trust'.[105] Published in five editions in early February 1714, the *Art of restoring* superficially examined the 'piety and probity of General Monck in bringing about the last Restoration', making the parallel between the events of 1659/1660 and Harley's involvement in advancing the claims for the restoration of a second Stuart exile. Toland imagined himself living under a republic: England in 1714 was like it had been in 1659, a free state that preserved 'all our liberties against Universal monarchy'. The public meaning of the historical parallel made between Monck and Harley was significant. Both men were portrayed as betrayers of republican institutions and complicit with tyrannical Stuart kings. Using Clarendon's history, to display 'the management' of the Restoration, Toland meant his readers to draw contemporary connections. Although he did not condemn Monck for the act of restoration, but for the 'wicked means that conduced to this happy end', his point was to expose the deceit of Harley. As he spelt out, 'our present case, 'tis true, is extremely different from what it was in the year 1659, just as different as light is from darkness. We are under the most noble, free, and legal constitution in the universe, whether the Dignity of the Prince, or the ease of the subject be considered'. Unlike the anarchy that confronted Monck, Harley was betraying a state 'free from priestly tyranny and popular superstition' where 'every particular man, and all communities of men, are as secure in the enjoyment of their property and privilege as the Queen is in her Imperial throne'.[106] In the pamphlet Toland skilfully established a complex series of parallels between Monck and Harley, describing the gap between the public commitment to the commonwealth/Hanoverian succession in speeches, letters and private negotiations, and the pursuit of restoration. Importantly as part of his strategy for making this comparative narrative, Toland reproduced *in extenso* the papers of General Monck in defence of the 'good old cause'. Here the re-deployment of discourses of liberty against 'tyranny and arbitrary power' from the 1650s, just like the editions of 1698–1700, could be usefully read as commentaries on the contemporary state of politics, as much as simple historical citation. 'Sir Roger' (Robert Harley) was engaging in similar hidden negotiations for 'making a King'. Just as pictures and prints of Charles II had been distributed in 1660, so images of the Pretender were deliberately put in circulation. Such a restoration 'would change this admirable constitution into popery and slavery'.[107] To reinforce this unfortunate parallel Toland also published two issues of a more complete edition of Monck's letters. Accompanying this discovery of Harley's supposed deceit were a number of political commentaries, which again made the connection between popish conspiracy and the incipient threat of tyranny. The *Grand mystery laid open* (1714) with its extract from William III's last speech to Parliament prominently on the title page, exposed the popish plot against civil and religious liberties inspired by corrupt ministers of state: 'if our liberties be invaded by the keepers of them, of whom shall we seek protection?'[108] In *Acts of Parliament no infallible security to bad peace-makers* (1714) Toland used the example of the attainder and execution of William de la Pole, Duke of Suffolk in the mid-fifteenth century, for making an 'ignominious peace with France' at the Treaty of Tours, as a warning to Harley of the punishment he might expect to receive for the disgraceful terms of the Treaty of Utrecht.

This survey of Toland's activities as an editor of republican works, as a political polemicist, as a private memorialist, and as a propagandist for the Hanoverian succession in the 1700s has intended to establish a number of related points. First, Toland, almost single-handedly (but importantly ultimately as one element of a grouping of elite politicians) imaginatively recast the republican tradition into a form compatible with the exigencies of politics after 1689. Republican languages were not excluded from mainstream political discourse, although they were powerfully stigmatised by clericalist polemics. Toland both recovered a tradition and invented new discourses. The use Toland (and others) made of the tradition of the 1650s was not a simple justification of the regicide, but carefully adapted for the conduct of contemporary politics. 'King-killing' after all was a defensive strategy rather than a blueprint for civic conduct. Toland did create a canon of eighteenth-century republican texts, but this was not his primary purpose. He had specific political intentions that were achieved by making a distinction between the central intellectual contents of the republican tradition and the narrower question of institutional form. The ideas of balance, liberty, of free and impartial government, and of political virtue, were reclaimed from association with the regicide of 1649, despite repeated attempts by clergymen to rivet them firmly in the public mind. The key intellectual development was the articulation of 'limited' and regulated monarchy encapsulated most effectively in *Anglia libera* and the writings projecting the 'republican' monarchy of Sophia. This process of adaptation certainly made republicanism 'respectable'. While defences of limited monarchy can justly be described as less controversial than the regicidal arguments of the 1650s, they were just as vital. Toland's political writings were powerful instruments in developing a working ideology to defend Protestant liberties against the urgent threat of popish tyranny. Killing kings in the 1700s was simply politically inappropriate.[109]

While regulated monarchy could be seen as a rather docile form of republicanism when compared with the achievements of the 1650s, to the audience of the time we should recall that any deviation from the shibboleths of divine government was tainted as dangerous subversion. *De jure divino* discourses were persistent and strong. The reinvention of republican ideas within the context of these divine arguments was difficult: making them acceptable was a major tactical achievement. Scholars have confidently argued that John Locke's contractarian account of the origins of government and the defence of 1689 was too radical for the pragmatic needs of Whig politics in the eighteenth century, yet if we compare the success of Toland's intrusion of a defence of 'limited' monarchy right into the heart of the Hanoverian court it may be possible to rethink the 'radical' nature of republican politics in the period.

A key practical difficulty for republicans like Toland, Shaftesbury and Molesworth in the 1700s was the dynastic insecurity of the platform for their vision of politics. Without a Protestant monarchy all prospects of liberty and virtue were damned. *Anglia libera* was reliant upon the successful coronation of Sophia or George rather than the restoration of James. Advancing the claims of Sophia may have been a respectable strategy, it was also a successful manoeuvre. After the safe accession of George I, men like Molesworth and Toland had not only the security of a 'free state' but also a political platform for the articulation of commonwealth reforms. With the collateral of George I's defeat of the Jacobite challenge, writers like Toland turned their attentions not simply to the business of constructing defensive ideologies about the regulation of regal government, but also to the positive business of establishing a free and virtuous community. None of these republican aspirations took the form of advancing antimonarchical constitutional innovations, but, especially in defending virtue, reason and 'liberty of conscience', focused upon reforming the corruption of the Church. Underpinning the politics of the war of reason on priestcraft was a series of very specific legal, cultural and political ambitions that became part of a programme for republican politicians between 1716 and 1721.

NOTES

1 Foster *Letters* pp. 97, 103

2 See *The Act of Settlement. Historical Association: Constitutional Documents – VI* 'Introduction'.

3 See M. L. de Miranda 'The moral social and political thought of the Third Earl of Shaftesbury, 1671–1713' (PhD Cambridge, 1994) p. 195.

4 *Limitations for the next foreign successor* (1701) pp. 11–13.

5 *Ibid.* pp. 16–17, 18, 19, 28–31.

6 *Remarks on a pamphlet, entitled Limitations for the next foreign successor* (1701) p. 24.

7 *Ibid.* p. 25.

8 Cited in F. H. Ellis (ed.) *Poems on affairs of state* (New Haven, 1970) vol. 6 p. 327.

9 See de Miranda 'Shaftesbury' pp. 196–197; *Tolandiana* pp. 81–82.

10 *Vindicius Liberius* p. 194.

11 A. Ward 'The Electress Sophia and the Hanoverian Succession' *English Historical Review* I (1886) pp. 470–506.

12 Toland *An account of the courts of Hannover and Prussia* (1705) p. 69.

13 Klopp 2, p. 266.

14 See *Tolandiana* pp. 78–80; *Anglia Libera, oder Das Freye Engeland* (Hamburg, 1701), and *Engelant, Vrygemaakt. Of De Bepaling en Successie Der Kroon Verklaart* (Rotterdam: Barent Bos, 1701).

15 Klopp 2 p. 265.

16 Klopp 2 p. 209.

17 Klopp 2 p. 276.

18 Klopp 2 pp. 333–334.

19 Klopp 2 p. 288.

20 PRO 30/24/20 Parts 1–2 fo. 28.

21 Klopp 2 p. 318.

22 Klopp 2 p. 333.

23 Klopp 2 p. 341.

24 Klopp 2 pp. 357–358; Toland passed on Sharp's Sermon on the Coronation of Queen Anne, as well as letters from Spanheim and Sir Robert Clayton.

25 Klopp 2 p. 376.

26 R. Doebner (ed.) *Briefe de Königin Sophie Charlotte von Preussen und der Kürfursten Sophie von Hannover* (Leipzig, 1905) pp. 14, 15–16.

27 *Ibid.* p. 20.

28 Doebner *Briefe* p. 22

29 Kemble *State papers* pp. 459–460.

30 Kemble *State papers* pp. 463, 465, 466, 467.

31 *Anglia Libera* 'Dedication'.

32 *Ibid.* pp. 1–2.

33 *Ibid.* pp. 4–5.

34 *Ibid.* p. 8.

35 *Ibid.* p. 14.

36 *Ibid.* p. 15.

37 *Ibid.* pp. 98–100.

38 *Ibid.* p. 105.

39 *Ibid.* p. 19.

40 *Ibid.* p. 26.

41 *Ibid.* pp. 30–32.

42 *Ibid.* pp. 44, 45–46.

43 *Ibid.* pp. 59–63.

44 *Ibid.* pp. 76–80.

45 *Ibid.* p. 83.

46 *Ibid.* pp. 85–86.

47 *Ibid.* pp. 90–92.

48 Q. Skinner *Liberty before Liberalism* (Cambridge, 1998) pp. 21–22 fn. 65, 67, and pp. 54–55 fn. 174, 176, 177.

49 *Anglia Libera* pp. 108–109.

50 *Ibid.* pp. 110–125, 126; see also 139.

51 *Ibid.* p. 188.

52 *The art of governing by parties* (1701), Dedication pp. i–ii, iv [unpaginated].

53 *Art* p. 4.

54 *Ibid.* p. 28.

55 *Ibid.* pp. 31–32, 33.

56 *Ibid.* pp. 37–38, 40.

57 *Ibid.* pp. 63–64, 70–71, 72.

58 *Ibid.* pp. 96–97, 104, 107.

59 *Ibid.* pp. 112–115. Citing *Discourses* II. 25.

60 *Ibid.* p. 135.

61 *Ibid.* pp. 173–174.

62 *Paradoxes of State* (1702) 1–2. William III's speech can be found in W. Cobbett

Parliamentary history of England (1803) V pp. 1329–1331.

63 See *Parliamentary history* V p. 1329.

64 *Paradoxes* pp. 4–5.

65 *Ibid.* p. 19.

66 *The memorial of the state of England* (1705) 'To the reader' A2.

67 *Memorial* pp. 11–13.

68 *Ibid.* pp. 34–35.

69 *Ibid.* pp. 43–44.

70 *Ibid.* pp. 47–49, 52, 53, 54–55, 58.

71 *Ibid.* pp. 76–78, 87.

72 *Collections* 2 p. 338.

73 *Ibid.* p. 350.

74 *Tolandiana* p. 197.

75 *Collections* 2 pp. 405–408.

76 *Ibid.* pp. 431–432.

77 See G. C. Gibbs 'English attitudes towards Hanover and the Hanoverian succession in the first half of the eighteenth century' in A. M. Birke and K. Kluxen (eds) *England and Hanover* (1986) pp. 33–53; R.Hatton 'George I as an English and a European Figure' in P. Fritz and D. Williams (eds) *The triumph of culture: eighteenth-century perspectives* (Toronto, 1972) pp. 191–209.

78 H. Isham Longden 'The Diaries (home and foreign) of Sir Justinian Isham, 1704–1736' *Transactions of the Royal Historical Society* (1907) p. 192.

79 See D. Hayton (ed.) *The Parliamentary diary of Sir Richard Cocks 1698–1702* (Oxford, 1996) p. 323; Cobbett *Parliamentary history* VI pp. 519–533.

80 See mss note BL copy of *Reasons for addressing his Majesty* (1702) call-mark 8135 b 54.

81 *Reasons for addressing his Majesty* pp. 1, 3, 4.

82 *Ibid.* pp. 14, 17, 20.

83 See *Relation des cours de Prusse et Hannovre* (A La Haye, Thomas Johnson, 1706).

84 *An Account of the courts* (1706: 2nd edition A. Baldwin) pp. iii, v, vi, vii–iii.

85 *Ibid.* Preface, p. xii; the Appendix reproduces the oath at pp. 81–87.

86 *Ibid.* pp. 53, 58, 67–69.

87 *Ibid.* Ordinances pp. 5, 6–7, 13–14.

88 *Ibid.* pp. 10–11, 23–24, 32–33.

89 *Ibid.* pp. 38–39.

90 It is noticeable that neither R. Oresko, G. C. Gibbs, H. M. Scott (eds) *Royal and republican sovereignty in early modern Europe* (Cambridge, 1997) nor J. Adamson (ed.) *The princely courts of Europe 1500–1750* (1999) devote serious attention to either Sophia or Sophie Charlotte's courts.

91 *Characters of the Court of Hannover* (1714) pp. 3, 10, 12–17.

92 See Toland *Her Majesty's reasons for creating the Electoral Prince of Hanover a Peer of this Realm* (1712) pp. 6, 7, 8.

93 *Reasons* (1714) pp. 4, 6, 12, 39.

94 *Funeral* pp. viii, 4–5, 6.

95 *Ibid.* p. 9.

96 *Ibid.* compare p. 10 with the Latin of p. 32.

97 *Ibid.* pp. 11–12, 13.

98 *Ibid.* pp. 16, 18, 19, 22.

99 *Collection* 2 pp. 405–406.

100 *Ibid.* p. 410.

101 *Ibid.* pp. 215, 216–217, 219.

102 *Ibid.* p. 222

103 *Ibid.* pp. 227–228.

104 *Ibid.* pp. 229, 230, 231, 234.

105 *Ibid.* p. 421.

106 *Art of Restoring* (1714) pp. 12, 13.

107 *Ibid.* pp. 37–38, 40, 43.

108 *The Grand Mystery laid open* (1714) p. 38.

109 Worden 'The Revolution and the English republican tradition' in Wootton *Republicanism* pp. 242, 260.

6

———◆———

Sapere aude:
'commonwealth' politics under
George I, 1714–22

O N the night of 1 March 1710, London was convulsed by rioting crowds.
During the course of the evening dissenting meeting-houses were
attacked and destroyed, lords, earls and bishops were insulted and affronted in
the streets, and many citizens were beaten, assaulted and even killed. Any who
refused to join in with the chant of 'High Church and Sacheverell' were
'knocked down' by armed and increasingly violent men.[1] Abigail Harley writing
to Edward Harley in Oxford the day after the tumult, commented that 'now we
hear nothing but drums'.[2] The cause of all this disorder was a conflict over
whether Christian culture was determined by men of reason and toleration, or
men of God and authority. The Whig prosecution defended the Erastian
principle, 'by which all ecclesiastical jurisdiction ... is made subject to the civil
power', and reinforced its commitment to Protestant civil liberties by prose-
cuting the High Church clergyman Henry Sacheverell.[3] Toland was intimate
with many of the leading actors in the public trial. Despite Sacheverell's
conviction, his reputation as a defender of 'the church in danger' set the scene
for the triumph of the Tory party that was swept to power in the following
General Election. Clerical politics was civil politics under another name.

Toland saw the trial as a critical moment in the republican war against
priestcraft. In a number of works published between 1710 and 1714 he struggled
to establish the dangers of such clericalism to public virtue, addressing much
of the argument to the Hanoverian court. His account of the trial itself, 'Fit to
be kept in all Families as a storehouse of arguments in defence of the Constitution' warned the Protestant population at large against the deceit and danger
of the High Church. Again by skilful editorial labour, he accented the extremism
of Sacheverell's hostility towards 'revolution principles'.[4] Pruning much of
Sacheverell's defence, and indeed, censoring some of the defence material
which cast aspersions on the religious integrity of his own work, Toland
established that the High Church was dangerous to the constitution of Britain.[5]

This clarion call against the incipient threat of dangerous priests, was reiterated in a number of other pamphlets which were shrill and unbridled in their critique of the Church. 'Busie and seditious clergymen' needed restraint.[6] 'High Church drummers' used their pulpits to broadcast sedition and encourage Jacobite restoration. Pulpits were 'wooden Engines' for the advance of passive obedience and other 'slavish notions'. They had been the 'armed instruments of Tyranny ... in most countries'. To allow oneself to be 'prated out' of liberty and property was foolish: 'will not the world think that we do not value as we ought our happy constitution if they see its greatest enemies permitted twice a week to banter, ridicule, libel and insult it?'[7] One implication of the Sacheverell trial was, as Toland pointed out, 'that Clergymen shou'd not (under penalty of incapacity during life) meddle with the civil government in their pulpits, nor pretend to decide questions in Politicks'. This 'protestant popery' was concerned only with 'advancing the pride and power of priests'. Sacheverell, like 'the Dunstans, the Anselms, the Becketts, the Huberts, or the Langtons', was in a long line of wicked priests who had challenged the authority of the civil state. Not only were the clergy immoral and drunk, haunting taverns and coffee-houses, but had become riotous and seditious, unhinging all 'wholesome order and Government'.[8] This battle of ideas against the priests, manifest in the public trial of Sacheverell, was fundamental to Toland's lifetime commitment as a public writer.

After the disastrous electoral defeats of 1710, Toland focused his energies on defending the succession and remaining vigilant against popish tyranny. It was his firm conviction that the enemy within, the false clergy, were the most dangerous threat to liberty. Most of this writing was defensive, establishing the legitimacy of the Hanoverians and exposing the menace of the priests. With the successful accession of George I, all of the years of writing for, and socialising with, the Whig political elite came to fruition. Now Toland had the opportunity to campaign for reforms that would have the possibility of real political effect. Between 1716 and 1719 there was a radical attempt to transform the confessional foundations of the constitution. Measures limiting the exercise of liberty of conscience were repealed, the Convocation of the Church of England was suspended, and a project to fundamentally remodel the constitutional balance between the three estates was attempted.[9] Toland, briefly, was right at the heart of these projects. Republican ambitions had come home.

That Toland saw radical opportunity can be seen in one of the first works he published under the new monarchy – *The reasons for naturalising the Jews* (1714) – which advanced one of the most radical defences of social toleration in the eighteenth century.[10] A deliberately provocative work, it was dismissed by contemporaries as the work of a violent 'Republican Atheist'.[11] Traditionally this text has been regarded as a key contribution to the evolution of 'Enlightened' attitudes towards Judaism.[12] At root Toland's arguments were political rather than religious. He wished to establish that there were 'common principles' in favour of a 'General Naturalisation'. These 'common reasons for a General Naturalisation, are as strong in behalf of the Jews, as of any other people whatsoever'. The point was not simply to tolerate Jews, but to break the confessional foundations of politics. All individuals (Jewish, Christian, whatever) should have rights of full citizenship as long as they 'wou'd not only be good subjects, but who wou'd also be as useful and advantageous to the public weal, as any of those Protestant Churches'. Aware that his proposal would not be popular he counter-argued that 'I may propose to serve my country ... [and] the most effectual way to do so, is the promoting of humanity, and the doing good to all mankind'.[13] Religious confession was irrelevant to civic identity.

Hostility to the Jewish community was one of the 'prejudices' that Toland aimed to dispel. Such attitudes were 'silly ... exciting at once laughter, scorn and pity'. For Toland, naturalisation was good policy because Jews were simply like other people: some were 'sordid wretches, sharpers, extortioners, villains of all sorts and degrees' but others were 'men of probity and worth, persons of courage and conduct, of liberal and generous spirits'. Jews as humans, deserved to be regarded 'under the common circumstances of human nature' and as 'creatures of the same species'. The diversity of manners 'and especially contrary rites or doctrines in religion' led to hatred, cruel persecution and murder.[14] The experience of dissenting Protestants under the lash of 'popery' was similar.[15] Typically, for Toland, the sad experience of the Jews was not the result of accident but the design of corrupt priests who acted like 'ravenous wolves'. 'Their most inveterate enemies were the Priests' who conspired with rapacious princes to plunder Jewish property, 'but also to acquire the reputation of zeal and sanctity among the credulous vulgar'. Driven by priestly prejudice, kings had turned the sword of state against them such 'that their condition under Christian princes was farr worse than that of their forefathers under Pharao'. The tragedy of Jewish suffering was an exemplar of how 'dangerous and destructive a monster is superstition, when rid by the Mob, and driven by the Priests'.[16]

The promotion of 'common humanity and genuine religion' was now a possibility which would benefit both 'private and public interest'.[17] Aware that many critics would claim that he was blind to the dangers of Jewish religion, he had taken 'no inconsiderable pains' to investigate their rites and ceremonies. His research suggested that Judaism was a tolerable and natural religion. Contrary to commonplace Christian accounts Toland, echoing Spinoza, insisted that the rites and ceremonies of that religion were 'solely calculated for their own Nation and Republic'. Jews did not wish to convert Christians but simply 'are every where enjoin'd to magnify to all the world the divine goodness, wisdom, and power, with those duties of men, and other attributes of God, which constitute Natural Religion'.[18] As humans, like other religious dissenters, Jews were 'safe and sociable'.[19] Religious ceremony, as long as it did not prompt execrable persecution (like priestly Christianity) was immaterial to the status of individuals in a civic sense.

Toland's defence of toleration was premised not upon the theological credibility of the Jewish religion but upon the nature of civil society. All individuals were equal regardless of religious confession. Human society was structured by 'ties of kindred, acquaintance, friendship, or confederacy'. Because human beings took longer to rear than other species they were 'absolutely incapable to subsist afterwards without the company of other men'. The web of dependent relations was intimate and social. Building on relations formed in the family, humanity developed 'notions of acquaintance, neighbourhood, friendship, affinity, association, confederacy, subjection and superiority'. All individuals experienced three forms of related obligation: to domestic community, to the welfare of the whole species, and thirdly 'in a special manner to the safe and flourishing condition of that country or society to which he immediately belongs'. These obligations were to be achieved by diligent industry and would thus benefit both public and private interests.[20] The promotion of naturalisation was a rational civic injunction. Toland's republican political agenda suggested that all dissenters, not only Jews, thus be given full rights of citizenship.[21] This ambition of establishing a tolerant and rational civic culture was taken even further in Toland's most successful political pamphlet, *The State anatomy of Great Britain* (which went through nine editions in 1717) and its supplement *The second part of the State anatomy* (two editions, 1717).

Published in the first three months of 1717 both works were enormously popular.[22] Toland had spent the previous two decades of his life trying to persuade both the public and the political elite of the merits of fundamental reform, finally his time had come to broadcast his ideas to a ministry who had parliamentary strength and intentions of implementing them. It was a repeated contemporary charge that Toland was not the sole author of *State anatomy*. As one hostile commentator wrote, the work 'has been long hatching, and had been much talk'd of so many days before it came abroad, pieces and parts of it handed about, and rehearsed amongst the people it is calculated to serve'. As Defoe commented, 'we shall find him as heterodox in politicks, as he is in religion'.[23] Toland was regarded as a spokesman for a radical political clique closely associated with the ministry of the day he could 'no more be called the Author, than the shopkeeper who sells watches, ought to be, tho he is corruptly and improperly, called a watchmaker'.[24] The work has been described as a 'manifesto for the Molesworth connection'.[25] Indeed, as we will see below, Toland's intimacy with Molesworth after 1716 was profound, if little noted.

This relationship was one of the most important conduits for the dissemination of Toland's ideas amongst a serious political elite.

Although there is still much work to be done on the political history of the early years of George I, it is clear that Robert Molesworth was a focus for radical commonwealth projects such as the repeal of the Test Act and the Peerage Bill. A prominent supporter of William III, and appointed to his Privy Council after 1689, he starting his political career as a country Whig in the 1690s in both the English and Irish Parliaments. Molesworth, an admirer of Algernon Sidney, made his republican reputation with the publication of his anti-absolutist *Account of Denmark* (1694) which displayed a mixture of contractarian political thought with a profound anticlericalism. Associated with John Methuen, Lord Chancellor of Ireland, Molesworth, an Irishman, may have known Toland from the late 1690s: typically in this period he acted as teller against the Blasphemy Bill. His parliamentary career in the 1700s was undistinguished by any major performance, although he opposed the Tithes Bill of 1707 and liased closely with Godolphin in an attempt to bring Shaftesbury into the government in 1708. At different points he seems to have been in the circle of Sunderland and Marlborough. Evidence of his anticlericalism is clear in his removal from the Irish Privy Council in 1713 after complaint by the prolocutor of Convocation. After 1714 he achieved some reward in appointment to the Irish Privy Council and as commissioner for trade and plantations but not as much as he expected. After 1716 he did however exercise political influence without access to patronage, in particular over the controversial issues of toleration and the peerage. It was a public sign of his continuing status that he was created Baron Molesworth of Philipstown and Viscount Molesworth of Swords in July 1719.[26]

Confirming Molesworth's public reputation, Toland aiming to defend the 'publick interest', enjoined the new monarch George I, as king of 'a free-born Protestant people', to establish true liberty. The new monarchy was 'not grounded on arbitrary prerogative, and a chimerical jure divino; but on the legal CONSTITUTION and PROTESTANT RELIGION'. The only opposition to his regulated rule was the malicious 'inferior Clergy and inferior people, or a mob of priests and peasants'.[27] George I was to emulate William III as a virtuous legislator. Explicitly calculated to defend the 'Whig supremacy' and the Hanoverian regime, Toland announced his republican purpose by citing Cicero on the title page: 'for just as the aim of the pilot is a successful voyage, of the physician, health, and of the general victory, so this director of the commonwealth has as his aim for his fellow citizens a happy life, fortified by wealth, rich in material resources, great in glory and honoured for virtue. I want him to bring to perfection this achievement, which is the greatest and best possible amongst men'.[28] George I was to be this model of Cicero's 'Prince in Idea'.[29] Hostile contemporaries, sensitive to the Harringtonian language of the work, accused him of dangerous innovation: 'he would now frame a new constitu-tion'.[30] It was Toland's point, though, that justly regulated kings could be legitimate governors. He enjoined all men to 'love King George'. Inverting accusations of sedition commonly attributed to republicans he noted that subversion was more likely to come from non-jurors and Jacobites who denied the Hanoverians their just title to the Crown.[31]

Once again Toland was keen to clarify the republican nature of his proposals. To accuse him and his friends of hostility to 'all regal government whether limited or unlimited, conditional or absolute' was wrong. Just as Cicero, Polybius and Aristotle had judged, monarchy was a essential part of the mixed constitution: the English crown was a medium between 'an absolutely hereditary, and an absolutely elective monarchy'. The meaning of the word commonwealth was 'the common weal or good ... just as the word *Respublica* in Latin, is a general word for all free Governments of which we believe ours to be the best'. Citing the examples of James I and Sir Thomas Smith, Toland asserted that there was no medium between free governments and 'unlimited arbitrary power in the monarch'.[32] While George I had been elected by 'a free people for his numberless virtues', his example was to be contrasted with the suggestions of 'court parasites' and a 'few aspiring clergy-men' who attempted to tarnish republicans with the reputation of 'levelling and democratical principles'. Drawing the distinction between 'our envy'd liberty' and anarchy and licentiousness, Toland summarised the nature of Hanoverian rule as 'a government of laws enacted for the common good of all the people, by their own consent and approbation as they are represented in Parliament'. Political liberty was established by the rule of law: this meant that 'our monarchy is the best form of a commonwealth'.[33]

Just as the Whigs were 'assertors' of liberty rather than 'antimonarchical or popular republicans' so Tories were 'abettors of tyranny'. The focus of Toland's enquiry was the consequence of these distinctions in matters of religion. Protestantism as a religion of liberty and reason, was 'an essential part of our constitution, adding the sanction of laws to the conviction of our minds'. The Protestant principle of toleration could not however be applied to Roman Catholics since their faith was a politically corrosive doctrine rather than a theological belief. Popery was a form of tyranny, 'a mere political faction, erecting a splendid, pompous, and universal empire over mankind'.[34] Beyond the distinction between Protestantism and Popery, all religious difference was tolerable. As Toland blandly put it, 'Tis impossible for reasonable men not to differ about the meaning of ancient books or intricate doctrines, but not at all necessary that they hate one another'. Controversy and contention within the Protestant communion ought to be avoided since its complication with civil power caused political distress. Battles between high, low and dissenting churchmen were ultimately about self-interest or matters indifferent.[35]

The resolution of this problem was the establishment of a statutory measure of liberty of conscience compatible with the continuance of a National Church. This did not imply 'licentiousness in morals (which has no plea from conscience) nor indifference as to all religions: but a free toleration both of such actions as are in their own nature allow'd to be indifferent, or in their circumstances unsinful'. Bare speculation, doctrine and opinion 'as are not destructive of humane society' were tolerable, because premised upon a liberty of 'the use of reason which is equally the right of all men'.

The regulation of such liberty was either entire or partial. Entire liberty was established when any man 'according to the dictates of his own conscience, may have the free exercise of his religion, without any impediment to his preferment or imployment in the state'. Partial liberty was when the free exercise of religion was not matched by liberty of civil status but meant 'he is thereby render'd incapable' of civil service.[36] As Harrington had noted, approved Toland, 'a national religion must not be a *Public driveing*, but a *Publick leading*'. This commitment to entire or partial liberty in religion was a litmus test for the nature of civil liberty. Toleration was the source of 'science', persecution ('the root of ignorance') produced 'sedition and troubles'. Establishing an entire liberty was then not only virtuous, but politically expedient too 'as it furnishes the King with more hearts, and the nation with more hands'.[37] The Occasional Conformity and Schism Acts ought to be repealed: so too did the 'political monopoly' of the sacramental test. Fracturing these statutes would be an effective method for destroying the institutions that bred up 'Protestant popery' which was a 'spiritual tyranny' based upon the independence of the Church from the State.[38] Toland was not alone in advancing the civil rights of the dissenting community. Other writings rehearsed the key arguments. The Dissenters had suffered for their conscience, but had proved stalwart for the cause of 'English Liberty'. Subscribing to a limited understanding of the prince's power as a 'trust', Dissenters had insisted that 'the liberties of the people are part of our constitution'. Defending the Protestant succession against the threat of absolute hereditary monarchy qualified Dissenters for public service in terms of 'policy' and 'common justice'. Allowing such men to serve as Sheriffs, Justices and Corporation officers would provide a bulwark against the corruption of Jacobite men in local society. Since every individual devolved their right of self-defence in consenting to the creation of a magistrate, so 'everyone has a right to a capacity for 'em to gain public office'.[39]

Foreshadowing the parliamentary proposals of 1717–19, Toland discussed the precise terms for reforming Church and State. Parliamentary corruption could be removed by 'restor[ing] the constitution' and securing it from such infamous acts of tyranny like Harley's creation of twelve peers ('the deadliest blow which was ever struck at the vitals of Parliament'). The judiciary should be rendered independent from 'court influence'.[40] Statutes for restraining the tumults and riots prompted by firebrands like Sacheverell were demanded. Perhaps the most significant series of recommendations advanced were those to regulate the universities and the pulpits. It had been a continual theme of Toland's polemic against the corrosive influence of the Church, that the universities were the breeding grounds of such false ideology. Unlike the institutions in Leiden, Helmstadt and Frankfurt, the English universities, but especially Oxford, taught 'a very opposite genius to our Constitution'. The constant assault upon 'revolution principles' coupled with the 'barbarism and ignorance, Turbulence and sedition' of the tutors, was a persistent corrosive. The King would, Toland promised, find 'effectual means to make them not only keep to their business, and to that precisely; but, if they shou'd neglect their duty, or depart from their province, he'll correct and punish them in proportion to their demerits'.[41] Just as the regulations of the universities would be severely enforced so would the 'pulpits' be adapted to the interests of civic virtue. The clergy were the 'veriest bunglers that ever dabl'd in politicks': wherever they exercised any power in civil matters 'the worse it is for both Prince and People'. A strict application of the statute of mortmain, or 'the 75th canon' enjoining sober conversation, would prohibit their intermeddling especially in the property and politics of the laity.[42] Citing Cicero, Toland confronted priests who 'wou'd go about to defend those things by Divine religion, which were condemn'd by human equity' with the Roman's reply, 'we must look out for other ceremonies, for other priests of the immortal Gods, for other expounders of religion'.[43] Once again republican political aspirations assumed the practical form of anticlerical measures.[44]

Toland had been preparing these policies for some time. He made his attitude to the new regime very clear in a scribal memorial circulated immediately after the accession of George I (and printed in the posthumous works). This memorial offered practical counsel 'presented to a minister of state'. One of the fundamental themes was an explicit attack upon the greed and tyranny of the clergy. As he insisted, 'I take it for granted, as a thing of public notoriety, that but too many of the clergy of England have no regard for any thing but profit and power'. The best way of restraining corrupt clerical ambition was 'to lay a strict and steady hand over them' by reinvigorating the medieval statute of Mortmain and discontinuing their 'rampant practices' of meddling in 'politicks or civil affairs'.[45] Made 'equally proud and insolent at the universities', these churchmen corrupted civil government by the authority they wielded over the nobility by 'governing their persons, families, estates and interest'. A step towards undercutting this cultural authority would be to remove the clerical qualification for teaching fellowships at Oxford and Cambridge.

Controlling the clergy was one means of resolving the current political divisions of the times because distinctions in religion and politics were driven by clerical interest. It was Toland's advice and judgement that a broad-based ministry would be most successful. By including men of 'virtue and merit', even if Tory, the benefits of impartiality would accrue authority to the government.[46] This counsel was based on fundamental principles. As he pointed out, although mankind was by nature a 'sociable species of animal herding together in communities for their common safety' they still quarrelled amongst themselves 'or oppress each other, just upon the same motives and topicks with other animals: such as food, venery, sickness old age and want of understanding'. Rather than resolving these differences the 'use of speech, and especially of hands, which manage weapons to their own destruction, as well as that of other creatures' made conflict worse. These conflicts should be healed by 'true virtue, religion and understanding' established by 'good education and wholesome laws'.[47] Since the rules for virtue and religion were a key part of 'the civil government' they ought to be 'plain and simple, or (as we commonly speak) the naked truth, unchangeable, void of craft, of gain, or of power'. It was the function and duty of the clergy to teach such a civil religion as 'the ready way to make humanity shine, justice flourish, and communities happy'.[48] Reform of the Church was then a pressing and urgent part of the programme to refurbish English virtues. Transformation of the Church could be achieved by the King and the diocesan bishops enforcing existing canon law. Similarly the universities could be 'settl'd on the foot of virtue'. Advancing a virtually Platonic model Toland suggested a balanced community could be cultivated by encouraging each person to develop to the best of their abilities undistracted by fears, hopes or passions. The defence of public virtue would be enforced by a strict application of the law: the disorderly, the seditious and the corrupt would have to be 'severely handled'. 'Gentlemen of virtue, understanding, and industry' should be magistrates, but on no account ought any clergyman or lawyer to be in the civil magistracy.[49]

To reform the dissolute and vicious morals of the people, strict laws against poaching should be enforced and a timetable of virtuous popular sports 'such as wrestling, cudgel playing, throwing the barr, and the like recreations serving to increase strength and agility in the body, no less than to procure or preserve health' should be introduced. With such an overhaul of the various civil and social institutions and led by the virtuous kingship of George, it would be possible to 'make these islands the most happy, flourishing and potent Empire of the whole world; especially, by the destruction of superstition and vice, the highest and most glorious conquest'.[50] In these ambitions Toland displayed his conviction that the English commonwealth could be brought back to virtue and liberty. As he was to underscore in the later printed work, the ministry in power had men capable of establishing this civic reform: men like Hoadly, Sunderland ('as famous for [his] unshaken love of liberty, as for his universal learning'), Walpole, Stanhope, the young Duke of Newcastle were all figures who Toland attempted to seduce to his vision.[51]

Although *State anatomy* was a bestseller, contemporaries were unconvinced. Defoe dismissed the arguments as a 'projected state tyranny'. Toland's attack upon the established church and his intention of tolerating not only different opinions, but also different religions, would compromise true religion, just as his flattery of the king would sacrifice the liberties of the people.[52] Another commentator was particularly incensed with Toland's glib assertion that men would always differ about religious truth.[53] A further critic condemned Toland's state surgery as mere quackery. The advice in favour of the Dissenters was corrosive of the established order, since they aimed at their own 'ecclesiastical tyranny' rather than parity. The suggestion made by Toland, and repeated by Benjamin Hoadly, the Bishop of Bangor, that men had 'a natural right of civil offices seems ... a very wild notion'. To allow Dissenters into civil government would infringe the 'common safety'; while dissenting tradesmen might benefit the community 'dissenting statesmen must be dangerous'.[54] The thrust of the counter-polemic against Toland in 1717 indicated the division within Whig ideology about the limits of toleration and the relationship between civil and religious liberties. Toland's strategy was twofold: to cultivate support for a suspension of the remaining statutes against conscience, and to encourage a renovation of the ecclesiastical institutions he saw as causing the problems of religious tyranny in the first place. Thus for Toland and his circle, toleration and anticlericalism were a central part of a political programme. In works like *State anatomy* Toland explicitly attempted as he put it, to prepare 'the minds of those without doors' because he was confident that 'some things will be done by those within'. His 'illustrious prompters' would ensure that the many things discussed in the tract would be 'accomplish'd by their means'.[55] The success of Toland's *State anatomy* suggests that there was a significant audience outside of the Court and Parliament for the thrust of such arguments.[56] To other figures, (with increasing conviction during the later 1710s) like Robert Walpole, while a measure of toleration was fundamental, preservation of the social authority of the Church of England took priority. In this assessment by Walpole of the power of allegiance to the established Church lay the seeds of defeat for the commonwealth programme. Consequently with Walpole's capture of ministerial primacy in 1720, just at the moment when the battle against the Church seemed won, the palms of victory were to be snatched away.

With the political rise of Walpole and the defeat (and ultimately the deaths) of Stanhope and Sunderland after 1720, Toland found himself once again writing a republican critique of the established order having followed the star of Molesworth's reputation into opposition. Just as he had sacrificed his friendship to Harley when the latter seemed to compromise his commitments to Protestant liberties, so Toland was loyal to Molesworth when he remained stalwart to these principles. Between 1717 and 1721 a fierce battle was fought within the Whig regime. After the so-called schism of 1717 when Walpole and Townshend left the ministry there was an increasingly bitter contest between the leading politicians, made worse by the fracture of relations between George and his son. During these last years of the 1710s there was a profound and sustained attempt to establish the fundamentals of republican ideology against persistent harassment from an apostate Whig opposition. The political and intellectual ambitions and dimensions of this conflict have rarely been examined. One of the central debates between the ministry and opposition focused on the urgency of the war against priestcraft and the need for securing the constitution against corruption. Just as the 'true Whigs' of the later 1690s had reviled those who compromised the 'revolution principles' of 1689, by invoking commonwealth writings of the 1650s, so some twenty years later, Toland re-invoked the writing of men like Shaftesbury and Molesworth.

The reputation of the third Earl of Shaftesbury who had supported, sponsored and collaborated with Toland in the 1690s and 1700s was central to the preservation of a true commonwealth tradition under the new regime. Shaftesbury had been a lynchpin in the radical milieu that included people like Prince Eugene, Queen Sophia and Benjamin Furly. By 1718, closely associated with the political star of Robert Molesworth, Toland fashioned a political authority invoking the heritage of earlier republicans like Shaftesbury. This was especially powerful because many of the figures involved in common-wealth politics after 1714 – Trenchard, Sunderland, Stanhope, and Molesworth – had developed their ideas and practical experience in the 1690s. Resonance with this recent past was a cultural resource that provided a motive for both political action and ideological conviction. That Shaftesbury was a model of republican virtue worthy of emulation can be seen in the publication of a collection of his letters of advice *To a young man at the University* (1716). Premised upon a celebration of 'inviolable Toleration' against the 'abominable Blasphemous representative of Church power', Shaftesbury was represented as defending the 'freedom of reason in the learned world and good govern-ment in the civil world'. Tyranny in the one was 'ever accompanied, or soon followed, by tyranny in the other. And when slavery is brought upon a people, they are soon reduced to that base and brutal state, both in their under-standings and morals'.[57] Hostile to clerical claims to knowledge, Shaftesbury reinforced the link between liberty, freedom and virtue. The recurrent theme of the letters was to apply republican conceptions of 'liberty' to the realm of religious belief. With such 'Christian liberty' Britons might 'cease to be slaves and drudges in religion'. A mind 'set at liberty ... from voluntary error and self-darkening conceit, aspires to what is generous and deserving'. The pursuit of 'self-interest' led naturally to 'inward slavery'. The tyranny of passion supported political slavery, but a man who asserted 'his inward liberty' was 'morally free'.[58] This moral theory drawing the connection between mental and civil liberty would become a key part of the republican defence of toleration after 1716.

Toland exploited this image of Shaftesbury as the stalwart of 'true whiggism' in his subtle electoral propaganda on behalf of Molesworth in 1721 by publishing an earlier correspondence between the two noblemen. The volume, circulated in scribal form before publication, was calculated to provide both a hagiography of Shaftesbury, and refurbish Molesworth's republican credentials. The letters, given to Toland by Molesworth in 1719 'as a memorial of the late Earl of Shaftesbury, whom I infinitely honour'd, and with whom I cultivated a most infinite acquaintance', were intended to provide models of virtuous private and public service. Shaftesbury, a man of learning was driven by a 'love of one's country' and a 'passion for true freedom'. Just as he adored 'liberty and laws', so 'he aborr'd licentiousness and tyranny'.[59] Paralleling Molesworth's disgust with the corruption of the Whig regime in 1720, Shaftesbury had withdrawn from London and the court in the 1700s. Shaftesbury was sickened by the perversion of the revolution by 'the sweet of places and pensions'. Importantly, especially for the opposition Molesworth had embarked upon against the corruption of the Whig ministry after the crisis of the South Sea Bubble, for Shaftesbury the apostate Whigs were as much to blame as the Tories.[60] Molesworth and Shaftesbury had a 'sworn friendship'. Both men 'had ever unalterably appear'd for the liberty of his country, and indeed of mankind, as well by writing as by word and action'. Disinterring the dynamics of elite politics of the 1700s, Toland portrayed Molesworth as a broker between Godolphin and Shaftesbury, 'he brought them to an interview and eclairisse-ment'. Molesworth's knowledge of the constitution and disposition of the people made him an indispensable instrument for Godolphin's management of national politics. Encouraged by Molesworth, Shaftesbury served 'the government disinterestedly', keeping 'clean hands' in giving advice for the pursuit of honest measures. As Toland noted, Molesworth's action was admirable and thus was especially relevant for 'present ministers'.[61] The political nation could be assured that Molesworth was a man of impeccable republican credentials.

A second theme, underscored to make contemporary analogies obvious, was Shaftesbury's 'uncommon aversion' for the court, which he blamed for the corruption of the revolution. The variety of acts against standing armies, places, pensions and dependence in the judiciary, had not stopped those who abandoned their principles for private profit. This was not to blame the 'Prince' but the self-interested advice of 'evil counsellors'. Shaftesbury's counsel that the antidote to such corruption was to be found in free elections was especially relevant in 1721 when under the terms of the Septennial Act an election was due. Frequent elections established the 'sense of the people' by 'free choice' and acted as a purge of malignant corruption. As a direct commentary on the contemporary government, Toland insisted that even 'the very best, the most freely elected, you can imagine, if continu'd too long, grows as it were stagnant, and falls by degrees into such corruptions, as they would have aborr'd at the beginning'. Shaftesbury's dictum that 'you can never be hurt but by a Parliament' had particular reference to 1721 according to Toland. Electors ought to be cautioned against bribery and 'any unreasonable gainer or spender', as well as those who were 'suspected enemies of his present Majesty's title and family'. Deliberately recalling the *Danger of mercenary Parliaments* (in both editions of 1698 and 1705) with lengthy citations against those ministers who became 'the most active instruments of enslaving their country', Toland made the parallel between the early 1700s and the late 1710s even more explicit. As he clarified, the tracts had been prompted not by any suspicion of William III who was not suspected of 'harbouring any design against that liberty, he so generally came to retrieve', but by doubts about his counsellors who 'might tempt him to be arbitrary; not to procure him power, but to themselves impunity'.[62] Even the Archangel Michael ought not to be trusted by any 'great patriot' especially 'in time of peace with a Standing Army'.[63]

Toland also set out to exploit Shaftesbury's commitment to republican discourses evident in his own collaborations with the peer by reprinting *The danger of mercenary Parliaments* (first published in 1698 and reprinted in the 1705 collection of *State tracts*) in 1722, complete with a new editorial introduction. This was, in fact, the last work Toland ever wrote, although his 'passion for liberty continued warm to the last moments of his life'.[64] As in the 1690s, so in 1722, the political context of the work was a forthcoming electoral campaign. 'Free and frequent parliaments' were the foundation of wealth, power, liberty and prosperity. The 'original freedom' of elections was the 'greatest happiness that any people can have'. Bribery, 'long' parliaments and 'packing' members was a fundamental threat to the constitution whether undertaken by Whigs or Tories. Reminding the public in 1722 that the revolution of 1689 was a 'Golden dream' and 'a full deliverance from their present miseries, and a sure remedy for their future fears' was a call to renewed virtue. Although William had been venerated as the 'most auspicious prince that ever sway'd the English Scepter', his title was only made legitimate by 'the general consent and election of his people'.[65] Defending opposition to Walpole's dominance of the ministry, the debates about the politics of place and pension of the later 1690s were rehearsed as pertinent to 1722. The corruption of self-interest 'like a universal leprosy, has so notoriously infected and overspread both our court and parliament'. Court life was ever the same; allurements and temptations were constantly present 'for the corrupting of mens minds, and debauching of their honest principles'.[66] The point of the tract in 1698 and 1722 was to encourage the election of honest men. Key to the arguments were republican accounts of the relationship between private interest and public virtue, the consensual origins of political authority and a fundamental critique of the corruption of courts.

One of the purposes of Toland's hagiography of Shaftesbury was to indicate how the baton of virtue had been successfully passed on to Robert Molesworth. The latter's claim to republican credentials was based on the reputation of his influential *Account of Denmark*.[67] Achieving three English editions in its first year of publication and a French translation, the work prompted the Danish Ambassador Scheel to demand that the printer be severely punished and all copies burnt.[68] One contemporary dismissed the work as an 'anti-monarchical project' written in defence of the 'specious pretence of the All-atoning Freedom of the subject'.[69] Such a 'snarling republican' intended both to 'trample bishops and blaspheme kings'.[70] These themes were echoed in some of the more popular material produced by Toland, such as the political engraving published in November 1721 which represented Molesworth as Cato complete with a fragment of Lucan's eulogy of Cato.[71] The treatise was as much a defence of 1689 as a commentary on the decline of liberty in Scandinavia. The revolution of 1689 had restored England to a 'legal state of Freedom'. Once again William III was presented as a king who reinstated liberty against the persistent threat of deviant churchmen who attempted 'enslaving the spirits of the people, as a preparation to that of their bodies'. True knowledge and learning established 'good principles, morals, the improvement of Reason, the love of justice, the value of liberty, the duty owing to ones country and the laws', while the false knowledge of the churchmen established 'submission to superiors and an entire blind obedience to Authority'. Molesworth set his face against all 'dangerous passive notions' and 'slavish opinions'. Critically, just as Toland was to do in his *Life of Milton*, Molesworth insisted that good education especially in the history of virtuous men was critical in developing a veneration for 'publick liberty'. The examples of Brutus and Cato were 'the true pattern and model of exact vertue'.[72] Tyranny had been built upon false doctrines of 'passive obedience and jus divinum' in the 'latter ages of slavery'.[73] In calling for the 'character of the Priest [to] give place to that of the Patriot', Molesworth identified the Church as a critical engine in the corruption of liberty. This was a republican polemic that became ever more redolent after 1714, when the security of a limited monarchy was only compromised by an element within the established Church that still pursued the dream of, as a minimum, the *jus divinum* of the Anglican episcopacy and, as a maximum, the restoration of the Stuart monarchy.

The continuity of Molesworth's commitment to this analysis of the menace of the clerical establishment to liberty can also be seen in his edition of the monarchomach writer François Hotman's *Francogallia* published in 1711 and again in 1721. Many earlier radical works were republished and translated in England during the 1680s and 1690s as a part of the ideological defence of resistance against popish absolutism.[74] Certainly library catalogues of men like Shaftesbury, Furly, Locke and others indicate that this canon of works was owned and presumably read. Molesworth's edition of Hotman is a generally accurate translation but he did add editorial material to make it relevant to contemporary politics in 1711 and 1721.[75] For Molesworth, Hotman's research established an account of 'the ancient free states' of Europe, a prequel to his own study of the decline of liberty in the *Account of Denmark*. He had translated the book for Englishmen, 'who of all people living, have the greatest reason to be thoroughly instructed in what it contains, as having on the one hand, the most to lose; and on the other, the least sense of their Right to it'. The English were 'the only possessors of true liberty in the world': instruction would explain the origins of that liberty, but also the miserable consequences of losing it.[76] The context of Tory triumph after the disaster of the Sacheverell trial and the consequent threat to the succession of Hanover provided an urgent tocsin to defenders of liberty. Choosing to promote such a glorious end 'in my study, which I would have promoted any other way, if I had been called to it', Molesworth commended Hotman's learning against Pierre Bayle's attack upon his scholarship. *Francogallia* contained 'only pure Matter of Fact' and thus 'truth exposes Tyranny'. Originally, Molesworth had intended to include a long commentary (published later in 1775 as *The principles of a real Whig*) written in 1705 but eventually included it in the edition of 1721 because while 'this piece being seasonable at all times for the perusal of Englishmen [it was] ... more particularly at this time'.[77]

Just as Toland had defended his republications in the 1690s, so Molesworth rebutted the 'heavy calumny' that books which promoted 'the acquiring or preserving the public liberty', were seditious. The claim 'that we are all commonwealths-men; which (in the ordinary meaning of the word) amounts to haters of Kingly government' was unjust. Such works, contrary to the decrees of Oxford University, were the 'very foundations of all our civil rights'. Reading such works would counter the commonplaces of traditional education which was 'so diametrically opposite to our Bill of Rights'.[78] Recounting his interpretation of 'revolution principles' as a version of the 'true old Gothic Constitution' of the three estates of monarchy, lords and commons, he defended the idea of kingship 'accountable to the whole body of the people in case of male administration'. Allegiance and obedience were in exchange for 'protection, liberty and property'. Much like Toland, Molesworth defined the 'commonwealth' in terms of free government: the model of Elizabethan government rather than the anarchy of the interregnum. As he explained 'for where the very frame of the constitution, the good of the whole is taken care of by the whole (as 'tis in our case) the having a king or Queen at the head of it, alters not the case'. Institutions of government could be instrumentally distinguished from the nature or character of that regime.[79] Molesworth insisted that the true etymology of 'loyalty' invoked obedience to the prince, only 'according to law'. The constitution of the nation was a 'government of law, not of persons'.[80]

Having established his republican credentials in the realms of civil government, Molesworth turned to the question of religious liberty 'a great and universal concern'. The starting point was that 'whosoever is against liberty of mind, is in effect, against liberty of body too'. Although defending the necessity of an established Church this was combined with tolerance and charity for all, including 'pagans, Turks, Jews, Papists, Quakers, Socinians, Presbyterians or others'. Tyrannising citizens for difference in opinion was the 'offspring of interest and ignorance'. Citing the golden rule, Molesworth insisted that there could be no religious grounds for restraint of liberty or 'to retrench the civil advantages of an honest man'. Churchmen who attempted to engross a monopoly on entrance to heaven were corrupt: invoking a profound relativism he insisted religious difference had no influence 'on moral honesty'. The pursuit of liberty and virtue was independent of questions of religious commitment: thus 'the thriving of one single person by honest means, is the thriving of the commonwealth wherein he resides'. This was the groundwork for a programme of republican reforms that included a defence of general naturalisation, arguments about electoral reform, the case for expanding the militia, and invocations in favour of 'maintaining liberty of the press' and restraint of priestcraft.[81] All these adjustments would encourage an expansive, and hopefully, pan-European liberty. It is important to stress that Molesworth's republicanism was not simply discursive – especially after 1714, he was an active parliamentarian. A powerful agitator against the Occasional Conformity and Schism Acts in 1717, he voted in favour of repealing them in 1719. A supporter of the controversial Peerage Bill in 1719 he turned against the ministry over the question of the subjection of Irish jurisdiction to the English House of Lords in 1720, and more savagely over the administration's conduct in the case of the South Sea bubble.[82]

Molesworth and Toland were not alone. There were others in the political firmament that shared these ambitions. Popular journals like *The Freethinker*, *The Independent Whig* and *Cato's Letters* reiterated these themes to a wider audience. *The Freethinker* was edited by Ambrose Philips, antagonist of Pope and pastoral poet. As Thomas Burnett commented, 'the government have sett the author up to it, and know that we are assisting to him'.[83] Philips was also secretary of the Hanover Club, an adjunct to the Whig Kit Kat Club, which was dedicated to giving Tories and Jacobites 'all the opposition they could give in their several stations'. Including MPs like James Craggs and Sir Richard

Steele, as well as men like Paul Methuen, the club had 'true Whig' credentials: many of the politicians held significant position in the post-1714 ministry.[84] Thomas Burnett admitted that 'though I am not the author, yet I am one of a club that reviews everyone before they go to the press'.[85] Running from March 1718 into the next year, and frequently republished as a collection in the early 1720s, Philips collaborated with Hugh Boulter, Richard West and Zachary Pierce. Boulter, associated with Sunderland, was Chaplain to George I in 1719 and became Archbishop of Armagh in the mid-1720s. Richard West became Irish Lord Chancellor. Zachary Pierce, another contributor, was Bishop of Rochester.[86] The collective authors are remarkable, not least, for their intimacy with the Whig supremacy of the 1720s.

The motto of *The Freethinker*, the name itself establishing its radical credentials (pre-empting Kant) was 'Sapere Aude'. The purpose of the journal was to encourage the destruction of prejudice and defend liberty of conscience: 'to think freely is not to think at random: it is not to think like a fool or a madman: but like a philosopher; it is not to think without the checks of reason and judgement; but without the incumberances of prejudice and passion'. Freethinking was the 'foundation of all human liberty: remove the one and the other cannot stand'. As the source of knowledge, the parent of the arts and sciences, freethinking supported virtue, good manners, 'order and government' and true religion. Great Britain was a 'land of philosophers' where reason stood as a bulwark against 'slavery, ignorance, superstition, idleness and poverty'. In Britain a man was 'not obliged to divest himself in any degree of his reason, before he can be a good subject'.[87] Discoursing about sensitive issues such as the crucifixion of Christ (which was compared with that of Socrates and Cato), the journal sponsored an anticlerical and almost irreligious attitude towards Christian doctrine and institutions. There was a clear republican intent to the paper: a 'free people' needed to use their reason to combat passion and interest, as well as error and delusion. Truth, like the 'bursting of a bomb in a crowd' alarmed modern statesmen and courtiers whose understandings 'are enslaved, and perpetually employed in journey work under their passions'.[88] Amongst a miscellany of discussion about air-pumps, duelling and Lucretius, there was a persistent assertion that 'every Briton not only may, but has a right to, Think aloud'. To encourage all to be rational was a fundamental maxim of free government and would 'dispose the people to vertue'. Antiquity showed that though the tyranny of 'authority' had often 'usurpt an arbitrary power' it had also often been deposed.[89] The collapse of the 'Protestant' language of liberty of conscience into a republican language of freethinking was achieved most effectively in the discussion of the relative merits of the atheist and the superstitious. The 'Protestant principle' was clearly defined as 'a right of thinking and judging for my self'. Since judgement was determined by reason 'without prejudice', both enthusiasts and atheists were compromised. However, using the distinctions, advanced by Shaftesbury, between the libertine and virtuous atheist, *The Freethinker* argued that the 'religious atheist ... delights in goodness, and in everything, that is reasonable and beautiful. He loves mankind; he is social and publick spirited'. Although there was a tendency amongst such men to muddle religion and superstition they were to be valued over the deranged enthusiast or popishly superstitious.[90] Fanatics, non-jurors and the High Church, especially those who believed in the 'Chimerical notions of a Royal, Rectilineal Priesthood, independent of the state', should be severely disciplined by the state for their threat to public peace.[91]

The articulation of such ideas from a government-sponsored journal gives an indication of the centrality of republican conceptions of virtue and liberty to the leading politicians. 'True religion' was a plain and simple matter that resembled 'good manners'. Such manners were to be distinguished from the 'unmanly politeness' of the courts of arbitrary princes: 'free states' should reject such politeness 'as the very laws of tyranny'.[92] One of the main areas for reform was, then, that of the Church. Citing Cicero *de natura deorum* against the dangers of 'superstition', the journal indicted the 'cunning and artful part of mankind' who exploited the natural tendency of humans to fear the unknown. Such priests 'imposed on the world all the wildest inconsistances, which the brain of man could invent' with the objective of terrifying 'men into every compliance'. Since the frailties of humankind were vice and 'a strong propensity of mind towards everything, that is mysterious, dark and incomprehensible', so the priests established their tyrannous empire.[93] War against such corruption was the purpose of the ministry. Toland was not alone in this public campaign.

Perhaps the most effective, and certainly the most humorous, writer projecting a political anticlericalism was the young Thomas Gordon, another associate of Robert Molesworth. In a number of pamphlets and journals, Gordon portrayed churchmen as greedy and devious manipulators of Scripture. Such churchmen, ambitious only to increase the value of their livings, were better described as the 'Lord's receiver general' than the 'Ambassadors' of God. Parodying clerical arguments about divine right in Church and State, Gordon dismissed their sanctity and insisted that their lies were easily exposed by reading scripture.[94] In *An apology for the danger of the Church* (1719), Gordon let slip his intentions in the sub-title 'that the church is, and ought to be always in Danger; and that it would be dangerous for her to be out of danger'. Countering the attempt to set up 'the parsons as the idols of the universe', Gordon (again by parody and satire) trounced the clericalist claims of the Church. There was no unbroken apostolic succession from 'Jerusalem to Lambeth'. He produced a mock catalogue of books: *The art of Holy foaming, The Holy monopoly, Church arithmetic* (that 'three is one), *The unreasonableness of understanding Scripture*, and *The Tribe of Issachar; or an argument to prove that the laity have a right to no liberty, but that of being slaves to the Clergy*. Such clergy only believed in two holy days: 30 January and 29 May.[95] In two further works, *Priestianity: or a view of the disparity between the Apostles and the modern inferior clergy* (1720) and *The Character of an Independent Whig* (1720), Gordon made the connection between the attack upon the Church and the preservation of liberty even more explicit. The thrust of the first pamphlet focused on the role the clergy had in corrupting the beliefs of their parishioners by insinuating themselves into the homes of the gentry. As Gordon explained 'when a shepherd will intrust a wolf with the care of his flock, then I shall consent that a priest may be a superintendent of my family'. Fortunately, Gordon exclaimed, 'the British spirit begins to reassume its reason; that is shakes off the Biggottry of Priestcraft, and daily disesteems the delusion of juggling impostors'.

Just as Toland, Shaftesbury and Molesworth had asserted, Gordon too posed the rhetorical question 'Is not the liberty of the mind preferable to the liberty of the body?' The sacrifice of reason to the 'arbitrary' will of the churchmen was a tragedy, since 'everyman living has a right to think freely, and reason ought to direct him'. Gordon's remedy was to propose a strict scrutiny of the morals, principles and characters of churchmen. Since they were 'servants' of the laity, they ought to be forced to display their testimonies and certificates of good conduct like any other servant seeking employment.[96] In the second work, Gordon reinforced the connection between the attack on the Church and the defence of liberty; as he claimed 'Reason and liberty are the two greatest gifts and blessings which man has given us, and yet where ever a priestly authority prevails, they must either fly or suffer'. Churchmen, in the tradition of Archbishop Laud, had laid a plot against 'conscience and constitution'. It was clear that 'abject slavery' was 'and always has been, the certain consequence of power in the priests'. The antidote was to be found in the 'unlimited Toleration of all dissenters, whatsoever': it was simply 'tyrannical' to punish religious difference, for 'in matters of conscience, he who does his best does well, though he is mistaken'. All Protestants ought to be equally employed by the state: provided a 'man loves liberty and his country, what is it to the commonwealth whether he sings his prayers or says them?' The high churchman made a 'prey of our property, and slaves of our persons'. Trouncing their influence in the parish and the universities by accommodating and rewarding Dissenters would be a secure route to preserving liberty.[97]

After 1714, Toland was convinced his time had come. Closely associated with the political interest of Robert Molesworth, he set out to exploit his connections and to circulate his ideas. Fundamental to his political agenda was a practical anticlericalism. He engaged not just in a cultural war against prejudice, but in the detail of practical politics too. He conducted a polemic on all fronts. He wrote memorials, manifestos, popular pamphlets and journal pieces for the public, but he also circulated scribal works in salons and coffee-houses. From the late 1690s to the early 1720s, he pursued a consistent and principled course. Celebrating a republican heritage, he subtly refashioned it to practical purpose. Clearly, Toland was an effective and skilful practical politician. The power of his ideas was not simply forged by exploiting an existing canon of writings. He also produced a series of compelling works that challenged the cultural authority of the Church. Not explicitly polemical, many of these works were profoundly learned. Erudition then became a tool of cultural deconstruction. Exploring these writings, especially those scribal texts we know he was circulating amongst the highest elites, will allow a further consideration of the intellectual context for his broader commitment to political action.

NOTES

1 See G. Holmes *The trial of Doctor Sacheverell* (1973) pp. 156–178.

2 See *Portland Mss* IV pp. 532–533.

3 Toland *The High Church displayed* (1711) pp. 4, 24.

4 So for example he inserted material about the mob attack on Burges' Chapel, and similar riotous behaviour in Wolverhampton and Barnstaple *High Church* pp. 95–96, 104–106.

5 See p. 305 on 'blasphemous books'.

6 *Mr Toland's reflections* pp. 9, 11, 12.

7 *Jacobitism, perjury and popery* pp. 3, 4–6, 8–10, 11, 13, 14, 15.

8 *An appeal to honest people* pp. 2, 4–5, 11, 14, 36–37, 38, 42–47, 56, 57.

9 J. Campbell *The lives of the Lord Chancellors* (1846) 4, pp. 393.

10 H. Mainusch (ed.) *Gründe für die Einbürgerung der Juden in Grossbritannien und Irland* (Stuttgardt, 1965) contains a modern English edition with a parallel German translation. All references will be to this edition. There is an important modern edition in French, see P. Lurbe (ed.) *Raisons de naturaliser les Juifs* (Paris, 1998).

11 See S. Parker *Censura temporum* (1709) p. 564.

12 For a broader discussion see J. A. I. Champion 'Toleration and citizenship in Enlightenment England: John Toland and the naturalisation of the Jews, 1714–1753' in O. Grell and R. Porter (eds) *Toleration in Enlightenment Europe* (Cambridge, 2000) pp. 133–156.

13 Toland *Reasons* pp. 52, 46, 44.

14 *Ibid.* p. 62.

15 *Ibid.* p. 64.

16 *Ibid.* p. 68.

17 *Ibid.* p. 82.

18 *Ibid.* p. 96.

19 *Ibid.* p. 100.

20 *Ibid.* p. 42.

21 *Ibid.* pp. 88–90.

22 See *Tolandiana* p. 200.

23 D. Defoe *An argument proving that the design of employing and ennobling foreigners, is a treasonable conspiracy against the constitution* (1717) pp. 7–8.

24 *Ibid.* p. 8.

25 C. Robbins *The eighteenth century commonwealthmen* (Cambridge, 1959) p. 127.

26 See entry in E. Cruickshanks, S. Handley, D. Hayton (eds) *History of Parliament 1690– 1715* (Cambridge, 2002); DNB; E. Turner 'The Peerage Bill of 1719' *English Historical Review* 28 (1913) pp. 250–251; G. Townend 'Religious radicalism and conservatism in the Whig Party under George I: the repeal of the Occasional Conformity and Schism Acts' *Parliamentary History* 7 (1988) pp. 24–43. The best account of Molesworth and his circle remains Robbins *Eighteenth century commonwealthmen* pp. 88–133.

27 Toland *State anatomy* Preface, pp. ii; 2, 3, 6.

28 See Cicero *de republica* V iii.6 (Loeb edition) p. 251.

29 Toland *State anatomy* (1717) Title page in Latin, p. 104 (English translation); compare with Cicero *de republica* (Loeb, 1977) pp. 250–251.

30 D. Defoe *A further argument against ennobling foreigners* (1717) p. 43.

31 *State anatomy* Preface.

32 *Ibid.* pp. 9–11.

33 *Ibid.* pp. 12–13.

34 *Ibid.* pp. 21–22.

35 *Ibid.* pp. 23, 25–26.

36 *Ibid.* p. 27.

37 *Ibid.* pp. 29–30.

38 *Ibid.* p. 35.

39 *Reasons for enabling Protestant Dissenters to bear public offices* (1717) pp. 12, 14–15, 25–26, 32–34, 36.

40 *Ibid.* pp. 39–41.

41 *Ibid.* pp. 70, 74–75.

42 *Ibid.* pp. 76, 77–78.

43 *Ibid.* pp. 80–81.

44 See S. Taylor 'Whigs, Tories and Anticlericalism: ecclesiastical courts legislation in 1733' *Parliamentary History* 19 (2000) pp. 329–355.

45 *Collections* 2, 'A memorial' pp. 239–240

46 *Ibid.* p. 244

47 *Ibid.* pp. 239–258; at p. 246.

48 *Ibid.* p. 247.

49 *Ibid.* pp. 248, 249–250, 252, 255.

50 *Ibid.* p. 257.

51 *Ibid.* p. 95.

52 Defoe *An argument* pp. 51, 71, 80–81, 95.

53 *Remarks upon the State Anatomy of Great Britain* (1717) pp. 10–11.

54 *Reasons against repealing the Occasional and Test Act* (1718) pp. 4, 5, 6, 17, 18, 24.

55 Toland *Second part of the State anatomy* (1717) pp. 3, 4–5, 6.

56 See C. B. Realey 'The London Journal and its authors, 1720–1723' *Humanistic Studies of the University of Kansas* 5 (1936) pp. 1–38.

57 Shaftesbury *Several letters written by a noble lord to a young man at the university* (1716) pp. 6–7, 8.

58 *Ibid.* pp. 12, 14, 15, 17.

59 Toland *Letters* Preface pp. v, vi, vii

60 *Ibid.* pp. vii–viii.

61 *Ibid.* pp. x–xi.

62 *Ibid.* pp. xix, xx, xxi–xxii, xxiii.

63 *Ibid.* p. xxiii.

64 Toland *Danger of mercenary parliaments* Preface pp. x–xi.

65 *Ibid.* pp. v, 1–8, 9, 20–21.

66 *Ibid.* pp. 9, 10–11.

67 *Ibid.* p. 25.

68 See E. Seaton *Literary relations of England and Scandinavia in the seventeenth century* (Oxford, 1935) pp. 134–135.

69 T. Rogers *The commonwealthsman unmasqu'd. Or a just rebuke to the author of the account of Denmark* (1694) pp. 2–3.

70 *Ibid.* p. 110.

71 See British Museum, Prints and Drawings B1656D. 'Thomas Gibson pinxit. P. Pelham fec. 1721' Sold by John Bowles, Mercers Hall Cheapside. On Toland's translation see *Tolandiana* p. 231.

72 R. Molesworth *An account of Denmark* (1694) 'Preface' p. 3, A3r, A4, A5, A5r, A6–A6r.

73 *Ibid.* pp. 34–35.

74 See J. H. M. Salmon *The French religious wars in English political thought* (Oxford, 1959) esp. chapters 7 and 8. See also G. Garnett (ed.) *Vindicae contra tyrannos* (Cambridge, 1994).

75 See R. E. Geisey, J. H. M. Salmon (eds) *Francogallia by François Hotman* (Cambridge, 1972) pp. 122–125. Comparison of chapter 6 on the election and deposition of Kings shows that Molesworth truncated some of the material in Hotman's original text. Compare Hotman 1972 p. 239 with Hotman 1721 p. 46, also 1972 p. 241 with 1721 p. 47.

76 Molesworth (ed.) *Francogallia* (1711) 'Preface to the reader' pp. ii, ii, iv, vi, 5–6.

77 *Francogallia* 'The bookseller to the Reader'.

78 *Ibid.* pp. v, vi.

79 *Ibid.* pp. vii, viii.

80 *Ibid.* p. x.

81 *Ibid.* pp. xii–iii, xiv, xxii–vi, xxxiv.

82 See R. Sedgwick (ed.) *The Commons 1715–1754* (1970) volume 2 pp. 262–263.

83 See L. Hanson *Government and the Press* p. 101. See also M. Harris *London newspapers in the age of Walpole* (1987) p. 101.

84 See personal communication from David Hayton, and *History of Parliament, 1690–1715*.

85 Harris *London newspapers* p. 101.

86 See DNB.

87 *The Freethinker* Number 1 24 March 1718 (Collected edition, 1722) pp. 3, 4, 5–6, 7.

88 *Ibid.* No. 10 and 12 pp. 64–65, 66, 77, 80.

89 *Ibid.* No. 16, pp. 107, 110–111; No. 17, p. 114.

90 *Ibid.* No. 22 pp. 151–153.

91 *Ibid.* No. 30, 31, pp. 231–232.

92 *Ibid.* No. 24 pp. 171–173; No. 25, pp. 174, 178–179.

93 *Ibid.* No. 34 pp. 240, 245–246, 249.

94 T. Gordon *A modest apology for Cardinal Alberoni* (1719) pp. 6–7, 14–15, 16, 19, 21–22.

95 T. Gordon *An apology for the danger of the Church* (1719) pp. 3, 4, 6, 27, 32.

96 T. Gordon *Priestianity: or a view of the disparity between the Apostles and the modern inferior clergy* (1720) pp. iv, xiii, xiv, 4, 6–8, 9, 19.

97 T. Gordon *The character of an Independent Whig* (1720) pp. 3, 6–7, 8–9, 11–12, 27.

Part III

Subversive learning

———◆———

7

Respublica mosaica:
imposters, legislators and
civil religion

TOLAND was, then, embroiled in the day-to-day cut and thrust of British politics, advancing a clear and profound defence of commonwealth principles especially by supporting the interest of the Protestant succession against popery. This was not simply a British project, but a European-wide campaign. Toland exploited all possible connections. His intellectual contribution was not just made in the form of printed works but (as we have seen in chapter 2 above) was also manifest in the conversations and scribal materials he circulated amongst his powerful friends. One potent relationship was the connection with Hanover. From the very moment Toland managed to intrude himself into the diplomatic mission charged with presenting the *Act of Settlement* to Sophia, he used his intimacy with her as a theatre for the display of his arguments. This relationship with Sophia (and her daughter) was both public and private: the series of public defences and *eloges* of her political legitimacy and rational character were matched by a private liaison manifest in a series of profoundly erudite and heterodox conversations about the nature of the soul, the sacred status of Scripture and political theory.[1] The textual remnants of these conversations are the closest we can get to capturing the power of Toland's intellectual charisma.

Taking advantage of the 'complete liberty of conscience' established at Hanover, Toland, often encouraged by Sophia (much to the anxiety of Leibniz), engaged head on in disputation with many more pious and orthodox Christian believers.[2] Although some historians have described Sophia as a wit rather than as seriously interested in matters of metaphysics and natural philosophy, it was Leibniz himself who insisted that 'Madame L'électrice, est entièrement pour la raison, et par conséquent toute les mesures qui pourrant servir à faire que les rois et les peuples suivent la raison, seront à son goût'.[3] 'Serenissima' while distinguished by great intellectual curiosity and linguistic skill, had little taste for dogmatic theology. Hostile to religious enthusiasm and mystery in ecclesiastical matters she pursued an Erastian toleration: Lutherans, Calvinists, French Huguenots as well as the Anglican liturgy all found a place in her regime. An insight into her religious character can be seen in Leibniz's comment to Toland in 1709, 'that she was accustomed to quote and praise particularly that passage of Scripture which demands whether it is consistent with reason that the Author of the eye should not see, and the Author of the ear should not hear'.[4] It was also reported that Sophia found fault with the Apostles for failing to inquire of Lazarus what death was like.[5]

The evidence of Toland's dispute with Isaac Beausobre which took place in Berlin in October 1701, orchestrated by Sophia, indicates that the Electress was keen to explore even the most controversial topics.[6] Toland, clearly eager to impress his auditors with his intellectual credentials, set out to discuss 'des ouvrages anti-religieux qu'il n'avoit pas encore publiés'. The thrust of Toland's arguments would 'rendre l'Ecriture douteuse'. The debate lasted for two hours. Toland refuted the inspired status of the Bible by arguing that it was defective because 'les anciens ayant admis dans le canon du livres douteux'. During the discussion, Beausobre became so disenchanted with the tone of Toland's arguments that he defied him to testify to his belief in God and Providence, a tactic that was unsuccessful, since Toland (typically) eluded any precise denial or commitment but merely moved the conversation along to a different matter. These oral discussions ultimately resulted in the composition of scribal text upon the Christian canon which was circulated amongst a broader community. Without the restraints of a public audience, and the danger of censorship or punishment, Toland's intellectual argument was destructive and hostile. Indeed, reports of his behaviour in the coffee-houses of Edinburgh and Oxford, where he was given 'to railing ... against all communities in religion and monarchy', confirm that Toland was a fierce controversialist in the right context.[7] As contemporaries were very well aware, letting Toland tell the potential Queen of Great Britain that the Bible was defective and corrupt, was a dangerous business. It did not stop there however.

One of the more heterodox discussions initiated in Sophia's company focused on an even more controversial issue. Conversations between Leibniz, Sophia and Toland in September 1702 had fixed upon the related issues of the nature of the soul and the relationship between matter and motion.[8] As Leibniz reported to Sophia, Toland's opinions about the soul were similar to those of Lucretius: 'c'est à dire sur le concours du corpuscules, mais il ne dit pas d'où il vient que le matière a du movement et de l'ordre, ny comment il y a du sentiment dans le monde'.[9] Sophia supported Leibniz's point that the relationship between matter and motion was the critical issue and that perhaps Toland understood little of the problem. As Leibniz clarified, Toland subscribed to the views of Hobbes, Epicurus and Lucretius in arguing 'qui'l n'y a d'autre chose dans la nature que ses figures et mouvemens'.[10] So, just as Toland was engaged in advancing a political defence of the Hanoverian succession in public, he was also discussing heterodox accounts of key metaphysical problems with the next successor. This convergence of public and private discourse was made more manifest by the publication of the substance of these discussions in 1704 in *Letters to Serena*, a work closely associated with the Hanoverian interest, which established the connections between such metaphysical speculation and more mainstream political thought.

Letters to Serena (1704) is an intriguing work. Although its first form was in a private disputation, the published text displayed a range of erudition and learning. Especially in the first three letters on the history of prejudice, idolatry and doctrine, Toland borrowed learning from Herbert of Cherbury, Gerard Vossius, Charles Blount, Robert Howard, Anthony Van Dale and Balthasaar Bekker, as well as a library of classical texts. The last two letters offered critiques of the metaphysical theories of Spinoza and Newton. The continuity and intellectual portability of Toland's intentions are indicated by the fact that the first three letters of the work were later translated into French by Toland and scribally circulated amongst the milieu of Prince Eugene and Baron d'Hohendorf in *c.* 1709–10. An anonymous Dutch translation of the first letter appeared in Amsterdam in 1710, while later on in the eighteenth century, French translations were published by d'Holbach and Naigeon.[11] Here is clear evidence of how Toland used works for different audiences, but also how he saw a continuity of purpose across these communities in Holland, Vienna, Hanover and England. The first three letters gave an account of the epistemology of prejudice, the history of opinions concerning the soul, and a history of the origins of idolatry. The last two letters engaged with the natural philosophy of Spinoza and Newton. Taking inspiration from Lucretius' *de rerum natura*, the work used a materialist metaphysics as a premise for a criticism of the politics of fear. Toland, building on these arguments, also justified a practical and radical political anticlericalism.[12] The text corroded belief in the immortality of the soul, and the associated system of priestcraft. It was conceived as an antidote to the damage false religion and superstition did to civic communities. That this agenda resulted from Toland's intellectual intimacy with the successor to the English Crown must have alarmed more orthodox contemporaries.

Unhindered by constraints of writing for a public audience where the radicalism of his insights were determined by the hegemony of mainstream Protestant discourses (and the letter of the law), in private Toland characteristically engaged in a much more pungent style of communication. Evidence for the literary remodelling of scribal work for a broader public readership is most profound for the case of his *Nazarenus* (1718) which saw life initially as a bespoke scribal work for Prince Eugene of Savoy and Baron d'Hohendorf a decade before its publication. The literary style of the original version of the work was polemic and abrasive – the irreligious assault upon Judaism, Christianity and Islam was obvious – unlike the printed version which translated the brusque irreligion of the French work into a more subtle and ambiguous text. It was so equivocal that in fact many readers thought of the work as an essentially pious one.[13]

In his scribal works, then, when communicating with powerful and influential people like Sophia, Eugene and Shaftesbury (people who had as much to lose as him), Toland was explicit in his heterodoxy. This intellectual honesty was an essential part of Toland's strategy of trying to persuade his audience. For a public, and probably hostile, audience he used a more subtle form of insinuation, but in private he let the full flow of his polemic rip. This can be seen most evidently in his contribution to the composition and circulation of the most dangerous clandestine work of the period, the *Traité des trois imposteurs* printed at The Hague by Charles Levier in 1719. This edition was the end-product of a complex series of manuscript traditions, literary shadow-play and intellectual conversation that dated back to the earlier 1700s.[14] Establishing precisely who was responsible for the composition of the clandestine work, and who transformed it into a semi-public text, has been the subject of much historical debate. Some years ago the suggestion was advanced that the work was the product of a semi-masonic group, 'The Knights of the Jubilation', and consequently was part of a radical, materialist and republican assault upon the shibboleths of the *ancien regime*.[15] More recently research, exploring the circle of men like Charles Levier, Rousset de Missy and Jean Aymon, has proposed a little-known Dutchman Jan Vroesen (friend of Furly and Shaftesbury) as the original compiler of the text.[16] Others have suggested that Toland was also intimately involved.[17]

The French manuscript has diverse forms. It is possible to construct a historical taxonomy for the variant manuscript versions of the work, indicating that there were at least three distinct types of families of the manuscript independent of the printed edition.[18] Establishing the inter-relations of text, distribution and chronology between these works is a profoundly complicated business. There is certainty that Benjamin Furly, Eugene of Savoy and Baron d'Hohendorf were all involved in the compilation and circulation of the text.[19] Extracting ideas and even paragraphs from a range of heterodox material (Spinoza, Hobbes, Cicero, Vanini, Pomponazzi, Herbert, Charron, Lucretius, amongst many others), the manuscript systematically destroyed and ridiculed the notion of a revealed religion. Moses, Christ and Mahomet were false prophets who manipulated religion to their own ends. Doctrines of the soul, spirit, heaven and hell were ridiculous. The majority of humankind was condemned for their superstitious ignorance. All priests were dismissed as agents of tyranny and prejudice. Some versions of the work included different materials, expanding on the crimes of the priests, the absurdity of Christian doctrine, or the imposture of Mahomet. One of the distinctive versions (known as *Le fameux livre des trois imposteurs*), included a larger account of Moses' life and conduct. These scribal copies are closely associated with the library and intellectual connection of Prince Eugene and the Baron d'Hohendorf.[20] While there is obscurity about the specific origins of these additions, it is possible to establish the role Toland played in the circle that produced the text.[21] As we will see he was also perpetrating similar ideas in his own writings to both public and private English audiences.

Toland was connected to the *Traité* in two ways. First, by his intimacy with the individuals who were central in the production of the work, and second, by the literary parallels between his work and the arguments of the clandestine text. As we have seen, Toland's connections with heterodox circles on the continent were manifold. Early in his career he had spent time in the Low Countries, especially in Leiden, studying at the University, which had brought him into contact with people like Benjamin Furly, in whose library it is known that Charles Levier made a copy of the *Traité* in 1711. Later in his career, while undertaking various diplomatic duties, Toland travelled throughout Europe: it was during these visits that he became friendly with, first, Baron d'Hohendorf and then with Prince Eugene of Savoy. During this period Toland established relations with many of the men involved in the work. He certainly knew the controversial figure of Jean Aymon who had a hand in revising the *Traité* in collaboration with Rousset de Missy before publication in 1719.[22] Toland first encountered Aymon when the latter was attempting to sell manuscripts stolen from the French Royal Library. Toland undertook a sales-catalogue describing the various manuscripts for Humphrey Wanley: it was through this connection that Toland had a sight of the source (the *Codex Armachanus*) upon which he based the second part of his *Nazarenus* (1718).[23]

Aymon was also an important connection for Toland's dealings with Thomas Johnson, the Scottish bookseller who lived and traded in Holland, and was deeply involved in the 1719 edition. Johnson was a significant, if much under-studied, figure in the clandestine Republic of Letters. Based in The Hague and then Rotterdam, Johnson was involved in the publication and distribution of a range of mainstream and more contentious literature. Publisher of the *Journal Litéraire* (1713–22) and the *Mercure Galant,* he also produced works by Anthony Collins, Shaftesbury, the Duke of Buckingham as well as Colerus' *Vie de Spinoza.*[24] A pioneer publisher of editions of single Shakespeare plays, he was a member of 'the association of booksellers at the Hague' and collaborated in joint ventures with publishers in England like Bernard Lintott. As a *libraire* he also had contacts in England with men like Anthony Collins, to whom he sent packages of books.[25] Johnson later collaborated with Toland in the publication of a number of books. The latter used his bookshop as a postal address in 1708 when writing to Leibniz. In 1709, Johnson published (at The Hague) one of Toland's most radical works: the Latin *Adeisidaemon* and *Origines Judaicae*. He was still in contact with Toland in 1715 when a second edition of the same work was mooted.[26] Toland, then, was intimate with many of the key figures involved in both the manuscript and printed version of the *Traité*.

Toland was not merely a hanger-on in this world of clandestine letters but made his own contributions. Toland supplied both Eugene and d'Hohendorf with scribal work as can be seen in the collection of 'Dissertations diverses' composed between 1708 and 1710. Dedicated to Eugene, and copied for d'Hohendorf, much of this scribal work, like the *Traité*, was concerned with the nature of religious imposture in general, and the *respublica mosaica* in particular. Toland's scribal energies were also devoted to distributing, and generating interest in, a new edition of Giordano Bruno's *Spaccio*, writing to Leibniz and others with a specimen of his intentions. Importantly, in trying to prompt interest in Bruno's work, Toland connected it with the tradition of imposture epitomised in the *Traité*. In 1711 M. de la Croze, reporting a conversation he had with Toland in 1702, commented that 'Monsieur Toland, qui a ses raisons pour faire beaucoup de cas de cet ouvrage, croit que c'est celui qui est si fameux dans la monde, sous le titre de Traité des trois imposteurs'.[27] That Toland was deliberately attempting to pass off Bruno's work as the *Traité* is confirmed by another letter written in 1709 (from Amsterdam) by John Bagford 'the book-hunter' and antiquary. Writing to his correspondent Bagford insisted that the attribution of a book 'intituled the three Grand impostores' to Toland was incorrect, indeed he continued 'nor dou I knowe thare is any book in the World which bare that Title'. On the other hand, Bagford recognised Bruno's *Spaccio* as the work which Toland had 'occasion' to pass off as the *Traité*. Bagford, who had read the *Spaccio* in Toland's company (and hoped to do so again), added the comment that when he first read the volume he too thought that it was 'the book meant by the title of the three Impostors'. Although Bruno's work scarcely mentioned 'Mouse Christ or Mahomet' the work was still impious because it treated 'all the authores of all revealed Religion whatsoever, as Impostour'.[28] Toland was clearly aware of the reputation (and probably the text) of the *Traité*: it was typical of his desire to be at the vanguard of radicalism that he claimed insider knowledge of the work.

Further evidence of contemporary association of Toland with the clandestine work is found in the fabricated provenance commonly attached to the *Traité*. In the fictionalised account of the discovery of the manuscript in a Frankfurt bookshop in 1706, a German officer named Tausendorf (surely a reference to the real Hohendorf) had offered three books for sale: the first was a copy of Bruno's *Spaccio* (described as 'the same one of which Toland had an English one printed'); the second was an edition of Cicero's *de natura deorum;* the final volume was the treatise on imposture. The naming of Toland (in association with the circulation of Bruno's work) is significant. It is also notable that Toland had connections with Cicero that tied him to the same circle. In 1712 he had printed a work called, *Cicero illustratus*, intended as an encouragement for subscribers to fund a complete edition of the Roman's works replete with critical historical and philological apparatus. Significantly, this work was dedicated to both Eugene and d'Hohendorf. In his extensive and influential article on the *Traité,* Prosper Marchand rehearsed these same discussions about 'the famous' Toland's role in the confusion of the *Spaccio* and the *Traité,* and also noted that as author of *Nazarenus* Toland was skilled at constructing fake literary lineages for supposedly ancient texts.[29] His association with many of the central figures involved in the production and circulation of the clandestine work, especially the intellectual intimacy with Eugene of Savoy and Baron d'Hohendorf which threw open to him their important collection of *libertin* and freethinking literature in Vienna, make it unlikely then, that Toland was not involved in the making of the *Traité.*[30]

Toland's works (both published and manuscript) during this period show that his attitudes to the divine mission of Moses were profoundly irreligious. Toland exploited his erudition to compose a heterodox account of Moses as a political legislator which challenged the Christian version of the divine religious patriarch. There was a good republican source for this depiction of Moses in the writings of the arch-heretic, Machiavelli. The Florentine's *Discourses* had treated Moses as a legislator with the same skills and 'virtu' as Numa, Solon and Lycurgus.[31] This laid the foundations for what contemporaries regarded as atheism. For orthodox believers the Mosaic legation was the prophetic foundation of Christianity. Although Christian theologians insisted Christ had perfected the Mosaic dispensation as a type or pre-figuration of the true faith, Judaism was treated as a Godly model. Christian scholarship became increasingly knowledgeable about the historical nature of the *republica hebraeorum.*[32] The primary document for exploring the Hebrew republic was the Old Testament. Historical scholarship became much more sophisticated in its exploration of the rites, ceremonies and practices of the ancient Jews, as philological and linguistic developments opened up new rabbinical and classical sources. Toland was aware of this Christian apologetic and indeed owned the learned works of men like Carlo Sigonio and the Buxtorfs. Although much of this work was driven by Christian theological imperatives it still valued the sacred meaning of the Jewish state.[33] Contemporary historians like Jacques Basnage carefully used their learning to defend a providential account of the meaning of Jewish history against the threats of 'atheists, deists, and apostates'.[34] Writing the history of Moses ought to have been, *au fond,* an apologetic exercise.

Evidence of Toland's heterodox opinion can be seen in the frontispiece to Harrington's *Works* (1700) where Moses was depicted as the first of the great political legislators that included Solon, Confucius, Lycurgus and Numa. Repeatedly Toland announced his ambition of publishing a major analytical study to be called 'Respublica Mosaica'. His first indication of these intentions was in the private manuscript written for Prince Eugene of Savoy, circulated between 1708 and 1710: 'vous sçavez que j'ai deja promis au publie LA REPUBLIQUE de MOYSE, laquelle de toutes les formes de Governement j'estime avoir eté la plus excellente et parfaite'. In this study, he continued, 'je donneray une face et un tour si nouveau (pourtant sincere et natural) non seulement au systeme politique entier et à la plus grande partie des loix particulieres de cet incomparable Legislateur: mais aussi à un si grand nombre des circonstances et incidens historiques qui se trouvent dans la relation fort defectueuse et tres-abregée du <u>Pentateuque</u>'.[35] Toland promised a full blown 'political' reading of Moses along the model of Spinoza's account in the *Tractatus theologico-politicus* (1670). Lamentably this work does not appear to be extant, even though Toland expressed the hope that it 'seroit un ouvrage que je pretendois faire vivre apres moi, sans craindre de passer pour fan faron'. The work was not conceived simply as a historical work but also for 'le temps present, auquel (comme j'ay lieu de l'esperer) il pourra n'etre pas inutile à plusieurs egards'.[36] Although the major work remains elusive, Toland did disseminate fragments towards this larger study from which it is possible to reconstruct some of his intentions. The first of these to be published was *Origines Judaicae* (The Hague, 1709). At about the same time Toland had also composed a couple of shorter pieces in French for private circulation. The longer of these, the 'Projet d'une dissertation sur la colomne de feu et de nuée des Israelites', was also circulated in an English translation in the 1710s, and eventually published in 1720 as *Hodegus, or the pillar of cloud and fire*.[37] The second shorter piece 'Deux problems historiques, theologiques & politiques' was originally included in the collection of 'Dissertations diverses' sent to Prince Eugene and Baron d'Hohendorf, and was eventually published as an appendix to Toland's controversial study in comparative biblical criticism, *Nazarenus* (1718).

Origines Judaicae was a full-blown assault upon orthodox Christian under-standings of Moses as the *vir archetypus*. This work was directed against Pierre-Daniel Huet's classic statement of Christian orthodoxy, the massive *Demonstratio evangelica* (1679), which took as its motif the Mosiac origins of all philosophical and ethical learning. Huet set out to safeguard the univer-sality of the sacred history of the Old Testament and 'to draw all of profane history together into the single course of sacred history and to state that all peoples knew the teachings of the prophets'.[38] Similar attempts had been made in writings like Edward Stillingfleet's *Origines Sacrae* (1662 and many subsequent editions), which had aroused a furious debate in the 1680s and

1690s about the relative historical priority of Egyptian and Hebrew learning.[39] Toland intended to replace this Christian *philosophia mosaica* with a civic *respublica mosaica*.[40] Notice of his views had been indicated in his first anonymous publication where he had described Moses as 'without dispute ... one of the greatest and wisest Legislators that ever appeared in the world, not excepting, Solon, or Lycurgus or Numa'.[41] *Origines Judaicae* opened with a unequivocal assertion (borrowed from Cicero) that religion was 'a mere ingine of state policy ... that a belief in the immortal Gods was an invention contrived by wise and profound legislators for the general benefit of the commonwealth, in order that those whom reason could not influence, might be trained to their duty by a sense of religion'.[42]

Arguing against Huet's use of classical sources to claim that Moses was the archtype of all learning, Toland pointed out that one of the Bishop of Avranches' sources – Strabo – 'compares Moses with Minos, Lycurgus, Zamolxis and many others of the same description, without any distinction, and what is more, that he has given an account of the Jewish religion, the origin of that nation, and of Moses himself, totally different from that which we find in the Pentateuch'.[43] As Toland made plain, Huet had 'distorted' and falsified his sources in trying to 'demonstrate' Moses as the originator of pagan mythology. Huet's work was composed of 'frivilous and empty trifles'.[44] Having illustrated how Huet had misinterpreted Diodorus Siculus, Toland concentrated upon his business of giving an exegesis of Strabo's account of Moses and the Jews found in the *Geography* (Book XVI chapter 2 §34–39). For Strabo, as understood by Toland, Moses was 'unequivocally ... a pantheist, or as we in these modern times, would style him, a Spinozist'. Moses maintained that 'no divinity exists separate from the universal frame of nature, and that the universe is the supreme and only God, whose parts you may call creatures, and himself the great creator of all'.[45] To identify Moses as a pre-figuration of Spinoza was calculated to provoke the Godly. Toland compounded this danger by reproducing Strabo's commentary in its entirety so that it might be compared with the (in his view) faulty account given in the Pentateuch.[46] Invoking a biblical hermeneutics, again learnt from Spinoza's work, Toland insisted that the difference between the two accounts of the fertility of Judaea and the Pentateuch's description of it as a 'flowing with milk and honey' was attributed to Moses' 'pardonable stratagem' of providing a stimulus 'to keep up the spirits of the wandering Tribes of Israel'.[47]

Aware of the Christian concern to distance the tribes of Israel from Egyptian foundations, Toland persisted in approving Strabo's suggestions, noting that, as he commented, 'Moses himself, when he fled into the land of the Midianites was immediately taken for an Egyptian'.[48] Exploring the question of the racial identity of the Israelites, Toland further muddied the matter by claiming 'that they were a mixt race': consequently 'they are blindly prejudiced therefore who obstinately maintain that all the Jews were the undoubted offspring of Abraham or Jacob, without any admixture of foreign blood'.[49] Citing another classical text as a means to contextualise scriptural descriptions, he pointed out that Tacitus was correct to claim that the Jews were emigrants from Assyria to Egypt. Further evidence from Diodorus Siculus suggested that Moses himself was 'an Egyptian Priest, and a Nomarch, or Governor of a Province'.[50] Moses was 'learned in all the wisdom of the Egyptians' which indicated his 'priesthood and temporal dignity' and 'not his skill in magic and miracles'.[51] Indeed Moses instituted a simple non-ceremonial religion that upheld the injunctions of natural religion. Most of the rites and ceremonies of Judaism were introduced by post-Mosaic figures 'from superstitious motives'.[52] The broader theme of *Origines Judaicae*, echoing Spinoza's historical arguments, was the denial of the providential revealed history of the Hebrew religion and people. Toland exploited pagan sources like Strabo, Tacitus and Diodorus Siculus to give a historical and 'disenchanted' account of Moses and the Israelites. The refrain of his writing was that this classical historical account could be constantly contrasted with the defective evidence of the Pentateuch. Indeed in the middle of the work Toland inserted an extended consideration of the nature of divine prophecy, dismissing it as the false and fraudulent impositions of dreamers and seducers. He robustly concluded that 'no intimation is ever conveyed to men by God, by means of dreams or visions'.[53] This was pure Spinoza.

This technique of establishing the historical context of biblical history, and then giving a political account of Moses' *res gestae* was given even more detailed treatment in *Hodegus*, a work originally written for Eugene of Savoy in 1710, and published in a much expanded form in 1720.[54] Unlike *Origines Judaicae* where the audience of such subversive ideas was restricted to those who could read Latin, this work although originally written in French had a broader English readership. As the text was transformed from clandestine manuscript to published form the blunt heterodoxy of the first was modulated and masked by a veneer of scholarly investigation.[55] Toland's starting point was an insistence that studying the history of the Jewish nation was to be wrested from the monopoly of the Church. The history of the Hebrew antiquity was as important if not more so than that of the Greeks and Romans. Toland's own researches led him to a higher veneration for Moses and the Hebrew republic: 'wherefore my design in this publication, is to make Moses better understood, and consequently more easily believed'.[56] The premise of Toland's argument was that the account given in the Old Testament was incomplete and abridged: indeed, even the 'hyperbolical' language of Scripture was problematic and prone to allegory and 'inpenetrable absurdity' in the hands of priestly exegetes. The principal head of his case was that the Pentateuch did not record the achievements of providence and that 'several transactions generally understood to be miraculous, were in reality very natural'.[57]

In *Hodegus* Toland attempted to substitute the orthodox miraculous understanding of an episode from Exodus (XIII 21) where Moses and the Israelites were guided by a pillar of cloud and fire through the deserts, with a non-providential historical account. Using a collection of classical sources like Quintus Curtius, Herodotus and Xenophon to establish a correspondence between the practices of Moses and Alexander and the Persians, Toland argued that the 'cloud and pillar' were no miraculous manifestation of God but a form of 'ambulatory beacon' which directed the Israelites 'with the cloud of its smoke by day, and with the light of its fire by night'. There was no prodigy but 'mere human contrivance'.[58]

Drawing together, and comparing, the descriptions scattered throughout Exodus and Numbers, Toland hoped that 'I have set in the clearest light the nature and use of the Pillar of Cloud and Fire, directing the marches and stations of the Israelites in the Wilderness; in such a light, I say, that no man of good understanding, or void of superstition, will any longer think it a miracle'.[59] To reinforce the human dimensions of the episode Toland continued to argue that the biblical description of the Israelites being guided by the 'Angel of the Lord' was again no providential manifestation, even though Christian commentators had interpreted it so, but simply a reference to 'a mere mortal man, the overseer or director or the portable fire, and the guide of the Israelites in the wilderness'.[60] Contrary to the allegorising interpretations of the Church Fathers and following some suggestions advanced by Hobbes, Toland examined the Hebrew usage of the word, to conclude that the 'word Angel of itself imports nothing extraordinary, much less supernatural'.[61] 'Angel' was simply a Hebrew word for messenger or ambassador. Using the minor Roman military author Vegetius to establish the meaning of descriptions given in Numbers, Toland identified this 'guide and director' as Hobab 'the brother in law of Moses' who since he was born and bred in the wilderness was 'consequently well acquainted with the several parts of it'.[62] While Toland was at pains to indicate that the evidence of the Pentateuch was not good enough to establish, without doubt, that the guide at that particular time was Hobab since it was not possible to be accurate about the precise affinity of Hobab to Jethro and Moses, he was confident that the 'angel' was simply a local guide. The point of Toland's dissertation was to establish, by exploring the historical 'circumstances' of the Israelites, that Moses had acted like any other general or legislator in exploiting the military and logistic traditions of his time.[63]

Toland's reading of Moses as a political legislator and of Judaism as a religion adapted to civic circumstances was reviewed briefly in his 'Two problems', originally included in the collection of clandestine manuscripts circulated on the continent post-1710 and published as an appendix to his controversial *Nazarenus* (1718). This work was a prospectus for his *respublica mosaica* which he claimed he was half a year away from completing. Toland applauded Moses' political prudence, especially his 'plan' of government, which if it had been successfully established in Judea 'cou'd never have been afterwards destroy'd, either by the internal sedition of subjects, or the external violence of enemies, but should have lasted as long as mankind; which is to make a Government Immortal, tho it be reckon'd one of the things in nature the most subject to revolutions'. Toland proposed to discuss whether this immutability was based on 'any promise and miraculous concurrence of God; or on the intrinsic nature and constitution of the form itself' by posing two questions about the nature of Judaism. The first question inquired why, given that the ancient institutions of the Egyptians, Babylonians, Greeks and Romans had disintegrated long ago, had the Jews 'preserved themselves a distinct people with all their ancient rites'? Secondly, why, after the collapse of their republic, had they persisted in their hostility towards idolatrous practices? Toland encouraged answers that did not have 'recourse to miracles, or to promises drawn from the Old Testament'. In his own view Moses' system was to be explained by using Cicero's *de Republica* rather than providential arguments. It was necessary to 'allow MOSES a rank in the politics farr superior to SALEUCAS, CHARONDAS, SOLON, LYCURGUS, ROMULUS, NUMA, or any other Legislator'.[64] As Toland concluded, indicating that he always contrived some practical implication from his intellectual speculations, such was the 'original purity' of the Mosaic republic, that if the Jews ever happened to be 'resettl'd in Palestine upon their original foundation, which is not at all impossible; they will then, by reason of their excellent constitution, be much more populous, rich and powerful than any other nation now in the world'.[65]

It was apparent from the reception of this corpus of works upon Moses that Toland's attitudes were regarded by contemporaries as dangerously perfidious towards Christian observance.[66] Erudite scholars like Leibniz, who corresponded with Toland about *Origines Judaicae*, were unhappy with his use of classical sources like Strabo to explain the Mosaic republic.[67] Indeed Leibniz painstakingly listed the faults derived from Strabo's account, encouraging Toland to correct his own work. Toland sternly defended both himself and his sources, confirming that he would not 'make the least alteration' in the projected second edition.[68] Pierre-Daniel Huet was less restrained in his attack, ridiculing Toland's rustic Latin and faulty attempts at a display of classical learning. Toland was an atheist who had falsely attributed pantheistical opinions to Moses: 'il est assez grossier pour s'imaginer que nous jugions de la doctrine de Moyse sur la temoignage de Strabon, et non pas de la doctrine de Strabon sur la temoignage de Moyse'. Toland made Moses a Spinozist and denied his authorship of the Pentateuch: similarly he objected to Toland's description of 'la republique de Moyse n'a point eté instituée de Dieu: c'est l'ouvrage de la politique de cet homme avise'.[69] In the *Journal Litéraire* (1714) Toland's work was reviewed as advancing the following principles 'que la Sainte Ecriture n'est qu'une production de l'espirit humain; que la Republique des Juifs n'est que l'effet de la politique de Moise, et c'est a tort qu'on lui à donne le nom de Theocratie; que l'inspiration des prophetes ne differoit en rien des songes ordinaire'. The reviewer rather tartly noted that Toland acknowledged the dangerous consequences of such positions with audacity.[70]

In the English language reviews Toland got a similarly jaundiced reception. Samuel Parker decried the fact that Toland had put 'Moses in company with Lycurgus and Minos' describing *Origines Judaicae* as 'such an outrageous libel upon God's word, prophets and people'. Parker was astonished at Toland's relation of Moses: 'one would think, it might have satisfy'd Mr Toland to transform him into an Egyptian priest, without loading his memory so far as to tell us again and again, that with some people he pass'd for a Pantheist or Spinozist, in plainer words, a downright Atheist'. For Parker, as long as the Bible existed Toland's absurdities could be refuted for "twill be impossible for him to persuade us the Word of God is a system of Atheism'. Point by point the reviewer challenged each of the claims Toland had derived from Strabo by contrasting them with the statements of Scripture.[71] As well as receiving extensive reviews in the major journals of the Republic of Letters, *Origines Judaicae* was also the subject of intensive and lengthy rejoinders in larger theological works and academic disputations published in the Low Countries, Germany and France. *Hodegus* did not generate quite so much attention either on the continent or in England, although it was reprinted in 1732 and 1753. The one substantial reply to the work, *Hodegus confuted* (1721), rejected Toland's political account of Moses: the redemption of 'the Jews from the Egyptian slavery was to be unto all ages a spiritual figure of the manumission of true Christians from the yoke and bondage of sin by the guidance of Messiah the eternal Son of God'. Contrary to Toland's assertion that the cloud and pillar described in Exodus was a 'machine on a pole' the author simply asserted that 'it was the Angel of God's presence'. In an exceptionally confident piece of work the evidence of Scripture was simply contrasted with Toland's odd claims. The Word of God was of more value than the errors of *Hodegus*: the Holy Book contained an 'unalterable meaning'.[72]

There are close affinities between Toland's *respublica mosaica* and the account in the *Traité*.[73] The earliest versions of the account of Moses found both in the early clandestine manuscripts (like BL Sloane 2039 dated 1709) and the 1719 printed edition, were short and to the point. Derived from a series of classical and renaissance sources, the narrative was possibly lifted from the clandestine manuscript *Theophrastus redivivus*. The only copy of this work, which included a section on 'de Mosaic religione', was in the possession of Eugene of Savoy.[74] Moses was represented as a 'magician', an impostor adroit in the manipulation of a credulous and ignorant people. Invoking obligation by the use of prodigies and pretended miracles, he convinced the Israelites 'de sa mission divine'. Having established his authority 'il songea à la perpétuer; & sous prétexte d'établir un Culte Supreme, pour servir le Dieu, dont il se disoit le *Lieutenant*, il fit Aaron, son frére, et ses enfans Chefs du Palais Royal'. Using 'ruse Politique', Moses joined the force of arms with imposture to confirm his 'Authorité Souveraine' against those who 's'appercevoir de ses Artifices, & assez courageux pour lui reprocher'. He became 'moins leur Pére que leur Tyran' of the Israelites, and under cover of 'de Vengeances Divines, il vècut toûjours absolu'.[75] This exposition of Moses as a manipulator and tyrant dominating an ignorant and credulous people was rather insubstantial. Although Moses showed skill in creating religious observance like keeping the 'sabbath' as the premise of political order, he is portrayed as a deviant model rather than a positive one. This description was expanded with more historical detail in the succeeding versions of the manuscript.

Between 1709 and 1716 the account of Moses in scribal versions of the *Traité* underwent significant expansion exposing the variety of stratagems employed to dupe the people. The two types of amplification were both associated with manuscripts originating from the circle of Eugene and d'Hohendorf. The nature and style of these embellishments have an affinity with Toland's contemporaneous writings. The first stage of elaboration was the most influential, in the sense that it was the version that became the standard text for the later printed editions of the eighteenth century.[76] In this version much more attention was given to the historical circumstances of the Mosaic 'revolution'. Using a much broader base of historical sources that importantly combined the scriptural account of Exodus with pagan histories like Diodorus Siculus and Strabo, Moses was located within an Egyptian context. This was precisely what Toland's *Origines Judaicae* had attempted. Describing the Israelites as a pastoral nation integrated with the Arabian tribes of Goshen and wider Egypt, originally tolerated by Orus I, but then persecuted by Memnon II, the text described the 'state of bondage' into which Moses was born. Rescued and adopted by Queen Thermutis, daughter and successor of the cruel Orus II, Moses was educated 'in the right way to acquire the utmost knowledge of the Egyptians'. Thus Moses became the 'profoundest politician, the best naturalist, and the most knowing magician of his time'. A 'deep politician', Moses, under the patronage of Thermutis, became nomarch of Goshen. While in Egypt 'he had leisure and sufficient opportunity to study, as well the manners, as the genius and disposition both of the Egyptians and of those of his own nation': here the schemes for his 'revolution' were made. Upon the demise of Thermutis 'a violent persecution of the Hebrews was renew'd', and Moses 'no longer protected, and apprehensive he should not be able to justify certain murders by him committed, betook himself to flight'. Retiring to Arabia Petrea, Moses took the opportunity of collaborating with Jethro of Midian, marrying his daughter: as the text commented, 'and here it may not be amiss to remark, that Moses was then so very indifferent a Jew and knew at the time so little of the tremendous God he afterwards imag'd out, that he readily espous'd a damsel who worship'd Idols and did not even once think of circumcising his children'.[77]

Conspiring with Jethro of Midian, Moses plotted military revenge, and 'lay'd a vast plan, and knew how to employ against Egypt all the science which he had learned of the Egyptians'. His strategy was to prompt a popular revolt against the Egyptians by cultivating in the populace a belief that he was sent by God to save them. Using his skills and talents 'he accordingly soon brought them to a belief that his God who he sometimes called an Angel of the Lord, the God of his fathers, the God of the Almighty had appear'd to him, that it was by his express order he took upon him the care and trouble of conducting them'. Such pretended prodigies 'bedazzled' the Israelites. Interestingly, lengthy treatment was given to the methods Moses took 'to induce this populace to submit to his jurisdiction', especially his manipulation of the episode of the cloud and pillar described in Exodus and Numbers. Undoubtedly this was the 'grossest of all cheats and impositions of this impostor'. Learning from his experience in the deserts of Arabia he noticed how 'customary' it was for travellers to use 'flaming lanterns' and 'smoak which issued from the same lanterns' as guides. Moses made such natural skills 'pass for a miracle and a token of his God's favour and protection'. Moses exhorted Hobab, his wife's brother, 'by the most pressing motive of interest' because of his experience of the countryside 'to undertake the office of being their conductor'. The credulous populace 'believed that the Almighty was actually and personally present in that Fire and in that Smoke'. This expansion, then, gave a far more historical or 'circumstantial' account of Moses than that given in the 1709/1719 version. By using both classical sources and Scripture the text now gave a more forensic picture of precisely how Moses established his imposture. It emphasised the 'Egyptian' origins of both Moses and the Israelites, but also by implication undermined the 'miraculous' nature of events reported in the Old Testament.[78]

The second series of expansions developed these points in greater detail by including passages that exposed the 'imaginary prodigies or miraculous operations' that Moses employed to dupe the people. Not only did the text expose how Moses used 'natural magick' and 'so dazzled even the most clear sighted of the Hebrews', but moved on to berate Christian commentators who insisted on such impostures as the grounds of 'the grandest of mysteries of Christianity'. Examining passages in Maccabees and elsewhere, where mysterious lights were interpreted as the manifestations of God, the author suggested that Moses and his confederates had used chemical phosphorus to create a 'pretended celestial light'.[79] Such tricks were readily available and exploited by Moses. Like the vulgar of the eighteenth century, 'those poor silly wretches were seduced and led astray by means of these subtil pranks ... which they believed real miracles, for want of knowing the natural causes of such fallacious appearance'. As the addition continued, Moses performed many other tricks with snakes and lice to seduce the credulous Jews. The thrust of this addition was both to expose Moses' fraud and also the ignorance of the vulgar: an ignorance that was still perpetuated by a stupid veneration for miraculous understandings of scriptural accounts. Further additions underscored 'the iniquity, the fallacy, and injustice of Moses' in his treatment of the Israelites. Again appropriating scriptural passages from Numbers and Deuteronomy, the text described Moses' 'tyrannical' treatment of the twelve tribes of Israel in general and of those who opposed him.

These revisions in the description of Moses' imposture have parallels in Toland's work. Not only the substance of the account, but also the approach of collating classical and sacred sources, was mirrored in his researches on the *respublica mosaica*. As we have seen Toland commonly exploited orthodox learning to compromise the authoritative status of scriptural texts. Like the *Traité*, Toland used his erudition both to give an unusual and heterodox account of Moses, and to appropriate scriptural authority for his own devices. Unlike the *Traité*, Toland's account of the significance of Moses was not unequivocally hostile. Moses was not simply an impostor, but was an exemplar of how a legislator could accommodate religion to the virtuous service of civil society. Just as Spinoza had used the books of the Old Testament to construct an account of Moses as a republican legislator, so too did Toland try to reclaim his reputation for non-sacerdotal 'political' purposes.

Clearly, Toland's writings (both the scribal and printed versions of *Hodegus*) had broadly different audiences than that of the *Traité*. Although it should be noted that Eugene and d'Hohendorf, were recipients and owners of both sets of writings. Evidence of the distribution of surviving copies of the French work suggest it had a broad circulation on the continent. Toland's scribal writings on Moses unlike the *Traité*, were also published in a widely distributed printed edition in 1720. Untangling the exact connections between these two traditions of writing will prove very difficult. It is unclear whether those who copied and distributed manuscript versions of the *Traité* included Toland himself, or whether they merely took the opportunity of exploiting Toland's work available in the same library. By 1719 Toland's reputation in relation to his account of Moses had already been compromised by the critical reception of *Origines Judaicae*. Given the careful attention paid by all the participants to covering up the historical origins and authorship of the *Traité*, inclusion of such an easily recognisable extract would have prompted much finger pointing from Christian critics.

What Toland was trying to do in these works is not immediately obvious. Possibly his intentions were merely impious – to corrode the commonplace Christian veneration for sacred Hebrew history. Certainly the force of his account was to compromise scriptural history with non-sacred sources, just as Spinoza had done in his *Tractatus theologico politicus*. Providing such material for men like Eugene and Hohendorf would have been providing more grist to their irreligious mill. But Toland also made public versions of his work, so clearly had a wider political objective. Comparing Toland's intentions with the reception of the *Traité* is less than helpful since the meaning of the accounts of Moses in both works is different. While the *Traité* gave a negative and hostile account of the Hebrew legislator, it is equally clear that Toland's attitude was one of admiration. For the *Traité* Moses exemplified tyranny, while Toland's laid much more stress upon Moses' skills as a (republican) legislator. Perhaps bound by Straussian imperatives of censorship, Toland simply adopted different attitudes in public and private. It is also possible that Toland simply had different intentions as a public writer. There is little doubt that the social context for reading a manuscript of the *Traité* was distinct from the audience that encountered a printed edition of Toland's writings. He was deeply aware of the power of public texts as persuasive devices for compromising the hegemony of orthodox belief. This attack on the commonplaces of established belief was more than intellectual hubris, but had political purposes. The priority Toland gave to the pursuit of civic virtue, meant that reform could only be achieved by destroying the confessional basis of political authority. As he put it, 'Civil liberty and Religious Toleration, ... [are] the most desirable things in this world, the most conducing to peace, plenty, knowledge, and every kind of happiness, [and] have been the two main objects of all my writing'.[80] Toland's Moses was a republican legislator and therefore an exemplary model for the conduct of contemporary politics.

Toland was by no means unique in drawing republican significance from the Mosaic model. James Harrington (whose works, as we have seen, Toland edited in 1700) represented a key moment in the republican development of a political account of the Mosaic theocracy. Drawing specific significance from the collaboration between the heathen Jethro of Midian and Moses, Harrington argued that human and divine prudence was 'first discovered unto mankind by God himself in the fabric of the Commonwealth of Israel'.[81] Moses had his 'education by the daughter of Pharaoh' and acquired political wisdom through a combination of prophetic understanding and an appreciation of ancient prudence. The perfection of Israel was achieved by the institution of a holy popular commonwealth: the degeneration of such theocracy was prompted by a crisis of republican virtue and the rise of priestcraft.[82] For Harrington, the Mosaic commonwealth was both divine and a human contrivance.[83] Such was Harrington's conviction that divine and rational prudence were complicit in Moses' commonwealth that he denied the irreligious implications of comparing it with the achievements of Numa, Solon and Lycurgus. This was the point of the scriptural convergence of the commonwealths of Midian and Israel: 'How then cometh it', he continued, 'to be irreverent or atheistical, as some say, in politicians ... to compare (though but by way of illustration) other legislators or politicians, as Lycurgus, Solon, with Moses, or other commonwealths, as Rome and Venice, with that of Israel?'[84] Human prudence was the 'creature of God', thus there were proper commonwealths before that of the Mosaic theocracy and might be afterwards.[85]

Unlike the more Godly accounts of the Hebrew commonwealth written by men like Cunaeus, Harrington's work embraced a republican reading of Moses as a legislator that had its roots in Machiavelli's *Discorsi*. For Harrington this was not to deny the theocratic nature of the *respublica mosaica* but to elevate the status of commonswealth politics to divinity. Following Moses' and Jethro's injunctions, the true commonwealth was popular and anti-hierocratic, which implied that political reform would involve both civic and religious renewal against the iniquity of both tyranny and priestcraft. Later republicans like Henry Neville and Algernon Sidney echoed Harrington in applauding the Hebrew state as a 'model fit to be imitated by all nations'.[86] Unlike Machiavelli, Harrington constructed his account of Moses from almost comprehensively scriptural sources: much of the defence of his position against the attacks of contemporary clergy rested upon his ability to establish his position from biblical material. So although Harrington undertook an unorthodox description of the Hebrew commonwealth it was not contrived as an underhand assault upon the integrity of Scripture. The authority of his argument was precisely because it was a credible biblical interpretation.

A far less orthodox account of Moses as a political legislator was advanced by the radical republican translator of Spinoza, Charles Blount. Moses was not the author of divine revelation but a legislator who expounded 'the first originals of things after such a method as might breed in the minds of men piety, and a worshipping of the true God'.[87] Importantly Blount used many of the classical sources that formed the basis of both Toland's work and that of the *Traité*.[88] Commenting on Moses passing the Red Sea, Blount noted (following Memphite tradition) that the legislator was 'well acquainted with the condition of the place, observed the flux and reflux of the waters, and so brought over his army by dry land'.[89] Alexander of Macedon had experienced the same sort of episode in his passage through the Pamphylian Ocean. Both Abraham and Moses 'were well skill'd in Egyptian learning' and (following Herodotus) this explained why certain of their customs such as circumcision were adopted from Egyptian practice. Judaism upheld the principal tenets of natural religion in the 'practices of Virtue and Goodness'. The laws, rites and ceremonies of Judaism far from being particular divine revelation 'were practised among the Gentiles indifferently, or at least did not much vary from them, as the diligent searchers into Antiquity well know'.[90] Unlike Harrington's more positive explication of the significance of the Mosaic commonwealth for contemporary politics, Blount's arguments simply indicated that Moses was as much a legislator as any other figure in antiquity, the point being that most religion (beyond the rational injunctions of natural religion) was a heuristic device either for civic measures, or twisted to deviant purposes by a corrupt and self-interested priesthood. There was a readily available public discourse articulated by English republicans from the 1650s to the 1700s which paid close conceptual and historical attention to the nature and import of the *respublica mosaica*. Toland's account of Moses drew then upon a well-established English republican tradition.

It is important to underscore that Toland's work on Moses was not simply impious but, as has been discussed in the previous chapter, laid the foundation for practical suggestions in reforming the confessionalism of political culture. Circulating clandestine manuscripts to elite figures was intended to provide impetus for the reception of practical political projects. The republican reading of Moses as a 'legislator' laid the foundations for establishing a tolerant rational state. His intentions were twofold, both making a point about the historical nature of Scripture and providing a prescriptive model for the relationship between religion and the state. As he repeatedly insisted, the Old Testament, as a historical source, was partial and abridged: it could claim no special evidential status as revealed material but had to be contextualised with other pagan sources. The veneration of the Mosaic institution was to be a prescriptive model for political and religious reform. Toland's applause for Moses was part of a public strategy for rendering republican institutions more readily accommodated to the dominant Christian discourses of his time. If Moses could be shown to be a republican pantheist who designed a rational religion for political purposes then Toland's arguments were less exposed to vilification as irreligious. Toland's took the radical arguments of the *Traité* right into the heart of the British establishment.

NOTES

1 *An Account of the courts* p. 67.

2 *Ibid*. p. 56.

3 A. Ward 'The Electress Sophia and the Hanovarian Succession' *English Historical Review* 1 (1886) pp. 470–506.

4   *Ibid.* p. 479.

5   A. Ward *The Electress Sophia and the Hanoverian Succession* (1909) p. 341.

6   See J. P. Erman *Mémoires pour servir à l'histoire de Sophie Charlotte reine de Prusse* (Berlin, 1801) pp. 200–211.

7   S. Daniel *John Toland* (Montreal, 1984) p. 146

8   See M. Jacob 'John Toland and the Newtonian ideology' *Journal of the Warburg and Courtauld Institutes* 32 (1969) pp. 307–331 especially at pp. 313–314. Klopp 2 pp. 361–364.

9   Klopp 2 p. 362.

10 *Ibid.* pp. 363–364.

11 See Vienna Ms 10,325 'Dissertations Diverses'. See also *Tolandiana* p. 105.

12 See J. H. Nichols *The Epicurean Philosophy: the De rerum natura of Lucretius* (Cornell, 1976). See J. A. I. Champion '"The Men of Matter": spirits, matter and the politics of priestcraft, 1701–1709' in G. Paganini (ed.) *Scepticismes, Lumières, Clandestinité* (Geneva, 2002) pp. 115–150.

13 See Champion *Nazarenus*.

14 S. Berti *et al. Heterodoxy*.

15 See Jacob *Radical Enlightenment*.

16 See S. Berti 'The first edition of the *Traité des trois imposteurs*, and its debt to Spinoza's *Ethics*' in M. Hunter, D. Wootton (eds) *Atheism from the Reformation to the Enlightenment* (Oxford, 1992) pp. 183–220.

17 See M. Benitez 'La coterie Hollandaise et la réponse à M. de la Monnoye sur le Traité de tribus impostoribus' *Lias* 21 (1994) pp. 71–94.

18 See F. Charles-Daubert '*L'Esprit de Spinosa* et les *Traités des trois imposteurs*: rappel des différent familles et de leurs principales caracteristiques' in Berti *et al. Heterodoxy* pp. 131–189.

19 Charles-Daubert 'Les principales sources de *L'Esprit de Spinosa*' in *Groupe de recherches spinozistes. Travaux et documents 1* (Paris, 1989) pp. 61–107, at p. 82.

20 See Charles-Daubert '*L'Esprit*' pp. 138, 153, 174, 179; idem 'Les *Traités des trois imposteurs* aux XVIIe et XVIIIe siècles' in G. Canziani (ed.) *Filosofia e religione nella letteratura clandestina secoli XVII e XVIII* (Milan, 1994) pp. 319. 320–321; idem 'Les principales sources' pp. 83–84.

21 M. Benitez 'Une histoire interminable: origines et développement du *Traité des trois imposteurs*' in Berti *et al. Heterodoxy* pp. 53–74.

22 On Aymon see A. Goldgar *Impolite learning: conduct and community in the republic of letters 1680–1750* (1995) pp. 174–176.

23 See P. L. Heyworth (ed.) *The Letters of Humphrey Wanley* (Oxford, 1989) pp. 265–267, 275–278, 429–430.

24 Marchand owned a copy of Shaftesbury's *Lettre sur l'entousiasme* (The Hague, 1709) published by Johnson: see C. Berkvens-Stevalinck *Catalogue du Manuscrits de la Collection Prosper Marchand* (Leiden 1988) p. 126.

25 On Johnson see J. O'Higgins *Anthony Collins: the man and his works* (The Hague, 1970)

pp. 25, 211, 226; J. Feather 'English books in the Netherlands in the eighteenth century: reprints of piracies?' in C. Berkvens-Stevelinck, *et al.* (eds) *Le magasin de l'univers* (Brill, 1992) pp. 151–154.

26 See G. Carabelli 'John Toland e G. W. Leibniz Otto Lettere' *Rivista critica di storia della filosofia* 31 (1976) pp. 412–431 p. 417; *Tolandiana* p. 194.

27 See *Tolandiana* p. 154.

28 G. Aquilecchia 'Nota su John Toland traduttore di Giordano Bruno' *English Miscellany* 9 (1958) pp. 77–86 at 85–86.

29 Marchand 'Impostoribus' in Berti *et al. Heterodoxy* pp. 494, 499.

30 See G. Ricuperati 'Libertinismo e deismo a Vienna: Spinosa, Toland e Triregno' *Rivista Storica Italiana* 79 (1967) pp. 628–695.

31 See A. Brown 'Savanarola, Machiavelli and Moses: a changing model' in A. Brown *The Medici in Florence: the exercise of language and power* (Florence, 1992) pp. 263–279.

32 See F.E. Manuel *The Broken Staff* (1992) *passim.*

33 C. Ligota 'Histoire à fondemant theologique: la République du Hebreux' in *L'Ecriture Sainte au temps de Spinoza et dans le systeme Spinozist* (Paris, 1992) pp. 149–167 at 158.

34 Cited in L. A. Segal 'Jacques Basnage de Beauval's L'Histoire des Juifs: Christian historiographical perceptions of Jewry and Judaism on the eve of the Enlightenment' *Hebrew Union College Annual* 54 (1983) pp. 303–324 at 317.

35 See 'Projet d'une Dissertation sur la Colomne de feu et de Nuée des Israelites: dans une Lettre à Megalonymus' ONB 10,325 fos. 4–5.

36 'Projet' fo. 5.

37 Toland lent a copy of this work, under the title 'The Cloud & Pillar', to Lord Castleton.

38 See P. Rossi *The Dark Abyss of Time* (Chicago, 1987) pp. 152–157.

39 See S. Hutton 'Edward Stillingfleet, Henry More, and the decline of *Moses Atticus*: a note on seventeenth century Anglican apologetics' in R. Kroll *et al.* (eds) *Philosophy, science, and religion in England 1640–1700* (Cambridge, 1992) pp. 68–84.

40 See D. B. Sailor 'Moses and Atomism' *Journal of the History of Ideas* 25 (1964) pp. 3–16.

41 See Toland *Two Essays sent in a letter from Oxford* (1695) p. 15.

42 See the English translation of *Adeisidaemon* and *Origines Judaicae* located in John Ryland's Library call mark 3 f. 38. Since this manuscript is not paginated or foliated I have used a combination of page openings and paragraph numbers. *Origines Judaicae* Dedication fo. 2.§ 1.

43 *Origines* fo. 5 § 2.

44 *Ibid.* fo. 11 § 5.

45 *Ibid.* fo. 16 § 6.

46 *Ibid.* fos. 18–26 § 7–9.

47 *Ibid.* fo. 28 § 10.

48 *Ibid.* fo. 32 § 12. At fo. 35 §12 Toland noted 'in my own private opinion' Jews could be regarded as Egyptians.

49 *Origines* fo. 37 § 13.

50 *Ibid.* fo. 39 § 14.

51 *Ibid.* fo. 42 § 14.

52 *Ibid.* fo. 52 § 18.

53 *Ibid.* fo. 63 § 21.

54 See A. Rosenburg (ed.) *Simon Tyssot de Patot: voyages et avantures de Jaques Masse* (Paris, 1993) pp. 91–92.

55 See *Nazarenus* 'Introduction'.

56 See 'Projet' f.1–2, 3; the manuscript passages were translated and expanded in passages in *Tetradymus* (1720) Preface pp. i–ii; and *Hodegus* pp. 3–4.

57 *Tetradymus* p. ii; *Hodegus* pp. 4–5; 'Projet' fos. 3–4.

58 *Hodegus* pp. 6–7.

59 *Ibid.* p. 27.

60 *Ibid.* p. 46.

61 See T. Hobbes *Leviathan* (1651) ed. R. Tuck (Cambridge, 1989) p. 276.

62 *Hodegus* pp. 48, 50–51.

63 *Ibid.* p. 14.

64 *Nazarenus* Appendix 1 pp. 2–3, 4–5, 6–7.

65 *Nazarenus* Appendix 1 p. 8.

66 *Tolandiana passim.*

67 See G. Carabelli 'John Toland e Leibniz'.

68 *Ibid.* pp. 421, 428.

69 See 'Lettre de Mr Morin' in *Mémoires pour l'histoire des sciences et des beaux arts à Trévoux* (1709) pp. 1589–1590, 1591, 1601, 1604, 1611–1612, 1618.

70 *Journal Litéraire* (1714) IV (The Hague, 1732) pp. 250–253.

71 S. Parker *Censura Temporum* 2 volumes (London, 1708–9) pp. 547–564 cited at 548, 559, 560–563. See also, *The History of the Works of the Learned* XI (1709) pp. 376–378.

72 See *Hodegus Confuted. In a plain demonstration that the Pillar of a cloud and fire which led the Israelites thro the wilderness; was not, as Mr Toland vainly imagines a fire of human preparation* (1721) pp. 7, 18, 42, 46.

73 See Charles-Daubert 'Les *Traités des trois imposteurs* aux XVIIe et XVIIIe' pp. 331–336.

74 See G. Canziani and G. Paganini (eds) *Theophrastus redivivus* 2 volumes (Florence, 1981) Part 3 Chapter 5 pp. 430–457.

75 See Berti (ed.) *Trattato dei tre impostori* pp. 110, 112, 114.

76 See P. Retat (ed.) *Traité des trois imposteurs 1777* (Saint Etienne, 1973) pp. 40–51; A. Anderson (ed.) *The Treatise of the Three impostors and the Enlightenment* (1997) pp. 18–22.

77 The passages can be found in BL Stowe 47 'The famous book entitled De Tribus Impostoribus' fos. 33–41 and Glasgow University Library, General 1185 fos. 104–153.

78 *Ibid.*

79 See J. V. Golinski 'A noble spectacle. Phosphorus and the public culture of science in the early Royal Society' *Isis* 80 (1989) pp. 11–39.

80 See *Tetradymus* p. 223.

81 J. G. A. Pocock (ed.) *The political works of James Harrington* (Cambridge, 1977) p. 161.

82 Pocock 'Introduction' p. 92.

83 *Ibid.* p. 95.

84 *Ibid.* p. 629.

85 *Ibid.* pp. 616–617.

86 See Worden 'Republicanism and the Restoration' p. 162. Rousseau continued this republican regard for Moses as a great legislator: see 'Des Juifs' in *Oeuvres Completes* III (Paris, 1964) p. 499.

87 C. Blount *The Oracles of Reason* (1693) p. 75.

88 *Ibid.* pp. 127–130.

89 *Ibid.* p. 131.

90 *Ibid.* p. 133.

8

De studio theologia:
patristic erudition and the
attack on Scripture

Toland had a clear and (to many contemporaries) dangerous political agenda. His public polemic on behalf of the Hanoverian succession had neatly blended a republican aspiration of establishing a government of reason with an internecine war against priestcraft and superstition. This warfare was fought on many fronts. The rules of engagement were diverse. In works like *Christianity not mysterious*, Toland articulated a public strategy of enfranchising the rights of the individual to read and understand Scripture without recourse to the interpretative guidance of the Church. His work on Moses showed (following the example of Spinoza) how it was possible to read the Old Testament in a republican and civic manner, providing a model for others to emulate. Much of Toland's status as a public writer derived from the patronage he displayed prominently in the dedications of the printed works. Although he was controversial, his arguments were condoned through this intimacy with powerful people. Toland's public persona was not determined simply by his confederacy with the great and the good, but also by the credibility of his arguments, and by the perceived quality of his learning. Although one of the central discourses of his polemic was to promote the sovereignty of reason, he also invoked the authority of erudition. Toland's ambition was to deconstruct the credibility of clerical knowledge, at the very least to expose the institutional processes that made clergymen's opinions masquerade as divine truth.

It should be recalled that Toland was as comfortable in Furly's library in Rotterdam, or Anthony Collin's in Great Baddow as he was in the courts of Hanover and Berlin, or salons of London and the home counties. Although Toland broadcast his ideas through the medium of print, scribal writings or conversation, he made his ideas in dialogue with other books – spectacularly with the Bible, but also critically with the *corpus* of clerical learning. His forensic scrutiny of the methods, findings and pronouncements of established erudition was a fundamental element of the strategy for transforming public culture. The evidence of Toland's intellectual conduct suggests a process of renovation by subversion (what Guy Dubord called 'détournement') from within, rather than one of revolutionary destruction. The starting point for Toland's cultural hostilities was the canon of orthodox literature – both sacred and critical. In order to engage in this battle with any prospect of success, he needed to be proficient in the routines and skills of orthodox learning. As we have seen from his own collection of books, most of these were such scholarly tomes, rather than subversive works.

The question of Toland's learning has been long debated. His contemporaries at Oxford remarked that he was a man of much learning if little religion, and implored him to employ his skills to pious ends. Educated at Edinburgh, Glasgow, Leiden and Oxford, Toland had a reputation in the 1690s as a skilled linguist, although his growing impiety prompted Edmund Gibson to decline Toland's assistance on the labours of preparing a new edition of Camden's *Britannia*. Toland was indeed proud of having been taught by the famous Spanheim at Leiden. While he admitted having differences with his tutor, he did not reveal that the Dutchman had refused him admittance after one quarrel 'upon which occasion he was hiss'd out of the school'.' The fundamental skills of the early modern scholar were linguistic. Claiming to be proficient in at least ten languages, Toland produced works translated from, and composed in, Italian, a variety of Celtic languages, as well as Greek and Latin. He claimed knowledge of Arabic, Spanish and Hebrew and had a fluency in French. That Toland had a facility with a variety of learning can be seen in his different works on Celtic learning and biblical scholarship. As contemporaries like Humphrey Wanley and Edmund Lhwyd were aware, Toland's knowledge of Irish languages (both written and oral) was broad. This skill, combined with his deep reading in the classical canon, enabled him to produce an original, if highly controversial, account of the origin and nature of ancient Celtic philosophy and religion. So for example, in *Nazarenus* (1718), Toland displayed the evidence of his wide reading in patristic studies and biblical criticism, to attempt to authenticate the spurious *Gospel of Barnabas*. As the prospectus *Cicero illustratus* (1712) indicates, his critical abilities also had classical pretensions projected in the ambition to produce a comprehensive and annotated edition of the works of Cicero.

For some contemporaries like Martin Aedler, an orientalist on the margins of the intellectual life of Cambridge, Toland's intellectual productions were indications of his serious learning, so much so that he thought Toland would be a good person to encourage such learning in the university. Other contemporaries derided this claim to erudition. Although Toland had talents and application he had 'for many years employ'd the best parts, and a great stock of reading to the worst purposes, namely to shock the Faith of Christians in the glorious person and Divinity of their redeemer, and to sap and undermine the principles and foundations of the orthodox Faith'. Another obituary commented that 'he had read many Books, but digested few, if any'. Toland's learning was shallow: 'he would reject an opinion, merely because an eminent writer embraced it ... he had a smattering in many languages, was a critick in none'. Affected, stylistically 'low, confused and disagreeable', and a rude controversialist Toland was 'always in the wrong'. His public notoriety was 'owing chiefly to the animadversions of learned men upon his writings, among whom 'twas a common trick in their disputes with one another, to charge their adversary with an agreement to, or resemblance, of Mr Toland's Notions'. While many agreed that 'learning, without all doubt he had', the moral quality of that erudition was fundamentally contested.[2] These descriptions raise some important issues about the nature and function of Toland's erudition. He was perceived as a man of broad reading, even though he commonly used such labour for the worst purposes.

The second theme to underscore is the relationship between Toland and other 'learned' men: he was thought to deliberately contradict received learned opinion, and in consequence such learned men self-consciously animadverted upon his arguments, projecting their significance to a broader audience. This controversial transaction between Toland's claims to learning, and learned rebuttal, allows insight into the communicative strategy that Toland developed during the course of his life. Toland was a master of the art of scholarly subversion.

There is little doubt amongst modern historians, as amongst Toland's contemporaries, that he was embroiled in a project aimed at compromising clerical authority. By examining his 'learned' works it will be possible to indicate how he both mastered, and turned to his own purposes, standards of citation and testimony. In doing so he not only produced 'learned' works that prompted furious rebuttal, but attempted to expose the knowledge claims that underlay the routines of learning. Modern historical studies have tended to dismiss Toland's learning as second rate and derivative: he 'dwelt outside the world of the *érudits*'.[3] Challenging suggestions that Toland's own work was parasitic upon the patrimony of orthodox erudition, others have described the work on the apocrypha, in particular, as surprisingly competent.[4] The quality of this erudition can be examined in detail by looking at the evolution of his *Amyntor* (1699) into a later work *A catalogue of books* (1726). This is an interesting text not simply because of its content, but also because of its longevity and existence as a printed and manuscript work.

The origins of the work are to be found in Toland's editorial recovery of the republican canon of political writers in the later 1690s. One of the controversies prompted by this project was the debate over the spurious nature of the

Eikon Basilike purportedly written by the martyred Charles I, but in Toland's view forged by his chaplain.[5] In the course of exposing the fraud, Toland made an off-hand remark about the number of supposititious works ascribed to Christ and the apostles. Joining doubts about the authenticity of the *Eikon Basilike* with an assault upon the integrity of Scripture, incited furious rejoinder. Offspring Blackall, using the powerful platform of his 30 January commemorative sermon to the House of Commons, argued that when 'the publick records and Evidence of our Christianity, are, without controul or censure, suffered to be called in question' this was a threat to the 'Foundation of all Revealed Religion'.[6] Toland's response to this was to write *Amyntor* (1699: two editions in April and May), a defence of Milton's life and his account of the forgery of *Eikon Basilike*. Toland expanded his brief remarks about supposititious Christian works into a detailed catalogue of materials listing references to over seventy titles.[7] In the following March, this work was condemned (along with *Christianity not mysterious*) by the lower House of Convocation.[8] The 'Catalogue' provoked sustained and intense critical examination in print. This episode illustrates the intimacy of the political assault upon the *de jure divino* monarchy of Charles I with the broader cultural assault upon the status of revelation.

The 'Catalogue' of 1699 was not however the final form of the work. It was revised and expanded over the succeeding two decades, a final version being published in Desmaizeaux's collection of 1726. There is evidence that this copy was in circulation in scribal form on the continent and in England between 1710 and 1720. Toland sent Eugene of Savoy a scribal work, 'Amyntor Canonicus', from Leiden in August 1710. Subtitled 'Eclaircissement sur le Canon du Nouveau Testement', the manuscript was said to contain 'un catalogue tres-ample de livres anciennement attribués à Jesus Christ, à ses Apotres, et aux plus considerables de leurs premiers sectateurs'. This expanded catalogue does not survive in the Viennese archive, although the description of it as including 'plusieurs remarques et questions importantes, concernant l'histoire des Ecritures Sacrées', suggests some similarity with the 1726 version. That this text was in wider circulation, at the same time, can be established by Toland's correspondence with Jacob Arminius, of Amsterdam, discussing whether he might forward that work 'que vous m'a dit de avoir entre mains pour quelque grand Seigneur, et que vous m'a promis de le copier'. Arminius was keen to have Toland's French translation of the English version, sheet by sheet, and confirmed that he would let no one else see it.[9] From internal evidence in the 1726 version it is possible to advance a termination date for final amendments from the publication dates of works cited. Since books are referenced from 1700 through to 1718, Toland was probably making additions to the catalogue, as he read new material. That the text was in circulation in England between 1718 and the early months of the

1720s can be established from the surviving list of 'Manuscripts of mine abroad' which noted that the Whig associate of Robert Molesworth, Thomas Hewett, had a copy (and had returned it) of a text called 'History of ye Canon' which seems likely to be similar to the work sought out by Arminius. Again Toland had sought out pan-European audiences, public and elite, for his work.

The expansion from the fragment of 1698 to a full-blown catalogue provides clear evidence of Toland's reading and research into the nature of patristic evidence for apocryphal material. The manifestation of this reading was a text composed almost entirely of massive annotation, reference and citation of scholarly sources. The progression from the first to the final version of the catalogue can be established with precision by collation of the two texts. The way the catalogue worked was simple: working through from Christ to the Apostles and disciples, the apocryphal works ascribed to each person were described and their authenticity evaluated. The structure of the catalogue parodied the form of more orthodox works. The first version (1699) contained seventeen general entries and discussed seventy-seven titles, while the final version (1726) had twenty general entries discussing over one hundred and ten titles. The exact nature of these expansions, inclusions and additions, illustrates some of the techniques of Toland's working practices. Although there were completely new entries included under the heading of 'Mark', 'Barnabas' and 'the Gospels of Valentine ... and others', the vast majority of new material consisted of sub-entries added to already existing headings. For example, the entries for non-canonical texts ascribed to Mary grew from five to nine, for Peter from nine to fourteen and for Paul from eleven to nineteen.

Toland revised, corrected and re-ordered his first draft. The example of the improvement of the first entry, 'of books reported to be written by CHRIST himself, or that particularly concern him', is characteristic of the form this revision took. References are expanded, explanatory commentary included, plus more material added.[10] The commentary on the correspondence between Jesus and Abgarus, King of Edessa, has identical sources. The main reference for the tradition was Eusebius, which Toland supplemented by a precise page reference to the Dominican scholar Francis Combefis' patristic editions. The final version also expanded part of the latter reference into the more detailed assertion, 'Nicephorus says he wrote it with his own hand. Hist. Eccles. l. 2. c. 7'. In the second item, 'The epistle of Christ to Peter', additional references are added as well as ironic authorial commentary: 'But the forger of this piece forgot, that Paul was neither a Christian, nor an Apostle, till after the death of Christ'. Item 4, on the 'Hymn which Christ secretly taught his disciples and apostles', displays an interesting alteration in reference. The 1699 edition cites 'Augustin. Epist. 253. Ad Ceretum Episcopum' while that of 1726 has '*Augustin. Epist. Ad Ceretium Episcopum. Edit Benedictin. 237*'. Clearly Toland adjusted the testimony for this evidence from one edition of Augustine's letters to another. Identifying the precise sources that Toland used to furnish his footnotes and reference allows an insight into his methods. Following the clue of these altered references it is possible to examine at least two books that we know Toland used (and in one case certainly owned). In this way we can reconstruct the routines of Toland's research practice, and his reading patterns.

The two works are Johann Grabe's *Spicilegium SS Patrum* (Oxford, 1699, second edition 1700, third edition 1714) and Johann Albertus Fabricius *Codex Apocryphi Novi Testamenti* (Hamburg, 1703 and 1719). These volumes were works of unquestionably orthodox scholarship that aimed (for entirely pious reasons) to recover the monuments of primitive Christianity. Toland mined them for bibliographical details about the various apocryphal texts. For example, comparing sections of Grabe's text (vol. 1, pp. 55–81) with both versions of *Amyntor* shows that Toland simply re-ordered the discursive original into a simple series of headings. Whereas Grabe discussed the various textual remnants before giving a separate series of extracts from contemporary witnesses, Toland simply identifies the name of the spurious text and indicates the location of sources. At the same time as extracting the ore from Grabe, Toland also synthesised Fabricius' research on 'De dictis Christo Tributas' which identified twelve items. Item 7, a completely new addition examining a letter 'written by CHRIST, and dropt down from Heaven' was derived from the Fabricius discussion. Whereas Fabricius had deliberated about the authenticity of the 'episcopal letter' and directed the reader to the tradition 'edita ex ms Ecclesiae Toletanae à Josepho Saenz de Aguirre Tom. 2. Collectionis maxime concilior. Hispaniae pag. 428 seq.', Toland merely cited 'Aguirr. Tom. 2. collect. max. Concilior. Hispan. pag. 428' with a facetious remark to the effect that such forgery ought to be ignored. Item 8, 'a great many *Sayings* attributed to Christ, but not recorded in the *New Testament*' was lifted directly from Fabricius' additions to the first edition of his work, 'De dictis Christi servatoris nostri, quae in quator Evangeliis canonicis non extant' (1719: volume 1, 321*–335*).[11] Further evidence of Toland's close readings of this source can be seen in the manuscript translation of the Latin passages in Fabricius that survives in his archive.[12] That Toland borrowed his learning from these sources can be seen most obviously in some of the changes where references derived from Grabe in 1699 are substituted by citations drawn from Fabricius in 1719.[13] Examples of such amendments and additions are manifold.

Toland devoted considerable effort to refurbishing the catalogue although the essential structure of the work remained intact. The majority of this new material took the form either of authorial comment and translation of sources, or of the inclusion of more citations of texts in support of the various apocryphal works. Not only did this make the catalogue look more scholarly but the incorporation of the culturally powerful erudition of Grabe and

Fabricius, also compromised their reputations by association with him. Toland also invoked the authority of 'original' manuscripts to accrue scholarly credit to the catalogue. [14] Even though in most cases it is unlikely that Toland had actually consulted the manuscripts, he did lay claim to original archival work in the case of an unidentified codex of 'the book of the Infancy of Christ, pretended to have been written by Thomas'. Noting that the Orientalist scholar, Henry Sike, Regius Professor of Divinity at Cambridge (1702–12), had printed a Latin and Arabic edition of the work 'with learned notes', he commented that 'I leant him a Latin version of it on parchment, which is very old; and which had it come into his hands, might have saved him a great part of his labor'. Unusually, Toland had lost track of the manuscript, he lamented, 'but what's become of it, since his unfortunate death, I know not: neither have I claim'd it, as having nothing to show my title'. [15]

The bulk of the references in the text were to patristic sources and the various commentaries, collections and editions of the 'documents' of the early Christian Church. Epiphanius, Eusebius, Jerome, Origen, Augustine, Philaster, Nicephorus, Theodoret and Clement of Alexandria were the most frequently cited sources. Beyond these, almost sanctified sources, were a range of more obscure patristic authors such as Isidore of Pelusium (d. 425), Turibus, Bishop of Asturica (fl. 440), Titus Bostrens (d. 378), Eustathius of Antioch (d. 337) and Paul Orosius (fl. 400). In citing these early Christian texts Toland was suborning authoritative witnesses to his project of compromising the canonicity of received Scripture.

At another level, Toland was also playing a complex inter-textual game, not only by implicating the Church Fathers in his schemes, but perhaps more importantly, by engrossing the editorial labours of his orthodox contemporaries to his own purposes. These patristic sources did not come to Toland's attention as unmediated texts. Surveying the list of printed books cited by Toland it is evident that he had access to the publications of many of his learned contemporaries. As well as the works of Fabricius and Grabe, Toland also cited the writings of eminent continental scholars like Jean Cotelerius, Christopher Pfaff, Henry Sike, Louis Le Nain Tillemont, Nicholas Rigaltius, Francis Combefis, as well as Englishmen of learned reputation like James Ussher, John Mill, John Gregory and David Wilkins. There were also works of a much older generation such as the enormous collections of early Christian material like Johann Jacob's *Monumenta S. Patrum Orthodoxographa* (3 volumes, Basel, 1569)[16] and individual works like William Lindanus' *Missa apostolica: seu, Divinius Sacrificium S. Apostoli Petri* (Paris, 1595). It is possible to identify, with some precision, many of the exact editions of the more obscure works Toland cited, because of the detail he gave regarding page references or volumes used. Contemporary readers were expert at decoding his references. One of the intentions of Toland's catalogue rested upon the capacity of the reader, both to recognise, and to pursue, the citations he gave to original sources. He was exploiting then not simply the products of particular scholarly labour, but the deeper structure of epistemic practice.

Christian erudition was critical to establishing the legitimacy of primitive (and therefore true) Christianity.[7] For both Roman Catholics and Protestants the recovery of the rituals, beliefs, and institutions of the early church was central to establishing the legitimacy of contemporary practice. As a number of modern scholars have established, these rival ambitions of reconstructing primitive Christianity from ancient sources led to many complex confessional polemics. Contested definitions of who were the 'best' Church Fathers was one powerful controversial issue: was the limit to authentic witnesses the third, fifth or tenth centuries? Even if some accommodation could be made amongst scholars of differing confessional identities about the core definition of legitimate patristic testimonies, there was further furious debate and controversy about the authenticity of the textual remains of these 'Fathers'. Advancing the claims of one Father against another resulted in differing textual editions according to the confessional interests of the editor: Gallican editions of St Cyprian differed from those made by Anglican figures such as John Fell. The recovery of primitive piety was then a means of reinforcing the claims of differing and competing definitions of 'orthodoxy'. The development of 'critical' methods to identify and disseminate 'good' editions of legitimate patristic sources was not simply an advancement of 'scholarly' research methods but also an investment in an epistemological strategy for making ecclesiological authority. Although there was a powerful Protestant polemic, most urgently developed by Jean Daillé in his 1632 *Traité de l'emploies saints Pères* (and republished in the 1650s in English and Latin), against the corrupt use of patristic 'tradition', English churchmen, expanding on the sixteenth-century Anglican apologist Bishop John Jewel's notion of the authority of the *quinquesecularis*, crafted a means for using certain patristic sources to establish the patriarchal independence of the Church of England. This cautious approach to patristic authority meant that, unlike the French Church, the English did not embark upon the scholarly enterprise of making a complete patrology like the *Bibliotheca Patrum*, but instead focused their efforts upon specific texts such as the *Ignatian Epistles*.[8] This confessional pursuit of the 'unanimem consensum patrum' created a vast printed resource of patristic editions, a textual database that could be deployed for a variety of theological purpose independent of the intentions of the original editors.

The testimonies of the 'Fathers' were then a powerful persuasive in a variety of confessional debates. The authority of such patristic sources lay in two interwoven procedures; the first relied upon establishing the textual integrity of the edition, and the second on the accurate citation of this

published resource. Literary technology conspired with epistemological authority. The task of criticism was to distinguish the spurious from the authentic
text; the function of print technology was to enable this critically purified text
to be 'read' in a theologically correct manner. Clerical scholarship thus
produced a cultural artefact that both reified their institutional authority and
acted as a testimony of that authority. The patristic edition was both a site for
making and contesting true knowledge. Caution in choosing to read only the
best editions of the Fathers was a central theme of Protestant advice. Daniel
Tossanus, Professor of Divinity at Heidelberg, in his influential *A Synopsis or
Compendium of the Fathers* (London, 1635) in giving advice to young divines
argued that, read carefully, the Fathers were a useful supplement to the
Scriptures. Reading incautiously they might become 'like one blind in the
darke, and saile in a wide sea without either North Starre or Compasse'. A
firm grounding in the 'sovereign command' of Scripture was the starting
point for a critical and historical assessment of 'what is authenticall, what
erroneous, irreptitious and inserted by monks'. There were 'many supposititious books' commonly forged by Jesuits, that could only be exposed by
'certain rules' of judgement. The determining voice was to be the injunctions
of true Scripture: any patristic source that contradicted such canons was
unlikely to be authentic.[19]

The ferocity of anti-Catholic polemic in the work of men like Tossanus had
been moderated in the mainstream of Anglican scholarship after the Restoration. While there were still many Churchmen who supported the fundamental
criticisms of Jean Daillé (indeed a new edition of the English translation of his
work was published in 1675), there were also those who deliberately challenged
'the most celebrated scourge of the fathers'. In 1709 the high churchman,
William Reeves, prefaced his edition of Justin Martyr, Tertullian and Minutius
Felix with a lengthy rebuttal of slanders against the integrity of the Fathers.
Corruption originated in deviant editorial labour, rather than being fundamental to patristic texts. The writings of the Church Fathers were 'the next
best books to the Bible' and a 'passage for the unlearned into the knowledge of
the purest times of Christianity'. The truth of Christianity was built upon the
two pillars of 'scripture and primitive Christianity'. Reeves acknowledged
Daillé's point that there might be minor discrepancies between the differing
patristic accounts of the minutae of Christian practice, but in central doctrine
(such as the Trinity) the testimonies of the Fathers converged into a coherent
truth. Understanding the contextual witnesses of the early Fathers was 'the
most rational and safest method to understand the Holy Scripture'. He con-
ceded that interpreting Scripture, especially in matters 'of Polity and discipline',
was made more complex by the achievements of modern criticism. Collating
scriptural statements with the 'authenticae literae' of holy contemporaries
side-stepped both the scepticism of the critics who had 'mended away the very

body of the Sacred text' and the enthusiasm of those that laid claim to 'the spirit for the interpretation of the letter'. Such patristic sources, 'not only the most faithful guardians of the canon, but of the sense of Scripture too', were 'witnesses of facts only'.[20]

The provision of credible and critically competent editions was crucial for the formation of authentic and instrumentally persuasive cultural authority. The 'test of antiquity' became an increasingly effective means of reinforcing the doctrinal and disciplinary claims of the Church of England against both Roman Catholic and Low Church Protestant challenges. In order to comprehend the game Toland was playing it is necessary to underscore the cultural value placed on the Fathers. The value of authentic patristic sources was not simply defended in the works of controversial polemics, but was also promoted in the works of bibliographical advice of the period. The claim that patristic learning made a more Godly and devout ministry was the premise of the various works of advice published after the Restoration. In capturing the cultural environment appropriate to Toland's context the works of Henry Dodwell, Thomas Barlow and Thomas Bray, composed between the 1670s and 1700s, are central: in the advice of these men it is possible to be precise about the exact books recommended to be read.

Henry Dodwell's reputation as a man of pious erudition ensured that his letters of advice, first published in 1672 and frequently reprinted, were considered as powerful incitements to Christian virtue. Written for novices and young divines, Dodwell included a 'Catalogue' of genuine Christian authors 'till the conversion of Constantine to Christianity, together with good Editions where they might find and furnish themselves with them'. Dodwell set out 'learnedly and impartially' to discuss the textual authority and integrity of his sources in order to discover their 'Testimonial Authority'. The form his catalogue took worked through forty-six early Fathers and patristic works from Clemens Romanus (mid-first century) to Pamphilus Martyr (end of the third century). The work of each author was discussed and identified as 'undoubted' or not. Specific details of the best editions were transcribed: so for example Clemens Romanus' two Letters to the Corinthians were available 'by Patricius Junius at Oxford, Anno Dom. MDCXXXVIII. Or by Cotelerius, if you can get it. If not, the 2nd edition of Oxford, divided according to Cotelerius's paragraphs is the best of those which are easily to be had and cheap. This is in the Year MDCLXXVII'.[21] Referring prospective readers to editions of patristic works published in France, Germany and the Low Countries, Dodwell provided an annotated guide to the best, most accurate and easiest obtainable editions.

Dodwell included careful advice about negotiating confessional bias in editorial scholarship: writing on the works of Tertullian, he commented 'Edit. By Rigaltius rather than any other, because of the improvement of that most ancient noble MS of Agobardus. Or, if you would have a Protestant Edition and of an easier price, get that of Franeker, 1592, rather than many others though later'.[22] In the supplementary counsel, Dodwell delivered thematic directions, establishing the order that the Fathers ought to be read in (Justin, Athenagoras, Tatian, Theophilus Antiochenus, Clemens of Alexandria, Tertullian, Minucius Felix, Origen, Cyprian, Arnobius, Lactantius), and recommending particular volumes for more focused issues like the study of heresy (Irenaeus, Tertullian, Epiphanius, Philastrius, Augustine and Theodoret).[23] Dodwell also included practical directions on how to make 'critical learning' from the reading of these books. The reader must make marks in the margin (if the books 'be your own') of significant passages, 'and when you shall meet with any thing parallel, compare them together'. For those passages of rare import, Dodwell suggested, 'note them in paper books prepared for that purpose'. From these acts of reading and note taking, a scholar might build an armoury of citations and references to establish a particular account of the primitive Church. Reading was done, then, with 'design and observation' which thus avoided the dangers of 'confusion and distraction': the paper notebooks became the place for observing and comparing evidence, and ultimately to 'exercise your own conjectures concerning what is singular, and worthy of special observation'.[24] Exactly these themes were echoed in the influential writings of Thomas Barlow.[25] From these acts of marginal annotation were built the infrastructure of cultural authority. These were scholarly procedures that Toland must have imitated in preparation of his own work.

For men like Barlow and his friends, knowledge was made by reading and reflecting upon that reading. By such constant practice and 'with great application of mind', the text of Scripture and the Fathers became 'imprinted on our minds'. The examination of 'such citations as he meets with; and see to what purpose their authority is urg'd on all sides' was how conviction was made. Tracing citations to sources and judging their significance was how men used learning.[26] The works of advice concerning study composed by Dodwell and Barlow were products of erudition: the *Bibliotheca parochialis* (1697) was written by Thomas Bray for the encouragement of learning amongst the poorest curates in the country. Such was Bray's concern to propagate Christian knowledge, that his aim of establishing a modest library in each parish was reinforced by Parliamentary Statute in 1709, resulting in some eighty foundations. Bray identified a minimum 'catalogue of books' which every parish clergyman ought to have access. Acknowledging that other learned men had made lists of authors 'they would recommend to our use', Bray complained that 'few or none seem to have adapted their catalogues to the *Proper* and *Immediate* business of a parish minister'.[27] Since the main function of the cleric was to 'draw forth the waters of life, both for his own and others benefit, from the Holy Scriptures', he needed to 'know the critical history of the original versions and various editions' of the Old and New

Testaments. Concordances, lexicons, glossaries, sacred geographies and zoo-
logies were all recommended.[28] As with scriptural texts, so with the Church
Fathers: the key was to distinguish the genuine from the spurious, or in other
words 'to know the edition'.[29] Although aimed at the clerical foot-soldier, the
works identified as suitable were erudite.[30] Learning and 'hard study' was a
means for refurbishing the authority of the Church and converting the world
to Christian truth. A lack of books created ignorance and immorality: 'where
the priests lips cannot preserve, cannot procure knowledge, how should the
people seek the law at his mouth?'.[31] Bray thus composed a *Bibliotheca
Catechetica*, valued at about £5, which would satisfy the basic requirements of
a learned ministry.[32] The point to be made here is that when Toland embarked
upon a public attack on the canon and on the authenticity of the Fathers, this
was a form of erudition that was not simply addressed to the learned in the
universities, but held implications for patristic libraries of every parish.

English patristic learning was sophisticated and comprehensive. A premise of
this learned culture was 'knowing the edition', of distinguishing genuine
from spurious witnesses. The 1680s and 1690s saw more and more scholarship being published, with increasingly sophisticated critical apparatus.
Toland was to exploit all of these resources in the compilation of his catalogue.
The scholarly quality of such editions encouraged and enabled readers to be
confident in the integrity and authoritative status of the texts. Toland's intention was to tarnish the distinction between spurious and authentic, and
between supposititious and canonical. His subversion of this system of
criticism was both covert and explicit. Initially, Toland denied that *Amyntor*
had any corrosive purpose against the established canon of Scripture. He
simply dealt with 'supposititious' works ascribed to Christ and the Apostles,
rather than true scripture. Despite the pedantry of 'som German divines', it
was generally accepted that Christ wrote nothing, 'there is none ascrib'd to
him in the whole Bible; nor do we read there that ever he wrote anything,
except once with his finger on the ground'. Jerome and Augustine confirmed
that 'the Lord himself wrote nothing'. Toland claimed his catalogue was
intended 'to convince all the world' that he was not attacking the authority of
the New Testament. Like his contemporaries, Toland insisted he followed
correct scholarly protocol in citation, 'I constantly refer to the books wherein
they are quoted, that everybody may inform himself of the fact'.[33]

Toland claimed to distinguish the genuine from the forged. Many 'spurious
pieces' were forged by 'more zealous than discreet Christians, to supply the
brevity of the Apostolic memoirs', others were made by Heathens and Jews 'to
impose on the credulity of many well dispos'd Persons, who greedily
swallow'd any book for Divine revelation that contain'd a great many
Miracles'. The 'suppos'd writings of certain Apostolic men' which were 'read

with extraordinary veneration' formed another category. Toland denied the merits of the 'apocrypha' (the *Epistle of Barnabas*, writings by Hermas, Polycarp, Clemens Romanus and Ignatius), despite the commonplace assumption of their spiritual value.[34] Such texts had been received by Rome and 'most Protestants' and indeed many scholars devoted considerable effort to making good editions of them. Toland dismissed them as inconsequential forgeries, foisted on the Church by the whims of the early Fathers who paid them the 'highest respect'. Toland reproduced (complete with referential footnotes) the evidences of this respect: Clemens Alexandrinus, Origen, Irenaeus, Eusebius all cited the 'apocrypha' as 'Canonical Scripture', even though in Toland's opinion the *Pastor of Hermas* was 'the sillyest book in the world'.[35]

This posed a problem of consistency in Toland's view. If the orthodox 'think 'em genuine, why do they not receive 'em into the Canon of Scriptures, since they were the Companions and Fellow Laborers of the Apostles, as well as St Mark or St Luke?' Raising the thorny problem of the identity of the inspired books and the evident historicity of canon formation, Toland wondered whether such works ought to be added to the received Scripture, and if not where that left the integrity of the canon. Toland worked hard to establish that the commonplace strategy of appealing to the witnesses of the Church Fathers to authenticate the canon was problematic too. Eusebius had argued against the authenticity of some of the material mentioned in *Amyntor* (specifically the 'Acts, Gospel, Preaching and Revelation of St Peter') because 'no ancient or modern writer ... has quoted proofs out of them'. But he was mistaken 'for the contrary appears by the testimonials markt in the catalogue, and which any body may compare with the originals'.[36] Toland's target was not simply the authenticity of the texts themselves, but also the practice of citing patristic sources to authorise them. If Eusebius had observed early fathers making use of such apocryphal texts then 'he would have own'd them as the genuine productions of the Apostles, and admitted them (as we say) into the Canon'. The fact that Eusebius had not read such citations 'he presently concluded there were none': as Toland showed by citation of other sources there were 'demonstrative proofs quoted out of some of 'em long before'. Not only were the 'apocrypha' dubious but the integrity of the early fathers was also suspect.[37]

The authority of the Church Fathers was contradictory. Not only did they selectively support false works, but commonly denied the authority of true scripture. Here Toland's claim not to be speculating about the authority of *scriptura* looked distinctly weak. Books of the New Testament (such as the Epistle to the Hebrews, James, the second of Peter, 2, 3 of John, the Epistle of Jude, and Revelation) had all at some time been 'plainly doubted by the Ancients'.[38] Toland hammered the point home: as the evidence of the Council of Laodicea established, the canon was not formed by revealed authority or inspiration but fabricated by the credit of 'testimony'. 'The parity of reason' therefore enjoined all testimonies to be considered impartially. The clerical privileging of particular sources and texts was condemned as a self-interested and subjective procedure.³⁹ Many had condemned books in the canon. Celsus and the Manicheans advanced serious and lengthy criticisms against 'the Genuiness of the whole New Testament'. In a lengthy extract from Faustus drawn from the reputable patristic source of Augustine, Toland reproduced as 'testimony' the (to orthodox contemporaries) heretical invective against the canonical gospels. The evidence of the Ebionites and Nazarenes, 'the oldest Christians' suggested that some early believers had different copies of Matthew's gospel; the Marcionites certainly had a different copy of Luke.⁴⁰

Questions about the canon were not as straightforward as they seemed. Citing the learning of 'Rivet, Father Simon, Du Pin, Ittigius, Dr Cave, Ernestus Grabius' in his support, Toland proffered his catalogue (which was 'much larger ... than was publish'd by any of these') as a suitable authority to update received arguments. As he noted 'I could add more not there mentioned, and other authorities for those which are there'. At some point he would write a history of the canon which would 'lay all the matters of fact together in their natural order, without making the least remark of my own, or giving it a Color in favour of any sect or opinion'. The emphasis on empirical evidences and witnesses mirrored the remarks made by defenders of patristic sources like Reeve and Cave. Such 'matters of fact', for Toland, would leave 'all the world to judge for themselves, and to build what they please with those materials I shall furnish them'. The catalogue then was designed as a resource, in the mould and style of orthodox learning, to encourage readers to 'judge for them-selves'.⁴¹ Toland reinforced his pretensions to pious erudition by completing his arguments with another act of citation: translating a lengthy extract from Henry Dodwell's writings on the early history of the dissemination of Christian literature, Toland furnished his readers with yet more 'curious disquisitions' on the issue.⁴²

The reaction of readers of Toland's work in the furious reception *Amyntor* provoked indicates that he had struck a major controversial nerve. The first substantive reply was made by the talented cleric Samuel Clarke, Chaplain to Bishop John Moore and subsequently a Boyle Lecturer. Clarke defended the received canon, while simultaneously supporting the value of the apocryphal writings of Hermas, Polycarp, Clemens Romanus. Although there were differ-ent forms of 'authority' for both types of book, a 'proportional veneration' was due to each.⁴³ The variation in the strength of 'authority' did not 'in the *least diminish from the authority of the New Testament, or tend to make the number of the Canonical Books Uncertain or Precarious*'. Citing the testimonies of patristic sources like Irenaeus and Eusebius (supplemented by Greek extracts in the margins), and the writings of men like Grabe, Cotelerius, Pearson and Wake, in favour of the apocrypha, Clarke directed the reader to further evidences that he saw no need to 'transcribe'. As he summarised, 'upon these *great Authorities* then, though we cannot be absolutely sure that these Writings are Genuine, yet we may well conclude and believe them to be so, notwithstanding the suspitions which some have raised to the contrary'.[44] Not only the ancients, but the 'learnedst and most judicious cricks of our times, as well laicks as those of the Clergy, have received them as genuine, and recommended them as *containing the true and pure Faith of Christ*'.[45] Both patristic and contemporary learning substantiated a just distinction between canonical and apocryphal works.

If Samuel Clarke's intention was to save the writings of Hermas *et al.* from the charge of being spurious, then the more substantial works of John Richardson and Stephen Nye engaged with not only the arguments but also the critical methods used by Toland. Their vindications fixed upon his faulty, corrupt and actively devious scholarship. A sometime Fellow of Emmanuel College, Cambridge, John Richardson's work *The canon of the New Testament vindicated*, circulated initially in manuscript form, was first published in print in 1700 and reprinted in 1701 and 1719.[46] The burden of his argument simply arraigned testimonies from the early Fathers against Toland's citations, showing how the opinions drawn from such evidences very rarely were sustainable by the texts. Toland's polemic had been built upon whether, when and how, various Fathers had cited and used non-canonical material. Many 'authoritative' Fathers had used 'spurious' texts as true 'scripture' even using them in public services. Checking Toland's 'references' showed how he had manipulated such textual authorities. Richardson's own footnotes scrutinised Toland's citations. Here the powerful image of the author and respondant poring over the same volumes to establish a pre-eminence of interpretative authority is illustrative of the spaces and processes of the making of cultural power.

A close examination of this war in the footnotes will enable a better appreciation of the cultural politics of citation and reading. Toland cited various early Fathers as favourably quoting the *Epistles* of Barnabas. Richardson identified the precise page references in specific editions: 'I find therefore that Clement of Alexandria (Ed. Par. G. L. 1641) cites Barnabas, *Stromat.* l. 2. p. 373, 375, 396 – l. 5. P.571, 577, 578. – Origen cites him l.1. against Celsus p. 49. – l.3. of Principles c.2.f. 144. Edit Par. 1522. Irenaeus quotes Hermas, l.4.c.37 (not c.3. as 'tis in our Author) p. 370, ...)'. Having identified the locations of these citations (presumably for the reader to follow up: certainly, scribal additions to one copy indicate that at least one reader did so, and then added further material) Richardson continued to assess 'how fairly the sense of these places is represented'. That these sources show the fathers quoting Barnabas 'as *scripture*' was 'not true ... For in the places referr'd to, they cite it indeed, but under no such Title'. The claim that Irenaeus cited Hermas as canonical was disputed: Irenaeus indeed and Origen calls it *scripture*, but not *canonical*, 'That's our Authors addition'. Toland was a 'vain boaster'. Richardson even doubted whether Toland had read 'those books he pretends to quote'. He damned Toland's credit, 'I believe, few, who shall consult the quotations produc'd above, will admire him either for an exact or faithful historian'. [47]

Toland made up 'testimonies for Spurious pieces'. Richardson was forced to acknowledge that he 'could not but smile ... at the ingenuity of our Author' when he discovered the source of Toland's references concerning the *Preaching* of Paul and Peter. Toland had cited exactly the same passage from Cyprian's *Discourse concerning the Baptism of Heretics* for both texts. The humour here was that he had exploited the editorial annotations of the learned Nicholas Rigaltius, who had conjectured that '*Paul* is by mistake set for *Peter*'. [48] This is good evidence both of Toland's facility with, and ludic appropriation of learned resources, and also of his readers' assiduity in tracing, checking and examining his citations. Even Toland's exploitation of heretical evidences like Celsus and Faustus was devious: the mischief of quoting the heretic without reproducing the 'answer, which is to be found in the same place' was obvious. To remedy the fault, Richardson transcribed Augustine's rebuttal of Faustus at length thus supplying his readers with an immediate antidote to Toland's critical misbehaviour. Toland's standards of citation were not simply poor but positively corrupt. He had claimed the existence of a letter from Christ to Peter and Paul by citing Augustine against Faustus, Book 28 chapter 13, 'which perhaps may make the unwary reader believe, that such an Epistle is there set down, as part of the Scripture receiv'd by, and peculiar to, the Manichees'. As Richardson pointed out there were only five chapters in the twenty-eighth book; the reference in the fourth chapter made no mention of Paul or Peter. Interestingly even though Toland acknowledged that he had read his critics' work he made no corrections to the later versions of the catalogue even though he had opportunity and indeed did include additional references in many places. [49] Richardson saw a remedy to Toland's corrupt practice in producing his own collection of testimonies (drawn from Irenaeus and Tertullian) for the established canon. Persuaded by a friend to make such a catalogue, from his own reading, Richardson carefully identified the editions he used and gave exact page references and detailed commentary to assist the reader in establishing a correct conviction. [50]

Stephen Nye's censure of Toland's catalogue, *A defence of the canon of the new Testament* (two editions, 1700), developed many of these same themes against Toland's devious citations and unsubstantiated assertions. For Nye, the work was not only corrupt but also inconsistent. Sometimes spurious works were claimed as suitable for the canon, at other points the same works were dismissed as forgeries. While Nye paid some attention to the broader arguments Toland made against the integrity of the canon, the focus of his efforts dealt with the details of the catalogue. Toland's claims for the comprehensivity of the catalogue were disputed: Nye offered further apocryphal works (a Valentinian Infancy Gospel, 'a letter that fell from heaven, an Ethiopian liturgy of Christ). His citation practice was inadequate: 'I observe also that, *Amyntor* very often confirms the books of his catalogue, by witness of Authors who never mention any such book or books'.[51] If Toland was to complete his 'non-such History of the Scripture Canon', Nye hoped 'he will oftner himself consult the authors he cites; and less trust the references of others'. Nye acknowledged that the first and second centuries after Christ was a time when the world was filled with Christian texts, many of which had not survived. The existing canon was however sufficient: the power of these orthodox books meant that many of the more marginal books 'fell (gradually) into disuse, and were afterwards lost'. The works in Toland's catalogue were these marginal books.[52] Contrary to Toland's implications, these listed works had not been suppressed or censored, but 'time; the sufficiency of the books preserved; and that, some of them came not to general knowledge, till the evidences that they were genuine, were not so certain'. Like Richardson, Nye noted that Toland's citation of Irenaeus, Clemens Alexandrinus and Origen was deeply flawed: 'he refers us to places in their writings. But in some of those places, nothing at all is said by those Fathers, concerning the books of which we are inquiring; in other places, the authors are named, but nothing is quoted out of them: elsewhere are citations out of them, but not under the names of Scripture or Canonical'. Many quotations simply did not have the pertinence Toland claimed for them.

Nye systematically exposed the duplicity of Toland's references. To the rhetorical question 'Has Amyntor any evidence?' Nye replied with conviction, that such 'a deceitful management of such subjects as this obliges his Reader to distrust all he says, and more especially his quotations'. He paid close attention to Toland's use of passages from Faustus the Manichee (a compromised source in Nye's estimation because anti-Christian). Although Toland had 'truly recited' the words, he had 'neither seen, how to rightly point them, nor truly translate them'. Even his use of an hostile and heretical source was dishonest. Nye reproduced the Latin passage from Faustus (as transcribed by Toland) and the incompetent translation, for direct comparison with an accurate transcription (correctly pointed) and translation. Toland's version was a 'pure piece of Jargon; it offers to prove a certain point, by a consideration quite contrary to it'. Translated authentically, Faustus' remarks were contrary to Toland's understanding; 'Briefly, Faustus meant not in the least to say; the books of the canon are falsely intitled to the Apostles, and Evangelists, whose names they bear: but that the *Testament of the Son* has been vitiated, and disgraced, by divers *other* Gospels, Acts, Epistles, meaning *those of the Catalogue*'. Examining further passages from Faustus, Nye complained, 'Reach me the Ferula, for they are Schoolboys Mistakes in this place, *Jam* is not, *already*; or *saepe, frequently:* much less is *à nobis, those of our party,* which it never signifies'.[53] As a final confutation of Toland's work, Nye appended 'An abstract of the foregoing dispute' wherein point by point he established his victory over the arguments advanced against the canon. The rhetoric of this abstract, with its language of proof, testimony and authority ('I have proved, ... I have shown ..., I have evinced'), is indicative of the controversial dimensions of scholarship. Nye's demonstration of Toland's scholarly worthlessness in acts of transcription, translation and hermeneutics, was authorised by his own mastery of patristic sources: 'I have produced unquestionable Testimony'.[54]

Toland steadfastly continued to work on the catalogue throughout his life despite the critical response, of which he took little notice. He seemed unconcerned with the damage to his reputation as a learned man. The generation of such a reception may have been precisely the point of the catalogue. To many contemporaries it did not seem that he meant to establish any firm arguments, but instead to simply question received wisdom: 'he saith, he will determine nothing, but suspend his judgement'.[55] The form of Toland's catalogue compelled orthodox critics to engage in the intricacies of his footnotes and references. By posing a series of controversial attacks upon the textual and historical integrity of 'Scripture', supported by what looked like authentic 'testimonies' from a series of patristic authorities, widely available in printed editions (many of which were written by his orthodox audience) Toland ensured that his claims received attention. The threat of his 'scholarship' persisted long after the initial publication. The most substantial reaction was the three volume work of the young dissenting scholar, Jeremiah Jones *A new and full method of settling the canonical authority of the New Testament* (1726–27). This work on the canon remained a standard work well into the nineteenth century. In its form, of assessing the testimonies for the authenticity of works ascribed to Christ and the Apostles, it remained faithful to the work it attempted to destroy. Whereas Toland compressed his material into perhaps fifty pages of print, Jones' consideration consumed hundreds of pages.[56] The irony here is that Toland's irreligious ambitions actually provoked a work that became the staple of orthodox scholarship. Toland's critical erudition spawned piety as well as irreligion.

The cultural function of Toland's learning was complex. Many contemporary readers despised his efforts: certainly those who responded in public replies were motivated not only by the need to correct his mistakes, but also by the urgent need to disable the public perception of the authority of his work. Toland probably laid claim to a broader learning than he possessed. He was expert at mining sources like Fabricius and Grabe for additional annotations and evidences. Sometimes he made real mistakes, sometimes he plagiarised references from sources he had not seen. These were however common practices in the scholarship of the day. Surveying the *corpus* of patristic editions and collections from the sixteenth to the eighteenth century, it is evident that much scholarship was incremental, building on the textual achievements of earlier editors. As other scholars have indicated there was a curious inertia in the reception of the exposure of fraudulent material: Toland trod heavily on very delicate grounds. At the heart of Toland's project was an attempted subversion of scholarly procedures of citation. As has already been discussed, contemporaries were deeply unhappy with the standards of his transcriptions and referencing. It is a moot point whether his practice was simply slipshod or actively malicious. Bibliographical citation was both an epistemological and rhetorical transaction: it was both a claim to knowledge and an assertion of status within the community of scholars. The evidential, corroborative, documentary associations conjured by referencing were a power-ful part of the rhetoric of persuasion in the period. Toland's repeated acts of citation were attempts to incorporate orthodox learning within his agenda. Deploying such references was an insidious attempt to persuade the reader, or at the very least an attempt to encourage the reader to pursue a course of textual examination. In Toland's catalogues the text is overwhelmed by the references: the words of the catalogues are a series of directions to other books. Here, Toland was doing cultural and political work with another community's intellectual property, he was 'living in another's space'. As an act of intellectual appropriation, Toland was trying to suborn one set of witnesses for another purpose.

Toland was not simply a plagiarist. His use of standard editions, contem-poraries' work, and of the Church Fathers, suggests he was exploiting both the form and content of these works. By exploiting recognised routines for the display of erudition, Toland used other works, instrumentally as fodder to sanction his own remarks. Toland made *Amyntor* and the scribal versions of the catalogue into a subversive text not simply by the substantive arguments advanced against the canon of scripture, but by the passive subterfuge of encouraging and undermining the commonplace reading strategy. As clergy-men like Barlow, Dodwell and Bray insisted, readers should check references and sources to confirm the truth of the citation. Toland led his readers to any number of volumes, ancient and modern: those expecting confirmation would have been disappointed. Erudition was collaborative as the circle around men like Grabe and Dodwell establishes: the subversive inter-textuality of Toland's catalogue could only work when enmeshed in an infrastructure of clerical learning and publishing. This implication, subornation and appropriation of orthodox scholarship exposed the subjectivity of the citation process: by leading his readers to texts that they would discover contradicted his own purposes, he was divulging the nature of citation not simply as a 'factual' process, but as a rhetorical device.

Erudition made cultural authority ultimately by making persuasive facts: clergymen made divine truth in the same way. Toland's (ab)use of this system compromised the perceived neutrality of the process. Exposing false erudition was an explicitly political act: Toland did his best to try to associate these anti-patristic attitudes with the Protestant legitimacy of the Hanoverian succession in the publication of works like *A letter against popery* (1712) by the deceased Queen of Prussia, Sophie Charlotte. Reinforcing the connection between true criticism and anti-popish superstition, Toland gave an account of Sophie Charlotte's disputation with the Italian Jesuit, Father Vota, over the status of the Church Fathers Augustine and Jerome. Not only a beautiful face, Sophie exceeded all men in 'the beauties of her mind' in matters of 'divinity and philosophy'.[57] Widely read, even in sceptical works like Bayle's *Dictionary*, Sophie Charlotte argued against taking the Church Fathers (even of the first three centuries) as a certain rule of faith. Such erudition was a device for creating 'the authority (that is, the domination) of the priests'. Neglecting the pure fountains of scripture for the 'muddy cisterns of the Fathers' such learning made superstition. The authority of patristic writings were 'dissonant and discordant'; ecclesiastical history was 'nothing else but a continual cata-logue of Clergyman's vices'.[58] It was imperative that the Church of England purge itself of the 'old leaven' of such popery. Condemning the 'Brittish admirers' of the Fathers 'who talk of nothing but the rights and powers of convocation', Toland opposed the 'slavish credulity' of such 'false Protestants'. Importantly, the account of Sophie Charlotte's disputation with Vota displayed the same strategy as Toland's catalogue had done by pointing out the contra-dictions between different patristic texts. We have no evidence to suggest that the Queen developed such a skill because of intimacy with Toland's work although such topics were evidently commonplace between him and her mother. Toland dismissed the 'exact study of the fathers' as a waste of time, because they were 'of all books the hardest to be understood or reconcil'd, being like a heap of rubbish without any order, accuracy or judgement'. Despite this view, he devoted considerable energies to developing an expertise in patristic scholarship because he saw potent opportunities for compromising false clerical authority.[59] Displaying the anti-patristic reputation of Sophie Charlotte in 1712 was a powerful device for exposing the potential religious corruption of the high church interest identified with Atterbury. Erudition was politics under another name.

The evidence of the 'catalogue' exposes Toland's own reading habits, and is also evidence of his engagement with the world of learning. Toland was accomplished in the routines of *ars critica*: his learning was neither profound nor shallow, but instrumental. The forensic use, and examination, of the critical and cultural procedures for establishing authentic attribution, were bent to the purpose of attacking the clerical monopoly of interpretative authority. This was a Trojan undertaking. The virulent, and insidious quality of such apparently innocuous work was evident from its hostile reception in England between 1700 and the late 1720s. This subversive learning was also circulated amongst a variety of elite figures ranging from Sophia of Hanover, Prince Eugene of Savoy and a number of British politicians associated with the Whig administration after 1714. To acknowledge that figures who might become the sovereign, or who lay at the heart of negotiating the military alliance against Catholic France, or who were responsible for the reforming ministry of the late 1710s, were reading and enjoying such material throws a different light on the role of irreligious ideas in the mainstream of British politics in the period. Publishing such works to confuse the unlearned public was crime enough in the eyes of the clergyman. Intruding such impiety into the elite circles of politics, not only compromised the divine status of revelation, but by consequence undermined the credibility of the Church, and was therefore fundamental blasphemy.

NOTES

1 F. H. Heinemann 'John Toland, France, Holland, and Dr Williams' *Review of English Studies* 25 (1949) pp. 346–349 at 346.

2 *Tolandiana* pp. 241, 244, 246.

3 Sullivan *Toland* esp. pp. 46–47.

4 See F. Schmidt 'John Toland, critique Deiste de la littérature Apocryphe' *Apocrypha* 1 (1990) pp. 119–145; B. E. Schwarzbach 'The sacred genealogy of a Voltairean polemic: the development of critical hypotheses regarding the composition of the canonical gospels' *Studies in Voltaire and the eighteenth century* 245 (1986) pp. 303–349.

5 See *Nazarenus*.

6 O. Blackall *A sermon preached before the Honourable House of Commons* (1699) pp. 16–17.

7 See *Amyntor* (1699), pp. 20–41.

8 See Cardwell *Synodolia* II pp. 705–706.

9 *Nazarenus* pp. 314–315.

10 The following passages are cited from *Amyntor* (1699) [abbreviated as A1699] pp. 20–21, and 'A Catalogue' (1726) [A1726] pp. 359–361.

11 On the non-canonical *agrapha* of Christ see Grabe vol. 1 p. 14 and following, 'Dicta aliqua Jesus Christi, non in quator Evangelis, sed alibi memorata'.

12 See *Nazarenus* pp. 296–300.

13 Fabricius *Codex* 1719: volume 1 p. 306.

14 See entries in A1726 pp. 363, 368, 369, 370, 372, 378, 379, 389.

15 A1726, p. 373. Sike's work was published at Utrecht in 1697, and then reproduced in both editions of Fabricius' work in 1703 and 1719.

16 Grynaeus also prepared an edition of Irenaeus' *Adversus Haereses* (Basel, 1571) an 'opus eruditissimum'. See BL Eve.a.91(1) for John Evelyn's annotated copy.

17 See B. Neveu 'L'erudition ecclesiastique de XVIIe siècle et la nostalgie de l'antiquité Chretienne' *Religion and Humanism. Studies in Church History* 17 (1981) pp. 195–225. J.-L. Quantin *Le Catholicisme Classique et les Pères de L'église* (Paris, 1999).

18 See J.-L. Quantin 'The Fathers in seventeenth century Anglican theology' in I. Backus (ed.) *The reception of the Church Fathers in the West* (Leiden, 1997) 2 pp. 996–999.

19 D. Tossanus *A synopsis* pp. iv–v, 1, 7, 16.

20 W. Reeves *The apologies of Justin Martyr, Tertullian and Minutus Felix* (1709) 'Prefatory Dissertation' pp. i, v–vi, vii, xi, xiv–xv, xxxv.

21 'Catalogue' p. 110.

22 'Catalogue' p. 116.

23 H. Dodwell *Two letters* pp. 223, 229.

24 *Ibid.* pp. 232, 236–238.

25 See Thomas Barlow *De Studio Theologiae* (1699) and especially 'A short method for the study of Divinity' appended to this work reproduced from a manuscript found in his study.

26 See 'A short method for the study of Divinity' pp. 75, 77, 78–79.

27 Thomas Bray *Bibliotheca Parochialis* (1697) p. 8.

28 Thomas Bray *Bibliotheca Parochialis* (1707) chapter 6, pp. 76–145.

29 *Ibid.* chapter 7.

30 *Ibid.* pp. 75–84, 149–161.

31 Thomas Bray *An essay* (1703) pp. 4, 5, 6.

32 *Ibid.* pp. 17–23; the list included Dodwell's *Two letters of advice* and Bray's own *Bibliotheca Parochialis*.

33 *Amyntor* pp. 17–18, 19.

34 *Ibid.* pp. 42–44.

35 *Ibid.* pp. 44–46.

36 *Ibid.* pp. 52–53.

37 *Ibid.* p. 55.

38 *Ibid.* pp. 57–58

39 *Ibid.* p. 57.

40 *Ibid.* pp. 60–64, 65.

41 *Ibid.* pp. 66–67.

42 *Ibid.* pp. 69–78.

43 S. Clarke *Some reflections on that part of a book called Amyntor* (London, 1699) pp. 8–9.

44 Clarke *Some reflections* pp. 11, 12, 13–14.

45 *Ibid.* p. 30.

46 J. Richardson *The canon of the New Testament vindicated* (1700). I have used the BL copy [call-mark 698.d.33] which has a number of manuscript annotations, adding in references to other patristic sources.

47 *Ibid.* pp. 25, 33, 43.

48 *Ibid.* pp. 45–46.

49 *Ibid.* pp. 61–63.

50 *Ibid.* pp. 107–118.

51 S. Nye *Historical Defence of the Canon of the New Testament* (1700) pp. 21, 23.

52 *Ibid.* pp. 60–61, 67–70.

53 *Ibid.* pp. 93–95, 96, 97–98.

54 *Ibid.* pp. 113–122.

55 *Ibid.* p. 20.

56 J. Jones *A new and full method of settling the canonical authority of the New Testament* (1726–27) p. 2.

57 J. Toland *A letter against popery* (1712) pp. 3, 4.

58 *Ibid.* pp. 6–7, 8–9, 12.

59 *Ibid.* pp. 18–19, 24, 32–37.

9

'A complete history of priestcraft':
The Druids and the origins of
ancient virtue

THE foundations of the cultural purchase of Toland's intellectual arguments were laid in a series of personal relationships with powerful men and women. Whether writing for German princes or queens, or for government ministers, or wealthy earls, or provincial gentlemen, Toland was capable of designing writing suitable for his audiences. Sophia and Leibniz enjoyed abstract metaphysical discussion – they got works like *Letters to Serena* (1704); Eugene and Hohendorf liked a variety of impiety – Toland drafted work on the *Gospel of Barnabas*, dissertations on Giordano Bruno and the history of the apocrypha. For men like Harley, Collins and Shaftesbury (as well as a list of more minor figures) Toland was able to produce a mixture of learning and prudential political commentary. For Harley he composed a series of printed pamphlets advancing various political schemes as well as more private memorials analysing the options prompted by political circumstances. It is clear in some cases that Toland was writing what he thought these powerful people would like to hear: the tone of the more personal works for Eugene and Harley, in particular, underscores the individual relationship of respect and service. It is also clear that he used the opportunities of intellectual intimacy to advocate a powerful defence of his central principles.

Toland's working relationships with powerful people took a variety of forms. In the cases of noble and imperial persons like Sophia and Eugene, the politics of international diplomacy and courtly access limited the intimacy of the relationship. His collaboration with the aristocratic Shaftesbury was routine: it was manifest in the concrete form of a series of pamphlets and political commentaries in the late 1690s and early 1700s. While direct written collaboration is not evident in the case of Toland's connections with Harley, and anxieties about the elusiveness of the minister's political identity are apparent in the cautious language of his correspondence, it is obvious that Toland saw some point, and advantage, to this relationship. When it became unmistakable that Harley was undertaking a very different set of policies than those which had cemented their relationship, Toland abandoned all association with him, and in fact turned to explicit and virulent public criticism. It may be debatable whether Harley saw any further use in his connection with Toland, but it is unequivocal that Toland saw little point in continuing to try to further his own agenda with Harley. Toland's aspirations were implicitly based, then, on the assumption that his liaison with the premier minister would have some sort of effect on the shape of national policy (in this case specifically in defending and securing the Hanoverian succession).

Aspirations, ambitions, influences and convictions are notoriously difficult to define with precision. Throughout his life, Toland was confident that he had something important to say, and that people would listen: he thought he was making a difference. Intellectual conversations in libraries, at after-dinner tables lubricated by fine claret in country retreats, or the more robust sociability of coffee-houses and refined politeness of metropolitan salons, were the venue for his projects. Toland described himself as always with 'a book in my hand or in my head', motivated by the desire to be entertaining in 'private conversation' and 'serviceable to publick society'.¹ Exploring in detail the intellectual transactions between Toland and Lord Robert Molesworth, one of the commonwealth politicians in his circle, will allow a more reflective appreciation of the function of his learning and ideas.

As has already been established, Molesworth was at the heart of the intellectual and political community that Toland exploited in the circulation of his scribal works. A politician of impeccable Whig credentials, Molesworth had made his republican reputation with the publication of his *Account of Denmark* (1694) that indicted civil tyranny and priestcraft in equal measure. On the margins of ministerial influence in the 1700s although a continuing member of the Irish Privy Council, Molesworth devoted considerable energies to preserving the declining fortunes of his estates in England and Ireland. After the accession of George I, his political *kudos* as torchbearer of the 'true Whig' tradition, projected him back into the turbulence of national and parliamentary politics. He was both an Irish Privy Councillor and a commissioner for Trade and Plantations. In 1720, Toland had been employed by Molesworth to produce a polemical pamphlet for the controversy surrounding the Declaratory Act defending the jurisdictional competence of the Irish legislature.² Toland was committed to Molesworth's political reputation. Indeed it was one of Toland's last political acts to reinforce his support for Molesworth's parliamentary candidature at Westminster by preparing electoral broadsides, representing him as a modern Cato. Closely associated with republican undertakings to reform the Church, the universities and even the constitutional role of the House of Lords, although not part of the inner circle of political managers like Stanhope, Sunderland, Townshend and Walpole, Molesworth attracted considerable political authority. His relationship with the series of successful journals, produced by Thomas Gordon and John Trenchard, which popularised a commonwealth critique of corruption in Church and State, similarly meant he was identified as a leading opposition figure. The deep concern that Molesworth held for Toland is immediately apparent from the tone of his letters to his dying friend in early 1722, signed off with the phrase 'your affectionate friend and servant'.[3]

Toland's intimacy with Molesworth has often been cited as evidence of the manifestation of an 'Irish' identity and affinity.[4] Recent historiography has suggested that there was an intimate relationship between Toland's ethnic origins and the literary and philosophical quality of his polemic. The ambiguity and equivocation found in Toland's writings are a 'symptom of Irish intellectual culture'. Responding to the contradictions and tensions of the rival claims of national identity and political authority, Toland's subversive writing was a consequence of conflicts within the 'Irish mind'.[5] As we will see Toland's interest in things 'Celtic' was part of an elaborate and learned joke. There is considerable evidence to establish Toland's connections with Ireland. The evidence of correspondence in the Bodleian (from 1694) between the non-juring scholar, Henry Dodwell (who later suffered some damage to his reputation at the hands of Toland's scholarly games) and Bishop George Ashe, indicates the obscurity of his origins. Dodwell, perhaps wary of the young Toland's character, had made inquiry of the Irish bishop about 'our Countryman'. Ashe had received testimony (which could, he suggested, be authenticated by 'sufficient vouchers') indicating that Toland was 'bastard son to Cornelius Tolan a popish priest of Enishowen near Derry'. Esteemed 'a very very talkative man' he noted that he had been 'bred in Glasgow, [and] has been in Rome and Leyden'. Ashe had passed on a letter from Richard Anderson on the same subject to Dodwell. In this earlier report, culled from conversations with a number of people in Dublin, further details emerged: Toland's father had been a priest in the parish of Donagh, Toland himself was born in France and 'speaks French very well now'. Described in the same terms as 'a black sclender man' both very angry and very talkative, Toland at this point was depicted as 'a great searcher after religion and that he said he had tried all sorts and found the Presbyterian Religion to be the best'.[6] Later he reflected with some nostalgia about his childhood in the parish of Clonmany in Inishowen, County Donegal in the 1670s.[7] Toland was educated as a Gaelic speaker. Although some contemporaries in Oxford in the early 1690s suspected that Toland had been born in France, Toland later sought out confirmation of his Irish lineage and ancestry from Catholic sources.[8] Baited by Abbot Tilladet and Bishop Huet 'upon the account of his pretended illegitimacy', Toland produced testimonial certification from 'the Irish Franciscans of Prague' to establish his Irish origins.[9] There is little doubt that Toland was of Irish extraction, and that he knew the Celtic languages.[10]

Toland was proud of his linguistic competence. It was the basis for a profound learning and erudition which he exploited, especially in his relationship with Molesworth, to fashion his intellectual credibility. Accomplished in a variety of Gaelic skills, he displayed not only the 'native' capacity to speak Irish, but also the more 'learned' and complex idiom of historical orthography that suggests he had received tuition at some point in his education.[11] We have already seen that his early reputation in Scotland, Leiden and Oxford was built on these linguistic and philological abilities, even if he was regarded as a man of little religious commitment. One of the important results of this Celtic learning was the composition of a scribal work, which displayed to full effect these skills, specifically for Robert Molesworth – *A specimen of a critical history of the Druids*. By exploring the themes of this writing, it will be possible to see how the relationship between erudition and polemic functioned in the text, as an instrument both for bonding Toland to his patron by defining a common political understanding, but also providing intellectual entertainment. As will be discussed below, in the three letters, Toland set out to reconstruct the institutions, practices, beliefs and material culture of Celtic antiquity. In each of the separate letters he adopted a different focus. In the first the 'system' of Druidical religion was exposed. In the second specimen he gave an account of the 'monuments relating to the Druids', exploring the remains, usage and meaning of their cairns, obelisks, cromlechs, altars and temples. The final letter combined discussions of classical mythology along with an assertion of the Pythagorean context of Druidical philosophy.

The work was read by a wide circle of people. The *Specimen of critical history* was one of the scribal texts that Toland distributed amongst a range of people between 1718 and 1720. The first printed version was published by Pierre Desmaizeaux in the 1726 posthumous collection of Toland's miscellaneous works. Translations into French and German were made later in the eighteenth century. Four variant editions were published between 1814 and 1815 in London, Dublin and Edinburgh: at least one of these editions (by Robert Huddlestone) came complete with critical notes that doubled the length of the work.[12] Just like work upon Christian apocrypha, Toland's study of Celtic culture had a durable and influential intellectual afterlife. Although eighteenth-century writers from William Stukeley to John Pinkerton read and engaged with this printed version of Toland's text, during his lifetime the work was only circulated in scribal form. The suggestion that *A specimen of critical history* was however a clandestine or private work is not supported by Toland's surviving archive. The original fragments were addressed to Robert Molesworth: Toland completed the writing of the three letters between June 1718 and April 1719. Again very much like the work on the apocrypha, the project had been, as

Toland noted, 'form'd several years ago at Oxford, and which I have ever since kept in view; collecting, as occasion presented whatever might any way tend to the advantage or perfection of it'.[13] That Toland was researching such a project was not a secret: indeed he systematically exploited his relationship with Molesworth to publicise it to a circle of the Irish peer's friends. Through such connections, Toland wrote to men like Lord Edward Southwell (1671–1730) enclosing extracts of his work ('wch are five sheets of the introductory book, and wch I beg you to preserve safe till I call for them after the holy-days'), asking for any assistance and advice which was 'fit to communicate towards bringing a work to perfection'.[14] In June 1718 Toland wrote to another interested party recapitulating the long gestation of the druidical research, noting that he had purchased 'all the printed books particularly treating of them',[15] and that he had a network of correspondents in 'Ireland, Wales, Scotland and Bretagne'. He had even travelled to Scotland in the course of his investigation. Accentuating his intimacy with the powerful he mentioned that Lord Chancellor Parker had offered his help too.[16] Molesworth repeatedly discussed the progress of the study with Toland. While pointing out that he had no learning to offer himself, he gave specific encouragement and suggestions about who might help.[17] In one of the last letters to discuss the progress of the text, Toland commented, 'I am farr advanced in my history of the Druids, which will rather be a thin folio or a thick quarto, with about six copper cuts'.[18] The work was destined clearly for print form. In gathering research materials, Toland was also building up a circle of intimate, interested people who by default were also implicated in the intellectual significance of the writing.

Far from being a work of solitary imagination, Toland set out deliberately to exploit and synthesise the scholarly resources available to him. In the course of his researches he had encountered the advice of erudite men such as Edward Lhwyd, John Aubrey, John Woodward and Edmund Gibson. As his library indicates, he had collected all of the available printed volumes on Celtic and druidical learning he could lay his hands on. Indeed the evidence of his library listing suggests that he was not exaggerating in this claim. Gathered on chairs in his Putney lodgings were antiquarian works by Englishmen, Irishmen, Frenchmen and Danes. Works by Rowland, Langhorne, Lhwyd, Camden, Sheringham, Sammes, Price, Charleton, Jones, Sachaverell, Brand, Ware, MacCurtin, O'Flaherty, Walsh, Rouillard, Picard, Gosselin, Pezron, Du Pleix, Worm, Rudbeck, Saxo, and Shefferius (amongst others) provided Toland with a pretty comprehensive resource for exploring the antiquities of northern Europe.[19] Many of these works would have provided him with accounts and evidences of the various national 'origin' narratives for France, England, Ireland and Denmark. The French works, in particular, are interesting combinations of mythopoetic construction and scholarly commentary. Jean

Picard's history of the antiquity of the Franks, Sebastien Roulliard's account of the *prisca theologia* of the Gallic Druids, Pierre Ramus' writings on the customs of the ancient Gauls, and Scipion Dupliex's history of the origins of the French monarchy, all provided Toland with an ample stock of learning for the compilation of his own views.[20] Further materials were drawn from the works of the Danish historians which described the Trojan origins of the northern nations.[21] Combined with these literary works, which concentrated on exploring the textual remnants of antiquity, was an up-to-date collection of works that decoded the meanings of the physical monuments of antiquity. These ranged from the works of Inigo Jones, Walter Charleton and Aylett Sammes on the cultural origins of Stonehenge (Danish, Roman or Phoenician),[22] to the works of men like William Sacheverell, Martin Martin and John Brand which gave detailed descriptions of the topography, antiquities and history of the western islands of England and Scotland. Supplementing these volumes were key texts describing the Irish past by James Ware, Peter Walsh, Hugh Mac-Curtin, and Roderic O'Flaherty.[23] Toland worked hard at his scholarship, even if his ambitions were scandalous.

The work prepared for Molesworth was complex and erudite. In other works like *Nazarenus* (1718), Toland had made Celtic learning part of a broader arsenal of erudition that included patristic and biblical criticism as well as a range of learning in classical, Islamic and rabbinical sources.[24] From his first recognition as a 'scholar' in Oxford he had played up his interests in the origins of Celtic culture. This erudition had a point beyond the display of knowledge. The early researches had been towards the preparation of an 'Irish Dictionary' which would, as the eminent philologist and antiquarian Edward Lhwyd put it, 'prove the Irish a colony of the Gauls'.[25] The careful reconstruction of an ancient Celtic Christianity in *Nazarenus* was calculated to condemn all forms of deviation from this pure (un-priestly, un-sacramental) model. Here an imagined primordial Celtic Christianity became a device for compromising the *de jure divino* claims of contemporary churchmen: implicitly it defended some form of true ecclesiastical institution. In the more confidential work on druids he set about inventing a different pre-Christian tradition, again with a specific exemplary purpose of condemning all forms of priestcraft. One of the powerful implications of the work was that there was no form of legitimate priestly institution. Toland's interest in the learning of Celtic antiquity is less evidence of his 'Irish' cultural commitments rather than another instrument in his intellectual project of refining the politics of religion from clerical corruption.

A good place to start thinking about the function of Toland's erudition in the *Specimen* is the nature of the sources he used to make his arguments. As we have seen in his experiments in biblical criticism, Toland was adept at mimicking the standard routines of orthodox scholars to produce authentic-looking books. Such was the success of this academic impersonation, that Toland provoked serious and laborious responses. One of the purposes of the biblical criticism had been to embroil clergymen in a forensic and interminable controversy. The Celtic research functioned in both similar and different ways. First, despite Toland's own claims to having undertaken 'original' research (even fieldwork), a close reading of the work indicates it is mainly from literary sources (in particular books that he owned himself), and very few others, that he put together his account of Celtic learning and the history of the Druids. These materials were orthodox, uncontroversial, and indeed, generally pious in intention. Such sources, again very much like the patristic and biblical scholarship, did not naturally lend themselves to Toland's heterodox purposes. Again the process of intellectual engagement was one of appropriation rather than destruction. One of the premises of these literary accounts and antiquarian descriptions was their commitment to the Judaeo-Christian framework of Scriptural and sacred time. Discussions about the 'nationum origo' by necessity required an integration of the particular national past with the sacred chronology of the Old Testament. Literary record and ancient monuments were synchronised with the genealogies of post-diluvian history. Whether describing the Trojan extraction of the Franks, or insisting that the druids of antiquity preached the pure patriarchal religion of Abraham, or that Ireland was populated by figures who survived the deluge; without exception, all of the sources to which Toland had access, harmonised their theories with the injunctions of sacred chronology. Even though, by the late seventeenth century, some of the fictions of influential authors like Annius of Viterbo had been exposed for fabricating foundation myths where scriptural text was obscure, the framework provided by the account in Genesis still determined such enquiry. Given that Toland denied the veridical status of revelation, the intellectual gymnastics he developed in appropriating these sources to his own agenda were agile.

William Stukeley, writing in the 1740s in response to the *Specimen of critical history* commented upon Toland's 'unreasonable prejudice against religion in general, & priestcraft, as he call'd it'. Regardless of Toland's hostility to clerical institutions , Stukeley (as did many others) still applauded the study which 'remains of good use to us' as a work of erudition.[26] Stukeley's own work, meticulous in its recording of the dimensions and material state of ancient artefacts, has been described as 'Trinitarian archaeology'. Following an earlier tradition of pious scholarship by men like Thomas Gale and Samuel Bochart, Stukeley meant his learning to establish the primitive monotheism of the Druids. Toland's achievement in *Specimen of critical history* was far from compatible with these objectives, for his politics of antiquarian scholarship described a different non-sacred aboriginal Celtic past.

It is possible to distinguish between Toland's scholarly method and technique and the substantive interpretations he advanced in the work. The texture of his scholarship was synthetic. In his studies of Moses, Toland had combined classical and sacred sources (using Strabo to explain *Exodus*). In the study of Druidical culture he brought together classical Roman and Greek material, with contemporary European commentary, and supplementary manuscript and antiquarian material. Although Toland did use a number of Irish sources (many in manuscript), he interlarded such material with the more traditional testimonies. Importantly, then, Toland treated ancient sources uniformly regardless of their cultural provenance or religious identity. The Druids he writes of are reconstructed from a miscellany of original ethnographic evidence of the so-called 'Posidonian' tradition, compiled from the works of Strabo, Diodorus Siculus, Athenaeus, Caesar, Pomponius Mela, Ammianus Marcellinus and Pliny.[27] Toland produced a work that recovered the culture and beliefs of the Druids of 'the antient Gauls, Britons, Irish and Scots'. His Celticism was pan-European, rather than specifically Irish. Texts that depicted French Druids were with equal application, descriptive of the 'systems' of 'all the British Islands'. As Toland's Irish sources (printed, manuscript and oral) established, long after Druidical institutions had been exterminated in 'Gaule and South-Britain' their memory was 'still best preserv'd in Ireland and the Highlands of Scotland, comprehending the Hebridae, Hebrides, or Western Isles, among which the Isle of Man'.[28] Throughout the work Toland carefully Latinised all of the references to Irish names in the main body of the text to emphasise that the figures were of equal value to those of more mainstream classical tradition.

Central to Toland's argument for the persistence of Druidical institutions in the Northern Isles was his display of the physical antiquities in the second letter. While the fragments of textual evidence might be thought of as fragile authorities, the gazetteer-like listing of the dimensions, location and usage of ancient monuments provided solid empirical demonstration for the authority of his arguments. One eighteenth-century critic, picking up on this, complained that Toland provided accounts of many monuments without providing particular details and measurements.[29] Toland thus wove his interpretation of the Celtic past into the fabric of contemporary landscape. Cairns found in the Isle of Man, in Caermarthenshire, or outside Londonderry were ritual beacons for 'La Bealtine' or Belen's Fire.[30] Drawing mainly from the accounts of such monuments found in the antiquarian books he owned, Toland used classical texts like Strabo, Caesar or Pliny to substantiate his interpretation of Druidical origins. Festivals and temples, obelisks and cromlechs, from the Isle of Lewis to Jersey, from Anglesey to the Orkneys were described and appropriated to the explanation of the remnants of Celtic antiquity. The remains of a pristine non-priestly culture were ubiquitous.

Although Toland presented himself as a field archaeologist describing, identifying, interpreting the physical objects, it seems more than likely that his accounts were lifted from secondary sources. There are only a handful of occasions when he indicates that he has seen, or remembers seeing, particular antiquities.[31] He intended to spend a summer in Scotland researching antiquities for himself. Empirical description would, like the deployment of footnotes from the works of Grabe and Fabricius, accrue credibility to his arguments. Emphasising this he insisted 'all such monuments ... I shall so accurately describe in every respect, and give such accounts of them where accountable; that I hope the curious will have reason to be satisfied'. As he continued 'whenever I am at a loss, I shall frankly own it; and never give my conjectures for more than what they are, that is probable guesses: and certainly nothing can be more amiss in Inquiries of this kind, than to obtrude suppositions for matters of fact'.[32]

Reliant upon the works of chorographers and antiquarians for 'matter of fact', Toland took great pleasure in advancing his own interpretation, and indeed exposing past ignorance. Whether describing the festivals of fire-walking, the reputation of the 'Fatal stone of Tarah', or the rocking stones of Balvaird, Toland rebutted superstitious interpretations and explained the natural significance of the objects. As he noted, very often the 'multitude (that common prey of Priests and Princes) ... [would swallow] the secrets of natural philosophy for divine miracles'. In explaining the mechanism by which the rocking stones operated, Toland not only debunked the supernatural element but also condemned the destructive use that priestly management made of such devices.[33] The point of Toland's lengthy descriptions was however not simply to expose fraud, but to establish the ubiquity of these ancient monuments in the British islands.

Toland did not merely elevate the antiquities of the British Isles to equivalent status with more traditionally 'classical' sources by using the latter to interpret the former, but also made an explicit claim about their relative cultural priority. In discussing the various festivals surrounding the cairns he suggested (via some pretty dubious etymological arguments) that it was 'hugely probable' that ancient Greek worship of Apollo was derived from the Gauls. By the conclusion of the second letter this remark had developed into a full-blown comparative argument. Comparing Herodotus' description of an antiquity near the Temple of Minerva at Sais in Egypt, with that of the Dwarfy-Stone in the Orkneys, Toland was at a loss to understand the 'original design'. Ridiculing Boetian suggestions of Egyptian influences (which he considered almost as absurd as 'the Britons fables about their Trojan ancestors') he made the suggestion that 'according to the ceaseless vicissitudes of things, there was a time, when the inhabitants of these Islands were as learned and knowing, as the present Egyptians and the Highlanders are ignorant'.[34] Contemporary

'Britons' had a cultural legacy to match those of Greek and Roman antiquity. By appropriating the cultural authority of classical antiquity to the remnants of Celtic history, Toland intruded the British past into the pantheon of ancient learning, at the same time as subverting the commonplace privileging of classical antiquity. It also unhinged such historical narratives from sacred time. Toland, was then, not simply elevating a Celtic exemplar, but exposing the process by which such standards were created. The invention of a primordial 'Celtic learning' was a playful device for disclosing the procedures for creating mythical narratives of sacred national origins. A closer look at the precise interpretations offered by Toland will perhaps help establish this point.

One of the digressions that Toland made in the first letter was on the necessity for elegant expression in the 'fields of antiquity and criticism'. Following Cicero *de oratore*, style, grace and eloquence, as well as learning, were key to the art of communication.[35] Reason needed the skills of oratory to be efficient and effective in the public sphere. Toland had indicated his commitment to the 'force of eloquence' in his earlier poetic work *Clito* (1700) by advancing the claims of the unsuperstitious orator Hercules. Toland was expert in the different techniques of rhetorical *color* and writing.[36] Indeed one antagonist suspected that Toland imagined he had such eloquence at his disposal and that 'he may move His Tongue long enough before his Prosaic Poetry can lead us into the mistake of making chains for ourselves, and seeking imaginary Good before that which is real'.[37] It was one of Toland's more controversial claims that the art of eloquence originated in Celtic culture. Aware of the innovation of his arguments he insisted that his knowledge of 'the Irish language and books' would transform the meaning of both 'words and things even in the Greec and Roman authors'.[38] Toland proposed a Celtic revision of one of the central mythical figures of early modern rhetorical practice: Lucian's 'Gallorum Hercules'. The 'Gallic Hercules' was one of the central representations of the rhetorical tradition that underpinned the power of eloquence which persisted in early modern intellectual culture.[39] Lucian gave a detailed account of the fable of Hercules. The latter was 'a man of great wisdom [who] had all men linked together by the eares in a chain to draw them and leade them even as he lusted'.[40] Lucian represented Hercules as a man who led the people by the 'force of his persuasions'. Toland reproduced the complete passage from Lucian's works in the third letter of the *Specimen*.[41] In this passage Lucian had given a distinct account of Hercules from the usual picture: the Gauls represented Hercules as an old man in a lion skin holding club, bow and quiver. The most remarkable feature of the portrait was described by Lucian that 'this ancient Hercules drags after him a vast crowd of men, all of whom are fastened by the ears with thin chains composed of gold and amber'. Since Hercules is holding a club and bow the chains are not hand-held but fastened to a 'hole in the tip of the God's tongue'. As Lucian noted, this God was known by the Celtic name of 'Ogmius'. This Celtic reading of the classical figure was Toland's prompt to propose a major revision of the tradition.

Lucian was informed (according to Toland) by a 'learned Druid who stood by, that Hercules did not in Gaule, as in Greece, betoken *strength of body*, but the *force of eloquence*'. Toland ridiculed the arguments of men like Samuel Bochart who claimed 'Phoenician' origins, or Edmund Dickenson who conjectured that Hercules was 'Joshua, who was surnamed OGMIUS, for having conquored OG King of Bashan'. There were many variant readings of the fable: 'Egyptian, the Indian, the Tyrian, the Cretan, the Grecian or Theban' but the only serious reading was the Celtic.[42] Toland proceeded then to give an account of the fable that combined classical references (Tacitus and Phurnutus) with manuscript Irish sources. Using the *Auriacept na n-eces* (the Scholars' Primer) found in the version of the Book of Ballymote, combined with the printed works of Ware, Forbes, and O'Flaherty, Toland constructed an innovative reading of the Gallic Hercules, premised upon the connection between OGIMIUS and the Irish tradition of OGAM or OGUM.[43] Making the connection between eloquence and language, Toland forged a synthesis between the fable concerning Hercules and the Irish account of the 'secret of writing'. Blending together material from the four books of the *Auriacept* compiled from the account by Forchern (poet to Conchabar mac Nessa) of Fenius Forsaid, with sources like Nennius, Toland linked the Herculean account of eloquence to the Ogam script of ancient Ireland. Just as Hercules was regarded by the Druids as the 'symboll of the force of eloquence' so was Ogam script the aboriginal language in which the Druids expressed their 'Divinity and Philosophy'. Toland gave an accomplished and intelligent account of Ogam, premised upon the materials he had read in the Book of Ballymote describing the alphabet and its usage.[44] Typically, Toland exploited his local knowledge of Irish literature to reinterpret a traditional fable. Indeed he insisted that if the full archives of Irish antiquity were examined critically it would be possible to reconstruct the philosophy of the Druids. Toland's catalogue of sources would be the premise of many new 'noble discoveries' in the antiquities 'not only of Gaule and Britain, but likewise to the numerous passages of the Greec and Latin authors'. This was an inversion of the usual patterns of cultural imperialism. That many scholars ignored the Irish literature was balanced by the fact that many modern historians used the sources credulously. Toland's critical skill would distinguish 'the dross from the pure ore, and distinguishing counterfeit from sterling coin'.[45]

Toland conflated two distinct types of sources to construct an innovative vindication of the cultural value of Celtic learning. This learning was pre-Christian. Again taking a side-swipe at Christian narratives, Toland insisted that Patrick's conversion saw not only the corruption of the Ogam script, but also the conceptual degeneration of learning which changed from beautiful Druidical allegory to 'scholastical divinity, metaphysical or chronological disputes, legends, miracles and martyrologies'. Celebrating the 'primevous Irish learning' of the heathen kings Achaius, Tuathalius and Cormac, who all successively contributed to the academy of Tarah, was a simple device for exposing the destructive achievements of early Christianity. Druidical learning was systematically destroyed in Patrick's time, 'book burning and letter-murdering humor' being a typical Christian practice. Citing Diogenes Laertius and Phurnutus, Toland asserted that ancient Celtic Druids were reckoned to be 'the chief authors of the Barbarous Theology and Philosophy, long anterior to the Greecs'.[46]

If, in his account of the Gallic Hercules, Toland had exhibited a scholarly creativity with his sources, in the third letter of the *Specimen* he excelled himself in his treatment of another classical tradition. This letter was much more miscellaneous in its contents: there are extracts from obscure classical sources, descriptions of persisting superstitions, and accounts of the history of the Manx legislator Manannan. The bulk of the text however is concerned to examine the history of Abaris and the Hyperboreans.[47] Abaris was a legendary servant of Apollo, one of the Hyperboreans who lived in the far north 'beyond the north wind'. Extracting material from (amongst others) Pytheas who had first speculated about a mysterious land of Thule in his *Tour of the Earth*, Toland argued that Abaris, 'a philosopher of the Brittish world',[48] was a Celtic Druid and that the Hebrides were the Hyperborean islands. In arbitrating between the different accounts of Pytheas, Strabo, Solinus and Antonius Diogenes, Toland drew the distinction between a hyperborean continent and the hyperborean islands. Abaris the Druid, inhabitant of Skye, was also intimate with Pythagoras: it was a matter of dispute whether the Druids learnt their 'symbolical and enigmatical method of teaching' from Pythagoras 'or that this philosopher had borrow'd these particulars from the Druids'. Abaris, described by Himerius visiting Athens, wearing plaid and 'trowzers' and dressed in the 'native garb of an aboriginal Scot', was a prudent 'searcher after wisdom'.[49] This placed Abaris at the source of all learning and philosophy. Not only did it challenge the primacy of Greek culture, but also denied the Christian assumption that Moses was the source of all philosophy.

If Toland represented Abaris as a candidate for the title of founding philosopher, then his description of the Hyperborean community was as a quasi-utopian republic. Again blending classical sources (Diodorus Siculus and Hippocrates) with the chorographical descriptions of contemporaries like Martin Martin, Toland delivered a picture of natural plenty and social virtue. Everything from cattle, 'amphibious animals', 'tame and wild fowl', 'from the shrimp to the whale' were (and are) 'exceeding numerous and prolific'. Although Martin Martin, as Toland admitted 'when he wrote his *Description* of these islands, was far from dreaming of the Hyperboreans', his evidence confirmed the fruitful descriptions of Diodorus Siculus. The archaeological evidence tended to confirm that 'in remote ages they were in a far more flourishing condition than at present'.[50] The 'original constitution' of the people matched the natural virtue of the land: they were strangers to vice, distempers and ornament owing 'everything to nature'.[51] Hospitable and judicious, 'in a word, they are equally void of the two chief plagues of Mankind, LUXURY and AMBITION'. Living 'according to nature' and avoiding disputes about 'dominion and commerce' they are 'rigid observers of Justice'.[52] In the course of providing this exposition Toland slipped from the past tense (in discussing the classical account of the Hyperboreans) into the present tense: not only were the Hebrides the site of a Hyperborean past, but there still persisted the material conditions for re-establishing that heritage.

It may be apparent then from this brief survey of the *Specimen* that the text is a very complicated one. The layers of meaning are only manifest when read in context with a series of commonplace contemporary assumptions about the nature of antiquity. Clearly Toland promoted the claims of Celtic learning in general, and Irish traditions in detail. Without doubt he advanced powerful arguments in defence of the cultural status of a non-classical tradition: it should be noted that this tradition is pan-Celtic, it is British, Irish, Scottish, Hebridean and Manx. Although commending the literary antiquities of Ireland, Toland does not give cultural priority to his own native country. Indeed, he noted that in a further dissertation 'concerning the Celtic languages and colonies' he was going to discuss the 'origins' both of the British colonies and the Irish. Contrary to the fabulous traditions of Trojans, Milesians and Nemetes, as the British were colonised by the continental Gauls so the 'ancient Irish, not one of their colonies excepted ... were all from Gaule and Great Britain'.[53] It is difficult then to read the purpose of the work as simply attempting to promote a proto-nationalist defence of specifically Irish culture, perhaps as a back-cloth to a defence of Irish Parliamentary independence in the early 1720s. Toland's targets were broader and more fundamental.

A deeper reading of the work suggests that the important point for Toland was to unshackle questions of national origins from sacred revelation, rather than to advance the claims of any particular culture. The *Specimen* was about 'revolutions' rather than 'origins', about the history of institutions and the 'ceaseless vicissitudes of things', rather than providing prescriptive models for applause.[54] This ambiguity of purpose is perhaps reason for the instrumental quality of Toland's discussions in the work. Take the example of the Druids. Toland's account straddles what has been labelled the Posidonian and Alexandrinian positions.[55] At some points in the argument, Toland condemned Druidical barbarity, but at other places, he applauded the sublimity of their philosophy. In many passages the religious institutions of the Druids become the models of superstition and priestcraft, in others they preserve the 'two grand doctrines of the Eternity and Incorruptibility of the Universe, and the incessant Revolution of all beings and forms'.[56] This was clearly inconsistent. What then was Toland trying to communicate to Molesworth and his other readers?

At least one reader was very sceptical about the piety of the work. Thomas Parker, the Lord Chancellor, had been sent the first (and more aggressively anticlerical) letter shortly after its completion. He showed it to John Chamberlayne, who reported to Toland rather snidely that, 'I saw my Ld Chanc. Yesterday, who among other papers gave me your project of a history of the Druids, which he told me he did not understand but which he suspected to be level'd against Christian Priests'.[57] Chamberlayne, associated with the SPCK, was sensitive to the dangers of irreligious discourse, also admitted that he was not intelligent enough to detect any 'poison lurking'. It was palpable, to Chamberlayne, that Toland intended to provoke contemporary implications in the readers' mind. So for example, the practice of the Druids 'seducing their followers' might teach us 'not to be so deceiv'd'. But beyond this injunction, however, Toland drew no specific lessons, but intended to 'leave the reader to make such applications himself, seldom making any for him; since he that is neither clear sighted nor quick enough of conception to do so, may as good purpose read the Fairy-Tales, as this History'.[58] Just like the work on the canonicity of Scripture Toland was raising issues to provoke debate rather than simply establish his own points.

The after-life of the work shows that later writers like William Blake explicitly used Toland's work on Druids as a source for indicting Christian priestcraft, while men like Stukeley attempted to provide critical antidotes to this hostility.[59] Toland's representations of the ancient Celtic past were not merely calculated for emulation, but were also a device for the display of his own learning and political principles. Toland used the scheme of Druidical religion, of the figure of Hercules as a motif for the 'force of eloquence', and of the semi-utopian community of the Hebrides, as literary exemplars to establish political principle. Unlike the pious scholarship of his contemporaries which employed erudition to reconstruct a prescriptive tradition derived from sacred history, Toland showed how easy it was, both to destroy the historical evidences of these models, and to construct better, more civil, alternatives. Toland's display of erudition and learning in the *Specimen*, was premeditated to reinforce his own credibility, but also to damage the authority of other work. He intended, as he arrogantly asserted, 'to leave no room for any to write on this subject after me'.[60] The materials he circulated to Molesworth and others were only sample chapters of much more detailed work in progress: in this polite scribal form he did not wish to 'crowd the margins with long passages'.[61]

There was a specific rhetorical purpose intended in the display of learning. It is important to remember that the *Specimen* was a scribal publication. The circle of readers focused upon Molesworth were all people who made a firm connection between political and religious liberties. Indeed they very commonly, either individually or collectively, were involved in articulating a commonwealth Whig ideology in the form of attacks upon the legal foundations of the confessional state, and in particular against priestcraft and intolerance. The significance of this affinity was its identity as a politically active grouping, intimate with the Hanoverian court and the political establishment after 1714. Toland's community of readers were not marginal and radical figures, but worked and acted at the very centre of national politics. The evidence of the circulation of scribal material like the *Specimen* suggests how such writing was engineered to intrude Toland into a circle of patronage, and in that sense was effective in creating a social connection that enabled the circulation of his ideas and opinions in an oral or conversational context. The texts themselves might be thought of as contrived to act as stimulants towards the development of political activity amongst this milieu. Implicitly, he was constructing a community of collaborators as well as of readers. The project bound together a collection of men and women, even before it maturated into scribal form.

The hub of this activity was Toland's relationship with Molesworth. Toland kept his noble friend up to date with the progress of the composition. In one of the last letters to discuss the text, Toland commented, 'I am farr advanced in my history of the Druids'. An indication of his confidence in the aristocrat's discrimination can be seen in the fact that Toland left the decision about the final appearance of the text to Molesworth. As he noted, 'I shall entirely submit to your Lordships taste'.[62] Since Molesworth had given Toland 'extraordinary helps' in arranging things like transcriptions from abroad and access to manuscripts in Britain it was only just that he was given the same 'absolute right' over the manuscript 'that Cicero did to Atticus'. The parallel of the republican ancients with Toland and Molesworth was deliberate and illuminating. Toland's forfeiture of authorial control to Molesworth was much more than an act of deference from client to patron. Combined with his lack of discretion about the project such renunciation was an effective instrument for incorporating Molesworth's social power into the textual form of the work. It was, after all, Toland's prerogative to determine the circulation of the text, although Molesworth's name might be invoked to facilitate the consequent passage and reception of the work.

The manuscript form of the work thus provided not just a forum for the communication of ideas but also an instrument of social integration. A powerful (and perhaps unique) glimpse of the intellectual understanding that existed between the two men can be seen in their copy of one of the books used in the *Specimen* – Martin Martin's *A description of the Western Island of Scotland* (1716) which is currently in the British Library. Martin's work, first published in 1703 to critical applause, was a natural history of Scottish culture that received warm support from the Royal Society in London because of its emphasis upon reporting credible 'matters of fact' when delivering an account of various strange phenomena and local traditions.[63] The copy Toland and Molesworth shared was the second edition 'very much corrected'. Toland had read the book three times by September 1720, and had lent it to Molesworth sometime in 1721. He had it back by October 1721. Toland described his reading habits in detail: 'after the first cursory reading of Dr Martin's book, I perus'd it a second time with pen in hand (as 'tis often my custom) and in the same manner a third time'. This repeated reading was with the purpose of explaining and correcting the text, 'as well by reading books as consulting men'. Toland took his criticism seriously: one can imagine him consulting, comparing and talking through his own ideas with other people: the result of this process was manifest in his marginalia. Again the echoes with the routines of reading he hoped to provoke in his work on the canon are significant. Molesworth, having received the book added his comments distinguishing his remarks from Toland's by his initials. Here is evidence of the intimate dialogue and intellectual banter between the two men.[64]

In his comments Toland constantly drew attention to the *Specimen* indicating that both he and Molesworth used the scribal work as a semi-permanent and authoritative literary resource. Toland's comments assumed a variety of forms, but included useful clarifications and definitions (presumably) for Molesworth's information (so 'usquebaugh' was the name for 'Brandy 3 times distill'd'). The general tenor of both sets of annotation was to impugn the credulity of Martin Martin's work. Remarking on Martin's account of 'men's being devour'd by whales', Toland noted that it 'is unworthy of a fellow of the Royal Society'. At another point one can almost hear Toland sighing 'why did he not go to see this rarity, I mean why did he not disprove this fable?' One passage of Martin detailing a report of 'viscous water' attracted the inquiry from Toland, 'why did he not try this experiment?', to which Molesworth tartly responded 'I'll tell ye why: your author is a foolish pretending coxcomb'. A repeated phrase, 'This is not so ...', often opens some correction or doubtful opinion. Marginalia indicating 'this is plain popery' or 'all impostures' were delivered with the intention of exposing the priestcraft of both Protestant and Catholic traditions. The language of popery, imposture, and priestly deceit runs like a thread through both series of commentaries, although Molesworth also displays a keen interest in fishing and techniques for catching sand-eels. The central points are however that superstition runs deep in all religions, and that it has a long history, and that it was 'generally hurtful or ridiculous'.[65]

Toland presents himself as a key authority on the various subject matter of Martin's book (indeed he cites his own *Specimen* and its 'explications' repeatedly throughout the annotations). With a typical lack of modesty, Toland noted that he could give a much more detailed and elaborate explanation but 'I have not room to set down what I know of this matter'. It is quite clear that Molesworth had an independent and anticlerical seam to his own contributions which are just as sceptical as those of his co-reader. In fact in one or two places Toland and Molesworth did not quite see eye to eye over the significance of the book. Responding to an intended correction from Molesworth (on matters piscatorial), Toland robustly defended himself, 'I am not at all mistaken My Lord: & if you have not been in every part of Scotland, that's none of my fault'.

While the dynamic of the exchange seems to have been driven by a combination of Toland's role as inquisitor of Martin's text in response to Molesworth's requests for explanations, it is obvious that in the margins of the book, both men engage in unrestrained criticism. This marginalia is evidence of uninhibited reader response. Although the rhetoric of scholarship is present (citations of other sources) and a sense of Toland's limited social deference to the aristocratic Molesworth ('My Lord') in some sense shape the form of the intellectual transaction, here the annotation is a sediment of how ideas were exchanged between these two men. In the margins of this work the cut and thrust of how controversialists engaged with ideas in books is manifest. Ideas did matter. Sentence by sentence both the arguments of his book, and Martin's own credibility, was ruined. In the same process of establishing their own opinions, the form of their transactions elevated the power of their own erudition and learning. From this communal reading of Martin's work there are gestures to the other texts Toland produced, both scribal and printed. Repeatedly, Toland advised Molesworth to 'see my H. of Druids'.[66] In the frequency of reference to the work on druids it is possible to draw out a number of implications. Toland was exploiting the fact that he knew that Molesworth had easy access to the work, and that it was considered as a solid enough scholarly resource to compete with (and indeed trounce) the authority of Martin's printed text. But he was also suggesting that there was an appropriate way of reading (and deriving meaning) from that text. Scribal works were then a way of getting inside a specific reader's head, and perhaps trying to shape, with some confidence of achievement, patterns of conviction and belief.

The function of the intellectual content of the *Specimen*, necessarily combined with its quality as a bearer and maker of social and political connections. As has been argued, Toland's work was calculated as a work of profound and comprehensive scholarship, at some points including footnotes of footnotes.[67] The first letter put together an analysis of the Druidical past as a 'complete

History of Priestcraft'. The Druids even invented the word. The text exposed the 'system' as one that combined sophistry, juggling and 'the art of managing the mob'. If there were parallels between Druidical religion and the modern experience readers 'ought not to impute it to design in the author, but to the conformity of things'. If this 'conformity of things' convicted the modern Church with the sins of antiquity then they ought to be 'blasted too, without a possibility of ever sprouting up again'. Part of Toland's rhetoric was to actively deny that he was prompting the reader in any way to form a specific opinion: he explained, 'all that I can do to show my own candour, is, to leave the reader to make such applications himself, seldom making any for him'. The display of erudition was meant to act as a prompt for the articulation of an attitude towards the Druidical past. In establishing and exposing the techniques of priestcraft, Toland hoped that his work was teaching philosophy by examples. Invoking standard classical tropes about the function of history, the work was meant to be both entertaining and instructive 'to all sorts of readers, without excepting the Ladies, who are pretty much concerned in this matter'.[68] Although the second and third letters were much less obviously polemical in their indictment of a persecuting Church, the attempts to parallel Egyptian and Celtic antiquities, and the examination of Pythagorean contexts for Druidical doctrines of the soul, undoubtedly had unorthodox implications, while being buried in layers of recondite scholarship.

Toland's scribal publications had a further, and perhaps different, purpose beyond the public intention of his printed writings. The social function of the act of circulation amongst the powerful was a critical platform for making their intellectual leverage more effectual: by persuading such people, Toland intended not only to achieve cerebral conviction, but hoped for practical political consequences. Ideas insinuated into the right minds could change the law. This might cause us to rethink one of the historiographical common-places about the nature of clandestine literature in the period. It is an assumption that such texts, because contrived for a limited audience, were more honest in the presentation of radical or irreligious ideas. Since they were hidden from the purview of the censor and the law, philosophic, religious and blasphemous opinions could be articulated in an unadulterated and sincere voice. Toland noted in his *Clidophorus* (1720), that the tyranny of priestcraft meant that the 'truth' could rarely be spoken in public. Only with 'doors fast shut and under all other precautions' could men communicate 'only to friends of known probity, prudence and capacity'.[69] The watchful surveillance of clergymen 'must of necessity produce shiftings, ambiguities, equivocations, and hypocrisy in all its shapes; which will not merely be call'd, but actually esteem'd *necessarily cautious*'. A model of 'private' reading could be derived from the classical example of Heraclitus, who had established that the 'secret meaning' of texts might be opened by readers with a 'key'. For Toland, 'such a key ... is to be, for the most part, borrow'd by the skilful from the writers themselves'.[70] This was an open invitation for his readers to examine his texts carefully (perhaps with the same sort of attention to detail evidenced in his reading with Molesworth). It was an enticement to his public audience to read his public printed books with strategic caution. But this injunction of 'reading between the lines', also raises the suggestion that those readers in his private circle (like Molesworth and company) would have access to a set of ideas and opinions articulated in his scribal works and in conversation, which could provide a useful means for decoding the meaning of his published works. As Toland knew to his own cost, in private, away from the observation of the mob and the priest, a man might ponder the truth, but it was 'dangerous ... to publish it to others'.[71]

Toland insisted that his printed writings contained the truth, but that the reader had to work hard to work out what these ideas were. In private (with 'friends of known probity, prudence and capacity') he had always eschewed all equivocation. We should be cautious of making too bold a distinction between the public and private, between print and manuscript texts, and between disguised and sincere meaning in Toland's work. The consequences of noting the difference of form and audience has sometimes obscured and fragmented the integrity of intentions articulated in his writings. For some historians the 'real' John Toland is only present in the clandestine, secret, shadowy Masonic coteries, while the public Toland was little more than a hypocritical gad-fly irritating the orthodox establishment. This understanding not only devalues the sophistication of Toland's public writing, but mis-characterises his similarly creative exploitation of manuscript publication. Manuscripts were not simply a different space for the unhindered utterance of ideas, but, for Toland, performed a much more subtle function of bonding a group of individuals into an intellectual community. This affinity of readers became a platform for intruding his ideas into the highest echelons of elite culture. There is a tension in much of the so-called radical clandestine works between textual form, intended audience, and their implicit objectives as works which would transform society. Certainly most of the intellectually subversive scribal works on the continent, although radical in aspiration, did not appeal to the sovereignty of the people or public opinion as the central agencies of change, but emphasised the rationality of a fundamentally elite audience.[72] Toland too had different strategies for communicating with a public and a more confidential audience: both of these were focused upon changing the political and religious culture of his society. Writing for politicians like Molesworth meant laying the foundations for cultural change.

It is clear from the trajectory of Toland's literary and political career, and the evidence of his political connections, that from the late 1690s to the end of his life in the early 1720s, Toland manoeuvred himself into relationships with patrons who held some intimacy with the mechanics of power: successively (and concurrently in some cases) he operated in the milieux of Locke, Shaftesbury, Harley, Molesworth and Eugene of Savoy. As the evidence of his archives suggests, in each of these relationships with more powerful men, Toland acted as a broker and producer of literary materials. While intimate with Shaftesbury he published his patron's works without his permission. For Harley he ghosted political pamphlets. His relationship with Eugene of Savoy was premised upon the exchange of clandestine literature. In all of these transactions Toland's literary skills were used for political ends. In the last five years of his life, he achieved the high-point of his political influence through his liaison with Molesworth. The erudition, literary skill and political intentions displayed in works like the *Specimen* acted to establish his credentials within this milieu. Toland was, however, more than Molesworth's tame *philosophe*; he sought out a more practical and engaged role. It would be wrong to separate this political relationship from the intellectual intimacy established between the two men represented in the exchange of scribal material like the *Specimen*, the catalogue on the apocrypha, and the history of the *respublica mosaica*. How far the intellectual content of this variety of manuscript material set the context for the development and articulation of 'political' tenets is difficult to establish with precision. However, it is possible to indicate that, far from consigning him to the radical margins, at least in England, Toland's scribal labours projected him into the swell of national politics. The affinity of readers involved in the circulation of the work became a platform for intruding his ideas into the highest echelons of elite culture.

NOTES

1   *Collections* 2 p. 118.

2   D. Hayton 'The Stanhope/Sunderland Ministry and the repudiation of Irish Parliamentary Independence' *English Historical Review* 103 (1998) pp. 610–636.

3   *Collections* 2 p. 494.

4   See J. A. I. Champion 'John Toland, the druids and the politics of Celtic scholarship' *Irish Historical Studies* 32 (2001) pp. 321–42.

5   R. Kearney 'John Toland: an Irish philosopher?' *John Toland's Christianity not mysterious* pp. 213–215.

6   See Bodleian Library MS Eng. Lett c28, c29.

7   See J. Simms 'John Toland (1670–1722), a Donegal heretic' *Irish Historical Studies* 16 (1968–69) pp. 304–320 at 304.

8   Heinemann 'John Toland, France, Holland and Dr Williams' pp. 346–347.

9   See *Collections* 1 pp. v–vi.

10   See *Collections* 1 p. lxxxviii ('Ac linguarum plus decem sciens') this is not noted in the

English version, see BL. Add Mss 4295 fo. 76.

11 See A. Harrison 'John Toland (1670–1722) and Celtic Studies' in *Celtic languages and Celtic peoples: proceedings of the Second North American Congress of Celtic Studies* (Canada, 1992) pp. 555–576.

12 See *Tolandiana* pp. 265–267.

13 *Collections* I p. 4.

14 BL Add Mss 4465 fo. 13.

15 See *Nazarenus* pp. 312–314.

16 BL Add Mss 4465 fo. 16.

17 BL Add Mss 4465 fo. 19.

18 See BL Add Mss 4465 fo. 36.

19 See *Nazarenus* pp. 312–14.

20 See R. E. Asher *National Myths in Renaissance France. Francus, Samothes and the Druids* (Edinburgh, 1993); C. Kidd *British identities before nationalism* (Cambridge, 1999).

21 See E. Seaton *Literary relations of England and Scandinavia in the seventeenth century* (Oxford, 1935).

22 See G. Parry *The Trophies of time: English antiquarians of the seventeenth century* (Oxford, 1995) and S. A. E. Mendyck *'Speculum Britanniae': Regional study, antiquarianism, and science in Britain to 1700* (Toronto, 1989).

23 See F. V. Emery 'Irish geography in the seventeenth century' *Irish Geography* 3 (1954–1958) pp. 263–276.

24 See *Nazarenus*.

25 See E. Lhwyd to J. Aubrey 9 January 1694 in R. T. Gunther (ed.) *Early Science in Oxford: life and letters of Edward Lhwyd* (Oxford, 1945) XIV p. 217.

26 See D. Haycock 'Dr William Stukeley (1687–1765): antiquarian and Newtonian in eighteenth century England' (London PhD 1998) p. 233.

27 See J. J. Tierney 'The Celtic ethnography of Posidonius' *Proceedings of the Royal Irish Academy* 60 (C) (1960) pp. 189–275.

28 *Specimen* p. 17.

29 See Haycock 'Stukeley' p. 137.

30 *Specimen* p. 67–68.

31 *Ibid.* p. 67, 104.

32 *Ibid.* p. 114 (see also pp. 31, 144 for statements about wishing to do more research).

33 *Ibid.* pp. 82, 106–07.

34 *Ibid.* pp. 75, 115, 118. Interestingly, Toland commented on the Dwarfy-Stone 'I wish it were in Surrey, that I might make it a summer study'.

35 *Ibid.* pp. 18–19.

36 See Toland, 'Preface' to *Nazarenus* (1718).

37 See Smith 'John Toland's *Clito*' p. 14.

38 *Ibid.* p. 33.

39 See Q. Skinner *Reason and rhetoric in the philosophy of Thomas Hobbes* (Cambridge, 1996).

40 Skinner *Reason* p. 92.

41 See *Specimen* pp. 121–124; compare with H. W. and F. G. Fowler *The works of Lucian of Samosata* (Oxford, 1905) III 'Heracles, an Introductory Lecture' pp. 256–259.

42 *Specimen* pp. 34, 35, 43.

43 See G. Calder (ed.) *Auraicept na n-eces: the Scholars' primer being the texts of the Ogham tract from the book of Ballymote* (Edinburgh, 1917).

44 On Ogam script see, D. McManus *A Guide to Ogam* (Maynooth, 1991) esp. pp. 147–151.

45 *Specimen* p. 47.

46 *Ibid.* pp. 48–49, 58, 59.

47 For some background, see C. F. C. Hawkes *Pytheas: Europe and the Greek explorers* (Oxford, 1975).

48 *Specimen* p. 177. Toland also cited Robert Sibbald's *Essay concerning the Thule of the Ancients*, see *Specimen* p. 157.

49 *Specimen* pp. 161–63, 181–2.

50 *Ibid.* pp. 169, 170–71, 173.

51 *Ibid.* pp. 175–176.

52 *Ibid.* pp. 176–177.

53 *Ibid.* p. 133 (see pp. 131–135).

54 *Ibid.* pp. 5, 118.

55 S. Piggott *The Druids* (1974) p. 77 and *passim*.

56 *Specimen* pp. 9–10, 46.

57 BL Add Mss 4295 fo. 27.

58 *Specimen* pp. 10, 16.

59 See S. Smiles *The Image of Antiquity* (New Haven, 1994) esp. pp. 75–112.

60 *Specimen* p. 31.

61 *Ibid.* p. 10.

62 See BL Add Mss 4465 fo. 36.

63 See M. Hunter *The occult laboratory* (2001) pp. 27–31.

64 See BL call-mark C.45.c1: manuscript additions opposite title page (dated 'Putney, September, 1720'). Molesworth's comments were added after 28 October 1721.

65 See Martin *Western Isles* 'JT' note p. 29 'In this story the superstition is pretty equal on both sides'; p. 172 'our author was a very poor philosopher, & no astronomer at all'; p. 230 'Protestants we see, may be very superstitious'.

66 See Martin *Western Isles* pp. 8, 26, 28, 35, 47, 60, 67, 68, 87, 88, 113, 141, 154, 249; there is also a reference to 'my Nazarenus, Letter 2' at p. 257.

67 *Western Isles* p. 5.

68 *Ibid.* pp. 14, 15, 16, 29, 30.

69 *Tetradymus* p. 66.

70 *Ibid.* p. 76.

71 *Ibid.* p. 100.

72 See M. Benitez *La face cachée des lumières* (Paris, 1996) p. 199–211.

Conclusion

Writing enlightenment

I N the early days of 1712 Prince Eugene of Savoy undertook a key diplomatic mission to London to reinforce the commitment of Robert Harley's ministry to the alliance against France in the negotiations over peace at Utrecht.[1] With the Tories in the ascendancy, Eugene's reputation as a stalwart defender of 'our common liberty' across Europe projected him as a defender of Whig principles. Long awaited by the Whig elites of London and Hanover, Eugene's military prowess had endowed him with a powerful public reputation in London. Tory figures like Lord Strafford (probably at the instigation of Robert Harley) had been involved in trying to dissuade him from visiting England, underscoring the mischief the 'mob' might pose. Eugene's reply 'was that he who had done so much for the liberty of Europe need never fear an English church mob, who always was on the side of those that were for liberty and property'.[2] Despite deliberate attempts to hinder his passage by refusing to provide suitable travel arrangements, Eugene arrived on 16 January, immediately dispatching Baron d'Hohendorf to Harley. It would be difficult to over-emphasise the importance of this moment, not just for national politics, but for the balance of power across Europe, and the perceived survival of Protestant liberty. This diplomatic crisis was a distillation of all the anxieties that confronted men like Toland – the security of the Protestant succession, the defence of true liberties in Church and State, the triumph of reason over superstition, and the war against popish priestcraft – ultimately rested on the shoulders of Eugene and d'Hohendorf.

Entertaining Eugene and his entourage became the focus of social life in London from January to March 1712. One contemporary commented, 'the mobb are so fond of Prince Eugen that his coach can hardly goe about'.[3] While Tory politicians did their best to compromise the diplomatic processes and the prince's public repute by blocking meetings and using the press to cast hostile aspersions, London's elite fell over themselves to entertain Eugene. As

Nicholas Tindal put it, 'multitudes of people crowded to see him, and with loud declarations attended him wherever he went'. Although Jacobite plotters endeavoured to rouse a 'rude rabble' to protest against the mission, 'for two whole months, the nobility and gentry of both parties vied with one another, who should entertain him'. Tory nobles like Lord Dartmouth snubbed Eugene. Plans for a lavish civic entertainment by the Mayor and Aldermen were spiked over issues of protocol 'to the great disappointment and mortification of most of the citizens'.[4] The many public demonstrations of support – bonfires, bells and 'illuminations' – were supplemented with dances, balls and 'drawing rooms' in the houses of the great and the good. Behind all of this public entertainment lay a deadly serious shadow play between Eugene and Harley through the medium of Hohendorf who acted as a covert messenger carrying memoranda back and forth. The public sociability that Eugene undertook – visiting the House of Lords, dining numerous times in public, attending the opera and dances, giving his own 'leveés', and having audiences with the Queen (on her birthday she presented him with 'a sword sett with diamonds') – was an instrument for the propagation of the political programme he supported.[5] Eugene had a notorious distaste for the rigid Anglicanism of the Tories, dismissing Tory ministers like Harcourt, Poulett, Dartmouth and St John, as 'reputed bigots to the Church ... brought into the administration as a demonstration to the world that the interest of the Church and the safety of the State are preferred before any private ends, and to rescue both out of the claws of anarchical, atheistical, antimonarchical Whigs, as they are generally called'.[6] It was precisely this quality of man – atheistic and antimonarchical – with whom Eugene associated in private.

Toland had been in contact with Eugene since 1709. The earliest work he had sent the prince and his adjutant d'Hohendorf, was the irreligious account of the *Gospel of Barnabas*, which became the basis for *Nazarenus* (1718), one of his most radical public works. Other manuscripts dealt with subjects like cosmology and physics, the life and thought of Giordano Bruno, and on the reputations of Cicero and Moses. As correspondence between d'Hohendorf and Toland indicates, their relationship was defined by a common interest in heterodoxy and clandestine writings. Hohendorf, again as his correspondence with other radical figures indicates, often acted on behalf of Eugene in the pursuit of 'dangerous books'. On the visit to London both men were reported to have used Christopher Bateman's bookshop, also frequented by intimates of theirs like Anthony Collins. So while Eugene and Hohendorf were embroiled in careful and intense negotiations over the future shape of world diplomacy, they were also trawling London's bookshops and leafing through clandestine literature. Toland's intimacy with these men was remarkable: it is evidence of the dimensions of his intellectual connections and consequent political significance. Added to his connections with Sophia and Hanover, as well as with leading Whig politicians, it is possible to suggest that Toland in the 1700s (and especially after 1710) had access to the key people who shaped the major developments in national politics. Enlightenment politics in England, at least, were being conducted right at the heart of the Whig establishment.

As this book has established, English political culture was in crisis after 1689 – the challenge that Toland (and his milieu) posed to religious commonplaces were not simply philosophical issues, but fundamentally linked to the power of contemporary civic and ecclesiastical institutions. Toland's cultural signifi-cance was determined not simply by the intelligence and acuity of his ideas, but by the fact that they were circulated in concert amongst the political elite and a wider public audience. Toland aimed not just to storm heaven, but to capture the citadels of political authority. In his example we can see how ideas worked in the period. Far from being detached intellectual exercises, the evidence of the composition, circulation and reception of his texts shows that ideas could have serious instrumental purchase in political life. One man and his pen – with the right support in powerful places – really could make a difference.

   Toland's affinity with men like Eugene illustrates the role his ideas played in the elite circles of early eighteenth-century European politics. It also indi-cates how receptive political and intellectual culture in the period was to the cultural intent of such ideas. Toland's example is both a symptom and a cause of the cultural conflict of the period. Fragments of evidence show how Toland's participation in an elite sociability was a means for insinuating his ideas into the minds of the great and good. This was most definitely enlighten-ment from above rather than from below. This offers a different model of 'Enlightenment' than the one commonly advanced which still emphasises the intellectual influence of philosophic ideas. The more sophisticated account suggested by Robert Darnton argues that the radical culture of the French high enlightenment, was disseminated by the circulation of forbidden ideas 'under the cloak' in clandestine and discrete networks. These 'bestsellers' corroded traditional Christian and royal culture by delegitimating these institu-tions in discourses that formed public opinion.[7] The print and scribal culture of England in the period examined here functioned with similar corrosive qualities. The difference was that the sort of anticlerical and heterodox ideas Toland promoted were central to the core debates in both the public and private sphere. Far from being marginal such ideas were both a currency of political debate and an instrument for creating cultural authority. The ideas that became powerful in France after the 1750s, were part of the mainstream of public political debate in England between 1690 and 1720.[8] Toland used his intellectual capacity and writing to make friends and influence people. We can see this in the shared reading and marginal annotation with Molesworth, the promises of novels to Sophia, and the use of manuscripts as tokens of love with unidentified noblewomen. In these transactions Toland exploited ideas to establish channels of communication. Although he died in relatively poor circumstances, he moved comfortably in more grand and privileged sur-roundings. Toland not only made ideas, he communicated and circulated them across political, social and cultural space.

Insight into Toland's awareness of the value of this sociability to the diffusion of ideas, can be read in his description of the 'humours and politicks' of Epsom (1711).[9] Written in emulation of the classical eulogies to country retirement by Pliny, Toland described the routines and habits of his life both in London and in 'retirement' in the Surrey countryside. In these descriptions it is possible to imaginatively experience the different cultural spaces in which Toland's 'enlightenment' ideas were voiced. Public life in Epsom was diverse – the main tavern and coffee-house attracted all sorts of people 'by the conversation of those, who walk there, you wou'd fancy your self to be this minute on the Exchange, and the next minute at St. James; one while in an East-India factory or a West-India Plantation, and another while with the army in Flanders or on board the Fleet in the ocean'.[10] No profession, trade or calling was absent, providing ample opportunity either for 'instruction or ... diversion'. Bowling greens, raffle shops, gaming tables supplemented the taverns, inns and coffee-houses as places of conversation and resort. Indeed the coffee-houses were the space for the display of 'social virtue' – they 'are equal'd by few, and exceeded by none, tho' I wish they may be imitated by all'.[11] Party distinctions, borne with honour in London, were set aside in Epsom. Even differences in religious identity did 'not ruffle men's tempers by irreli-gious wrangling'. Priests and politicians, who 'industriously propagate discord and humanity', were cursed. In 'plain terms', he wrote, 'we are not so fond of any set of notions, as to think 'em more important than the peace of society'. Whether attending 'sumptuous banquets' or 'a genteel collation', the theme of life in Epsom was a blending of the exotic and luxurious from metropolitan London, with the 'most relishing dainty' of local produce. Toland was not then coy about the material benefits of mixing with the ruling gentry. Aristocratic houses, public walks and private entertainments were natural haunts, where he got his business done. Although solitary at times – walking in the long groves at Woodcote conversing with himself, or at Box Hill 'that temple of nature' – or in more sociable company 'angling for trouts at Leatherhead, watching 'contending villagers' play cricket, following the hounds or racing horses, Toland participated in a variety of companionable forms of elite life, whether in London or Surrey. Ideas were the staple of his contributions to these encounters.

Although sociable, Toland also liked a quiet life. He had a preference for 'retirement' rather than solitude, and 'so would have it in my power to be alone or in company at pleasure'.[12] The proximity of Epsom to London meant he could do both, be back at the centre of power within two or three hours, or keep in touch by means of the frequently visiting stage coaches and daily post. Toland described a social life driven by his own perception of the demands of conversation or retirement. His own desires were modest – 'let me have Books and Bread enough without dependence, a bottle of Hermitage and a plate of Olives for a select friend'. This 'luxurious tranquillity' was to be preferred to the anxieties and corruptions of those that sought out inglorious titles and preferment. Meeting the nine muses in 'every lawn and every grove, in every shady bower and solitary glade', he was as likely to encounter Minerva as Diana. The picture of Toland, ever ready with 'a pocket book and a pencil' to record any ideas that may have occurred to him during all the various enter-tainments, is testimony to his pursuit of the life of the mind. In hyperbolic terms he composed a celebration of the natural charms of his country retreat, 'far more pleasant than the well known Courts of Princes'. Tired with sport or study 'and sleeping on the grass under a spreading chestnut beech. I enjoy not a more solid and secure repose, than the proudest monarch in his guilded Palace'. These retirements had intellectual purpose: as he described, on his wanderings he always had 'a book in my hand or in my head' with a design of 'returning more entertaining to private conversation, or more serviceable to publick society'.[13] The duality of intention – entertainment and instructive service – is an apt summary of how Toland's intimacy with the powerful allowed the circulation of his ideas. Ideas were the currency of sociability and entertainment, but also for brokering radical belief amongst a powerful community.

Evidence of the connection between ideas, elite sociability and entertainment can be seen in the example of perhaps his most enigmatic work – *Pantheisticon*, printed and circulated in 1720. The work has generated enormous interest amongst historians of clandestine philosophy but its significance is to be found as much in its role in creating a pan-European community of readers, as in its intellectual components. Written in Latin, it consists of three parts – a dissertation on the infinite nature of the universe, a liturgy used by a society of 'pantheists', and a discussion of the 'two-fold' philosophy of the pantheists incorporating a short work on 'de viri optimi & ornatissimi'. The intellectual sources and significance of these dissertations are complex and still contro-versial. The account of natural philosophy that starts the work is difficult and perplexing – the overwhelming intellectual influences have been attributed to Lucretius, Giordano Bruno, Spinoza and Newton. An extension of the dis-cussion raised in *Letters to Serena*, the ideas are materialist and heterodox in their account of the relationship between matter and motion, the nature of time and intellect. But discussions of astronomy, anatomy, the nature of latitude and longitude, as well as the climate and cell biology are also evident. It is clear that the arguments are derived from eclectic sources – Lucretius, Hippocrates, Copernicus are just a few of the works cited. The readership for this sort of material would have to be erudite and well-informed.

The second substantial part of the work is much more reader friendly being a 'formulae celebranda sodalitatis socraticae'. This included a three-part celebration of pantheistical principles of morality, philosophy and liberty. Conducted as a series of responses between a President and his companions, friends and brothers of the society, the description mirrors the symposia of antiquity rather than any more obviously Masonic ritual. Celebrating 'the coming together and conversation of friends', much of the ceremonial language derives explicitly from the works of Cicero, underscoring the notions 'that we might live pleasantly, and die peaceably ... free from all fears, neither elated by joy, nor depressed by sadness, we might always retain an unshaken constancy'.[14] If parts one and two developed a stoic approach to questions of religion, and applauded the classical defence of moral philosophy ('to lead a happy life virtue alone is sufficient, and is itself an ample reward'), the final section advanced a republican defence of the converging benefits of political and intellectual liberty enshrined in the rule of 'right reason'.[15] Toland proudly acknowledged 'we are willing to be brought up, and govern'd by this law, not by the lying, and superstitious fictions of men'.[16] Firmly premised both on the ideas and explicit extracts from Cicero's key works (especially *de republica, de legibus, de natura deorum* and *de diviniatione*) the central point of the work was to 'study the safety of the republick and the common good of mankind'.[17] Importantly the book asserted the necessary connection between reason and politics; cultivating reason meant both understanding the place of humanity in the wider context of the universe but also providing a platform for true liberty: true knowledge of nature would liberate the mind from the dark shadows of superstition and consequently dissolve the grounds of political tyranny. The society was a defender not only of the 'liberty of thought, but also of action, detesting at the same time, all licentiousness, and are sworn enemies of all Tyrants, whether despotic monarchs, or domineering nobles, or factious Mob-leaders'.[18]

This was then, a serious and profound book. It was also entertaining. Citing the aphorism that 'mirth is the characteristic of a freeman, sadness that of the slave', *Pantheisticon* took delight in stressing the elegant, pure and simple pleasure indulged in at their meetings. Explicitly modelled on the Greek *symposia* or the *suffitia* of the Spartans, the pantheistical 'banquets' were designed to 'bring together friends and relish the sweets of conversation' under the common government of reason. As 'the bottle is in common to all, so is the discourse': the society 'bigotted to no one's opinion, nor lead aside by Education or custom, nor subservient to the Religion and Laws of their country; they freely and impartially, in the silence of all prejudices, and with the greatest sedateness of Mind, discuss and bring to a scrutiny all things, as well sacred (as the saying is) as prophane'.[19] 'Serious amusement' seems to have been the purpose of the work.[20] Exploring the origins and circulation of the text will indicate how the text may have been read in the sort of circles around Eugene and in Epsom described above.

Although printed in 1720 at 'Cosmopoli' the origins of the work may lie directly in the contacts between Toland and the Eugene circle in 1711–12. As has already been noted, Toland was in correspondence with these men from 1709, probably having access to both d'Hohendorf's and Eugene's library collections in Vienna from this date. He certainly inscribed a dedication to Eugene in a copy of his own *Adeisidaemon* in 1709.[21] By 1710 he was supplying both men with clandestine works. Towards the end of 1712 he dedicated his elegantly printed prospectus for a modern edition of Cicero's works to both men, perhaps trying to reinforce in public his association with their pro-Hanoverian political agenda. During their diplomatic mission in London the only evidence of contact with Toland is the singular letter between him and Hohendorf, dated 7 March 1712. The main part of the letter is a learned discussion of sources related to Toland's ongoing history of scriptural apocrypha. Appended to the letter is reference to a 'formula, sive liturgica philosophica' that was not yet transcribed but would probably be sent in the next post.[22] At this stage the work may have simply been the section that would form part two of the printed volume. Like many of his other works, Toland constantly refined and updated his writing, expanding the contents over the next eight years.

If the origins of the work lie in this rather obscure scribal exchange, the printed versions are also enigmatic. Published in two different (but lexically similar) versions possibly by different printing houses (certainly on paper with different water-marks) one copy had elegant rubric and ornamentation, while the other (whilst containing some decoration) was a plainer copy.[23] The more ornate copy contained a number of sophisticated emblem-ornaments that reflected some of the themes of the text. It seems likely that the engraver Francis Hoffman was responsible for the decorations in at least one of these versions, which suggests the work was produced in England rather than the Netherlands. Certainly one of the emblems was used in an edition of Lucretius' *de rerum natura* published by Jacob Tonson in 1713 and edited by Michael Maittaire.[24] Toland's involvement in the work, which was printed, but not published in the conventional sense, was shadowy. Continental journalists were convinced they had identified his hand in the work, but it seems likely that rather than distributing the work publicly, that Toland sent copies to specific individuals, sometimes with additional scribal comments. Certainly after the print versions were distributed there was a thriving afterlife of scribal editions of the work both in Latin and in French. One manuscript indicated a provenance for the work, suggesting that there had only been fifty copies produced at a price of 50 guineas. Written originally for 'une société choisie des plus beaux Espirits et des plus grands Seigneurs de la Cour de Londres', a copy had been given to the Duc d'Orlean regent of France, by the English ambassador, John Dalrymple. This scribal copy was made immediately in the course of one night for distribution.[25] Here we have a fragment of evidence for both the audience and forms of circulation of this sort of work. Toland's preferred audience was elite rather than public.

Toland's archive shows that copies were sent to some of his more adventurous friends in England. One letter, written by Toland from Anthony Collin's estate at Baddow Hall in October 1720 to Barnham Goode in London replied to inquiries made by Mr Ingram about passages in *Pantheisticon*. In this letter a glimpse of the geographical and social network made by the circulation of the work is apparent. Toland revealed that he had deliberately left a hint of his authorship in the name used in the preface of the work. 'Janus Junius Eoganesius', was derived from a combination of his original Christian name and the Latin name for where he was born: as he explained it 'serves as good a cover as any I cou'd feign or invent'. Toland begged the two men to 'keep this foolery to your self ... since I hope it will be a long time, before it can be of use to any other'.[26] He noted that while he was willing to have his 'doctrines scann'd during my life' for either instruction or diversion, he was not keen to have 'critical descants on my name'. Content to let his friends in on the secret, Toland was concerned to keep both the text, and his authorship, out of a wider public view.

Convincing the powerful of the value of his ideas was a central part of his politics: getting them to read his books was imperative. Making the books entertaining, palming them off in salons and sending them as gifts to princes, ambassadors and regents was the starting point for his political strategy. Such books were intended to have an effect on national policy through convincing the influential figures of the time, rather than having a more historically nebulous 'influence' on public opinion.

Toland's role in the distribution of ideas amongst this European elite shows a very different model of cultural diffusion than is commonly proposed. This was no covert, marginal, radical figure, but an individual comfortable with social and political hierarchy who aimed to use his position to achieve reform, rather than to overthrow order. One of the central themes of recent accounts of parliamentary politics in the first three decades of the eighteenth century has been the importance of the social context of political management. The routines of political action were achieved by negotiating access to the Court and the Queen in the 1700s, or by being part of the networks of dining rooms, private houses and inns and coffee-houses, that co-ordinated parliamentary business in both the Houses of Commons and Lords. A descending hierarchy of meetings from county houses, to London town houses, to dining-clubs and regular coffee-house societies were venues where policy was formulated co-ordinated and disseminated. By communicating with figures near the apex of this social network, Toland was able to insinuate his ideas at an effective point in the chain of command.[27]

Toland was not just a *philosophe* devoted to enlightening the rich and power-ful, but also a public author of considerable reputation and skill. While committed to persuading the powerful and elite, making the public rational and free, was also a central part of his project from the earliest moment in his career in the 1690s. This was the point of his involvement in politics. Indeed one of the intentions of this work has been to underscore the practical and public dimension of his polemic. Unlike some accounts of 'Enlightenment' ideas that have emphasised the philosophical and intellectual achievements of authors (detached from their milieu or context), this study has established how entrenched Toland's project was in the everyday conflicts of political life. Writing in the late 1690s, Toland asserted that 'To employ one's thoughts on what he pleases, and to speak as freely as he thinks, is the greatest advantage of living in a free government'.[28] Although he never completed his full-blown history of republican traditions ('Brutus, or the history of Liberty and Tyranny'[29]) from the 1690s to the 1720s he was committed to the promotion of an authentic and politically engaged republicanism. Whether writing on behalf of Shaftesbury, Harley, Molesworth or the Electress of Hanover, Toland was unswerving in this commitment to liberty and free government. Although he built his ideas from the conceptual architecture of ancient and early modern discourses, Toland was not simply a conduit for the rehearsal of an earlier tradition of thought. His role was that of adaptation, adjustment and engage-ment. By detaching the political theory of the writings of Milton and Harrington from the question of the nature of monarchy, Toland made the texts functional for the central ideological conflicts of the 1700s. Free govern-ment was defined less by the relationship between monarchy and parliament, than by the quality of civic and religious freedom. For Toland, the unpre-judiced, non-dependent, rational exercise of human intellect in the cause of the common good was possible in a regime governed by the limited and regulated monarchy of the post–1689 polity. Here was a form of republican thinking that had practical purposes, and was unanchored from the straightforward issue of 'monarchical' government.

Following in the republican footsteps of Milton's *Areopagitica*, Toland underlined his commitment to the liberty of public reason in *A letter to a member of Parliament* (1698). Written in the context of debates about the lapse of the Licensing Act and the parliamentary discussion of a 'blasphemy' act, the tract identified the *esse* of humanity in its rational agency. The language of

Lockean 'reasonableness' was entangled with a republican vocabulary of tyranny and slavery. It was man's duty to use reason to judge of the truth and falsehood of beliefs and propositions; it was also the communal duty of each individual 'to inform each other in those propositions they apprehend to be true'. Men had, then, 'the same right to communicate their thoughts, as to think themselves'. While priestcraft dominated contemporary Rome, the city of antiquity had celebrated such freedom: there 'to think on what one had a mind to, and to speak one's thought as freely as to think them, was looked on as one of the chief blessings of a free government'. For Toland, the issue of the liberty of the press was a question of 'whether we ought to be free, or slaves in our understandings'. The role of the clergy (of all confessions) had been to impose upon the consciences and reason of the people. Protestant churchmen had been as deviant as Catholics: the question of the legitimacy of belief was not determined by standards of truth, but by sincerity of commitment to rational enquiry. Restraint of the liberty of thought and expression was not simply a religious crime but had dangerous civil consequences. Ignorance destroyed 'the English nation and enslave[d] the Nation'. The baneful influence of sacerdotal slavery corroded civil society for 'when men are once enslaved in their understandings (which of all things ought to be most free) it's scarce possible to preserve any other liberty'. Priestcraft and slavery went hand in hand, so 'there never was a nation which lost their religious rights that could long maintain their civil ones'. The endorsement of arbitrary and absolute notions of divine right monarchy from the pulpits throughout the Restoration had tarnished true notions of government. Securing the liberty of the press would 'in all probability, secure all other liberty'.[30] The press was to be a rational engine for the manufacture of public opinion.

The adjustments made over the course of Toland's life in his practical commitment to the printing press as an agent of intellectual reform can also be seen in his scribal *A project of a journal* composed about 1704. Intended to be published weekly, to advance the 'beauty, harmony, and reasonableness of Virtue', Toland saw the role of such a paper as supplementing the ambitions of the magistrate and legislators in cultivating a civil society. To be 'published to the world' on Wednesdays (the day most suitable 'because most people are in town') the paper was to be instructive and entertaining. The content of the paper was to follow this principle of public utility, but chiefly 'the moral virtues, remarkable passages of History, philosophical disquisitions, and the detection of popular errors'. Although Toland intended to extract materials from a variety of 'antient and modern, foreign and domestick books' he was insistent that no one should 'imagine that this will be a work above his sphere or capacity'. The work was calculated for 'the good of all' and especially the 'ladies'. Detailing the typographical layout, the continuous pagination and the indexing system, Toland was anxious to make the work accessible and useful for a variety of readers 'because they have no trouble in reading the Book by parts, which would deter them in one volume'. The journal was to be above faction and party but to serve the 'Publick and the Government' by rendering the people 'wise and vertuous'. The projected journal was to accomplish the philosophical ambitions of Cicero: it was to be a guide to life, a reformation of understanding and manners just like the *acta diurna* of ancient Rome.[31] Toland had ambitions then both 'within and without doors'. It is no surprise then that the true Whig journals of the later 1710s and early 1720s produced exactly this sort of discourse – republican and anticlerical – for a broad public audience.

Evidence from Toland's own publishing career suggests that he was well aware of the dangers of censorship and persecution. It is important to note however that Toland's commitment to freedom of the press was, like his commitment to republican liberty in general, a regulated conception rather than one of pure licence. This can be most simply demonstrated in his memorial 'Proposal for regulating ye news-papers' composed about 1717 (probably for Robert Molesworth). In one sense the proposal is indicative of the changed political circumstances that were in operation after 1714. In the early 1700s Toland was intimately engaged in opposition polemic against Tories, renegade Whigs and corrupt churchmen; after 1714 Toland was writing from a less defensive position given his intimacy with the Whig regime. 'It becomes every day more and more necessary, to put the public newspapers under some better regulation' to protect the King's reputation and person and the revenues of the government. Toland acknowledged the seeming contradiction of calling for regulation since he could 'truly say yt no man in the world is more zealous than myself' for the liberty of the press, but 'I would not have the Liberty of writeing turn'd into licentiousness, no more than any other liberty'.[32]

The circulation of seditious insinuations under the title of news needed supervision. The fact that 'papists, non-jurors or other disaffected persons' were in general the authors of such works made the need for regulation even more pressing; such works 'being industriously calculated for the taste of the mob, contribute more perhaps than all other artifices to poison the minds of the people against his majesty, to vilify his ministers & disturb the public peace, to the scandal of all good government'. Toland's draft act defined the parameters of regulation, taxation and penalties with precision. In his concluding remarks, Toland returned to the issue of the sacred liberty of the press: his measure was not intended as an encroachment but merely a regulation that would stop the nation 'running to an anarchy'. The point to make here is an important one for understanding the nature of Toland's republicanism. Liberty was not licence, the promotion of republican conceptions of government was radical, not because it advanced a 'modern' or democratic account of political society, but because it challenged the commonplaces of divine right discourses. For Toland, subscription to principles of a virtuous regulation of the press was as acceptable as advancing the legitimacy of a limited monarchy: these convictions were not compromises of an earlier authentic republican discourse but the application of core principles to the pragmatics of political context. As he noted in a later work, 'we are servants of the law, that we may be free'.[33]

For Toland the task of citizens was to free themselves from the corruption of passion, ambition and envy by the pursuit of reason.[34] Human beings were fundamentally sociable creatures who formed themselves into communities for mutual support. Promoting the cause of 'true and never deceiving reason' was a fundamental political duty.[35] Toland's commitment to the publication and propagation of a republican tradition, suggests that far from becoming a marginal and ineffective political discourse after 1689, it was still a vibrant and potentially effective political option. This political ideology brought him into a political intimacy with leading figures like Harley, Shaftesbury and Molesworth, but also took him as far as the court at Hanover. Fundamental to Toland's reinvention of republican politics was an emphasis upon the religious underpinnings of the tradition. A theory of religious liberty was elemental. This republicanism concerned itself almost exclusively with the relationship between the freedom of subjects and the powers of the Church. One of the political conditions necessary for the establishment of civil liberty was liberty of thought. By consequence the relationship between the Church and State, and between Church and laity were as significant as that between subject and monarch because of the republican emphasis upon the relationship between reason and citizenship. Liberty was not simply a political category but had a religious and rational context too. 'Liberty' was not only the unconstrained exercise of a bundle of civil rights, but for Toland and his circle included both *libertas philosophandi*, as well as the more narrow conception of the liberty of religious expression and worship. This dimension of republican thinking has not been explored with any serious intent by current historiography, which may account for the general impression that eighteenth-century republicanism was both insipid and derivative.

Republican ambitions were vital for Toland. He was also convinced that such aspirations were more than idle dreams. The immediate and pressing point to underscore was the connection between the attack on tyranny and the corrupting function of the Church. Fundamental to Toland's perception of the problem with contemporary politics was not simply a default case against the institution of monarchy, but a hostility to tyrannous government inspired by the passionate self-interest, not just of princes, but of priests too. Importantly, this meant that Toland (and others in his circle) was able to detach regicidal aspirations from his political agenda. Unlike the battle of the free and rational

Englishman against the Stuarts before 1689, the battle he saw himself engaged in was not so much against an actively deviant monarchy, but against the incipient potential for corruption of the current system of governance by 'wicked Levites'. All princes were latent tyrants, but this dormant form was habitually only cultivated by the corrupt 'pulpit stuff' of clergymen.[36] The war against tyranny then was fought on the front-line of theological discourses.

The dominance of *de jure divino* discourses, which legitimated both monarchical and ecclesiastical institutions, meant that, almost by default, the starting point for thinking and writing about political power was theological and ecclesiological rather than civic or jurisprudential. 'The power of Kings' was first and foremost a sacred discourse: in terms of corroding the affective power of this discourse, the starting point was divine.[37] Republican writers then, were engaged as much in a theological debate as a civil controversy. After 1689 ecclesiological issues were most manifest in the central issue of toleration. Despite men like Locke attempting to make a firm distinction between political theory and claims of conscience, for most in the political elite (in particular those involved in parliamentary politics and successive national administrations) the inter-related questions of the security of the established Protestant church and its rights of jurisdiction (and coercion) over the laity were fundamental. It was impossible to critique the nature of the monarchy without drawing implications for the status and authority of the Church, or the rights and duties of subjects or citizens. As we have seen, it was no accident that contemporaries vilified Toland both as a commonwealthman and a heresiarch. Like Spinoza, Toland saw republicanism as fundamentally an ecclesiological discourse.

The evidence of Toland's emphasis upon the liberty of reason and the defence of the regulated rule of the Hanoverian monarchy poses some difficulties for the claim that republicanism in the strict sense was only characterised by hostility to the institution of monarchy. His example shows it was both possible and practical to develop a theory of liberty which was compatible with regulated forms of monarchical government. Moreover it also establishes that it was practicable to fashion this political theory out of the canonical writings of Harrington, Milton and Sidney. Certainly no one in the late 1690s was more familiar with these authentic republican writings than Toland. After 1689, most politicians abandoned a regicidal agenda. Resistance against the tyranny of the Stuarts was most effectively undertaken after 1700, by a defence of the legitimate claims of the Hanoverian monarchy. 'Tyranny' rather than simply monarchical government became the focus of criticism. The most pernicious agent of tyranny in post-revolutionary England was the Church. Erastian defences of regal supremacy became (ironically) a fundamental weapon in the war against priestcraft. This was why, for example, Thomas Hobbes's writings, despite their perceived absolutist tendencies, persisted in being so popular amongst freethinking circles. Liberty could only be built on public reason rather than superstitious prejudice. Following Hobbes and Spinoza, Toland argued that the vulgar were incapable of rational conduct because they had been led astray by the corrupting influence of the Church. Since priestcraft made people ignorant, the attack upon it became a key part of a practical political agenda. A consequence of this was that Parliament and nobility, as bearers of reason and virtue, were the best agencies of republican reform.

Late seventeenth-century republicans shared the view with their earlier sources that loss of liberty reduced both the individual and the state to the condition of slavery. Importantly for Toland, and many of his circle, it was not just the subjection of the body that created slavery, but also that of the mind. Dependence and corruption was not simply a physical condition, but fundamentally a mental state: any institution that hindered such liberty was corrupt. The claims of the Church to 'independent' (sacerdotal) jurisdiction or authority over the laity made an elemental challenge to republican understandings of the consensual origins and function of government. Both Hobbes and Harrington were consequently concerned to derive religious authority from popular sources, or at least civil sources. The constitutional anxieties of earlier republicans about the 'king's negative voice' could easily be matched by the alarm about the clerical claims for the constitutional authority of Convocation in the 1690s. The hostility to the 'flattering clergy and courtiers' was profound in the 1650s: by the 1700s it was the overwhelming focus of republican disquiet. The continuity of such concerns can perhaps best be explored in the repeated importance of the attack upon the *Eikon Basilike* in the 1650s and 1690s: in the earlier period the focus of Milton's attack was against its misuse in civil tyranny, by 1698 Toland treated it as evidence of the conspiracies of priestcraft.[38]

Toland's polemic was shot through with references to religious tyranny. The influence of self-interested priests, or persecuting and partial ecclesiastical law corroded all forms of liberty. Priesthood, by its claim to interpretative or sacramental authority was a form of tyranny over conscience that became reified into persecuting law. For Toland, the claim to be able to think for someone else was tyrannous. For those republicans living under a secure limited monarchy in the 1700s the immediate cause of dependence and corruption was not monarchy but priesthood. The republican critique of clericalism argued that the Church caused two forms of dependence: by epistemic claims (their ability to understand the 'truth') and by the imposition of sacramental tests, which was a more active form of coercion. Liberty then, for later seventeenth century republicans like Toland, was premised upon an assertion of the relationship between reason and human identity. To be a good human was to have rational autonomy and self-mastery, and to be bound by laws of one's own making, independent of both passion and external coercion. Arguing that 'reason' was an eternal pattern for virtue, by necessity implicated the republican agenda in a war against a more traditional theological understanding of the relationship between human reason and sin. Sceptical of the human capacity for true knowledge, churchmen in the 1690s dismissed this veneration for reason as 'the vanity of fallen and darkened mankind'. As one critic of Molesworth's *Account* insisted, if mankind was in a condition of slavery this was caused by human sin, rather than tyrannous governments. The 'specious pretence of the all-Atoning Freedom of the subject' was rebutted in favour of the arguments of obligation and 'prudential' restraint. That which the republicans called 'slavish and unintelligible' was true Christianity: obedience and the 'passive state' was not a 'state of slavery' but 'glorious liberty'. Human pride was the prompt for sedition, it 'filled men's hearts with coarse and sordid desire, and makes their heads swell with the wind of Fantastical doctrines about liberty, without a just restriction; till at length the Distemper or malignancy breaks out into a vain outcry against tyranny and slavish opinions'.[39]

Almost by default, confronted with these theological definitions of the language of liberty, reason, and virtue, Toland felt compelled to engage with tyranny in all its forms: spiritual as well as civil. Unlike other neo-Roman theories of free states that were regarded as subversive because they attached a language of liberty to radical forms of representative government, the republicanism of Toland was elite and hierarchical. Its radicalism was found in the fact that it challenged fundamentally the traditional and dominant accounts of political authority that were built on theological foundations. The 'political' problem of tyranny could only be resolved by attention to religious issues. Toleration was the foundation of free citizenship. Toland's republicanism was not radical in either social or institutional ambition. His writings (drawing from Sidney's work) indicate a preference for the rule of an aristocracy of virtue: he did his best to mingle with such people. The high point of this 'aristocratic' republicanism can be seen in the constitutional proposals enshrined in the Peerage Bill of 1719, where the conceptual assertion 'that it is only possible to be free in a free state' was deployed as a justification for reinforcing the independence of the Lords. As many contemporaries noted, this was not a radical form of representative government.[40]

Working close to the heart of the political machine Toland's ambitions were to overturn the cultural system of superstition by compromising the theological structures that underpinned 'tyranny'. As a good republican, the keywords in his political vocabulary were the trinity of virtue, liberty and reason. Although he was concerned with the nature of political institutions, the thrust of his understanding of republican politics was as a moral discourse: making men free, rational and virtuous. By default the promotion of these ambitions projected him into a full-frontal assault upon the enduring structures of theological and ecclesiastical authority. If man was to be free, his soul had to be unshackled from the dominance of priestcraft. Politics necessarily involved contesting the social power of the Church and the cultural practices that legitimised that authority. Anticlericalism was as much a political as a religious discourse. Toland's intention was both to explain, and change, the world he lived in. Assessing the practical power of his discourses is a complex matter. Certainly his challenge to the cultural shibboleths of the established orthodoxy – both monarch and priest – was regarded as deeply subversive by contemporaries.

Reconfiguring the content and political viability of republican tradition was a significant achievement. There is no doubt that contemporaries in England, and on the continent, saw Toland as a dangerous, powerful and well-connected figure. There was little ambiguity about his reputation as a freethinker, absolutely hostile to the culture and authority of the established religion. Whether he had a long-lasting impact on the vitality of this Christian culture is still a matter of considerable debate. Certainly his ideas and scholarship had a persistence beyond the time and communities he wrote for. Contemporaries were profoundly anxious about his insidious influence both on public attitudes and political policy. A man who argued that atheists might be good subjects challenged the shibboleths of Christian society. Churchmen worried about two elements in his writing – the attack upon Revelation, and the promotion of republican political theory. These irreligious discourses were connected in denying a *de jure divino* authority for both Church and State.

The historiographical treatment of Toland has often made a distinction between the theological and political dimensions of his thought and polemic. The intention of this work has been to argue that they were inherently intertwined projects. Toland had (in Spinoza's vocabulary) 'theologico-political' objectives. The political, theological and cultural arguments that Toland articulated, were all part of an entrenched war against priestcraft. Unlike many other accounts of Toland which place him either at the radical margins of political society, or just caught within the carapace of Christianity, this work argues that he operated right at the core of a powerful political elite. This intimacy with the influential created a platform for the development of a series of public discourses aimed at persuading a broader audience. Toland's objectives were transformative in the sense that he wished to change the habitual structures of Christian culture. Although labelled a 'deist', 'freethinker', even 'atheist', none of these words fully captures either his strategy or character. Although he loudly proclaimed the sovereignty of reason, and indeed of the people, he was more than a simple rationalist, and certainly no democrat.

As this work has suggested, the intellectual origins of Toland's project are not easy to pin down. In many of his writings he appropriated, adapted and tuned contemporary (sometimes very pious) works to his own purpose. Plundering orthodox clerical scholarship on patristic and scriptural texts, or the antiquarian researches of Godly men, or even the writings of John Locke, Jean Leclerc and other people he had some friendship with, Toland was able to recycle ideas with facility. His innovation was to compromise cultural authority by exposing the conventional foundations of such knowledge. His function was viral; it set the immune system of orthodox culture against itself. Many contemporaries were convinced that Toland was merely a conduit for an older subversive tradition represented by the materialism of Hobbes or Spinoza, or even Lucretius and the ancients. It is possible to identify elements in his writings lifted from all these people and more – Hobbes, Spinoza, Herbert of Cherbury, Milton, Blount, Bekker, Van Dale, Simon, Livy, Cicero, Lucretius – to name but a few. But influence spotting will not unlock the secret of Toland's identity.

A frequent accusation, echoed by modern historians, was that Toland merely vulgarised the more complex and innovative ideas of the most philosophically original of thinkers: Benedict Spinoza. Nicknamed 'Tractatus Theologico-Politicus' and 'Spinoza in abstract' Toland was closely identified by contemporaries as a man who was, as one critic put it, 'Genuinus Spinozae pullus'.[41] As his writings show, Toland was certainly familiar with Spinoza's writings (both the *Ethics* and the *Tractatus theologico-politicus*), but it would be inaccurate to suggest he was simply derivative of this source. Where Spinoza's work was clandestine, Toland's was public. Where Spinoza was prosecuted and his works proscribed, Toland wrote for Queens and Princes. Where Spinoza had a rigorous and philosophically robust metaphysical system, Toland was eclectic, ludic and erudite.

Toland undoubtedly developed key approaches evident in Spinoza's works. The general influence of the *Tractatus theologico-politicus* (1670), which was available in English translation after 1689, pervades Toland's methodology and political thought. Toland's application of historical criticism, to both Scripture and patristic sources, was undoubtedly inspired by Spinoza's writing on the ideas of revelation and canon. The connections between virtue, liberty and a materialistic metaphysics evident in *Pantheisticon* (1720) show Toland thinking through the arguments linking republican politics and the rule of reason made by Spinoza in the second half of the *Tractatus*. The influence of Spinoza should not be overstated however. In making these arguments, Toland used more sources than simply Spinoza. Toland's unique skill was his eclecticism, binding together a wide variety of different types of writing – orthodox and impious, scholarly and popular, Christian and Judaic, literary and antiquarian.

While Spinoza's writings do provide a useful device for understanding the distinctive nature of Toland's intellectual and political republicanism, they do not explain it all. Toland's war against prejudice was a war against tyranny in the mind and in society. In the first instance, it was a specifically English campaign: its most obvious targets were intolerant churchmen. Theological prejudices were not only erroneous notions of revealed doctrine but also false political injunctions. While Spinoza gave a powerful example of how to combine a radical biblical criticism with a full defence of republican political institutions, there were also other sources for a defence of *libertas philosophandi* as the grounding of rational political liberty. Clearing away the undergrowth of false doctrine was an essential prerequisite for establishing the politics of virtue. Cultural criticism was then as essential to the war as political reform. While Jonathan Israel has powerfully reinstated the Dutch Enlightenment as a significant model for the radical assault upon Christian culture, the evidence presented here suggests that English society also had a notable role to play. Importantly the war of ideas in England was a battle for the minds of powerful men as well as the public, it was won by corroding religious certainties as much as by the positive affirmation of political principle. It was fought out, not just in clandestine circles, but in public: in aiming to convince the hearts and minds of the political elite, Toland hoped to capture control of powerful national institutions. In much of this Toland undoubtedly followed Spinoza. However, where Spinoza deployed his rabbinical learning in a single-minded account of the status of *Old Testament* scripture, Toland drew on a much wider range of erudition. Where Spinoza condensed republican political theory into a few chapters of commentary on the contemporary writing of people like Peter de la Court, Toland produced a massive canon of commonwealth writings, carefully made bespoke for contemporary purposes. Where Spinoza wrote in Latin and his posthumous ideas were circulated clandestinely, Toland used a full range of vernacular styles for both public and private polemic.

Toland (and by default the notion of an English Enlightenment) has been dismissed as a second-rate, isolated, marginal and mediocre figure, ultimately a failure because he was a man with no friends or adherents. Just as Toland was second-rate, isolated and derivative, so was the broader contribution of English thought to the cultural process of 'Enlightenment'.[42] As this book has been at pains to show, nothing could be further from the truth. At his best Toland was completely original. At his most powerful he stood on the threshold of influence right at the centre of British politics. He had friends everywhere – in the Royal court, in the salons, in coffee-houses, universities and private houses all over England and throughout Europe. His case is also good evidence for rethinking the significance of this period of English history. That Toland operated at the heart of national politics, that he produced such works for public and private audiences, surely tells us much about the nature of English public culture in the period. Fundamental issues about the certainty of Revelation, the power and authority of the Church, the status of the monarchy, and the rights of conscience, were all part of the everyday business of public debate.

Ultimately, Toland won a few famous victories against theological prejudice, but he lost the war against priestcraft. In England at least, churchmen, although perhaps more polite, retained their social authority into the distant future. That he lost, is not the same as saying he was unimportant. While to claim too much for one man would be to fall into temptations of exaggeration, it is clear Toland acted as a broker and mouthpiece for a radical milieu that was fundamentally opposed to the orthodox confessional structures of political and cultural life. Toland worked furiously to design tracts that would convince many different audiences of the authority of his views – with people like Sophia of Hanover, Eugene of Savoy, Shaftesbury, Harley, Molesworth, Collins and Furly listening, Toland always had the hope that his ideas would prompt national policy. Projecting the same ideas to the broader public community Toland intended to provide a context for the reception of this policy. Tragically, these 'enlightened' ambitions dribbled into the sand with the defeat of the commonwealth party by the more pragmatic Whiggism of Robert Walpole who recognised that the social power of the Established Church was a critical component of political hegemony. Toland did however leave a potent archive that became an important resource exploited by later 'High' Enlightenment assailants of irrationalism and superstition. We still live in a modernity shaped by this afterlife.

NOTES

1 See P. R. Sweet 'Prince Eugene of Savoy and Central Europe' *American Historical Review* 57 (1951) pp. 47–62. The best account of the background to this is E. Gregg *The Protestant succession in international politics, 1710–1716* (1986).

2 J. J. Cartwright (ed.) *The Wentworth papers 1705–1739* (1883) pp. 241–242.

3 *Ibid.* p. 244.

4 See N. Tindal *The continuation of Mr Rapin de Thoyras's History of England* 2 volumes (1751) ii pp. 237–238; PRO SP 34/17/48.

5 *Wentworth papers* p. 247.

6 *Portland Mss* V 'Characters by Prince Eugene' pp. 156–158 at 157.

7 Darnton *The forbidden bestsellers of pre-revolutionary France* (1996), *passim*.

8 See J. A. I Champion '"May the last king be strangled in the bowels of the last priest": irreligion and the English Enlightenment, 1649–1789' in T. Morton and N. Smith (eds) *Radicalism in British literary culture, 1650–1830* (Cambridge, 2002) pp. 29–44, 220–226.

9 See P. Lurbe 'Epsom as emblem: John Toland's *Description of Epsom*' *Eighteenth Century Ireland* 9 (1994) pp. 129–136. For a broader consideration of the politics of sociability between provinces and city see, S. E. Whyman *Sociability and power in late-Stuart England: the cultural worlds of the Verneys 1660–1720* (Oxford, 1999).

10 *Collections* 2 p. 100.

11 *Ibid.* p. 105.

12 *Ibid.* p. 115.

13 *Ibid.* p. 118.

14 *Pantheisticon* (1751) pp. 66–67.

15 *Ibid.* p. 73.

16 *Ibid.* pp. 85–86.

17 *Ibid.* p. 100.

18 *Ibid.* p. 57.

19 *Ibid.* pp. 11–14, 58.

20 *Collections* 2 p. 92.

21 See Vienna ONB Autogr. 45/83–1.

22 BL 4295 fo. 20r.

23 See the comparison between the BL copies C 69.E.5 and 4015.a.20. Pierre Lurbe is undertaking a scholarly edition of both the manuscript and printed editions. I am grateful to him for sharing his ongoing research.

24 See G. Cherchi *Satira ed enigma dice saggi sul Pantheisticon di John Toland* (Lucca, 1985) p. 34; and *ibid.* 'Atheism, dissimulation and Atomism in the philosophy of John Toland' (Unpublished PhD, London, 1994) p. 87.

25 Nicastro (ed.) *Pantheisticon* p. 90.

26 BL Add Mss 4295 fos. 39–40.

27 C. Jones 'The parliamentary organisation of the Whig Junto in the reign of Queen Anne: the evidence of Lord Ossulston's Diary' *Parliamentary History* 10 (1991) pp. 164–182. For a useful case-study see H. Snyder 'Godolphin and Harley: a study of their partnership in politics' *Huntingdon Library Quarterly* 30 (1966–67) pp. 241–271.

28 J. Toland *The Militia reform'd* (1698) p. 4. This phrase also occurs in *Pantheisticon* (1751) p. 108.

29 *Ibid.* p. 63.

30 J. Toland *A letter to a member of Parliament* (1698) pp. 3–5, 8, 11–12, 16–17, 21–22, 24, 26–27.

31 Toland 'A project of a journal' in *Collections* 2 pp. 202, 203, 205–206, 211–212, 213–214.

32 See BL Add Ms. 4295 f.49–50; also reproduced in L. Hanson *Government and the press 1697–1763* (Oxford, 1967) pp. 135–138.

33 *Pantheisticon* p. 84.

34 *Ibid.* pp. 1, 2, 3, 4.

35 *Ibid.* pp. 9, 11, 14, 57, 62.

36 See J. Toland *A defence of the parliament of 1640* (1698) preface p. 2–3 [unpaginated].

37 See P. Monod *The power of kings: monarchy and religion in Europe 1589–1715* (New Haven, 1999).

38 See Champion (ed.) *Nazarenus* 'Introduction' *passim.*

39 T. Rogers *Commonwealthsman unmasqu'd* (1694) pp. ii, 2, 62, 123, 148, 159.

40 See C. Brooks 'The debate on the Peerage Bill, 1719' in *Bicameralism: Tweekamerstel vroeger en nu* (eds) H. W. Blom, W. P. Blockmans and H. de Schepper (s-Gravenhage, 1992) pp. 261–277; C. Jones '"Venice preserv'd; or a plot discovered": the political and social context of the Peerage Bill of 1719' in C. Jones (ed.) *A pillar of the constitution* (1989) pp. 79–112.

41 Carabelli *Tolandiana* p. 95, Carabelli *Errata* p. 197.

42 See J. Israel *Radical Enlightenment* (Oxford, 2001) pp. 609–614, 627.

Select *Tolandiana*

All printed titles below are published in London unless otherwise stated. Both printer and bookseller are indicated where known. Full bibliographical descriptions are in Carabelli *Tolandiana*.

MANUSCRIPTS

Bodleian Library (Oxford) 'Livius Vindicatus' Rawlinson Collection Cod. D. 377, fos. 132–139. Modern edition in G. Carabelli 'Un inedito di John Toland: Il *Livius Vindicatus*, orvero la prima edizione (mancata) dell'*Adeisidaemon* (1709)' in *Rivista critica di storia della filosofia* 31 (1976) pp. 309–318.

British Library: BL Add Mss 4465 'A Collection of Miscellaneous Papers by John Toland'; BL Add Mss 4295 'Miscellaneous Letters and Papers by John Toland'.

Österreichische Nationalbibliothek, Vienna: ONB Ms 10325, 'Dissertations Diverses de Monsieur Tolandus'.

PRINTED WORKS

An account of the Courts of Prussia and Hanover (J. Darby, 1705; A. Baldwin, 1706; T. Johnson, The Hague, 1706).

Acts of Parliaments no infallible security (J. Baker, 1714).

Adeisidaemon (T. Johnson, The Hague, 1709).

Amyntor (The Booksellers of London, 1699).

Anglia libera (B. Lintott, 1701; B. Bos, Rotterdam, 1701; Hamburg, 1701).

An apology for Mr Toland (1697).

An appeal to honest people against wicked priests (Mrs Smith, 1713).

The art of canvassing at elections (J. Roberts, 1714).

The art of governing by partys (B. Lintott, 1701).

The art of restoring (J. Roberts, 1714).

Characters of the Court of Hannover (J. Baker, 1714).

Christianity not mysterious (Anon, 1696; S. Buckley, 1696; Anon, 1702).

Cicero illustratus (J. Humphreys, 1712).

Clito (Booksellers of London, 1700).

A collection of letters by General Monk (J. Roberts, 1714).

A collection of several pieces of Mr John Toland (J. Peele, 1726; 1747).

Select Tolandiana

A complete collection of the historical, political and miscellaneous works of John Milton (Amsterdam, 1698; J. Darby, 1699).

The danger of mercenary Parliaments (Anon 1698; J. Peele, 1722).

Declaration de L'Electeur Palatin, en faveur de ses sujets Protestans (T. Johnson, The Hague, 1707).

The declaration lately published in favour of his Protestant subjects, by the Elector Palatine (A. Baldwin, 1707; 1714).

A defence of Mr. Toland (E. Whitlock, 1697).

The description of Epsom (A. Baldwin, 1711).

The destiny of Rome (J. Roberts, A. Dodd, 1718).

Dunkirk or Dover (A. Baldwin, 1713).

The funeral elogy of Princess Sophia (B.Lintott, J. Roberts, 1714).

The great Mystery laid open (J. Roberts, 1714).

Her Majesty's reasons for creating the Electoral Prince of Hanover a Peer (A. Baldwin, 1712).

High-Church display'd (1711, 1713).

The Jacobitism, perjury, and popery of High-Church priests (J. Baker, 1710).

A lady's religion (T. Warren, R. Baldwin, 1697).

A letter against Popery (A. Baldwin, 1712).

A letter to a Member of Parliament, shewing that a restraint on the press is inconsistent with the Protestant religion (J. Darby, A. Bell, 1698; 1706).

Letters from the right honourable the late Earl of Shaftesbury to Robert Molesworth (W. Wilkins, J. Peele, 1721).

Letters to Serena (B. Lintott, 1704).

The life of John Milton (Amsterdam, 1698, J. Darby, 1699).

Memoirs of Denzil Lord Holles (T. Goodwin, 1699).

Memoirs of Lieutenant General Ludlow, the third and last part (Vevay, 1699).

A memorial concerning England in 1714 (in *A collection of several pieces*) (1726).

A memorial for the Earl of *** (in *A collection of several pieces*) (1726).

The memorial of the State of England (Booksellers, 1705; B. Bragg, 1705; Dublin, 1705).

A memorial presented to a Minister of State (in *A collection of several pieces*) (1726).

The militia reform'd (J. Darby, 1698; D. Brown, 1699; 1706).

Nazarenus (J. Brown, J. Roberts, J. Brotherton, 1718; J. Brotherton, J. Roberts, A. Dodd, 1718).

A new description of Epsom (in *A collection of several pieces*) (1726).

The Oceana of James Harrington (Booksellers, 1700).

The Ordinances, Statutes, and Privileges of the Royal Academy of Prussia (J. Darby, 1705; 1714).

Origines Judaicae (Thomas Johnson, The Hague, 1709).

Pantheisticon (Cosmopoli, 1720; S. Paterson, 1751).

Paradoxes of State (B. Lintott, 1702).

Oratio Philippica (E. Sanger, J. Chantry, 1707: 1709).

A Phillipick oration to incite the English against the French (E. Sanger, J. Chantry, 1707).

The reasons and necessity of the Duke of Cambridge's coming (J. Baker, 1714).

Reasons for addressing his Majesty to invite into England their Highnesses the Electress Dowager and Electoral Prince of Hanover (J. Nutt, 1702).

Reasons for attainting and abjuring the pretended Prince of Wales (B. Lintott, 1702).

Reasons for naturalising the Jews (J. Roberts, 1714).

The second part of the State anatomy (J. Philips, J. Roberts, J. Brotherton, P. Meadows, 1717, two editions).

Socinianism truly stated (1705).

A specimen of the critical history of the Celtic religion (in *A collection of several pieces*) (1726).

State anatomy of Great Britain (J. Philips, J. Brotherton, J. Roberts, 1717; 8 subsequent editions (J. Philips, J. Roberts, J. Brotherton, W. Meadows, 1717).

Tetradymus containing 1. Hodegus ... 2. Clidopherous ... 3 Hypatia ... 4. Mangoneutes (J. Philips, J. Roberts, J. Brotherton, W. Meadows, W. Meres, W. Chetwood, S. Chapman, J. Graves, 1720; 1732).

Two essays sent in a letter from Oxford (R. Baldwin, 1695).

Vindicius liberius (B. Lintott, 1702).

Index

Note: 'n' after a page number indicates a reference in an end-note.

Index

Lightning Source UK Ltd.
Milton Keynes UK
UKOW031351140413

209196UK00003B/39/P